OXFORD HISTORICAL MONOGRAPHS

Editors

M. G. BROCK	BARBARA HARVEY
H. M. MAYR-HARTING	H. G. PITT
A. F. THOMPSON	H. R. TREVOR-ROPER

ROGER,
BISHOP OF WORCESTER
1164–1179

MARY G. CHENEY

CLARENDON PRESS · OXFORD
1980

Oxford University Press, Walton Street, Oxford OX2 6DP
OXFORD LONDON GLASGOW
NEW YORK TORONTO MELBOURNE WELLINGTON
KAULA LUMPUR SINGAPORE JAKARTA HONG KONG TOKYO
DELHI BOMBAY CALCUTTA MADRAS KARACHI
NAIROBI DAR ES SALAAM CAPE TOWN

Published in the United States
by Oxford University Press, New York

© Mary G. Cheney 1980

All rights reserved. No part of this publication may be reproduced, stored in a retrieval system, or transmitted, in any form or by any means, electronic, mechanical, photocopying, recording, or otherwise, without the prior permission of Oxford University Press

British Library Cataloguing in Publication Data

Cheney, Mary G.
 Roger, Bishop of Worcester, 1164–1179 – (Oxford historical monographs).
 1. Roger, *Bishop of Worcester*
 2. Roman Catholic Church – Bishops – Biography
 3. Bishops – England – Worcester – Biography
 I. Title II. Series
 282'.092'4   BX4705.R/   79-41665

ISBN 0-19-821879-6

Printed in Great Britain by
Lowe & Brydone Printers Limited, Thetford, Norfolk

PREFACE

My first researches on Bishop Roger of Worcester were undertaken for the Oxford degree of Bachelor of Letters between July 1938 and July 1940; the second year's work was made possible by the grant of a research studentship at Westfield College, University of London. It is startling to recall that at that time there were only two scholarly studies of twelfth-century English bishops, those of Lena Voss on Henry of Winchester, and Dom Adrian Morey on Bartholomew of Exeter; the latter was an admirable model for a beginner studying Bartholomew's younger colleague.

For many years after 1940 other interests and duties prevented me from amplifying and amending my study of the bishop's career. When I was able to do so, more than twenty-five years later, both the direction of my research and the shape of this book were to some extent determined by the advances made in the meantime in the fields of twelfth-century history and canon law, as seen in the writings of Raymonde Foreville, David Knowles, C. R. Cheney, Walther Holtzmann, and Stephan Kuttner, to name only those whose work most directly affected my own. Professor Foreville's work made it possible to see more clearly Roger's part in the affair of Archbishop Thomas, and enabled me to discuss it here without relating the whole story afresh. In dealing with the structure and organization of the diocese of Worcester, I have been much helped by Professor Roy Haines's meticulous account of the diocese in the early fourteenth century, and this has made superfluous further discussion of its geography and territorial divisions. Above all, Holtzmann's work made it desirable and possible to devote more thought to Bishop Roger's work as a papal judge-delegate and as a keen observer of the legal scene, if not as a professional lawyer. I was also able to profit from the work of Stephan Kuttner and Eleanor Rathbone on the Anglo-Norman canonists, and from Charles Duggan's researches on the English decretal collections.

In the process of recasting my early work and adding to it, I have received help and advice from many scholars, librarians, and archivists in England and northern France, so many, indeed, that it is impossible to name and to thank them all individually. I owe a special debt to Professor Stephan Kuttner, both for his encouragement and for making possible two visits to the Institute of Medieval Canon Law at Berkeley, California, and for permission to use the papers left in his care by Professor Holtzmann; I must also thank him for permission to make use of material from my article 'Pope Alexander and Roger, bishop of Worcester'. Sir Richard Southern has long taken a kindly interest in my work; he and Dr Barbara Harvey read the greater part of the book in typescript and gave me the benefit of their friendly criticism. Professor David Luscombe kindly read a section which required an excursion into the unfamiliar paths of theology. My debt to the printed work of Dr Charles Duggan will be obvious to readers of this book; I have also referred on several occasions to parts of his doctoral thesis which are still unfortunately not in print, and benefited from his suggestions on some important topics.

I am grateful to the following for help with particular problems: Dr J. J. G. Alexander, the Revd Professor Leonard Boyle O.P., Professor C. N. L. Brooke, Dr G. R. C. Davis, Professor J. C. Holt, Dr B. R. Kemp, Dr N. R. Ker, and Mrs Dorothy Owen. I wish also to thank the custodians, past and present, of the diocesan and capitular archives of the cathedrals of Durham, Gloucester, Hereford, Salisbury, Wells, and Worcester, the librarian and archivist of His Grace the Duke of Devonshire at Chatsworth House, the librarians or archivists of Lambeth Palace, the College of Arms, King's College, Cambridge, Jesus and St John's Colleges, Oxford, and Christ Church, Oxford. In all cases permission was generously given to print the texts I required. Appendix I, no. 3 is printed by permission of the Trustees of the Berkeley Estates, nos. 2 and 37 by permission of the Controller of H.M. Stationery Office.

In conclusion, I should like to thank the Editors of the Oxford Historical Monographs and the Delegates of the Oxford University Press for accepting this book for publication in the series.

CONTENTS

List of books and articles cited, with abbreviations	ix
List of decretal collections, with abbreviations	xv
1 The early years	1
2 Church and king: Bishop Roger's part in the affair of Archbishop Thomas	17
3 The bishop in his diocese	56

The pastor (p. 56); the secular clergy (p. 69); monasteries, churches and patrons (p. 78); the judge (p. 90); the bishop's staff and household (p. 99); the Red Book of Worcester (p. 107); conclusion (p. 111)

4 The judge-delegate	113

The sources (p. 113); the background (p. 116); Bishop Roger as judge-delegate (p. 124); disputed jurisdiction (p. 139); undisputed jurisdiction (p. 151); possession, right and restitution (p. 162); conclusion (p. 164)

5 The bishop and the law	166
Part I Bishop Roger and the making of new law	166

Introduction (p. 166); papal pronouncements elicited by Bishop Roger (p. 170); papal pronouncements addressed to Roger at the request of litigants (p. 185); a request for a papal ruling (p. 187); contacts with the pope (p. 190)

Part II The 'English' contribution	193

The problems (p. 193); reforms and the making of law (p. 195); some decretal collections (p. 197); Master David of London (p. 206); conclusion (p. 208)

6 The later years, 1172–1179	213
Appendix I Acta of Bishop Roger, with related texts	228
Appendix II Calendar of papal letters to Bishop Roger, with related letters, and evidence for lost commissions	313
Appendix III The priors of Great Malvern, 1177–1191	374
Appendix IV Itinerary of Bishop Roger	377

Illustrations
(*between pp.* 228 *and* 229)

Plate I   Notification in chirograph form

Plate II   Bishop Roger's seal

BOOKS AND ARTICLES CITED, WITH ABBREVIATIONS

Ann. Mon.: *Annales monastici*, ed. H. R. Luard, 5 vols., RS 1864–9
Arnulf: see *Letters of Arnulf*

BL: British Library, London
BMCL: *Bulletin of the Institute of Medieval Canon Law*, new series
BN: Bibliothèque nationale, Paris
Bodl.: Bodleian Library, Oxford
Brett, M., *The English Church under King Henry I*, Oxford 1975
Brooke, Z. N., 'The Register of Master David of London and the part he played in the Becket crisis', *Essays in History presented to R. Lane Poole*, ed. H. W. C. Davis, Oxford 1927, pp. 227–45

Van Caenegem, R. C., *Royal Writs in England from the Conquest to Glanvill*, Selden Soc., 77, 1959
Cal. Docs. France: *Calendar of Documents preserved in France, illustrative of the History of Great Britain and Ireland*, I, A.D. 918–1206, ed. J. H. Round, HMSO 1899
Cal. Pat. Rolls: *Calendar of Patent Rolls*, HMSO 1901 onwards
Cheney, C. R., *English Bishops' Chanceries 1100–1250*, Manchester 1950
——, *From Becket to Langton*, Manchester 1956
Cheney, M., 'The Council of Westminster 1175', *SCH* xi, 1975, pp. 61–8
——, 'William FitzStephen and his Life of Archbishop Thomas', *Church and Government in the Middle Ages*, ed. C. N. L. Brooke *et al.*, Cambridge 1976, pp. 139–56
——, 'Pope Alexander III and Roger, bishop of Worcester: the exchange of ideas', *Proceedings of the Fourth International Congress of Medieval Canon Law*, 1972, pp. 207–27, Monumenta Iuris Canonici, series C: Subsidia, v, Città del Vaticano 1976
Chew, Helena M., *The English Ecclesiastical Tenants-in-Chief and Knight Service*, Oxford 1932
Chodorow, S. and Duggan, C., *Decretales ineditae saec. XII*, and *Regesta Decretalium saec. XII*, Monumenta Iuris Canonici, Series B: Corpus Collectionum, Città del Vaticano [forthcoming]
Chron. de Abingdon: *Chronicon monasterii de Abingdon*, ed. Joseph Stevenson, 2 vols., RS 1888
Chron. de Bello: *Chronicon monasterii de Bello*, [ed. J. S. Brewer], Anglia Christiana Soc. 1846
Chron. de Evesham: *Chronicon abbatiae de Evesham ad annum 1418*, ed. W. D. Macray, RS 1863
Chron. Stephen: *Chronicles of the reigns of Stephen, Henry II and Richard I*, ed. R. Howlett, 4 vols., RS 1884–9
Cirencester cart.: *The cartulary of Cirencester Abbey*, ed. C. D. Ross and Mary Devine, 3 vols., Oxford 1964–77

BOOKS AND ARTICLES CITED, WITH ABBREVIATIONS

Collectiones decretalium: see pp. xv–xvi

The Complete Peerage: by G. E. C(ockayne), revised by V. Gibbs *et al.*, 13 vols., London 1910–59

Constable, Giles, *Monastic Tithes from their Origins to the Twelfth Century*, Cambridge 1964

Councils and Synods, with other Documents relating to the English Church, vol. II, ed. F. M. Powicke and C. R. Cheney, Oxford 1964. (Vol. I, ed. D. Whitelock, M. Brett and C. N. L. Brooke, forthcoming)

Curia Regis Rolls . . . as preserved in the PRO, 15 vols., HMSO 1922–72

Darley cart.: The cartulary of Darley Abbey, ed. R. R. Darlington, 2 vols., Kendal 1945, for the Derbyshire Archaeological Society

Davis, G. R. C., *Medieval Cartularies of Great Britain: a Short Catalogue*, London 1958

D. and C. mun.: Muniments of the Dean and Chapter

Decretal Collections: see pp. xv–xvi

Delisle, *Recueil: Recueil des actes de Henri II . . . concernant les provinces françaises*, ed. L. Delisle and E. Berger, 4 vols. and album, Paris 1909–27

Denton, J. H., *Royal Free Chapels, 1100–1300*, Manchester 1970

Diceto: *Radulfi de Diceto decani Londoniensis opera historica*, ed. William Stubbs, 2 vols., RS 1876

Duggan, *Collections:* C. Duggan, *Twelfth Century Decretal Collections and their Importance in English History*, London 1963

Duggan, C., 'The Trinity collection of decretals and the early Worcester family', *Traditio* 17 (1961) 506–26

——, 'English decretals in continental primitive collections, with special reference to the primitive collection of Alcobaça', *SG* 14 (1967) 53–71

Early Yorkshire Charters, vols. 1–3 (1914–16), ed. W. Farrer; vols. 4–12, ed. C. T. Clay, Yorkshire Archaeological Soc., Record series (1935–65)

EHR: English Historical Review

English episcopal acta, [in progress]. Vol. I, Lincoln 1067–1185, ed. D. M. Smith, British Academy/Oxford 1980

Extra, Liber Extra: see X

Eyton, *Itinerary:* R. W. Eyton, *Court, Household and Itinerary of King Henry II*, London 1878

Fasti: John Le Neve, *Fasti Ecclesiae Anglicanae 1066–1300*, new ed. in progress, i, St Paul's, London (1968), ii, Monastic Cathedrals (1971), iii, Lincoln (1977), ed. D. Greenway

Foliot: see *Letters of Foliot*

Foreville, Raymonde, *L'Église et la royauté en Angleterre sous Henri II Plantagenet (1154–1189)*, Paris 1943

Fransen, *Les décrétales:* G. Fransen, *Les décrétales et les collections de décrétales*, Typologie des sources du Moyen Âge occidental, ed. L. Génicot, Fasc. 2 A-III, 1*, Turnhout 1972

Friedberg, E., *Quinque Compilationes Antiquae*, Leipzig 1882

BOOKS AND ARTICLES CITED, WITH ABBREVIATIONS xi

——, *Die Canones-Sammlungen zwischen Gratian und Bernard von Pavia*, Leipzig 1897

Gervas. Cant.: *Historical works of Gervase of Canterbury*, ed. William Stubbs, 2 vols., RS 1879–80
Gesta regis Henrici secundi Benedicti abbatis, ed. William Stubbs, 2 vols., RS 1867
Gilberti epistolae: *Gilberti ex abbate Glocestriae episcopi primum Herefordensis deinde Londoniensis epistolae*, ed. J. A. Giles, 2 vols., Patres ecclesiae Anglicanae, London, Oxford 1846. See also *Letters of Foliot*
Giraldi opera: *Giraldi Cambrensis opera*, ed. J. S. Brewer *et al.*, 8 vols., RS 1861–91
Glanvill, *Tractatus de legibus et consuetudinibus regni Angliae* . . . , ed. G. D. G. Hall, Nelson's Medieval Texts, 1965
Gloucester cart.: *Historia et cartularium . . . monasterii Gloucestriae*, ed. W. H. Hart, 3 vols., RS 1863–7
Guernes de Pont-Sainte-Maxence, Vie de S. Thomas . . . , ed. E. Walberg, Lund 1922, and with reduced apparatus in Les Classiques français du Moyen Âge, Paris 1936

HMC: Royal Commission on Historical Manuscripts
HMC *Wells*: HMC, *Calendar of the manuscripts of the Dean and Chapter of Wells*, 2 vols., 1907–14
HMC Worcester: HMC, *Fourteenth Report, Appendix, Part viii* (1895), Muniments . . . of the Dean and Chapter of Worcester pp. 165–203; Muniments of the Bishop of Worcester, pp. 204–5
HMSO: His/Her Majesty's Stationery Office
Haines, R. M., *The bishopric of Worcester in the first half of the fourteenth century*, London (S.P.C.K.) 1965
Heads of Houses: *The Heads of Religious Houses in England and Wales, 940–1216*, ed. David Knowles, C. N. L. Brooke and Vera London, Cambridge 1972
Hereford Charters: *Charters and Records of Hereford Cathedral*, ed. W. W. Capes, Cantilupe Soc., Hereford 1908
Hist. S. Augustini: *Historia Monasterii sancti Augustini Cantuariensis by Thomas of Elmham*, ed. Charles Hardwick, RS 1858
Holtzmann, *Studies*: *Studies in the collections of twelfth-century decretals*, from papers of the late W. Holtzmann, edited, translated and revised by C. R. and M. G. Cheney, Monumenta Iuris Canonici, Series B: Corpus Collectionum, vol. 3, Città del Vaticano 1979
Holtzmann, W., 'Die Register Papst Alexanders III in den Händen der Kanonisten', *QFIAB* 30 (1940) 13–87
see also *PUE*
Holtzmann and Kemp: *Papal decretals relating to the diocese of Lincoln in the twelfth century*, ed. W. Holtzmann and E. W. Kemp, Lincoln Record Soc., 1954

xii BOOKS AND ARTICLES CITED, WITH ABBREVIATIONS

Hoveden: Chronica Magistri Rogeri de Houedene, ed. William Stubbs, 4 vols., RS 1868–71

JEH: Journal of Ecclesiastical History
JL: *Regesta Pontificum Romanorum . . . ad annum 1198*, ed. P. Jaffé, 2nd ed. S. Loewenfeld *et al.*, 2 vols., Leipzig 1885–8
Jocelin of Brakelond: The chronicle of Jocelin of Brakelond, ed. H. E. Butler, Nelson's Medieval Classics, 1949

Ker, N. R., *Medieval Libraries of Great Britain: a list of surviving books*, 2nd ed., Royal Historical Soc., 1964
Knowles, David, *The episcopal colleagues of Archbishop Thomas Becket*, Cambridge 1951
Kuttner, S., see *Repert.*
Kuttner, S. and Rathbone, E., 'Anglo-Norman canonists of the twelfth century', *Traditio* 7 (1949–51) 279–358

Landboc sive Registrum monasterii . . . de Winchelcumba . . . , ed. David Royce, 2 vols., Exeter 1892, 1903
Landau, P., *Ius Patronatus: Studien zur Entwicklung des Patronats im Dekretalenrecht und in der Kanonistik des zwölften und dreizehnten Jahrhunderts* (Cologne/Vienna 1975), Forschungen zur kirchlichen Rechtsgeschichte und zum Kirchenrecht 12
The letters of Arnulf of Lisieux, ed. F. Barlow, Camden 3rd series 61 (1939)
The letters and charters of Gilbert Foliot, ed. Adrian Morey and C. N. L. Brooke, Cambridge 1967
The letters of John of Salisbury, i, ed. W. J. Millor, H. E. Butler and C. N. L. Brooke, 1955; ii, ed. W. J. Millor and C. N. L. Brooke, 1979 (also ed. J. A. Giles, 2 vols., 1848; PL 199)
Liber Pensionum Prioratus Wigorn, ed. Clement Price, Worc. Hist. Soc. 1925
Liverani, F. (ed.), *Spicilegium Liberianum*, vol. i, Florence 1863
Loewenfeld, S. (ed.), *Epistolae Pontificum Romanorum Ineditae*, Leipzig 1885
Luffield Priory Charters, ed. G. R. Elvey, Bucks and Northants Record Socs., 2 vols., 1968–75

MTB: *Materials for the history of Thomas Becket*, ed. J. C. Robertson and J. B. Sheppard, 7 vols., RS 1875–85
Magna vita S. Hugonis episcopi Lincolniensis, ed. James F. Dimock, RS 1864
Mansi, J. D., *Sacrorum Conciliorum nova . . . collectio*, 31 vols., Florence 1759–98
Martène, E. and Durand, U., *Veterum Scriptorum et Monumentorum . . . amplissima collectio*, 2 vols., 1724. (Reg. epistolarum Alexandri papae III . . ., vol. ii, 624–1011)
Mon. Ang.: W. Dugdale, *Monasticon Anglicanum*, ed. J. Caley *et al.*, 6 vols. in 8, 1817–30
Morey, A., *Bartholomew of Exeter, bishop and canonist*, Cambridge 1937

BOOKS AND ARTICLES CITED, WITH ABBREVIATIONS xiii

Nash, T. R., *Collections for the History of Worcestershire*, 2 vols. (London 1781–2, 2nd ed. and supplement 1799)

OHS: Oxford Historical Society
Oseney cart.: *The Cartulary of Oseney Abbey*, ed. H. E. Salter, 6 vols., OHS 1929–36

Pd: printed
PL: *Patrologiae cursus completus, series latina*, ed. J. P. Migne, 221 vols., Paris 1844–64
PR: Pipe Roll, as published by the Pipe Roll Soc., 1884 onwards
PRO: Public Record Office
PUE: *Papsturkunden in England*, ed. W. Holtzmann, 3 vols., 1930–1, 1935–6, 1952. Abhandlungen der Gesellschaft der Wissenschaften zu Göttingen, Phil.-hist. Klasse, Neue Folge 15, Dritte Folge 14–15, 33
PUF: *Papsturkunden in Frankreich*, vol. 2 (Normandie, 1937), vol. 5 (Touraine, Anjou, Maine und Bretagne, 1956), both ed. J. Ramackers, Abhandlungen der Gesellschaft der Wissenschaften zu Göttingen, Phil.-Hist. Klasse, Dritte Folge nos. 21, 35

QFIAB: *Quellen und Forschungen aus italienischen Bibliotheken und Archiven*

RS: (Rolls Series) *Rerum Britannicarum Medii Aevi Scriptores, or Chronicles and Memorials of Great Britain and Ireland during the Middle Ages*, HMSO
RTAM: *Recherches de Théologie ancienne et médiévale*
Red Book of the Exchequer, ed. Hubert Hall, 3 vols. RS 1896
Red Book: *The Red Book of Worcester*, ed. M. Hollings, Worcester Hist. Soc., 1934, 1937, 1939, 1950, with continuous pagination.
Reg. antiquiss.: *The Registrum antiquissimum of the cathedral church of Lincoln*, ed. C. W. Foster and K. Major, 10 vols., and plates (2 vols.), Lincoln Record Soc., 1931–73
Registrum Malmesburiense, ed. J. S. Brewer, 2 vols. RS 1879, 1880
Registrum . . . Prioratus . . . Wigorniensis, ed. William H. Hale, Camden Soc. 1865
Repert.: Stephan Kuttner, *Repertorium der Kanonistik, 1140–1234*, (Studi e Testi, vol. 71) Città del Vaticano 1937
Rot. Chart.: *Rotuli Chartarum* I.i., ed. T. D. Hardy, Record Commission, 1837
Rymer, Thomas (ed.), *Foedera, conventiones, litterae . . .*, ed. A. Clarke *et al.*, 3 vols. in 6, Record Commission, 1816–30

Salisbury charters: Charters and documents . . . of the cathedral, city and diocese of Salisbury, ed. W. Rich Jones and W. Dunn Macray, RS 1891
Salisbury, John of: see *Letters of John of Salisbury*
Sayers, Jane E., *Papal judges delegate in the province of Canterbury 1198–1254*, Oxford 1971
SCH: *Studies in Church History*

SG: Studia Gratiana
Singer, *Beiträge:* H. Singer, *Neue Beiträge zu den Dekretalen-sammlungen vor und nach Bernard von Pavia*, Sitzungsberichte der Kaiserlichen Akademie in Wien, Phil.-Hist. Klasse 171.1, 1913

Thomas, William, *Survey of the Cathedral Church of Worcester*, 1736
Thorne: Chronica W. Thorne, monachi s. Augustini Cantuariensis, in *Historiae Anglicanae Scriptores Decem*, ed. Roger Twysden, 1652
Torigni (or de Monte) Robert of, Chronicle, in *Chron. Stephen*, vol. iv, (which incorporates much of the annotation of the slightly earlier ed. of L. Delisle, 2 vols., Soc. de l'hist. de Normandie, Rouen 1872–3)
TPN: Taxatio ecclesiastica Angliae et Galliae auctoritate papae Nicholai IV circa A.D. 1291, Record Commission, London 1802
TRHS: Transactions of the Royal Historical Soc.

VCH: *Victoria County History*

Walberg, E., *La Tradition hagiographique de S. Thomas Becket avant la fin du xiie siècle*, Paris 1929
——, *See also* Guernes
Warner, George and Gilson, Julius P., *Catalogue of Western manuscripts in the old Royal and King's collections*, 4 vols., London 1921
Wilkins, David (ed.), *Concilia Magnae Britanniae et Hiberniae, A.D. 446–1717*, 4 vols., 1737
Worc. cart.: The cartulary of Worcester Cathedral Priory (Reg. I), ed. R. R. Darlington, PR Soc., NS 38 (1968)

X, *Extra:* Decretalium Gregorii pp. IX compilatio, ed. E. Friedberg, *Corpus Iuris Canonici*, vol. ii, Leipzig 1881

ZRG: Zeitschrift der Savigny-Stiftung für Rechtsgeschichte (Kan. Abt.)

LIST OF DECRETAL COLLECTIONS WITH ABBREVIATIONS

A comprehensive list of the decretal collections of c.1170–1210 with particulars of mss, editions, analyses etc, will be found in Holtzmann, *Studies*, pp. xx–xxxi. The following list includes only collections cited in the present work, and its chief purpose is to direct readers to printed texts where these exist.

Abr.	=	Abrincensis I, analysed Singer, *Beiträge*, pp. 355–400
Alc.	=	Alcobacensis I, analysed Holtzmann, *Studies*, pp. 8–25
ACL	=	Appendix Concilii Lateranensis, pd Mansi, *Concilia*, xxii, coll. 248–433
Aur.	=	Aureaevallensis, analysed Holtzmann, *ZRG* (1927), 77–115
Belv.	=	Belverensis, analysed Duggan, *Collections*, pp. 154–62
Bridl.	=	Bridlingtonensis, Bodl. Bodley MS 357 fos. 80^r–133^v, see Duggan, *Collections*, pp. 85–95
Brug.	=	Brugensis, analysed Friedberg, *Canones-Sammlungen*, pp. 136–70
Cant.	=	Cantuariensis, analysed Duggan, *Collections*, pp. 162–71
Cantab.	=	Cantabrigensis, analysed Friedberg, *Canones-Sammlungen*, pp. 5–21
Chelt.	=	Cheltenhamensis, BL Egerton MS 2819 fos. 11^r–102^v, see Duggan, *Collections*, pp. 99–103
Claud.	=	Claudiana, BL Cotton Claudius MS A. iv fos. 189–216, see Duggan, *Collections*, pp. 85–95
Claustr.	=	Claustroneoburgensis, analysed, and many items printed, F. Schoensteiner, *Jahrbuch des Stiftes Klosterneuburg* 2 (1909), 1–154
Comp. I, Comp. II	=	Compilatio I, II, analysed Friedberg, *Quinque Comp.*, pp. 1–65, 66–104
Cott.	=	Cottoniana, BL Cotton Vitellius MS E xiii fos. 204–288, see Duggan, *Collections*, pp. 103–10
Dert.	=	Dertusensis I, analysed Holtzmann, *ZRG* 16 (1927), 39–77
Duac.	=	Duacensis, Douai, Bibl. municipale MS 590 fos. 1^r–2^v, 247^r–248^v, see Holtzmann, *Traditio* 18 (1962), 452–5
Dun.	=	Dunelmensis 1, analysed Holtzmann, *Studies*, pp. 75–99
Flor.	=	Florianensis, analysed Holtzmann, *Studies*, pp. 43–63
Font.	=	Fontanensis, analysed Holtzmann, *Studies*, pp. 100–115, and see Duggan, *Collections*, pp. 80–1
Francft.	=	Francofortana, analysis forthcoming by P. Landau. Cf. Holtzmann and Kemp, p. xiv, and *Repert.* p. 295
Lips.	=	Lipsiensis, analysed Friedberg, *Quinque Comp.*, pp. 189–208

Par. I, Par. II	=	Parisiensis I, II, analysed Friedberg, *Canones-Sammlungen*, pp. 45–63, 21–45
Pet.	=	Petrihusensis, Cambridge, Peterhouse MSS 193, 114, 203, 180 (quires used as flyleaves), see Duggan, *Collections*, pp. 103–9
Reg.	=	Regalis, BL Royal MS 15 B iv fos. 107^v–118^v, see Duggan, *Collections*, pp. 81–4
Roff.	=	Roffensis, analysed Duggan, *Collections*, pp. 173–84
Rot. I	=	Rotomagensis I, analysed Holtzmann, *Studies*, pp. 160–207
Sang.	=	Sangermanensis, analysed Singer, *Beiträge*, pp. 68–354
Tan.	=	Tanneri, analysed Holtzmann, *Festschrift zur Feier des 200 jahrige Bestehens der Akad. der Wissenschaften in Göttingen* (1951), 83–145
Wig.	=	Wigorniensis, analysed H. E. Lohmann, *ZRG* 22 (1933), 36–187
Wig. alt.	=	Wigorniensis altera, analysed Duggan, *Collections*, pp. 152–4

I

THE EARLY YEARS

Herbert of Bosham, writing the life of St Thomas of Canterbury, allowed himself a digression when he came to record the election in 1163 of Roger, son of the earl of Gloucester, to the bishopric of Worcester. He says:

> To the see of Worcester a man was elected, young in years but old in virtuous living and seriousness, Roger by name. He was a nobleman, the son of the great Robert, late earl of Gloucester; already his outstanding virtue exceeded the nobility of his birth. If only the plan of the work I have undertaken would allow it, if only it were possible for me now to exalt this man with praises such as his merits deserve! He would shine out in this history of the martyr like the morning star in the heavenly firmament, or a blazing light burning and shining above all others in the shadows of our present life. When I think of him, I think of another great priest, Simon, son of Onias, who in his life repaired the house and in his days strengthened the temple, who was as the rainbow shining among clouds, as the lilies at the waterspring, as the flower of roses in springtime, as incense burning in fire and as a vessel of solid gold, a most precious vessel sanctified with honour and truly serving the house of God. But the plan of my present work calls me back. I may not with my pen cause the river of praise, or even a tiny stream, to flow through the pleasant pastures of his goodness, or compare the variety of his virtues to the variety of most beautiful flowers, though in his purity he was like the lily, in his modesty like the rose, in holy living like the violet, and yet like music for his joyful friendship. Above all, how great a pillar of justice was this man, how solid a rock of constancy for the support of others![1]

In all the biographies of the archbishop, no other individual receives praise of such warmth.

Herbert never came back with his pen to those pleasant pastures, no *vita*, no *gesta* of that great priest was written by those who knew him. Gerald of Wales did indeed in his later years, long after Roger's death, select him as one of the six most influential bishops of his time; he jotted down a few notes, hardly more than anecdotes, about him and the others, and appended them to his work on St Remigius and his successors at Lincoln.[2] Gerald linked Roger with his older contemporary

[1] *MTB*, iii. 259, with reminiscences of Ecclus. 50:1–10.
[2] *Giraldi opera*, vii. 43.

Bartholomew, bishop of Exeter, introducing them as: 'bishops of great repute, outstanding in fame and virtue, rightly to be compared in their zeal for ecclesiastical justice. They were indeed like twin candelabra, illuminating all Britain with their brilliance, so that Pope Alexander used to say these two were the two great lights of the English church, and to them, trusting in their probity, he issued commissions for almost all the lawsuits which in his time were referred to England by way of delegation. In addition to their other merits, the one was renowned among learned men for his eloquence and his knowledge of the disciplines of letters, the other was conspicuous among the nobility and great men of the land for his nobility both of birth and mind.' Gerald had known Roger personally,[3] and been impressed by his courage, his resolute avoidance of nepotism, and his support of Archbishop Thomas. But if one may judge his interest by the space devoted to different topics, he particularly admired Roger's quick wit and bold tongue, especially as directed at the hot-tempered and violent king of England. Where Herbert speaks of the modest rose, the pure lily, Gerald tells a couple of racy stories. Roger, he says, once came across two men about to appear before the court on the serious charge of speaking insulting, perhaps treasonable, words of the king. On the bishop's advice, they promptly admitted the offence, adding that this was nothing to what would have been said if the wine had not run out. The king laughed; the culprits escaped. On another occasion, at which Gerald, as archdeacon of Brecon, may well have been present, Roger himself deflected the king's anger. In March 1176 the prelates of England had assembled for a council at the summons of a papal legate. At the very start of the proceedings there was something like a riot. The archbishop of York tried to seize the place of honour on the legate's right hand, and was unceremoniously picked up and removed by some of the southern prelates. The archbishop, an old supporter of Henry II, complained to the king, who was disposed to treat the matter as a case of assault; had not the archbishop been roughly handled, and his cope torn? Not so, said the bishop of Worcester, the cope was certainly decades old, and

---

[3] Ibid., i. 43; Bishop Roger soothes Gerald's wounded pride after his failure to obtain the bishopric of St David's.

would have fallen to bits in the crush anyway. Outrageous words, but they had the desired effect; the king and the bystanders laughed, and the archbishop was put to shame, for he was apparently a notorious miser.

We must regret that both Herbert of Bosham and Gerald wrote so much, and yet told us so little, about Bishop Roger. But at least Gerald's trivial stories, which may be quite inaccurate in detail, confirm other more sober evidence about the bishop's quick tongue. There is not much jesting in the tragic story of Archbishop Thomas, but twice the word *jocatus* is applied to the bishop of Worcester.[4] With Gerald's examples in mind, it is easier to accept that some joke or jibe was uttered on these serious occasions, though the exact purport of them is not made clear. Perhaps the memory of light-hearted words, spoken in happier times, prompted Herbert's carefully planned antithesis, 'and yet like music for his joyful friendship'. The earl of Gloucester's son may have been old before his time in virtue and holy living (a conventional trope); he was not remembered as a dull man.

Herbert's rhetorical praise and Gerald's anecdotes are the only contemporary accounts of Bishop Roger. History-writing seems to have been at a low ebb at Worcester in this period. Annals were kept,[5] but they are brief and parochial, more concerned with the convent's perquisites from abbots blessed at Worcester than with the Lateran Council or the murder of the archbishop of Canterbury. In the kingdom at large, there is something of a dearth of chronicle-writing, or at least of surviving writing, for the period from the accession of Henry II to about 1170. Information then becomes fuller; Roger of Howden, William of Newburgh, Gervase of Canterbury, Ralph de Diceto offer, each from his own point of view, a full account of the last quarter of the century, and each provides occasional information about Roger of Worcester.

For the period 1163–72, the Lives of Archbishop Thomas provide a welcome, if sometimes confused and confusing, source of information. Their narratives are supplemented by the collections of letters and documents assembled by Thomas's clerks and admirers, by his chief clerical opponent, Gilbert

[4] *MTB*, iv. 47, vi. 321.
[5] *Ann. Mon.*, iv. xxxviii.

Foliot, bishop of London, and by other contemporaries.[6] There are references, in these collections and elsewhere, to letters from Bishop Roger to Archbishop Thomas, Gilbert Foliot, and Pope Alexander, but apart from reports on lawsuits only one text survives, of a letter of no general importance, which was preserved by the man in whose favour it was written (App. I, 17).

There is no trace of any collection of Bishop Roger's letters, nothing to compare with the letters of Foliot, Arnulf of Lisieux, or John of Salisbury. It might be deduced that neither Roger nor his clerks were keenly interested in fine epistolary style, but against this it must be remembered that Roger was probably well under fifty when he died; he had not been able to solace his declining years, as Gilbert and Arnulf may have done, in looking over his papers and polishing his letters for publication. No letters from Roger are preserved in the archbishop's collection, though there are references to such letters; were they too sharp in their language, or simply too unimportant, to be selected for preservation? The surviving texts of Bishop Roger's letters and charters are found, as we have long learnt to expect, almost exclusively in monastic and cathedral archives. Charters and letters concerning individual laymen or secular clerks, however important, had little chance of survival. References to lost texts are noted along with surviving *acta* in Appendix I; they help a little to restore the balance between monastic and other business.

Gerald of Wales mentioned in his account of Bishop Roger the *commissiones* of Pope Alexander, that is, the papal mandates delegating to this bishop all or part of the hearing of a case that had been taken to the Curia. Gerald was exaggerating when he said that almost all Alexander's commissions to England were addressed to Roger and Bartholomew of Exeter, as we shall see when the bishop's judicial activity is examined in detail, but

---

[6] The texts assembled in *MTB*, v, vi, vii, are drawn from the collections of Gilbert Foliot, John of Salisbury, Master David of London, and other manuscripts, as well as from the collections deriving from the archbishop's archives. For the MSS of these collections, see A. J. Duggan, 'The manuscript transmission of the letter collections relating to the Becket dispute, and their use as contemporary sources', unpublished Ph.D. thesis, University of London 1971. A short summary by the same author is in *Thomas Becket, Actes du Colloque de Sédières, 19–24 août 1973*, ed. Raymonde Foreville (Beauchesne 1975), pp. 1–7.

THE EARLY YEARS 5

there are some seventy mandates of which the text survives, addressed to Bishop Roger (alone or with others) or mentioning his involvement in cases for which the mandates are lost. The information contained in the mandates has to be treated with caution, for many, if not most, were based on statements made at the Curia by one party in the absence of the other. None the less, they can add considerably to our knowledge of the bishop's activities, particularly in the years after the death of St Thomas. Nearly all these commissions would be unknown had they not been collected by canon lawyers trying to keep up to date with the latest pronouncements of the supreme ecclesiastical lawgiver. Their collections, loosely called decretal collections, are discussed more fully below; they form a specially copious and useful source for the history of the English Church in the second half of the twelfth century, in the period before the first continuous series of surviving papal registers, the first royal chancery rolls, the first bishops' registers.

The nature of the sources explains the sharp limitations to our knowledge of Bishop Roger, and the inevitably unbalanced character of any discussion of his life and work. Trivial anecdotes and mere rumours must be noticed because they are recorded, while information on much more important topics is entirely lacking. It is necessary always to keep these large areas of ignorance openly and clearly in mind, and to resist as far as possible the temptation to fill them with conjectures, and with information drawn from the lives of other men; only this rather bleak and austere approach allows the material to be presented in a form that can be accepted and used with confidence. The surviving evidence, patchy though it is, makes it possible to offer some comments on Bishop Roger's part in the conflict between Archbishop Thomas and King Henry II, in spite of enormous gaps in our information. The nature of this evidence also compels us to devote considerable space to the bishop's judicial activity, particularly as a papal judge-delegate, and to his part in the development of the canon law, but we cannot tell whether this work occupied most of his time or much of his deepest interest. We do not know if he could speak English, the only language of most of his subjects, and there is not a single reference to his preaching. His formative years, up to his election to his bishopric, are almost entirely unknown; there is nothing to show how many of those years were spent in England, how many in northern France. Even after his election, there are many periods of months at a time when his whereabouts are unknown and his activities can only be guessed. And yet, since in the last resort all history relates to the doing and thinking of individuals, it is worth making the effort to assemble and examine all the available shreds of evidence about one who, as several contemporaries have told us, was thought to be both an influential and a good man. We shall at least get intermittent glimpses of a single, many-sided individual, who can take the place of that synthetic, artificial creature, the typical twelfth-century man, with a typical 'medieval mind'. Though we can never know him intimately, we can at least perceive a real person. And since he was by birth and office one of the great men of his time, in a position to experience and influence great events and great movements, a careful study of his career serves to illuminate and also to test general accounts of some aspects of this restless, inventive, age.

The date of Bishop Roger's birth is nowhere recorded. He was almost certainly the youngest son of Robert, earl of Gloucester, illegitimate son of King Henry I. A letter from Archbishop Thomas to Roger refers to Robert's special affection for this son of his old age.[7] Roger's mother was Mabilia, daughter of Robert FitzHamon, who brought to Robert FitzRoy great estates in England and Normandy, and a claim to the earldom of Gloucester. Earl Robert had many sons, legitimate and illegitimate; one bastard, Richard, was bishop of Bayeux from 1135 to 1142. It may be because of confusion with Richard that Roger is occasionally called illegitimate by modern writers.[8] Robert of Torigni, abbot of Mont St Michel, states in his chronicle that Roger's mother was the daughter of Robert of Bellême, and that his maternal grandfather was lord of Torigni. It was this last point that interested the abbot; the

---

[7] *MTB*, vii. 258, no. 649. 'The noble Earl Robert of Gloucester, your father, though he had many sons, is said to have loved you with a deeper affection than the others, because you were the son of his old age, and because your natural abilities showed that by God's grace he had transmitted the spark of his own wisdom and virtue to you, whom as his most precious offspring he dedicated from the first to God.'
[8] e.g. J. F. Dimock, annotating the works of Giraldus, *Opera*, vii. 57 n. 1.

rest of his statement was not quite exact, for Mabilia was the daughter of Robert of Bellême's sister.[9]

By an odd chance, Becket's biographer, William FitzStephen, has preserved what purport to be the bishop's own words about his mother. Soon after the coronation of the young Henry in 1170, the older Henry accused Bishop Roger of treachery, and exclaimed that he could not be the son of Robert 'the good earl, my uncle, who brought us up together in that castle, and had us instructed in the first elements of learning and good behaviour'. To which the bishop answered, 'You say that I am not Earl Robert's son. How do I know? But I am my mother's son, with whom my father received all his rights, and the inheritance of her estates, and the earldom.'[10] FitzStephen wrote his life of Becket within a few years of these events, and he was well acquainted with his *dramatis personae*. The speeches he puts into their mouths are inevitably semi-fictitious, but the basic facts can be accepted.

Henry's words about his years spent with Earl Robert tell us all we know of Roger's childhood. They suggest that he and his cousin the king were much of an age. Henry was born in March 1133; if Roger was born in 1132 x 1134 he would have been about thirty, which was commonly regarded as the minimum age for a bishop,[11] at the time of his election to Worcester in March 1163. The unusually long interval between his election and his consecration in August 1164 may have been due precisely to his not having reached that age, in which case he will have been a little younger than Henry. 'That castle' was probably Bristol, the headquarters from which Earl Robert for some years controlled much of southwest England on behalf of his sister Matilda 'the Empress' during her struggle with King Stephen. Henry is known to have been for some time in Earl Robert's care, and to have arrived in England with the earl late in 1142, probably in October. According to Gervase of Canterbury, his teacher in England was for four years a certain Master

---

[9] *Chron. Stephen*, iv. 286.
[10] *MTB*, iii. 104.
[11] C.3 of the Third Lateran Council restated the rule, 'lest what has been done in some cases, because of the pressures of the times, should be cited as a precedent by others'. Roger's contemporary, William, bishop of Chartres, brother-in-law of King Louis VII, was certainly under age at the time of his election, and his consecration was long delayed.

Matthew;[12] it seems reasonable to assume that Roger was his fellow-pupil at this time. But Gervase, who wrote more than fifty years later, must have been mistaken about the duration, or else about the place, of Master Matthew's instruction, for Henry was sent back to his father in Normandy before Easter 1144.[13]

Roger, who at an early age had been destined by his father to a career in the church, probably remained for some time in England. He appears as a witness to four, but only four, of the many surviving charters of Earl Robert his father and Earl William his elder brother. The earliest relates to the foundation of the Cistercian abbey of Margam in South Wales, which was undertaken by Earl Robert in the months before his death on 31 October 1147.[14] The charter was issued at Bristol, perhaps between late July and 28 October, and was witnessed by Hamo and Roger, the earl's sons. Roger was perhaps thirteen or fourteen at the time. He also witnessed an undated charter of Earl William (Patterson no. 280) for Goldcliffe Priory, recording gifts made for the welfare of the souls of their father and mother and William's heirs; William's wife is not mentioned, which may indicate a date before his marriage in 1150. Two further charters (Patterson nos. 34, 35), issued on separate occasions by William after his marriage, were witnessed by 'Roger my brother'; these record grants to St James's Priory at Bristol. The first of these is probably the latest, since it was also witnessed by Robert, Earl William's son, who can hardly have been born before the end of 1150. None of the charters gives him any title other than that of son, or brother, of the earl; presumably all were issued before he held any high ecclesiastical office.

Only once in his early years is Roger found as a witness to a royal charter. On or about 10 January 1156 he was at Dover with the king, their uncle Reginald, earl of Cornwall, Roger, archbishop of York, Thomas Becket the chancellor and a number

---

[12] *Gervas. Cant.*, i. 125.
[13] Gervase says that Henry left England in 1146. This was shown to be incorrect by R. L. Poole, 'Henry Plantagenet's early visits to England', *EHR* xlvii (1932), 447–52. Poole's dating is accepted by H. A. Cronne and R. H. C. Davis, *Regesta regum Anglo-normannorum*, iii (1971), xlvi.
[14] *Earldom of Gloucester charters*, ed. Robert B. Patterson (Oxford 1973), no. 119, and see also nos. 280, 34, 35.

of other great men, who witnessed a charter for Archbishop Theobald and the church of Canterbury.[15] Roger is styled simply 'son of the earl of Gloucester'; he appears among the clergy after the bishops and the treasurer of York, but before two archdeacons. It would appear that he was placed in this eminent position because of his princely birth, and that although he was now about twenty-one he still held no dignity in the church; though we have to reckon with the possibility that the scribe regarded his rank as sufficient to identify him, and more important than any clerical office. But there is no reference to his holding any such office before his election, and no reason to identify him with any of the numerous Rogers in England and Normandy in this period.

He does not appear as a witness to any of the other surviving royal charters of January–February 1156, and therefore there is nothing to show whether he, like the king and many of the party, was about to cross to Normandy to meet the king of France. But why else should he have been at Dover, in the furthest corner of Kent, at just this time? Possibly he was travelling to the schools of Paris, not necessarily for the first time. Herbert of Bosham noted that his 'great priest' had been a disciple of Robert of Melun *in scholis*,[16] and his evidence is amply confirmed by other sources. Robert of Cricklade, prior of St Frideswide, Oxford, tells an anecdote in which he recalls a visit to Paris, perhaps in 1158.[17] Roger 'now bishop of Worcester' came to visit him, in the company of one 'of the chief disciples' of Peter Lombard. Robert, who publicly accused Peter of heresy, was relieved to learn that his guest was a pupil of Robert of Melun and not of the Lombard.

The connection between Roger, Robert, and the schools of Paris was not forgotten. Archbishop Thomas, writing in 1166 to Roger, now bishop of Worcester, and his former teacher, now bishop of Hereford, referred to their common study of the holy scriptures, *sacrarum iuge exercitium litterarum*,[18] and probably in the same year John of Salisbury advised the exiled archbishop that the bishop of Hereford should be exhorted to support his

[15] *Mon. Ang.*, iv. 538, Eyton, *Itinerary*, p. 15.
[16] *MTB*, iii. 260.
[17] R. W. Hunt, 'English learning in the late twelfth century', *TRHS* xix (1936), 32, 37.
[18] *MTB*, v. 344.

cause, by means of letters from the masters of the schools of Paris, and by religious persons such as the prior of St Victor, and others who were his friends in France, 'and the same is advised for the bishop of Worcester'.[19] It is commonly assumed, on the basis of this one letter, that Robert of Melun taught in the schools of St Victor in his last years in Paris. The evidence seems rather thin, but if the inference is correct it would follow that Roger was his pupil there, and this might explain why Roger lived for some time, at an uncertain date, in St Victor's priory of Ste Barbe-en-Auge in Normandy.[20]

In the same letter, John of Salisbury suggested that Robert should be exhorted 'to show himself now as the sort of prelate whom he was accustomed to describe in the schools, and to free himself now from those defects which he used to condemn in others'. Robert must have touched in his lectures on the qualities required of a bishop, and painted a picture of a model prelate, while condemning as 'sons of dogs' those who were corrupted by riches and comforts.[21] The text of the lectures is lost; we do not know in what connection this topic was introduced. Robert's views on the dangers of riches perhaps influenced his pupil; Archbishop Thomas himself observed that Roger had always despised riches.[22] Perhaps Robert also instilled in him, in the course of their studies, other and more dangerous thoughts. Discussing St Paul's words on obedience to authority, Robert was the first commentator to justify active resistance to a tyrant. Bishops, he said, might excommunicate even a king, if he offended against the church.[23] Roger evidently kept his textbooks; much later we hear of him lending 'certain sentences of Master Robert' to Master David of London.[24]

---

[19] Ibid., vi. 20.   [20] Below, p. 53.   [21] *MTB*, v. 457.
[22] Ibid., vi. 578, 'nobilitatem vestram, quam constat pre honestate semper contempsisse divitias . . .'.
[23] B. Smalley, *The Becket conflict and the schools* (Oxford 1973), pp. 52-3. Robert's surviving works are edited by R. M. Martin and R. M. Gallet in *Spicilegium sacrum lovaniense*, 3 vols. 1932-52.
[24] F. Liverani, *Spicilegium Liberianum*, p. 621. Master David says 'Miseram quendam meorum Turonis pro defendendis mihi quibusdam sententiis magistri Roberti quas gratia domini Wigor' mihi commodaverat'. David's letter seems to have been written late in 1171 or early in 1172, before peace had been made between the king of England and the pope.

Roger's appearance in the schools of Paris was a sign of the times. He was the first of the Anglo-Norman royal family to begin an ecclesiastical career by attending a university. Noble prelates of a slightly earlier date would have been more likely to go to Cluny, like Roger's older cousin, Henry of Blois, bishop of Winchester.

There is no direct evidence to show whether Roger, the future judge-delegate who received so many of Pope Alexander's commissions, had studied canon or civil law, in any specialized or intensive way, before his election. His teacher, Robert of Melun, knew and often cited Gratian's *Decretum*, according to the editor of his works; he will accordingly have introduced his pupils to that learned work. But he can hardly have attempted to give anything like professional instruction in law. Herbert of Bosham says nothing of legal training, but Herbert had a low opinion of lawyers; he records with satisfaction that the crowd of lawyers in Archbishop Thomas's household sat at a lower table, suitable for men who dealt with worldly, rather than theological, matters.[25] Gerald of Wales too says nothing of legal training, but Gerald was a snob and a rhetorician; he wanted to contrast the learned bishop of Exeter and the princely bishop of Worcester.

Other indirect evidence is equally inconclusive. Roger received a commission to act as judge-delegate within a few months of his election; so did Samson, abbot of Bury St Edmund's, whose biographer tells us that Samson was at that time unlearned and unpractised in such matters, in spite of his former study of the liberal arts and the scriptures. Samson promptly hired two professional lawyers to advise him, and set to work to study the 'decrees and decretal letters', so that by means of study and practice he became a discreet judge, and was able to proceed in legal matters according to the rules of the law.[26] The bishop of Worcester could have done the same. Certainly he always had two or three *magistri* in attendance, but so did every English bishop, including those who had had some formal legal education, like Archbishop Thomas and Robert Foliot of Hereford. An undated letter from Gilbert Foliot to

---

[25] *MTB*, iii. 207.
[26] *The Chronicle of Jocelin of Brakelond*, ed. H. E. Butler, Nelson's Medieval Texts (1949), pp. 33-4.

Roger may provide evidence that Roger was at first, like Abbot Samson, unlearned and unpractised in legal, or at least in procedural, matters. The letter complains of hasty action and gross ignorance in the handling of a dispute; Gilbert is moved to give a little lecture on the basic legal rule that no man may act as judge, witness or *publica persona* in his own case.[27] But he also complains of the 'most villainous' character who has brought Roger's letter; this and the elementary nature of the blunders must raise a doubt. Had the villain forged or tampered with the letter? Once again, the evidence is not clear-cut, though it does suggest that Gilbert thought it possible that Roger needed this sort of instruction, and reminds us that, as far as we know, Roger had had no administrative experience before his election to Worcester.

Archbishop Thomas did indeed on one occasion apply the term *iurisperiti* to Roger and his teacher.[28] Writing to the two bishops in 1166, the exiled archbishop expressed his confidence that they were not among those 'qui habeantur iurisperiti, cum prodentes se et alios perdiderint iura'. But did he mean *iurisperiti* to carry the sense of having professional legal training? This must be doubted, for only a few lines earlier he had used the common phrase 'Loquimur scientibus et docentibus legem' (reminiscent of Romans 7:1), in which *legem* seems almost always to have the general meaning of divine law, or even simply of correct opinion. Taken as a whole, this letter does not provide any incontrovertible evidence for supposing that the two bishops were canon lawyers in any technical sense.

More general considerations point towards the same conclusion. Robert of Melun was primarily a theologian; his habits of mind were formed and most of his academic work done before canon law was established as an independent discipline in the schools of northern Europe.[29] Roger, a noble cleric with ascetic leanings, had no need to support himself by a career as a bishop's or a king's clerk, or in the rising profession of advocate in the courts; he had therefore no need to equip himself with a

---

[27] *Letters of Foliot*, p. 314, no. 243.
[28] *MTB*, v. 345.
[29] On the unspecialized character of academic thinking and teaching, as it existed roughly up to the time when Robert of Melun and Roger of Worcester were elected to their bishoprics, see Walter Ullmann, *The Growth of Papal Government* (1953), p. 366 n. 2, and the literature there cited.

knowledge of legal draughtsmanship and judicial procedure. If he contemplated becoming a bishop, he knew he could, like Abbot Samson, hire experts. Like Samson, he eventually learned the rules of the law, perhaps through study, certainly through hard practice as a judge, so that in about 1174 Pope Alexander could write to him in terms which assume his knowledge of a technical point of law, and one which had only recently been evolved and clearly defined.[30]

It must be assumed that Roger was maintained in the schools by his father and his brother, the earls of Gloucester, or by benefices in their patronage in England or Normandy. One of these was probably the church of Keynsham in Somerset. In 1167 Pope Alexander gave permission to Roger to establish a monastery there in memory of his nephew Robert, Earl William's only son (App. II, 46). The pope's letter, copied on to the flyleaf of a Worcester book, refers to the 'ecclesia de Chainesham, que in patrimonio tuo consistit et quam ad manus tuas diutius habuisti', words which must echo the bishop's own petition. The words suggest that Roger may have held the whole substantial manor as well as the church, but of this we cannot be certain; the manor would have been held of the earls, and it was recorded as Earl William's gift in the abbey's charters.

In March 1163 Roger was elected bishop of Worcester. Herbert of Bosham is careful to note that this was the wish of all concerned, 'communi omnium ad quos spectabat voto electus', a form of words which implies a canonical election but reflects the vague definitions of the old canon law on this subject. It would be easy to assume that the election was prompted by the king, finding a place of honour for his cousin and expecting a loyal supporter for the future. But it is not certain that he would have initiated the election of the earl of Gloucester's brother to Worcester, which could be seen as a dangerous concentration of family influence in one area. Roger himself is said to have accused Henry at a later date of ingratitude and active hostility to the family of Earl Robert (below, p. 48), and it would not be surprising if Henry remembered very vividly the earl's power

---

[30] The pope's letter to Bishop Roger begins: 'You know, as a wise and learned man, that . . . G. called elect of Lincoln has no right to grant dignities or prebends or in other ways to dispose of possessions of the church, because his election has not yet been confirmed'. (App. II, 64.)

to destroy a king's authority. Bishop Alfred of Worcester had died on 31 July 1160 and, according to Herbert, the archbishop had for some time been pressing the king to allow the filling of this and other vacancies. Was Roger the archbishop's choice?[31] Herbert says: 'the king at last, under great pressure from the archbishop, agreed that bishops should be appointed. And so bishops were elected to the two . . . sees, men conspicuous for every virtue.' William FitzStephen definitely ascribes to Thomas's influence the election of Robert of Melun to Hereford, saying that he induced the king to find places of honour for poor but distinguished natives of England living abroad.[32] Roger did not quite fit into this category, and is not mentioned in this connection. Yet another influence may have been at work, for in 1166 the archbishop, writing to the bishops of Hereford and Worcester, asserted that they were specially bound (*obligatos*) to the Roman Church, which had procured both their elections.[33] The pope was indeed more likely than usual to have been in close touch with English affairs at the appropriate time, since he was in France from April 1162 to September 1165. For much of that time he resided at Tours or at Sens, while from February to April 1163 he was actually in Paris. During this time both Robert of Melun and his noble pupil could very easily have become personally known to the pope. The archbishop would hardly have made such an assertion to the two men about their own elections unless it was based upon fact, but the circumstances remain entirely obscure.

In June 1163 Pope Alexander held a general council at Tours, designed as a counterblast to that held at Pavia in January 1160, at which the prelates of the empire had declared for the anti-pope Octavian. Ralph de Diceto noted that King Henry allowed the bishops, abbots and priors of England to attend.[34] A letter from the pope, carefully preserved in the royal archives, thanked the king and his council for their decision to send all the bishops to the meeting, and promised

---

[31] Knowles, *Episcopal colleagues*, p. 9 makes this assumption, but compare p. 22, where the king's influence is stressed.
[32] *MTB*, iii. 259 (Herbert); ibid., iii. 24 (FitzStephen).
[33] Ibid., v. 345.
[34] *Diceto*, i. 310. The bishops of Winchester, Lincoln and Bath are named as absent owing to illness.

THE EARLY YEARS

that this should not constitute a precedent for the future.[35] These general statements are confirmed by a list, only recently identified, of prelates who attended the council.[36] The last name in the list of bishops of the southern province of England is that of the elect of Worcester. Thomas Becket sat at the pope's right hand; Roger will have taken his place as his most junior suffragan. He will have heard, as Archbishop Thomas heard, the eloquent opening sermon of Arnulf, bishop of Lisieux, who took as his theme the defence of the unity and liberty of the Church, the inevitability of victory in the struggle, and the spiritual blessings promised to those who suffered in the great cause.[37] Arnulf was thinking of the struggle of Pope Alexander against the emperor and the anti-pope; he observed that most of those present were safe and rich and eminent, and prayed for an opportunity to play his part. Professor Foreville has said: 'Le concile de Tours acheva d'orienter Thomas Becket dans la dévotion aux interêts de l'église Romaine';[38] this is perhaps a more definite assertion than the evidence warrants, but the effect of the council should not be ignored, as it generally is, when the question is asked, why did the conflict of jurisdictions, already imminent in Archbishop Theobald's time, come to a head precisely in 1163, and why did the bishops of England resist the known wishes of their king, reject his proposals for the treatment of accused clerks, and refuse for some time even to promise to respect the king's ancestral rights?

The decrees and actions of the council must have provided a stimulating and revealing introduction to the affairs and the leading personalities of the church for a new young bishop. The decrees, apart from those concerned with the papal schism and with the heretics of Languedoc, were based on the idea of reform by legislation, and dealt with a wide variety of topics,

[35] JL 10834, printed *MTB*, v. 33 and Rymer, *Foedera*, I. i. 44.
[36] The list is in BL MS Cotton Vitellius A. xvii fo. 16ᵛ. The British bishops named are Canterbury, London, Ely, Salisbury, Norwich, Chichester, Rochester, Exeter, Coventry, Llandaff, St Asaph, Worcester (elect), York, Durham, Dunkeld. This list was identified and printed independently by two scholars: T. A. Reuter, 'A list of bishops attending the Council of Tours (1163)', *Annuarium historiae conciliorum* 8 (1976), pp. 116–21; Robert Somerville, *Pope Alexander III and the Council of Tours* (1977), pp. 27–9.
[37] On Arnulf's sermon see *Letters of Arnulf*, p. xli n. 4, and Robert Somerville, op. cit., pp. 12–18.
[38] *Église et royauté*, p. 116.

such as the appointment of priests to the cure of souls on an annual basis, demands for payment for burials, chrism and holy oil and for admission to the religious life, the practice of farming out for a fee the judicial duties of bishops and archdeacons, the grant to laymen of churches, tithes and offerings. The assembled prelates were encouraged to see legislation as an aid, almost a necessity, to the pastoral work which their predecessors had done for centuries in a more personal, less uniform way than was now expected.

After the council, the archbishop returned to England. There is no clear indication of Roger's movements, or of the date on which he received the temporalities of his see, which disappear from the Pipe Rolls in 1162. Nor do we know whether he was in England, and in his diocese, between his election and the council. There are, as will appear, indications that he was present during the early stages of the conflict between the king and the bishops of England, but his first precisely recorded appearance after the council is at Clarendon in January 1164. It will therefore be convenient to treat the next phase of his life in relation to the dominant issue of the years 1163–72, the dispute between the king and Archbishop Thomas, and to this we may now turn.

CHURCH AND KING: BISHOP ROGER'S PART IN THE AFFAIR OF ARCHBISHOP THOMAS

This is not the place for a new account of the causes, the personalities, the rights and wrongs, of the long dispute between King Henry II and Archbishop Thomas Becket. In the present work, interest must be focused on Roger of Worcester, examining afresh the evidence for his actions and the development of his opinions, and observing the occasions on which he was required, or was able, to make his views known, to act upon them, and in any way to influence the course of events. For the general history of the dispute and of the issues at stake, the account by Professor Raymonde Foreville remains unsurpassed.[1] The dispute was always fundamentally a dispute about jurisdiction, that is, about the exercise of power. Decisions had to be made in England about the claim of the church to special status for the clergy, to sharper separation from the laity, and to a greatly extended competence for its developing judicial system. The church's claim was opposed by the secular, royal, government, and the conflict crystallized round the strong personalities of the king and his former friend and chancellor, now archbishop of Canterbury. For the bishops of England, the result was an agonizing conflict of loyalties, and for none was the conflict more acute than for the young bishop-elect of Worcester.

All the bishops had sworn fealty to the king; all except York and Durham had professed obedience to Canterbury. But for Roger the king was his cousin, to whose cause his father had devoted the last ten years of his life. The importance of his cousin's hereditary rights must have been the dominant theme of his early years; how could he now oppose the exercise of those rights? On the other side of the scales lay his recent training in

[1] Foreville, *Église et royauté*, which has at p. xxx a table showing the dates and relationships of the contemporary Lives of Thomas, based on Walberg, *Tradition hagiographique*. See also David Knowles, *Thomas Becket* (1970) and *The episcopal colleagues of Thomas Becket* (1951).

theology, inevitably deeply imbued with notions of the supreme functions of the church in society, and the theoretical superiority of clerk over layman, priest over king. And it was to Archbishop Thomas that he had to look for consecration, which formed a personal bond no less binding than that of fealty to the king. The following pages will show, so far as the very inadequate sources allow, how Roger attempted to respect the just claims of both masters, and so earned the criticism now of one side, now of the other, and the judgement of an eminent historian that his conduct 'was on more than one occasion equivocal'.[2] To incur such judgements is perhaps the usual fate of the man who, in a great conflict, cannot persuade himself that one side has a monopoly of virtue.

There is no precise information about the date when Roger first became personally involved in the conflict. But there are some shreds of evidence, all slight and difficult to assess, which have some bearing on his movements and opinions in the months before the Council of Clarendon in January 1164, at which he was present. That he was in England before the end of December 1163 is all but certain. A letter of Gilbert Foliot (App. II, 101), addressed to the bishops-elect of Hereford and Worcester, must have been written before the consecration of Robert of Melun on 24 December. It shows that the two bishops-elect were acting together to hear a lawsuit, presumably as papal judges-delegate. And since the defendant had heard of the commission, and had come to Gilbert for a letter in support of his rights, possibly from Herefordshire, where the disputed benefice lay, it is probable that the commission had been issued at least some two months before Gilbert wrote his letter, and therefore that by about the end of October 1163 the Curia was acting on the assumption that the two bishops-elect were available to act as judges in England. The commission could, of course, have been issued much earlier, at any date after about the middle of April.

A second piece of evidence points in the same direction, but it is more difficult in this case to know how much reliance can be placed upon it. It is contained in a passage found only in two manuscripts of William FitzStephen's Life of Archbishop

[2] Knowles, *Episcopal colleagues*, p. 108.

Thomas; these are both texts of what appears to be a revised version of the Life. The passage, of which the form suggests a marginal note taken into the text by a later copyist, runs:

> The first coolness (*distantia*) between the king and St Thomas [arose] because of a clerk in the territory of Worcester, who was said to have slept with the daughter of a good man, and to have killed the father on her account. The king wished this clerk to be tried and sentenced by the lay court. The archbishop refused, and had the clerk kept in the custody of the bishop, so that he should not be handed over to the king's justice.[3]

If there is any truth in this story, and particularly in the assertion that this was the first incident that caused trouble between the king and the archbishop, it must have been at an early stage in his episcopate that the bishop of Worcester, not yet consecrated, found himself involved in the thorny problem of the trial of accused clerks. The form of words used by the chronicler must imply that the bishop fell in with the archbishop's policy, and refused to hand over the suspected murderer. There are some indications that FitzStephen himself was the author of this passage. The rather unusual word *distantia* recurs elsewhere in the Life, and FitzStephen was an acute observer of judicial matters. He also produces other information about the bishop of Worcester which is recorded by no other writer. If he was indeed the author of the passage, it must be taken seriously, for he was at this time a lawyer in the archbishop's service, and therefore well placed to observe the growing friction over the treatment of accused clerks. There is, as it happens, other evidence which suggests that at an early stage in the dispute the bishop elect of Worcester was known to hold opinions that would have made him sympathetic to the archbishop's views in the matter of ecclesiastical jurisdiction, though this evidence too presents some problems.

The Life of Thomas sometimes ascribed to Roger of Pontigny, describing the proceedings at Clarendon in January 1164, mentions, as do several others, two bishops who begged Archbishop Thomas to give way to the king, because they were already out of favour and feared that they would be the first to suffer if the dispute could not be resolved. These bishops were Jocelin of Salisbury and another, variously named as Henry of

---

[3] *MTB*, iii. 45. On FitzStephen's Life, see M. Cheney, 'William FitzStephen'. *Distantia* in this sense recurs on pp. 52, 73, 101.

Winchester (Herbert of Bosham, an eye-witness), the bishop—unnamed—of Norwich (Guernes of Pont-Sainte-Maxence, William of Canterbury and Edward Grim) and Roger of Norwich (Roger of Pontigny).[4] Roger of Pontigny followed his usual sources here, in naming the bishop of Norwich. But he added the personal names which they omit and, as he wrote, he was thinking of the bishop of Worcester, for he calls him Roger instead of William, and proceeds to a comment that can only apply to that bishop. The bishop in question was, he says, closely related to the king (which as far as we know the bishop of Norwich was not) and, though he was young (the bishop of Norwich was described as 'iam centenarius' within a few years),[5] he was devout and zealous for ecclesiastical liberty, and he had incurred the king's anger by criticizing his excesses very freely. It is difficult to interpret the evidence as to the bishop who was involved in the incident at Clarendon, but there can be no doubt that the additional comment of Roger of Pontigny refers to Roger of Worcester. It looks very much as though the writer was led astray by his source, and supplied the rest from personal knowledge. If this information can be accepted, it shows that by January 1164 the bishop of Worcester had already incurred the king's anger by opposing his wishes in the matter of jurisdiction, and by personal criticism, probably of his private life rather than his public policy.

So when the prelates and barons of England met the king at Clarendon, the bishop-elect of Worcester had probably been at work in his diocese for at least a few months, had been instrumental in protecting an accused clerk from royal justice, had become known for zeal for ecclesiastical justice (whatever that meant), and had angered the king by his free criticism. And yet there is no mention in the Lives of the archbishop of any support at this time from any bishop. A royal council had been held at Westminster in October 1163, at which the question of jurisdiction was for the first time the subject of public and acrimonious debate. There is no list of participants; the sources

---

[4] Knowles, *Episcopal colleagues*, pp. 161–2. *MTB*, iii. 279 (Herbert); *Guernes*, lines 938–9; *MTB*, i. 16 (William of Canterbury); *MTB*, ii. 391 (Grim); *MTB*, iv. 34 ('Roger of Pontigny' = Anonymous I). Similar confusion between Winton', Wigorn', and Norwic' occurs frequently in contemporary decretal collections.
[5] Liverani, *Spicilegium*, p. 746.

report only that 'the bishops' resisted the procedure demanded by the king for the trial of accused clerks, but weakened when asked to promise general respect for customary, undefined, royal rights.

Writing of the situation just after the council, Herbert of Bosham describes the isolation of the archbishop and his household, saying, 'we remained alone, and the few who supported us did so secretly, because of their fears'. He did not choose to reveal the names of these unheroic supporters. Referring to a period only a few months later, the Thomas Saga, which uses the lost Life by Robert, Prior of St Frideswide's, is more explicit. 'There were three bishops only in the land who steadfastly stood beside him with a good will, Henry of Winchester, his father by consecration, and his two sons by consecration, Roger of Worcester and Robert of Hereford. Yet their good will stood as it were behind the archbishop, without at all defending him, because awe of the king took away all their strength.'[6] These biographers stress the archbishop's lonely struggle, and suggest that fear was the only motive that prevented the other bishops from supporting him. Were they being quite honest? At Clarendon, the king required the archbishops and bishops to promise to respect the royal customs without the saving clause *salvo ordine nostro*. Gilbert Foliot, writing to Thomas a few years later, was prepared to assert that the bishops at Clarendon presented a perfectly united front against this demand. 'We stood immovable,' he says, 'we stood unafraid. We stood firm at the risk of the loss of our fortunes, torture of our bodies, exile, and even, if the Lord should permit, the sword.' And he listed his heroes, all the bishops of the province of Canterbury, omitting only William of Norwich and Walter of Rochester.[7] The retreat of the bishops, Gilbert suggests, was entirely due to the collapse of their leader. Was Gilbert any more honest than Herbert of Bosham? John of Salisbury's account is more subtle, and probably nearer the truth. 'The weight of the battle,' he says, 'fell upon the archbishop; the bishops dared do nothing

---

[6] *MTB*, iii. 274 (Herbert). *Thómas Saga Erkybyskups*, ed. E. Magnússon, (RS 1875, 1883), i. 181–3.
[7] *MTB*, v. 527–8, *Letters of Foliot*, pp. 229–43. This letter 'Multiplicem nobis' is discussed by Knowles, *Episcopal colleagues*, p. 171, and by A. Morey and C. N. L. Brooke, *Gilbert Foliot and his letters* (1965), pp. 166–87.

without his advice, because he was their head, and they were afraid to advise him to give way.'[8] Even here, though the heroes seem much less heroic, the bishops do not advise capitulation; it was Thomas who gave way. Where he led, the bishops followed. Their names were listed in the threefold chirograph recording 'a certain part of the customs and liberties and dignities of the king and his predecessors', which became known as the Constitutions of Clarendon. All accepted them, each promised solemnly, without reservation, to keep them. Roger, elect of Worcester, appears last on the list.

The clergy could now hope for peace, if not for privilege. Roger was able to arrange his long-delayed consecration; it took place at Canterbury on 23 August. He was ordained priest by the archbishop, and made the formal profession of obedience which still survives in the archives of Canterbury, with its neat cross drawn by his hand.[9] But peace was not to be had. Thomas showed at once that he regretted his weakness and his promise, and did not intend to keep it. The bishops of England refused to follow him in this volte-face. He could not persuade them to commit perjury in support of a cause which they had solemnly forsworn at his express command.

The archbishop's personal position was now the chief problem, and this posed new conflicts of loyalty for the bishops. The king obviously wished to ruin him financially and to drive him to resignation, or failing this to obtain his conviction for perjury and treason. To these ends the king summoned a council to Northampton early in October 1164. He required the bishops to sit in judgement upon the archbishop, along with the lay barons, as laid down in chapter eleven of the Constitutions. The bishops respected their promise and participated with the laymen in the first two judgements. They attempted, however, to fulfil their ecclesiastical obligations to Thomas, and all, except Gilbert Foliot, stood surety for him in respect of the fines demanded. Three laymen also stood surety. One was William, earl of Gloucester, Bishop Roger's brother. It has been suggested

---

[8] *MTB*, ii. 311.
[9] Canterbury Cathedral, D and C mun. C 115 no. 37, reproduced in N. R. Ker, *English MSS in the century after the Norman conquest* (1960), pl. 18d. This reproduction does not include the cross. Noted also in *Canterbury professions*, ed. M. Richter, Canterbury and York Society (1973), p. 50, no. 104.

that the appearance of the earl as a surety arose from the king's wish to punish the family for Roger's support of the archbishop. But FitzStephen, always clear on legal questions, speaks as though this was a matter of feudal obligation. The archbishop, he says, 'laicos fideiussores, comitem Gloecestrie et Willelmum de Eisnesforda et tertium quendam, homines suos, interposuit'.[10] William of Eynesford had recently been excommunicated by Thomas in the course of a dispute about patronage; he will hardly have counted as a supporter. Probably the archbishop was naming as sureties three of his more substantial tenants.

Still fulfilling their obligations, the bishops met to advise him when yet another charge was brought against him, about money which had passed through his hands as chancellor. They protested that Thomas had been received with an explicit promise of freedom from such liability; when this protest was brushed aside, they met again to discuss the next step. It is probably the discussions of this meeting, on 13 October, that are recorded in some detail by Alan of Tewkesbury.[11] Alan was a canon of Benevento before he became a monk of Christ Church, Canterbury, in about 1174. Where he obtained this information, recorded nowhere else, remains doubtful. He professes to be able to report the opinions of six of Thomas's suffragans. Four advised that he should resign, and throw himself on the king's mercy. Henry, bishop of Winchester, opposed them, saying that this would set a disastrous precedent. Last, the bishop of Worcester was asked for his advice, a convincing touch, for he was at this date the last in seniority. He 'so tempered his answer that in saying nothing he showed what was in his mind. "I give no advice in this matter," he said, "for if I say that the cure of souls received from God should be given up because of the wish and threats of the king, I should speak against my conscience and to my own damnation (*in capitis mei condemnationem*). If I advise resistance to the king, there are some here who are on his side, through whom it will be known to him, and I shall instantly be ejected from the synagogue and my fate will be that of public enemies and condemned men. So I do not say the one, or advise the other." ' He made his opinion clear, and rebuked

---

[10] *MTB*, iii. 53. The suggestion about Earl William is made by Robert B. Patterson, *Earldom of Gloucester charters* (1973), pp. 4–5.
[11] *MTB*, ii. 326–8.

the group of bishops who were now openly working with the king and for the resignation of the archbishop. And his judgement was sound; there was now no honourable, no canonical, no safe way out of the impasse. Thomas did not resign. Instead, he awaited the debate of the council, putting on a brave face though his knights renounced their fealty and his clerks were deserting him.

Thomas came to the meeting expecting the worst. According to Herbert of Bosham, he carried the host with him; according to FitzStephen his remaining clerks debated the question: ought he to excommunicate his attackers if the worst befell? To emphasize his priestly character, he proposed to go in his vestments, from which they dissuaded him, and to carry his cross in his own hands as a protection and a symbol of his priestly status, instead of having it borne before him in the customary way. This last part of his plan he carried out, to the surprise and dismay of all present, who saw that it would be regarded as a reflection on the integrity of the king. In this highly charged atmosphere, the archbishop's action produced one of those sudden storms in which men have no time to think, but act violently and speak hastily. Perhaps no bystander saw and heard it all; certainly different tales were told of it later. All agree that the bishop of London was involved, that he used insulting words, and that he, and perhaps others, tried to wrench the cross from the archbishop's hands. In this undignified wrangle the bishop of Worcester came to Thomas's defence, and reproved Gilbert Foliot, adding some jest or crack of which the sense remains obscure, and drawing from Gilbert a prophecy that Roger would pay dearly for the words he had uttered. If the story is anything more than fiction, it shows Bishop Roger supporting Thomas with a certain impetuous courage, at a time when such support was likely to bring retribution. Perhaps he did not appreciate as fully as the older man the probable consequence of the cross-carrying; Herbert of Bosham says that on hearing of it, King Henry was beside himself with rage.[12]

So the archbishop carried his cross. He had forbidden his suffragans to take part in any judgement against him, and

[12] Ibid., iv. 47 ('Roger of Pontigny'). *Guernes*, lines 1678–85. *MTB*, iii. 305 (Herbert).

appealed against them to the pope because they had already presumed to judge him, their ecclesiastical superior; both the prohibition and the appeal were offences against the Constitutions of Clarendon. The bishops, with the king's permission, respected the prohibition and appealed against Thomas in their turn. Thomas refused to hear the judgement of the lay lords, and left the castle. In the evening he sent three bishops, Robert of Hereford, Roger of Worcester and Walter of Rochester to the king, to ask for licence to depart and safe conduct out of the country.[13] Again, the bishops of Hereford and Worcester, 'his sons by consecration', are associated with the archbishop. The king put them off; he would answer tomorrow. Did the three bishops advise Thomas to escape while he could? According to William FitzStephen, it was the king's refusal to reply at once that convinced Thomas of his danger and led to his flight. According to Herbert of Bosham, 'those who knew the king's secrets' advised Thomas to 'do the best thing for himself and the king' (*ut et regi et sibi provideat*), and therefore he fled, few being aware of his plans except Herbert himself, the archbishop's chaplains and a few of his household.[14] It is hard to believe that the bishops, and particularly those who had gone to the king, had not thought of this possibility, and that they did not pause to discuss the implications of the king's answer. But none of them wrote an account of the business.

It was assumed that Thomas was hurrying to prosecute his appeal to the pope, then residing at Sens. The king therefore selected a group of bishops and eminent laymen to present his account of the affair, and to request that Thomas should be condemned at once, or sent to England with a papal legate, who would have power to hear the dispute between him and the king, without right of appeal. The bishops in the party were York, London, Chichester, Exeter and Worcester. All except Bishop Roger were mature men with considerable experience. The archbishop of of York was an old enemy of Thomas Becket, and also as it were an *ex officio* opponent of the church of Canterbury; the bishop of London also had his private feud with the archbishop. He and Hilary of Chichester had shown

[13] Ibid., iii. 308–9, 312 (Herbert).
[14] Ibid., iii. 69 (FitzStephen), iii, 312–13 (Herbert).

their disapproval of Thomas's actions at an early stage in the dispute. Bartholomew of Exeter had a reputation as a lawyer, which might be useful if the pope chose to hear the appeals at once, and he was, according to Alan of Tewkesbury, one of those who desired Thomas's resignation, believing that the king's anger was directed against him personally rather than against the clergy in general. Bishop Roger's appearance with this group is a little surprising. Was he sent as a test of loyalty? Or because his presence might help to counter suspicions that the prelates were all personal enemies of the archbishop, as was said to be the case on a later occasion? Gervase of Canterbury says that the king chose those who most hated Thomas, or those who loved him but dared not speak.[15] This may have been no more than an intelligent deduction, but it is one of the few additions which Gervase made to the information provided by his sources. Though as a monk, newly professed in 1163, he will have known nothing of the king's motives at the time, he will have met many of the leading figures in the drama, and could have spoken to many of them in the 1170s, including Roger himself.

The king's envoys, especially the bishops, are said to have met with hostility in France, and according to FitzStephen they found it necessary to disguise themselves, and to travel as members of the household of the earl of Arundel:[16] an improbable story, though the king of France showed from the first a shrewd capacity to exploit the dispute to his own advantage. Accounts of the meeting with the pope at Sens are numerous, detailed and in some respects contradictory. But on one point they agree, that in the formal discussions all the other bishops spoke, but Roger of Worcester remained silent. He did not, like Roger of York, Gilbert Foliot and Hilary of Chichester, speak against Thomas, or even second Bartholomew of Exeter in asking for legates to be sent to judge the case in England. The archbishop's biographers do not record, and few will have known, that at Sens Roger met the banished John of Salisbury, and promised to help him if he should ever need help, thus deliberately, though perhaps not openly, flouting the policy of

---

[15] *Gervas. Cant.*, i. 190.
[16] *MTB*, iii. 72.

the king.[17] He also used the visit to the pope for his own purposes, for on 26 November the pope addressed to him an important statement, of which more must be said later, defining the law relating to clerical marriage and the status of priests' sons, and instructing him to enforce it in his diocese.[18]

In spite of the pope's desperately weak position, he refused to act hastily against Thomas, or to send legates to England with full power to settle the matter. The envoys left promptly, as they had been commanded to do, and found the king at Marlborough on Christmas Eve. The day after Christmas, writs went out for the seizure of the archbishopric and of the possessions of all, clerks or laymen, employed by, or related to, the archbishop, and their immediate expulsion from England. There is no record of any protest; the archbishop had now no advocate.

While Thomas settled into his refuge with the Cistercians at Pontigny, the leaders of the church in England continued as far as possible to conduct business as usual. Bishop Roger was enthroned in his cathedral on 2 February 1165; he may not have returned to Worcester between his consecration and that date. He was at Bath on 14 March, where he witnessed, and perhaps arranged, a settlement between the elderly bishop and a group of laymen claiming lands of the church of Wells. This settlement was a minor triumph for the church. The dispute was of long standing, and the laymen had sued the church, the bishop and the precentor of Wells in the lay court *contra canones* (App. I, 72). Roger also heard one or two cases as papal judge-delegate, arrested some heretics who had settled in his diocese, and attended the council at Oxford, late in 1165 or early in 1166, at which their fate was settled.[19] He had reported their appearance to Gilbert Foliot, perhaps treating him as head of the province in the absence of the archbishop.

But however much the bishops might wish to forget the archbishop, his shadow lay across the land. In June 1165 the pope wrote to the bishop of London, ordering him to press the king to make peace with Thomas, and to associate the bishop of

---

[17] Ibid., vi. 109, John of Salisbury to the bishop of Worcester; 'nec immemor sum consolationis quam Senonis a vestre liberalitatis verbo percepi'. Knowles, *Episcopal colleagues*, p. 106 n. 4, interprets this as evidence for a gift.
[18] Below, p. 69, and App. II, no. 61.
[19] Below, p. 68.

Hereford with himself in the enterprise.[20] Gilbert followed the king 'to the very borders of Wales', where he was campaigning, and delivered the pope's exhortations. The place of the meeting, or meetings, is not stated. John, bishop of Poitiers, heard of a meeting of bishops with the king at Shrewsbury, and a royal charter shows Bishop Gilbert with the king at Oswestry, along with Roger, archbishop of York, Roger of Worcester, Robert, earl of Leicester, Richard de Lucy and Alan de Neville.[21] This formidable group may have discussed with the king the carefully-drafted reply which Gilbert transmitted to the pope.[22] Roger of Worcester appears here among some of the most important of the king's advisers, all, with the possible exception of the earl of Leicester, strongly opposed to the archbishop. As reported by Gilbert, the king's reply included an offer to accept the judgement of 'the whole church of his kingdom' on some at least of the disputed issues.

A letter composed by Herbert of Bosham suggests that towards the end of 1165 Henry added to that reply a proposal that the obnoxious 'customs' should be examined by a commission consisting of the archbishops of York and Rouen, and the bishops of London, Hereford, Worcester and Bayeux.[23] Again it appears that the bishops of Hereford and Worcester were selected to give respectability to a group of 'king's men' (Henry of Bayeux was one of the king's nominees for the archbishopric after the death of Thomas). Herbert, whose letter-collection is the only source of information about the proposal, immediately condemned it, observing that 'among these bishops the king seeks as examiners of those evil laws the very men who were the authors of them'. Evidently Herbert and the archbishop had no confidence in the intervention of the bishops of Hereford and Worcester. Nothing more is heard of the proposal.

At this time, the bishop of Worcester does not seem to have been regarded as an active partisan of the archbishop. John of

[20] *MTB*, v. 175–8 (JL 11205).
[21] *MTB*, v. 198; Delisle, *Recueil*, i. 389–90, no. 243; *Cal. docs. France*, p. 116.
[22] *Letters of Foliot*, pp. 202–7; *MTB*, v. 203–9.
[23] *MTB*, v. 287. The letter occurs only in the single MS of the letters of Herbert of Bosham. It is addressed to Pope Alexander in Thomas's name. The date is uncertain; the letter refers to a past Michaelmas, and seems to fit the circumstances of *c*. Oct. 1165–Mar. 1166.

Salisbury reported in 1165 that he had written, probably about the revenues of his benefices, to a number of old friends, the bishops of Hereford, Worcester and Chichester, and the archdeacon of Poitiers, of whom only Chichester had replied. It is not therefore surprising to find John telling Archbishop Thomas that he had no great hopes of support from Robert of Hereford or the bishop of Worcester. None the less, John thought it might be worth while to prompt letters of exhortation to them from the masters of the schools at Paris, and others, such as the prior of St Victor. The abbot and prior of St Victor wrote as suggested to Robert, and must have sent a copy to Thomas for information; it is preserved among the archbishop's papers. It urges him to live up to his former opinions about the duties of bishops and the dangerous effect of riches, and it reports the disappointment and the criticism caused by his behaviour among his former students.[24] No letter survives to Bishop Roger; if any was sent it cannot have been in the same terms. That John of Salisbury thought he might be impressed by a letter from acquaintances in Paris is interesting, but there is no means of knowing whether one was sent, and if not, why not.

In April 1166, Pope Alexander, now back in Italy, evidently judged that his own position was sufficiently improved, and the archbishop's sufficiently serious, to warrant a move in his favour. On, or about, Easter Day, letters were issued from the Lateran palace, announcing Thomas's appointment as legate of the apostolic see for all England except the diocese of York, and informing the prelates of England, instructing them to obey Thomas as legate and to come to him when summoned, without making difficulties (*sine contradictione aliqua*).[25] These letters will have been handed, according to normal practice, to the archbishop's representatives at the Curia, for transmission to him. It was then his responsibility to decide when and how they should be delivered to England. It was probably already the recognized duty of the bishop of London, as dean of the province, to circulate to the other suffragans of Canterbury

---

[24] *MTB*, v. 218; vi. 20; v. 456.
[25] *MTB*, v. 328–9, JL 11270; *MTB*, v. 329–31, JL 11271. See also *PUE*, ii. 311–12 no. 123.

documents sent to him for that purpose by the archbishop.[26] Thomas was able to exploit this custom; indeed it was highly convenient to do so, since he could only with difficulty find and pay messengers for such potentially risky work. But the bishop was hostile, and his obligations may not have been clearly defined, so that it was not prudent to rely on him exclusively. The archbishop therefore sent the letters to the two bishops on whose obedience he had the strongest claim, his 'sons by consecration' of Hereford and Worcester, with a covering letter stressing their obligation to the Roman Church and to himself.[27] He commanded them, with all the weight of his new legatine authority, to show the papal letters to the bishop of London, so that he should in turn make them known to the prelates of the province, and to the bishop of Durham. The two were also ordered to make the grant of the legation known quickly to the near-by bishops of Bath, Salisbury, Exeter, Chester and St David's, and to the bishop of Winchester. This was a wise precaution; it would ensure that the news reached at least nine bishops, and made it easier for the bishop of London to act correctly, without incurring the king's anger, since the content of the papal letters would already be public knowledge.[28]

With his letter to the two bishops, copies of the pope's letters announcing his new honour and increased authority, and probably other papal letters, Thomas will have sent his letter with instructions to the bishop of London,[29] and his letters to the other bishops, which Gilbert had to forward; the whole packet was presumably addressed to the bishops of Hereford and Worcester. Normally it seems that papal letters addressed to two or more persons would be delivered to the most senior. But just at this time, Robert of Hereford was taking part in a meeting of clergy in which a formal appeal was made to the

---

[26] The special status of the bishop of London as dean of the province was recognized early in the twelfth century, cf. Eadmer, *Historia novorum in Anglia*, ed. M. Rule (RS 1884), p. 211.
[27] *MTB*, v. 344–6.
[28] According to FitzStephen, Gilbert refused to circulate the letters (ibid., iii. 85).
[29] Ibid., vi. 35–7. Other letters which may have been sent at the same time are *MTB* v. 294 no. 157, 329 no. 173, 343 no. 178. They are mentioned in a letter of Foliot to the king (ibid., p. 417) reporting delivery of the papal letter about the legation.

pope against the archbishop, and he was one of the three bishops who set his seal to the appeal. This meeting took place on 24 June, and neither in the appeal nor in the letter about it from the clergy to Thomas, is there any mention of the grant of the legation. Possibly the carrier of the letters avoided Robert and turned instead to Bishop Roger, who will thus have found himself responsible for acting on the archbishop's instructions. The letters were delivered without excessive delay. Six weeks was reckoned a reasonable time for the journey from Rome; in this case they cannot have left the Curia before 3 May. In Pontigny the archbishop added his various covering letters, and Gilbert Foliot received those addressed to him on 30 June, as he was celebrating the beheading of St Paul in his cathedral.

Perhaps this episode contributed to a cautious revision by the archbishop's adherents of their attitude to Bishop Roger. At any rate, John of Salisbury felt emboldened to write again, reminding him of the promise of help made at Sens, and asking him, at the archbishop's request, to provide as if for himself, for the bearer, 'one of Christ's poor', probably one of those proscribed because of some connection with Thomas.[30] John took the opportunity to slip in a little exhortation to the bishop, spiced with praise of his father, 'worthy to be numbered in the list of kings'.

With this letter may be associated another, from John to Master Simon Lupellus asking him to support the bearer 'apud dominum Wigornensem . . . ut meipsum'.[31] A great part of this letter consists of thinly veiled criticism of the bishops of England; those who know the law ignore justice; it is from priests and prophets that pollution has spread over the land. And everyone is amazed, says John, that the bishops of the province have never once decided to consider the peace of the church, nor once admonished the king, to whose innocence they have publicly and collectively borne witness. 'And why I write this to you, I think you know.' It was surely a message intended for the bishop.

Master Simon Lupellus, whom John expected to be in touch with Bishop Roger, is pretty certainly Simon Luvel, who

---

[30] *MTB*, vi. 109.
[31] Ibid., vi. 184–5. *Letters of John of Salisbury*, ii. 285.

was appointed archdeacon of Worcester by the bishop, probably before the end of 1167, and was perhaps already in his service (below, p. 101). Simon, like John, was a canon of Exeter.[32] There is no evidence about the bishop's reaction to John's letter, and indeed no proof that he received it.

It was probably in the later part of 1166 or early in 1167 that Bishop Roger first became involved in a dispute about the archdeaconry of Bath, of which the details remain obscure. Robert, bishop of Bath, died on 31 August 1166. The archbishop's letter collection preserves a letter from Pope Alexander to John Cumin, an important royal official, expressing the pope's grave displeasure because John has presumed to claim the archdeaconry of Bath on lay authority, and had not been afraid to seize it from the bishop of Worcester *in magistro Baldewino* (a curious form of words), to whom the pope had confirmed it when Robert was alive. The pope commands John to resign it to the bishop, and not to trouble him about it himself or through a third party. If he does not obey within twenty days, the bishop will denounce him as excommunicate and, if the bishop 'by chance' refuses to do this, the archbishop of Canterbury will denounce John, and the pope himself will order the bishops of England to observe the sentence.[33] The papal letter has lost its dating clause; at the time of writing, John Cumin's offence was not recent, for the pope had heard of it *iampridem*. Whenever it was written, its threats and commands, and the archbishop's subsequent censures, had absolutely no effect. John Cumin, as Armitage Robinson showed, was probably in possession of the revenues of the archdeaconry from before Michaelmas 1167 until at least the consecration of Bishop Reginald in 1174, and no other archdeacon, certainly not Master Baldwin, occurs during all the long period from 1166 to 1181, when John became archbishop of Dublin.

When the pope wrote to John Cumin, he knew that the bishop of Worcester might, for reasons which he did not choose to specify, refuse to carry out the order to excommunicate John, and there is no evidence that the order was in fact

---

[32] Morey, *Bartholomew of Exeter*, p. 92.
[33] *MTB*, vi. 422, JL 11399. For John Cumin's earlier career, and an account of this episode, see J. Armitage Robinson, *Somerset Historical Essays* (1921), pp. 90–9.

obeyed. Possibly it was known that he would honour the oath sworn at Clarendon to respect the king's rights, one of which was that royal officials should not be excommunicated without his knowledge and permission. Whatever the early history of the case, and whatever the bishop's motives, the episode demonstrates the futility of the most peremptory papal commands, unless some bold spirit could be found to execute them. Master Baldwin, who had laid his case before the pope or Archbishop Thomas, or both, never obtained the archdeaconry, while John Cumin, the offender, probably enjoyed its profits for some fourteen years.

In his letter of April 1166 to the prelates of England, announcing the grant of the legation to Archbishop Thomas, Pope Alexander had stressed their duty to come to the archbishop's presence when summoned. A few months later, perhaps in July or August, John of Salisbury and some of the archbishop's friends advised him to exploit his legatine authority and the pope's command, and to summon the bishops, particularly those who had sealed the appeal of 24 June, and also the bishops Salisbury and Worcester. John did not expect them all to respond, but he felt that there must be some bishops and many dignitaries (*personas*) who favoured Thomas. As for the others, their protestations of obedience would be shown to be dishonest, and their true position revealed.[34]

Thomas's surviving letters do not make it clear how many bishops he summoned, or when or how often the summons was repeated. But in the autumn of 1166 a clerk of the bishop of Hereford informed the king that his bishop and *Dominus Rogerus* intended to leave England and visit the archbishop at his summons 'nisi regis auxilio et consilio remanerent'; that is, unless the king could help them to evade their obligation. The king, it seems, helped them by forbidding them to leave, adding that they could always appeal, and that if they left they would not be allowed to return.[35] He also, so the report went, complained a great deal about *Dominus Rogerus*, perhaps because he was known to be in touch with John of Salisbury, perhaps because he was sheltering proscribed men, perhaps because he had transmitted the papal letters about the legation. John of

[34] *MTB*, vi. 18–19.
[35] Ibid., vi. 74.

Salisbury heard a rumour that Roger of Worcester (who must surely be identical with *Dominus Rogerus*) and Bartholomew of Exeter were in danger of being treated as traitors (*capitales inimicos regni*).[36] He hastened to warn Bartholomew, and to advise the bishops to apply to Gilbert Foliot if any action was taken against them. This advice, like John's suggestion about summoning the bishops, was carefully calculated. If Gilbert proved unable to help, this would show up the hollowness of his assertions about the king's moderation and his willingness to receive correction.

These schemes were all frustrated by the skilful diplomacy of the king's agent, John of Oxford, at the Curia in November–December 1166. John seems to have persuaded the pope that the king and the archbishop could be reconciled, or at least that papal legates could judge the issue between them in a way acceptable to both parties, provided that the archbishop did nothing more to anger the king. Therefore everything was to remain in suspense till the coming of legates; a form of words was found which enabled those excommunicated by Thomas to be absolved, and the bishops of England were told that they need not answer the archbishop's summons. Robert of Hereford and Gilbert of London had already set out on the journey; they were met at or near Southampton (perhaps late in January) by John of Oxford, who, on papal authority, forbade them to go to Thomas, to Gilbert's joy and Robert's distress.[37] Having turned back the two bishops, John called a general meeting of bishops at Oxford to hear the papal mandate he had brought with him, 'summoning all the bishops as though he was your legate', as an observer told the pope. The bishop of Worcester was present at this little-known gathering, and made use of it to discuss a legal problem with his fellow bishops (App. I, 16). Possibly he too had set out in response to the summons, and turned back. He remained in England for some time; papal letters of 16 March and 22 April 1167 show the pope acting on the assumption that he would be at home, and available to deal with some tricky and politically sensitive litigation (App. II, 10, 46ii).

[36] Ibid., vi. 62–6.
[37] Ibid., vi. 150–4; iii. 87, vi. 193–4.

It was not until November 1167 that the legates, promised at the time of John of Oxford's visit to the Curia before Christmas, began the serious part of their work. They called the archbishop to a meeting between Gisors and Trie, just on the French side of the Norman frontier, on 18 November. To this meeting there came from King Henry's lands only Rotrou, archbishop of Rouen; the bishops and abbots of the province of Canterbury, whom the king had chosen to summon, were kept at Rouen. Among them were four bishops, three—York, London and Chichester—who supported the King, and with them was summoned Roger of Worcester, 'so that under his cloak the malice of the others may be concealed', as Thomas reported to the pope.[38] They had been summoned so as to be available in case Thomas agreed to a formal hearing of the dispute between himself and the king, or of the appeal of the preceding summer. But Thomas expected that none of his suffragans would dare to say anything on his behalf, and, as the legates had not been given power to compel him, they could take no judicial action. The English prelates did not therefore come to the meeting. Thomas's comment about Bishop Roger shows that he counted him among his friends, and assumed that the pope would be of the same opinion; his actions show that he was well aware that one friend was not enough.

The legates met the king for further discussions at Argentan on 27–9 November. On this occasion the four English bishops were present, and also the bishop of Salisbury, who had his own case against Thomas. As before, the bishop of London led the criticism of the archbishop. The appeal of the previous summer was renewed, as a device to impede Thomas in the exercise of jurisdiction in England. The bishop of Winchester was named as joining in this renewal; as he was certainly not present, it has been suggested that there may have been confusion here between Winchester and Worcester. But Henry's name was needed because he had sealed the earlier appeal;[39] this need was all the more urgent because Robert of Hereford, the third appellant, was now dead. There is no clear record of any action at this time by Bishop Roger. There was little he could do to help Thomas, since the king insisted on judicial proceedings,

---

[38] *MTB*, vi. 252.
[39] Knowles, *Episcopal colleagues*, p. 98 n. 2.

knowing that the archbishop would refuse them until his demand had been met for restitution of his possessions.[40]

Nonetheless, the archbishop's friends were disappointed by what they heard of Roger's behaviour. John of Salisbury included Roger in a sarcastic remark about those 'wise and religious men' who had told the legates of the king's humility and the *sinceritas* of his case. Writing to Archdeacon Baldwin at Exeter, he reported a rumour that Roger was involved in a proposal designed to make trouble for Bishop Bartholomew; the rumour seems to have been unfounded. Roger was also said to have spoken flippantly about the archbishop, 'plusquam tante modestie virum deceat, in archiepiscopum suum jocatus est'. In a second letter to Baldwin, John was more informative.[41] He writes, he says, because of rumours about 'our bishop' (*Wigorniensis noster*). The bishop is said to have spoken imprudently and irreverently about the archbishop, and to have criticized him for not resigning on condition that the king granted lawful freedom (*debitam . . . libertatem*) to the church in perpetuity. He himself, the bishop had said, would resign his bishopric on those terms. These words had caused distress, said John, among those who loved the bishop and had thought him a wiser man. If this advice were followed, it would create a dangerous precedent, and the king's goodwill could easily be revoked, and the church thrust back into its former slavery, or worse. Who after that would dare to preach liberty? Who would support a cause in which and for which they remembered that so great a pontiff had given way? The bishop must give other advice to his friends, but he may try for himself if he can buy freedom for his church in this way. 'I write this to you', says John, 'so that you can persuade our lord and friend to clear himself of this suspicion'. This second letter to Master Baldwin was obviously intended, like the letter to Simon Lupellus, as a message for Roger, to be transmitted by John's friends at Exeter. And it was not simply a message from John. The letter makes it clear that John was with Thomas when the rumours reached him, and tells how Thomas checked the tale-bearers, saying that rumours should not be believed, especially when told of such a man.

---

[40] *MTB*, vi. 251, cf. pp. 258–9. 'Diximus enim nos et nostros . . . bonis omnibus spoliatos; cum ad omnia fuerimus restituti libenter . . . iudicium subituros.'
[41] *MTB*, vi. 276, 317–19, 319–26.

John's letter not only reproves; it also informs the bishop of Thomas's intentions, no doubt to prevent him from repeating the suggestion about resignation. The archbishop will not accept such a plan, nor will he accept translation, nor will he cease to claim his rights, nor will he make peace while the customs, about which the dispute began, remain in force.

When John wrote these letters, he was under the impression that Roger was returning, or had returned, to England from the November meeting at Argentan. But the archbishop seems to have sent a further summons to him while he was in Normandy, ordering him, since he had crossed the sea, not to return without a visit, 'for we have much to say to you'.[42] He too assumed that Roger would be returning shortly to his diocese, for he gave orders about a dispute with the archbishop of York about St Oswald's, Gloucester, on which more must be said later.

There is no record of a visit by Roger to the archbishop. But the annals of Tewkesbury, followed by those of Worcester,[43] note that in 1167 Roger, bishop of Worcester, crossed the sea. This was clearly a matter of some importance, for these brief annals tend to note only the elections and deaths of prelates and a very few major events. But Roger's absence was so prolonged, and the cause of it so unusual, as to jolt the monastic writer out of his normal habits. After the meeting with the legates at Argentan there is no certain evidence of Roger's presence in England for several years. That he left England, and endured some kind of voluntary exile, is mentioned by several writers, though not one tells precisely when he left, or precisely why he did so.

Three Lives of the archbishop have something to say on this subject. Herbert of Bosham, elaborate and imprecise, says of Roger that he always obeyed Thomas, in good times and in bad, even to the extent of enduring loss, proscription and many dangers. But Herbert's long history passes very briefly over events between November 1167 and January 1169; Roger's departure from England is not mentioned. William FitzStephen is equally imprecise, and his account of this period is even shorter than Herbert's. Introducing an episode that must be

---

[42] Ibid., vi. 193–4.
[43] *Ann. Mon.*, i. 50, iv. 382.

placed in the summer of 1169, he says that the bishop of Worcester had been summoned to follow the archbishop, to give counsel to his lord and father, and to help the cause of the church. He obtained permission to cross the sea once, as if for study, since he was young, and from time to time visited the court of the king, because he was closely related to him. 'The outstanding memorial to his fame is this, that he alone of the bishops of England dared and decided to be exiled with his exiled father, to endure poverty with the poor, to stand up for the liberty of the church, and in the day of clouds and darkness to resist the king in his misdeeds.' FitzStephen was interested in legal, though not in chronological exactness; the reference to permission to cross the sea *once* recalls the king's earlier threat to the bishop of Hereford and *Dominus Rogerus*. His story does not suggest a total breach with the king, or explain Herbert's remarks about proscription and many dangers.

The account of Guernes of Pont-Sainte-Maxence, which again does not appear in his usual sources, is:

> Then St Thomas summoned his bishops in turn,
> None would go save Roger, son of the earl.
> He crossed the sea at once without the sheriff's leave.
> He did not shame his primate or the church.
> Seven years he was in exile, he borrowed much money at interest.

Guernes and FitzStephen wrote within three or four years of Thomas's death; Herbert in the late 1180s. Later still, Gerald of Wales also gave his account of Roger's action. 'He endured voluntary exile in the kingdom of the Franks in the city of Tours, where later he died. He determined that he would not return to his country unless his father was first reconciled, and restored to his possessions, even if he should have lived for many years.'[44]

Herbert, Guernes and FitzStephen all mention, in one way or another, poverty endured by the bishop in France. It does not appear that the revenues of the see of Worcester were confiscated because of his departure. They never appear on the Pipe Rolls. As we shall see, the king threatened to seize them in July 1170, but apparently did not pursue the matter. This does not

---

[44] *MTB*, iii. 258–9 (Herbert), iii. 86 (FitzStephen); *Guernes*, lines 2676–80; *Giraldi opera*, vii. 67.

mean that it was easy for the bishop to obtain money from England, or that he could live for some years away from his manors without incurring debts, which were the normal and almost invariable consequence of any prelate's prolonged absence from home. Possibly he had help from another source; there is a single, passing reference to the king of France supporting exiled bishops at this time. Roger and Thomas himself were the only exiled bishops from King Henry's lands. The situation may not have remained static throughout the whole period; the additional controls imposed by King Henry *c.* July × October 1169 may well have made the bishop's position more difficult.[45]

It is impossible entirely to reconcile the evidence of these writers with each other and with the contemporary letters and records. Guernes is misleading in suggesting that Roger responded promptly to the archbishop's summons, and conflicts with FitzStephen in saying that the bishop crossed the sea without permission. He certainly exaggerates the length of the exile, though Roger may not have returned finally to England till after the second coronation of the Young King on 27 August 1172 after an absence of about five years. Guernes was inclined to be complimentary about the bishop; perhaps he had met him, or hoped for his patronage.

A clue to the bishop's motives may be provided by the words of Gerald of Wales, that Roger had decided not to return to England 'nisi patre prius reconciliato ac restituto'. At the meeting with the legates in November 1167, the archbishop had refused to submit to judgement until his confiscated possessions were restored to him. Bishop Roger was present at that meeting, and his voluntary exile probably began soon afterwards; it may have been intended to impress upon the king the opinion that restitution of the archbishop's property was the essential preliminary to peace.

Roger may, as Gerald of Wales reports, have passed his exile at Tours, or at least made it his principal home. As we have seen, Master David of London mentions in a letter (written after the archbishop's death) that he had sent a servant to Tours to borrow a book from the bishop (above, p. 10).

---

[45] On the additional controls (*MTB*, vii. 147–51) see *EHR*, lxxxvii (1972), 757–71. For the reference to the king of France, see *MTB*, vi. 259.

Further, Roger's death at the abbey of Marmoutier, and his wish to be buried there, are most easily explained by supposing some previous connection, such as residence in the abbey during at least part of his five years' absence from England. His stated intention to study may have been quite serious. Master Philip of Calne, whom Herbert of Bosham listed among the 'eruditi sancti Thome', is said to have been recently at Tours, studying theology and teaching roman law.[46] Roger, like his archbishop, may have used some of his enforced leisure to improve his knowledge of law; a papal letter (or two letters, App. II, 63, 91) of September 1167 × 1169 answers questions on law and procedure raised by the bishop. The presence of teachers and students, the hope of hospitality in a famous monastery, and the curious territorial situation at Tours, where the rights of the kings of France and England interlocked, may all have influenced the bishop's choice of a refuge.

Proof of Roger's sympathy and courage was naturally welcome to Thomas and his friends, as a letter shows which must have been written not long afterwards to the archbishop.[47] The writer may be John of Salisbury, who was certainly in touch with the bishop at about this time, and was interested in his plans. 'We know', says the writer, 'that many at home are exiles in the spirit with their friends, but we have not heard of anyone who, leaving heart and soul at home, has shared the exile of his friends in the flesh. Your true friend the bishop of Worcester had chosen the nobler form of compassion, following the way of your exile and suffering with you; he has not looked back towards his see, or bowed his courage before the threats or the blandishments of the secular power. He alone has been found, who would bear his father's burdens both in body and spirit, and put respect for his superior before comfort and riches.' But the writer felt that this voluntary exile was not necessarily the best use of a loyal friend. Just because of his proved loyalty, it was perhaps better to use him as a defender in a more important position, where he could speak for the archbishop as opportunity arose. 'He should therefore go home at the summons of his prince; he will find there plenty of ways

---

[46] *MTB*, iii. 101, 527, v. 166, and Kuttner and Rathbone, 'Anglo-Norman canonists', p. 289.
[47] *MTB*, vi. 393–4.

to show his love for you, while here, as far as I can see, he cannot help you as much or demonstrate his goodwill towards you.'

Perhaps faced with conflicting opinions, Roger turned to Pope Alexander himself for advice, and sent a copy of the reply to Thomas or John, with the result that it was preserved among the archbishop's papers (App. II, 65). The reply was strictly conditional. 'It would please us very much, and it would be in every way expedient for your salvation, that you should return to the church committed to your care, if you can exercise your office there in freedom. But if you fear being forced to observe either those evil customs, which God and the church and we ourselves have utterly condemned, or any other evil, then we would not advise you on any account to put your foot in the trap, or your person into prison.'[48]

The whole letter expressed very strong support for Thomas and his friends, so much so that John of Salisbury made use of it, sending a copy to Baldwin at Exeter, 'so that you may be more strongly encouraged to the virtue of obedience'. John had the reply before him; did he know the terms of Roger's letter to the pope? He tells Baldwin that the bishop had asked whether he should go back to his diocese and obey the king, or help the Lord of Canterbury, enduring unspeakable perils for himself and his followers for the liberty of the church and the defence of divine law. The pope's letter and John's, taken together, suggest that one reason for Roger's removing to, or remaining in, France, was the increasing difficulty of acting according to his conscience if he remained in England.

It does not appear that Roger attempted any further action in favour of the archbishop for some time. He is not recorded as present at the negotiations between Thomas and the king in 1168. But he was useful, for we hear of papal mandates sent to the bishop of London by his agency. This was a matter of increasing importance, for messengers sent by the archbishop had been imprisoned and were threatened with mutilation, and the ports were watched with increasing care, so that it was difficult for Thomas to send letters, or to receive information

---

[48] This letter (JL 11406, *MTB*, vi. 390–1) is misleadingly summarized by Knowles, *Episcopal colleagues*, p. 107, who states that the pope ordered Roger to return home, though with a warning against obedience to evil principles.

from England. Roger, however, had not broken with the king, and the king had no wish to drive him entirely into the arms of the opposition, so that his agents may have moved more freely. Thomas evidently expected Roger to be able to send messengers to his diocese, for he ordered him to publish there the names of excommunicated persons.[49]

At the same time, Thomas tried to use Roger in another way. Being out of England, he could communicate more easily with the pope; the archbishop therefore asked him to follow the example of some French supporters in writing to Alexander in favour of the church of Canterbury against Gilbert Foliot. Gilbert, in addition to his past offences, was now accused, as the archbishop of Sens told the pope, of changing from a dragon into a lion, and boasting that he would obtain the transfer of the archbishopric from Canterbury to London. Thomas was anxious that Roger should support the rights of Canterbury: 'You', he said, 'will write more effectively, since you are more closely connected, and love more ardently.' He tried pressure, blandishment and exhortation, and included some hints about the content of the hoped-for letter. But no such letter survives among the archbishop's papers, where letters in the desired sense from six French prelates are preserved. Perhaps Roger did not share Thomas's passionate belief in Gilbert Foliot's wickedness.

In the spring of 1169 Roger decided to make a personal effort to break the deadlock. He wrote to Thomas, announcing his intention of speaking to the king in the archbishop's favour, more urgently than before. Thomas, a little ungenerously, thanked him, but complained that he and other bishops should long since have reproved Henry more boldly.[50] He also expressed pained surprise at Roger's request to be allowed, while engaged in this mission, to communicate with excommunicates. The times were evil, the bishop had observed, and Thomas was threatening to excommunicate some of the king's counsellors. If Roger was to exhort the king, he must go to court, where he would have difficulty in avoiding them. The archbishop would have none of this; the bishop was perhaps remembering, he

[49] *MTB*, vii. 50–2.
[50] *MTB*, vi. 574–9.

said, the edict according to which anyone who issued sentences of excommunication against the king's will was to be treated as a traitor. He ought rather to remember that he who ignores the reproof of the church should be considered a publican and a sinner. It was hardly a gracious or an endearing letter, though it was a little softened by a final request to the bishop not to resent the failure to grant the desired dispensation, for not even the pope had such authority.

Roger fulfilled his promise, and also obeyed the archbishop. He visited the king, probably soon after 29 May,[51] when Thomas carried out his threat to excommunicate Richard de Lucy, Richard of Ilchester, Geoffrey Ridel and other great men in the king's service. The king received him graciously, says FitzStephen, for he listened to him willingly, though he did not take his advice. But one day, when he and the king were hearing mass, the excommunicated Geoffrey Ridel entered the chapel. The bishop left as soon as he saw him, to the surprise and anger of the king. After a sharp exchange of messages, Henry ordered his cousin to leave his lands at once. The bishop's reply came back promptly, 'his foot was already in the stirrup', and he left, his servants and companions following. But the king's advisers saw that he had made a mistake. He had driven away, they said, a bishop closely bound to him by blood and loyalty, and given the archbishop some welcome and much desired help. The pope had not until now had a really evident and just cause for acting against the king, now he would use the proffered opportunity. So a messenger was sent to recall the bishop, but he refused to return. Others were sent, also in vain; Roger knew how to handle his cousin. Finally a third group, headed by an earl, was despatched on fast horses, with orders to persuade or force him. This time he returned (we do not hear of force), and 'spoke to the king very severely . . . And as long as he remained at court, that archdeacon never entered the chapel, or came into the king's presence when the bishop was with him.'

It was not a great victory. FitzStephen, who tells the story, treats it simply as an example of the bishop's personal courage

---

[51] *MTB*, iii. 86. The printed text reads 'qui multo post ad curiam venit'. But at least one early MS, Bodl. Douce 287, reads 'non multo post'. This seems likely to be correct, since the excommunicates were absolved in the autumn by the legates.

and integrity. The king did not make peace with Thomas. But he had been shown that there was a point beyond which perfectly loyal men would not follow him, and that he could not continue indefinitely to ignore the archbishop's ecclesiastical censures. This was the crucial matter, the weak point in the king's otherwise impenetrable armour. It was for this reason that Henry had to place ever stricter watch on the ports, to arrest and ill-treat the archbishop's messengers, to pour out his money in the Curia and still to come dangerously near to a breach with the pope himself. In the end it was fear of personal excommunication and general interdict that drove him first to negotiate and eventually to make some kind of peace with Thomas. All this would have been unnecessary if he had not known that men like his cousin would feel bound to obey those sentences. Only a year earlier, he was said to have boasted to Roger that there was no need to fear any threats, because he had the pope and all the cardinals in his pocket.[52] The situation was changing, in the archbishop's favour.

In the summer of 1169 two fresh envoys were sent by the pope to negotiate with the king. Both were prominent lawyers who became cardinals in the next decade, Gratian, nephew of Pope Eugenius III, and Vivian, archdeacon of Orvieto. The negotiations dragged on for some time, following the king, first at Domfront on 23 August, then at Bayeux on 31 August, thence to Caen on 8 September and finally to Rouen, 'cum multo labore', as the legates reported. The bishop of Worcester joined in the discussions from 24 August. He was the only English bishop present, though the king had summoned one other friend of the archbishop, John, bishop of Poitiers. The king, acting on the advice of the prelates and magnates, agreed in principle to grant the pope's request, and to allow Thomas and his fellow exiles to return and to be restored to their possessions. He instructed the bishops to draw up the precise *forma pacis* on which everything depended. This was a thankless task; according to the legates the king twice refused to accept the form of words worked out by the bishops. The negotiations broke down upon his insistence on inserting a clause saving the 'dignity' of his kingdom, and refusing a parallel clause saving the 'liberty'

---

[52] *MTB*, vi. 416–17.

of the church.⁵³ The archbishop of Rouen, the bishop of Nevers and the 'bishops and clergy' of Normandy, wrote to the pope conveying the king's version of what happened. It may be supposed that on this occasion it will have been the king who would have welcomed a letter of support from Bishop Roger; again, there is no trace of such a letter.

Later in the year, the archbishop prepared for the extreme measures from which he had been restrained in the past by the pope. Letters were prepared to seven English and three Welsh bishops and six of the greatest abbeys in England, commanding them to declare, or to observe, an interdict unless the king had come to terms before the feast of the Purification (2 February). One of these was addressed to the bishop of Worcester.⁵⁴ It is not known whether any of those intended for addressees in England reached their destinations, for though peace was not made, negotiations were resumed.

In the winter of 1169–70 the archbishop became aware of a new problem. The king wished his eldest son to be crowned king of England. The archbishops of Canterbury had commonly, though not invariably, performed this ceremony. Now there was obviously a danger that this custom might be set aside, and that it would be set aside in favour of Canterbury's rival, the archbishop of York. Thomas therefore obtained from Pope Alexander a mandate to Archbishop Roger, and the other bishops of England, forbidding them to crown the king's son, unless certain conditions were fulfilled.⁵⁵ It appears that at about this time Thomas wrote several times to Roger about the possibility of crossing to England, but ordered him to remain in France. In a letter to Roger, Thomas praises his obedience, and renews the prohibition, pending receipt of further orders and a fresh mandate from the pope.⁵⁶ At the same time he commands Roger on no account to agree to the coronation of the king's son 'contra . . . Cantuariensis ecclesie dignitatem', and to send a copy of this letter to the bishops of Winchester and Exeter, with a covering letter of his own encouraging them to stand firm in the matter. King Henry crossed to England, with this

---

⁵³ Ibid., vii. 70–82.
⁵⁴ Ibid., vii. 104–7.
⁵⁵ Ibid., vii. 217 (JL 11734), cf. ibid., vii. 216 (JL 11733).
⁵⁶ *MTB*, vii. 301–2.

coronation in mind, on 3 March; news of his move may have prompted the writing of this letter.

It is nowhere recorded that the bishops of Winchester and Exeter received any personal prohibition relating to the coronation; when it took place, Bartholomew was present, and Thomas himself wrote later to the pope in his defence. The bishop of Worcester presumably failed to find a messenger to run the gauntlet. But he decided to go himself to England, probably in response to an order from the king; FitzStephen puts into the king's mouth the words 'I myself ordered you to be present at the coronation of my son, and I told you the day in advance'. Roger evidently informed Thomas of his resolve, and promised 'personally to resist those who had for so long afflicted the church of Canterbury'. Thomas replied expressing his belief that it was by divine inspiration that he was to cross the channel at this time, and providing him with papal letters 'tanquam armis bellicis', presumably letters forbidding the coronation. The bishop was ordered to show these letters to the archbishop of York and the other bishops, forbidding them, on papal authority, to consecrate or crown the king's son. Thomas's letter begins with a glowing tribute to Robert, earl of Gloucester, and his courage in defending his sister's rights, and ends on the same note, urging the bishop not to disgrace his noble blood or destroy the fame of his family.[57] Possibly the bishop had spoken in person to Thomas, for the letter refers to words 'que de ore vestro processerunt', as well as a letter from him. If this was so, it is one of the very few traces of a meeting between the two.

Thomas may not have relied exclusively on the bishop of Worcester as his messenger. There is a letter addressed to a woman, which may belong to this period, instructing her to show a papal mandate to Roger of York; John of Salisbury certainly wrote to the monks of Canterbury, urging them to defend the rights of their church in the matter of the coronation.[58] The affair had some political importance, quite apart from the affront to Canterbury, the triumph for York, and

---

[57] Ibid., vii. 258–61. The papal letters to be carried were presumably, ibid., vii· 216–17 (JL 11733), and ibid., vii. 217 (JL 11734), possibly also ibid, vii. 256 (JL 11735). Thomas's own letter is ibid., vii. 256–7.
[58] *MTB*, vii. 302–7 (John's letter), vii. 307–9 (Thomas's letter to Idonea).

perhaps a more personal grief, for the Young King had been educated in Thomas's household, almost as his own son. As long as the ceremony was reserved for Canterbury, the archbishop had a useful bargaining counter; once it was performed, the counter was worthless.

But once again, the archbishop's plans were thwarted. The bishop of Worcester had reached Dieppe when he was forbidden to leave Normandy by the constable and the queen, who instructed local officials and ship-owners not to allow him to cross the sea. News of his intentions, and perhaps of the letters he was carrying, must have reached them from spies, or possibly from the notoriously unreliable Arnulf, bishop of Lisieux, to whom there is a brief reference in Thomas's last letter to the bishop of Worcester, which suggests that Arnulf may have known of Roger's plans.

The coronation took place at Westminster on 14 June, the archbishop of York presiding over the ceremony. William FitzStephen, who is often well-informed about events both at court and in London, asserts that the papal prohibition reached the archbishop of York and the bishop of London the day before the ceremony. Herbert of Bosham says that 'some bishops' received it before the coronation, while others, being warned, refused to receive it.[59] Neither writer tells, probably neither knew, which letters reached London, or by what messenger. Thomas must bitterly have regretted forbidding the bishop of Worcester to cross to England, when he had the opportunity to do so.

After the coronation, King Henry returned to Normandy. His meeting, three miles from Falaise, with the bishop, is described in unusual detail by FitzStephen.[60] Henry immediately began to abuse the bishop for not attending; insults and threats pour out; he is a traitor, he favours the enemy, he is unworthy of his bishopric, its revenues will be seized, he is no true son of Robert the good earl, who brought us up together. The bishop reported what had happened, at which the king broke out again, suggesting that he was trying to blame the queen and the constable.

[59] *MTB*, iii. 103 (FitzStephen), iii. 459 (Herbert).
[60] Ibid., iii. 104–6. The rendering of the bishop's words is deliberately free, and occasionally a little condensed. That he failed to reach England, but remained faithful to Thomas, is confirmed by an anonymous correspondent (*MTB*, vii. 318).

Not the queen [says the bishop], for if from fear of you she conceals the truth, you will be still angrier with me, and if she confesses the truth you will rave irreverently at that noble lady. The matter is not so important to me that she should hear one bitter word about it from you. In fact I prefer that it should have happened as it did, rather than that I should have been at the coronation, which was unjust and an offence to God, not because of him who was crowned, but because of the presumption of the man who crowned him, and if I had been there I would not have allowed him to crown him. You say I am not Earl Robert's son. How do I know? But I was my mother's son, with whom my father received the inheritance of the whole earldom and honour. As for you [and now he turns to the attack] you never showed by due reward that Earl Robert was your uncle, that he maintained you with fitting honour, that he fought King Stephen for you for sixteen years and was even taken prisoner in battle. If you had remembered my father's services, you would not have reduced my brothers to poverty and exile. My brother the earl should have a fee of a thousand knights, which King Henry your grandfather gave my father; you have diminished it by two hundred and forty knights. Another younger brother, said to be a good knight, you left so poor and so hopeless that he gave himself for ever to the Hospital of Jerusalem. This is how you reward your friends and repay them. What do I care if you threaten me, and want to rob me of my revenues? Expel me if you wish [*ut libet moveor, non moveor*]; the revenues are yours, if you have not enough already with what you receive from the archbishopric, six vacant bishoprics and many abbeys. And you receive this unjustly and to the peril of your soul, and turn to secular use the alms of the good kings, your fathers, and the patrimony of Christ.

All this, says FitzStephen, was said in the hearing of those who rode with the king, and a knight of Aquitaine, on learning who the speaker was, said, 'Well, it's lucky for the king that the man is a priest; if he was a knight he would not leave the king two acres of land'. Another companion abused the bishop, hoping to please the king, but Henry rounded on him and abused him in his turn, saying: 'Do you think, you villain, that if I say what I please to my cousin and my bishop, you and the rest can insult him? I can hardly keep my fingers from your eyes! You and the rest are forbidden to yap at the bishop.' So they arrived at their lodgings, and after dinner they talked together privately and peacefully about the restoration of the archbishop. 'Hec et hujusmodi dicta sunt', says FitzStephen. Nobody was expected to believe in exact reporting. But FitzStephen, if he was not at court himself, had good contacts there. This episode, like that involving the excommunicated Geoffrey Ridel, was of a kind to impress the king's followers.

The general effect of the story is convincing. The king appears as he is known from other sources, violent and changeable, and cunning too, for when the conversation takes an awkward turn he slips away. The bishop, too, as we have come to expect, is quite prepared to stand up to the king, and to reprove him where he feels sure of his ground. But above all, the whole business is a family affair, and the interference of outsiders is resented. The links that bind the two men are very strong; the king will not, in fact, break with the bishop; the bishop, though no coward, will respect his family ties, in spite of his Parisian training, his consecration by the archbishop, his profession of obedience. If this was the attitude of the one man who felt he must leave his country because he could not in conscience obey both his king and his primate, is it any wonder that the archbishop's cause never prospered?

FitzStephen treats the coronation of the Young King as part of a deep-laid plan. The king had been advised, he says, that it would be better for him to have the archbishop in England; 'he will be controlled better shut in than shut out'. Therefore first the Young King was crowned, so that if anything evil should happen, the kingdom should not be punished because of King Henry, who was no longer its king. Then the king hastened to a peace conference, and granted all that was asked of him.[61]

The peace conference took place at Fréteval on 21-22 July, following a meeting of the kings of France and England in this frontier area for other purposes. No English bishop was present except the bishop of Worcester, who had been with King Henry in Normandy barely a month before. The peace made was no credit to the negotiators. Henry did indeed promise to restore the property of the archbishop and his adherents. Earlier legal proceedings against him were to be dropped, and the king's anger formally remitted, but this last concession was vitiated by refusal to give the vital kiss of peace. The customs defined at Clarendon were not apparently mentioned, though the issues were bound to recur, and nothing was put down in writing about the treatment of the bishops who had crowned the Young King, though several writers state that Thomas had

[61] Ibid., iii. 107.

Henry's verbal assurance that he might pursue his case against them.⁶²

Thomas returned to England in December. There is little evidence about the movements of the bishop of Worcester, but that little makes it certain that he did not return with the archbishop, and very unlikely that he came to England. He may have remained at Tours, near the scene of the last discussions; he was probably there late in 1171 or early in 1172.⁶³ After Thomas's murder, he was at once involved in negotiations on behalf of the king, appearing at Sens on 25 January. It is most unlikely that he could have reached Sens on that date if he had spent Christmas at Worcester, and been summoned by the king after the news reached France. Nor was he at, or near, the court of the Young King in England in December, for the accounts of this period by Herbert of Bosham and the other biographers show that the archbishop and his agents were desperate to find supporters; they would certainly have turned to him if he had been within reach. William of Canterbury reports a meeting to organize elections to vacant bishoprics, to which the bishops of Winchester, Exeter, Worcester and Ely were not called; Guernes, embroidering upon his source, says that they were excluded because of their loyalty to Thomas.⁶⁴ But as Nigel of Ely had been dead for over a year, and Henry of Winchester was probably already past travelling, the episode must be misplaced or fictitious.

Bishop Roger figures once more in Guernes's account of the archbishop's doings in December 1170. The excommunication of the archbishop of York, and the bishops of London and Salisbury, was a major grievance of the king's party against Thomas (indeed it was the direct cause of his death), and he was pressed many times to absolve them. Guernes states that on one of these occasions Thomas replied that if they would swear to accept the judgement of the church he would act mercifully, taking advice of the king, Roger of Worcester, and other bishops.⁶⁵ This offer is otherwise unknown; it too may be fictitious, or it may have been reported to Guernes during his

---

⁶² Ibid., ii. 5, iii. 109–10, 466.
⁶³ See above, p. 10 and n.24.
⁶⁴ *MTB*, i. 106; *Guernes*, lines 4785–90.
⁶⁵ Lines 4915–20.

stay at Canterbury. Roger could have been mentioned in this connection because he was known to be in France, within reach of the king.

According to Gerald of Wales, Roger had intended to remain abroad until the archbishop was restored. The king had promised his peace, and restoration of possessions to Thomas and his adherents; why did Roger now remain in France? Strict control of the ports was certainly still in force; Thomas had encountered it on landing in England. Not long afterwards he complained to the Young King that 'the ports are closed, and those on this side may not leave, *nor those abroad come over to me*'.[66] His words suggest that Roger may again have been prevented from crossing the Channel, and this in turn gives some support to the assertions of William FitzStephen (the only biographer with good contacts at court) about the sinister intentions of the king.

Roger will have known little of what happened in England in December 1170, and that little will not have been reported by the archbishop's friends. This makes it easier to understand how he could, with a clear conscience, accompany a group of the king's supporters and officials in an attempt to prevent any damaging reaction by the church to the scandal of the murder of the archbishop in his cathedral, and to plead the personal innocence of the king. From Henry's point of view, it was most desirable that at least one English bishop should support his protestations, and best of all that the bishop should be Roger, who had been in exile for Thomas's sake. The other members of the party were Normans: Rotrou, archbishop of Rouen, Arnulf and Giles, bishops of Lisieux and Évreux. The pope had ordered Rotrou and William, archbishop of Sens, to pronounce an interdict on Henry's French lands if Thomas was imprisoned or ill-treated; the first object of the mission was to prevent William from executing the order, or to cause him to suspend it by appealing to the pope. William very properly spurned this manoeuvre, whereupon the king's party set out for the papal court.

One of the officials went ahead; the others travelled together to Siena, where they divided, according to a report sent to the

[66] *MTB*, i. 118.

king.[67] The officials left secretly by night and went by byways to Tusculum, leaving the bishops to follow in a more dignified way when opportunity allowed. The first objective of the officials was to prevent the personal excommunication of the king and the laying of an interdict on his English as well as his French lands, or at least to delay the business till the coming of 'your bishops'. They were desperately anxious to achieve this before Maundy Thursday, when such sentences were, as they reported, habitually pronounced at the Curia.

The bishops did not arrive till after Easter, by which time the dangerous day had passed, and the critical stage of the negotiations was over. Seeing no other way out of the difficulty, the king's men took it upon themselves to swear that they had received his orders to promise on oath in the pope's presence that Henry would obey any papal command, and that he himself would swear to the same effect. By this means they achieved their immediate purpose. The bishops did not take this oath; the king's men did not know if they had been asked to do so. But all the envoys, including the bishops, maintained that Henry had not ordered or desired the murder, though he, and they, accepted that his words had been the cause of it. Once again, as in the case of the embassy to Sens six years before, there is no evidence about Bishop Roger's motives, or about any contribution of his to the negotiations. A fortnight after Easter, the whole group was summoned to hear Pope Alexander's formal reply to the king. He confirmed the interdict on the French lands, ordered Henry to refrain from entering a church, and confirmed the excommunication and suspension of the three prelates who had crowned the Young King. Legates would be sent 'to see and know the king's humility'. There was now no fear of interdict on England, or deposition of the prelates, and the envoys retired from the Curia. The main party was at Bologna on 9 May. Some of them are found with the king in Normandy in the summer;

---

[67] The proceedings at Sens are described in two letters, *MTB*, vii. 440–3, and 443–5. The report to the king is ibid., 471–5; a second account is ibid., 475–8. Professor Foreville (*Église et royauté*, pp. 324–5) suggests that the bishops were left behind to spare them embarrassment at the Curia. This is possible, but the wording of the report seems to imply that the object was to prevent the 'dedecus et malum' being prepared by the king's enemies for him, rather than for the envoys.

Bishop Roger and Reginald, archdeacon of Salisbury, probably made a detour to avoid Rome, and may have arrived after the rest.[68]

In August Roger crossed from Normandy with the king to visit their dying relative Henry, bishop of Winchester. Here Roger renewed contact with Bartholomew of Exeter; together they witnessed the king's charter confirming Bishop Henry's deathbed restoration of property to his cathedral priory.[69] The king went on to Wales; there is little to indicate the movements of his cousin. Probably Roger returned to Normandy to await the coming of the promised papal legates. A charter issued by him and Daniel, prior of Sainte Barbe-en-Auge, concerning St Stephen's Abbey, Caen, may belong to this year (App. I, 7) like certain related documents, one of which records proceedings at Sainte Barbe in the bishop's presence. It may be to this period that the chronicle of Sainte Barbe refers when it notes that Roger, bishop of Worcester, spent some time at the priory, 'apud nos diu familiariter conversatus.'[70] Daniel, the prior, was probably an old acquaintance. He had come to Normandy from England, and been sent back during Stephen's reign to take charge of Sainte Barbe's little cell at Beckford in Worcester diocese. As we have seen, Roger may also have had links with Sainte Barbe through its mother house of Saint Victor of Paris.

The promised legates seem to have arrived in Normandy in the autumn. In December 1171, nearly a year after the murder, they arranged for the reconciliation of the cathedral church at Canterbury; the necessary services were conducted by Bartholomew of Exeter and Richard, bishop of Coventry. Roger's absence adds to the evidence which suggests that he was not in England at this time. It was not until 17 May 1172 that King Henry met the legates at Savigny, by which time his agents had probably conducted the essential preliminary negotiations;

---

[68] For the return journey, see *MTB*, vii. 485. Eyton, *Itinerary*, p. 157, places in June–July a royal charter issued at Rouen and witnessed by Roger. Delisle, *Recueil*, i. 562 no. 433 dates it 1168 x 1173, so that some doubt remains about the date of the bishop's presence in Rouen.

[69] *Registrum Johannis de Pontissara episcopi Wyntoniensis*, ed. C. Deedes, Canterbury and York Society (1924), ii. 628–9, calendared in A. W. Goodman, *Chartulary of Winchester Cathedral*, p. 12.

[70] 'Chronique de Ste Barbe', ed. R. N. Sauvage, *Mémoires de L'Académie de Caen* (1906), p. 54.

Arnulf of Lisieux and Reginald, archdeacon of Salisbury, both members of the embassy to Tusculum, are mentioned as acting for Henry, with Richard of Ilchester, archdeacon of Poitiers. On 21 May at Avranches the king was formally reconciled to the church, and the ceremonies were repeated a little later at Caen in the presence of the archbishop of Tours and his suffragans.

The great collection of letters and documents, which was assembled as a memorial to Archbishop Thomas, tails off after the murder; the surviving information becomes more spasmodic and less detailed. There is a report of the meetings between the king and the legates, but few of those present are named, though 'many bishops and nobles' are said to have been present. Roger of Worcester was probably among them; he seems to have been in Normandy. When Henry had made his settlement with the church, he made peace with King Louis, and sent the Young King and his wife, Louis' daughter, to England for a second coronation. This was designed to repair the injury done when she was excluded from the first ceremony in June 1170, and perhaps to ensure a valid coronation for her husband, since the propriety of the first might be questioned. With the royal pair, according to the *Gesta Henrici*, went Archbishop Rotrou, who performed the ceremony, and Bishops Giles of Évreux and Roger of Worcester. The coronation took place at Winchester on 27 August; about 8 September the archbishop and bishops returned to Normandy.[71] Presumably they attended the final reconciliation at Avranches on 27 September, which followed receipt of the pope's confirmation of the settlement made by his legates.[72]

With these ceremonies a chapter closes. Thomas was dead; the bishops who had opposed him were absolved and restored to office; his principal opponents in the king's service were clearly marked out for high honours. The church in England was released from the tensions of the previous few years, and

---

[71] *Gesta Henrici*, i. 31. Robert of Torigni (*Chron. Stephen*, iv. 254) mentions only Rotrou and Giles. *Diceto*, i. 352, says that Rotrou, Giles and Geoffrey, dean of Chartres, crossed with the Young King, and that some suffragans of Canterbury attended the ceremony. Gervase of Canterbury (i. 237–8) is chiefly interested in the further affront to Canterbury from Rotrou's performing the coronation; he also names only Rotrou and Giles. The *Gesta* are certainly better informed on the event than Diceto.

could move into a time of new problems and different possibilities. Here both the emphasis in the story and the sources available for its study change, and we may pause for a brief review of the bishop of Worcester's part in the drama of 1164–72.

Clearly he was never one of the leaders in the dispute. When it began, he was too inexperienced to carry much weight, and he was so closely tied to both the king and the archbishop that it was difficult for him to give outright support to either. The evidence also suggests that though he was shrewd and bold, he was not prepared to 'go into politics', to throw himself fully into the diplomatic and political intriguing and organizing without which great conflicts are seldom resolved. He was prepared to take personal risks in order to observe the law, when the law seemed clear, and Thomas himself observed that he was not interested in wealth; it was not for comfort or money that he failed to press the archbishop's case. That Thomas could not, in the event, get more support from such a man, is a measure of his failure as a leader, and of his misjudgement of the political situation in England. It is also an indication of the great strength of the king's position, whatever the truth may have been about rights that he claimed over the church.

3
THE BISHOP IN HIS DIOCESE

The pastor

Herbert of Bosham's approval of Bishop Roger was no doubt inspired primarily by the bishop's attitude to Archbishop Thomas; no doubt too it suited Herbert to depict Thomas's outstanding episcopal supporter as a model of virtue in general. But his rhetorical words are not mere rhetoric. They follow many pages devoted to his hero's behaviour as archbishop, his strict living, his careful examination of candidates for ordination, his efforts to eliminate corruption from among his officials. Herbert had a clear idea of what a bishop ought to be; his praise of Roger, imprecise though it is, and his chosen epithet—'that great priest'—suggest that Roger accepted the same standards, strove towards the same ideal. In this chapter an attempt will be made to test this suggestion, and to add a little detail to Herbert's impressionistic picture, in spite of the enormous gaps in the available information.

The nature of this information requires some initial comment. Neither chronicler nor annalist—neither the general nor the local historian—will report the normal activity of any bishop or pastor and administrator in his diocese. Even the biographer, who is commonly a hagiographer, will tend to mention only matters in which his subject was exceptional, as, for example, St Hugh was, in dismounting to confirm children.[1] Episcopal records cannot be pressed into service to fill the gaps left by the literary histories. As far as we know, no bishop of this period kept anything resembling the registers of later times, or any record of ordinations or of court proceedings, and none survives of the records some were just beginning to keep, the matricula containing information about parish churches and chapels, about which more must be said later. We must, of course, be very wary of assuming that records never existed

---

[1] *Magna vita*, p. 140; *Giraldi opera*, vii. 95. Cf. *MTB*, ii. 164.

because they do not now survive,[2] particularly at Worcester, where a warning is given by the loss of the matricula and the survival, by a series of chances, of a survey of the bishop's estates made c. 1164–7, which also must be discussed in more detail later. But two personal letters from Pope Alexander to Bishop Roger (App. II, 46, 58) were copied onto the fly-leaves of books; the persistence of this ancient custom at Worcester, both then and later, suggests that the bishop had no better place in which to enter copies of documents of special personal interest.[3]

For Bishop Roger, therefore, as for almost all his contemporaries on the episcopal bench, it is the cartularies of ecclesiastical corporations that provide the bulk of the available evidence about his diocesan activity. Cartularies were designed primarily as collections of title-deeds; the documents they preserve illustrate above all the activity of bishops as guardians and judges in matters relating to property, lands, churches, tithes, pensions and miscellaneous rights. A valuable supplement is provided by the papal letters to English prelates, mostly commissions to judges-delegate, which form a large proportion of the contents of the decretal collections of the later twelfth century. Here again the majority of texts deal with property, with only a sprinkling of matrimonial and other cases. Although these texts, dealing with property and lawsuits, can be used to throw light on many other topics, it yet remains true that the functions of bishops as administrators and judges are relatively well documented, while more spiritual duties and interests are illuminated only by a passing reference, or by the chance survival of an unusual text. This study of Bishop Roger, like many studies of the twelfth-century church, will inevitably have more to say of government than grace, of charters and courts than prayer and preaching, but no judgement is implied about the relative importance of these things, nor any suggestion that the former, rather than the latter, were the chief concern of the prelates of the time.

To redress the balance a little, we will begin by assembling

[2] Cf. J. Campbell, 'Observations on English government . . .', *TRHS*, 5th ser. xxv (1975), 39–54, and S. Harvey, 'Domesday Book and its predecessors', *EHR*, lxxxvi (1971), 753–73.
[3] N. R. Ker, *English manuscripts in the century after the Norman conquest* (1965), p. 20.

the evidence relating to Bishop Roger as shepherd of souls in his diocese, and such information as can be found about his convictions, opinions and interests. Gerald of Wales, in his account of the bishop, makes one or two points that are instructive. He gives us our only glimpse of the bishop celebrating mass, and a dramatic glimpse it is. The scene is Gloucester Abbey. All the congregation has come up towards the high altar to receive the episcopal blessing, when a great western tower, just completed, collapses suddenly because of a defect in the foundations. The shock is like an earthquake; a thick cloud of dust fills the air, and almost everyone rushes to the side walls for safety. But the good father stands unmoved and intrepid, as though he had heard nothing, 'wholly carried away on high in spirit'. It could be considered a miracle, says Gerald, that, though so many men and women had come to hear the bishop's mass, not one was hurt.[4] The story suggests a reputation for religious devotion of no ordinary intensity. To Gerald also we owe the information that Roger never gave revenues, in lands or benefices, to his relations, following in this respect in the footsteps of Archbishop Thomas.

The surviving sources throw very little light on the activity of most English bishops of this time as the chief authority in the diocese in matters of conscience, confession and the enjoining of penance. But chance has preserved a text which shows Bishop Roger pondering on these questions, expressing opinions and doubts which are of some interest in the general movement of practical theology. His doubts prompted the composition of a little treatise on problems connected with penance, absolution, and the large question of the nature of the church's judgements, and the power to bind and loose.

At an unknown date, Bishop Roger appointed a learned monk of his cathedral, Senatus by name, to an office which might later have been called that of penitentiary. Senatus held various offices in the course of his career at Worcester. In 1175 he witnesses as cantor (App. I, 77), in 1186 × 1189 as camerarius, and he became prior in 1189; the Worcester annals,

---

[4] *Giraldi opera*, vii. 64–6. Gerald probably misplaced the episode. A tower fell at Worcester in 1175 (*Ann. Mon.*, iv. 383); cf. *Medieval art and architecture at Worcester cathedral*, British Archaeological Association, Conference Transactions 1 (1978), 80–1.

recording his resignation, call him *Magister Senatus theologus*.[5] Addressing Bishop Roger, Senatus describes the burdensome office imposed on him by the bishop as that of 'archpriest of the church, having the care of penitents and the judgement of confessions'. In this capacity he was asked by the bishop to set out his opinions on some difficult theological-penitential problems, and his reply has been preserved in a single manuscript, probably from the library of Worcester Cathedral Priory.[6] The treatise is presented, like so many of its time, in the form of a letter, beginning with greeting, ending with valediction. It falls roughly into four sections. An initial display of fine writing, learned allusions and expressions of modesty, shows that the bishop had reproved the monk for his silence, and ordered him not only to preach, but also to write for the benefit of posterity. Reference to his appointment as archpriest leads to thoughts of the responsibility of such office; 'who will not be filled with terror at sitting in Christ's judgement seat?'. The second section deals with the effect of indulgences granted by bishops, the third with the effect of absolution given to duellists. The fourth and longest section replies to doubts expressed by the bishop about the effect of absolution and condemnation in general, given that the judge may be ignorant, or be deceived. The extent of the treatise, and the fundamental nature of its basic theme, have been obscured in recent times because separate sections have been printed separately, the second in one place, the first and third in another, while the last has been ignored.

The form of the bishop's question about indulgences (Senatus regularly uses the word *remissio*) is made clear in the reply:

---

[5] *Ann. Mon.*, iv. 388; for his other appointments see *Worc. cart.*, p. lviii and C. H. Turner, *Early Worcester manuscripts* (1917), p. xlv. See also R. W. Hunt, 'English learning in the late twelfth century', *TRHS*, 4th ser. xix (1936), 30, and B. Smalley, in *Recherches de théologie ancienne et médiévale*, xlv (1978), 159.

[6] Ker, *Libraries*, p. 208. Senatus's treatise occurs only in Bodl. MS Bodley 633 fos. 197ʳ–199ᵛ. The opening passage on fo. 197ʳ, and the section on the judicial duel on fo. 198ʳ⁻ᵛ, are printed by E. Rathbone as an appendix to 'Roman law in the Anglo-Norman realm', *SG*, xi (1967), 270–2. The section on indulgences on fos. 197ᵛ–198ʳ had been printed by Ph. Delhaye, 'Deux textes de Senatus de Worcester sur la pénitence', *Recherches de théologie ancienne et médiévale*, xix (1952), 206–7. The longer section, fos. 198ᵛ–199ᵛ, on the nature of the church's judgements and the power to bind and loose, remains unprinted and was not discussed by either editor, though the whole forms a single treatise.

On this subject (almsgiving), you have asked what is its value, its efficacy before God, when remission of penance is granted for good works, such as the building of hospitals and bridges, and at the dedication of churches, with the object of encouraging the faithful to give more abundantly? You say that this remission is arbitrary and leads souls astray (seducens animas) since the prelates who grant it cannot remit the offence (culpa) for God alone does this, nor the penalty, for they cannot know the contrition of these men's hearts, or the purity of their confessions. By remissions of this sort, and the giving of money because of them, the payments of the rich are made to seem more meritorious than the good disposition of the poor, whose poverty denies them the means of payment.

Senatus begins his answer with a distinction: 'if we investigate the matter more thoroughly' we shall find that the prelates in such cases remit neither the offence nor the penalty for which we are liable towards God, though they relax the penalty imposed by man. For the punishment is two-fold: the first is inspired by God through contrition, the second is imposed by the priest, in the form of almsgiving, fasting and so on. 'In case you want an authority for this', he cites a conciliar decree allowing the sinner to redeem part of his penance by paying a penny or reciting a psalter, which the poor and the ignorant cannot do. Answering the bishop's complaint that the rich are made to seem more meritorious than the poor, he agrees that the poor are no less worthy in the sight of God, and that, in the sight of men, those who do not avoid fasting by payment should be considered most virtuous. But he had not completely answered the main question. It was easy to find authority for the alleviation by a superior of penance enjoined on an individual whose condition he fully understood; it was another matter to clarify the theology of the broadcast indulgence. Senatus was probably aware of this, for he ends abruptly: 'If these considerations do not calm your doubts, perhaps they will calm those of others, like things thrown to the crowd, to catch as catch can' (Matth. 19:12).

Indulgences of this sort had been known in the eleventh century, and were common in England before the middle of the twelfth; there are some twenty-five among the *acta* of Archbishop Theobald. Abelard seems to have been their first recorded critic. Like Bishop Roger, he thought they endangered men's souls (*decipiunt animas*);[7] perhaps his influence had

[7] *Peter Abelard's Ethics*, ed. D. E. Luscombe (Oxford Medieval Texts 1971), pp. 110–11.

reached Roger in Paris. Roger was not alone in his doubts; it was probably his friend, John of Salisbury, who as bishop of Chartres put to Pope Alexander III a question about 'remissions given at the dedication of churches and for the building of bridges', and received an answer which defined the law on one point (X 5.38.4 with address to Canterbury). Another Englishman, the canonist Alanus, glossing that answer early in the thirteenth century, commented: 'What these remissions are worth is an old dispute, and is still highly uncertain'; he could only list a string of conflicting opinions.[8]

This is not the place for a study of the theological positions of Bishop Roger's time. What is interesting for the present purpose is to observe him addressing himself to this thorny problem, which affected, as he thought, the welfare of many souls, and ordering the best local theologian to set down his opinions on the subject. No indulgence survives that was issued by him, though churches were dedicated in his diocese and no doubt bridges and hospitals were built there as much as elsewhere.[9] Gilbert Foliot in much the same period issued at least seventeen indulgences as bishop of London.

The second problem put by the bishop to Senatus was of a different kind. Instead of dealing with a relatively new, and developing practice, the bishop was turning his attention to an old custom now attracting criticism, the judicial duel. The duel was one of those irrational methods of proof traditional among the Germanic peoples, which depended upon supposed supernatural intervention. The Roman Church, from ancient times, had frowned on all ordeals on theological grounds, but it had long tolerated what it could not suppress, and had allowed the clergy to take a prominent part in the administration of this primitive form of justice. But opinion was changing fast. Already at the end of the eleventh century, the sceptical William Rufus had expressed angry doubts about the outcome

---

[8] Gl. Ord., X 5.38.4 ad v. *ut prosint*.
[9] A privilege of Pope Innocent III (*Cirencester cart.*, i. 163 no. 164/96) refers to an indulgence granted by the bishops of Worcester, Hereford, Exeter and Bath at the dedication of the church. A dedication ceremony took place at Cirencester on 17 Oct. 1176; if this was the dedication in question, Bishop Roger may have been associated with the indulgence, the text of which has not apparently survived. His presence at the dedication is not otherwise attested (*Gesta Henrici*, i. 127-8).

of an ordeal; he was probably exceptional only in being able to express his doubts in public.[10]

In the question put by Bishop Roger, and in the reply of Senatus, the duel is treated simply as a fight between two angry men, each desiring the death of the other. There is no trace of the notion that divine justice would direct the outcome. The bishop's concern was with the spiritual condition of the duellists, and the priest's duty towards them. Perhaps this reflects his deepest interests; perhaps he was simply addressing his question to the appropriate authority, and would have discussed the legal aspect of the matter with his iurisperiti. The crux of his 'almost insoluble' problem (*nodum inexplicabilem fere*) was this: should penance (and absolution) be given to men about to take part in a judicial duel? And if given, what is its effect? 'For they receive penance out of fear of punishment, not from contrition of heart or love of virtue, and they do not perform the penance, but proceed to battle; their minds are inflamed with anger and burn to inflict injury. It is too late to advise the claimant to withdraw; if you advise the accused to confess or to restore stolen goods, you might as well say, "Now be hanged".'[11] Therefore it makes no difference to them if penance is not enjoined, or is given without effect. And if penance is enjoined, it will not be fruitful for the remission of sins, for what is promised by human agency is not instantly granted by the divine majesty'.

Senatus begins his reply by noting that contradictory opinions have been expressed on the first point; some say that penance should be enjoined upon both duellists, others that it should be denied to the claimant, whose claim is the cause of the duel. But the accused may indeed be guilty, and it is not a mortal sin to make use of trial by ordeal.[12] Senatus therefore decides firmly in favour of enjoining penance on both parties, so that they shall not fall into despair or into anger against the church. Whether the enjoining of penance will have effect, he

---

[10] *Eadmeri historia novorum in Anglia*, ed. M. Rule (RS 1884), p. 102. On ordeals see R. van Caenegem, *The birth of the English Common Law* (Cambridge 1973), chapter 3, and the literature there cited; also Colin Morris, 'Judicium Dei...' *SCH*, xii (1975), 95–111, and J. M. W. Baldwin, 'The intellectual preparation for the canon of 1215 against ordeals', *Speculum*, xxxvi (1961), 613–36.
[11] 'Iam pasces in cruce corvos.' Cf. Horace, Ep. I, 16.48.
[12] Senatus refers to Numbers 5:12, perhaps from Gratian's section on ordeals, Decretum C.2 q.5 c.21.

leaves to the mercy of God, quoting Augustine's words, that sin must always be corrected, just as efforts must always be made to cure the sick.

These were sufficiently serious questions, but the bishop had touched on a still larger issue when he said 'what is promised by human agency is not instantly granted by divine majesty'. Pursuing this problem, he had evidently expressed doubts about the interpretation of Christ's words to Peter, 'Whatever you shall have bound or loosed on earth, shall be bound or loosed in heaven', saying that the words seemed to express the wrong order, 'videtur vobis ordo preposterus', Senatus says, 'quasi rectius dixisset, "Quod ego ligavero vel solvero in celis erit a vobis ligatum vel solutum in terris".' It is not, the bishop says, the decisions of priests that weigh with God, but the lives of the accused, and God does not follow the judgement of the church, which sometimes judges as a result of deception or ignorance. Senatus seems startled. 'Did not David's key lock and open? [Apoc. 3:7]. Are not Peter's keys the keys of the kingdom of heaven? Do they not lock and unlock?' But he addresses himself to the problem: 'Until you meet with a better opinion, I will say what I think, so that all may be brought back into the way of concord.' His discussion turns on the distinction between God's action on the inner man——'opus quod interius operatur Deus'——and the action of the priest, which must depend on external indications and has external effect; 'noxium exteriori pena ligat', and it is this external *pena* that is ratified by God. From this, he advances to a general discussion of the nature of the judgement of ecclesiastical judges, including both the confessor and the judge in the law court. Again, Senatus stresses that the judge deals with external matters. The judge in the courts must be guided by lawful proofs, particularly the evidence of sworn witnesses. His duty is to preside over the dispensing of a special kind of justice, defined by Senatus as *iustitia probatoria*, the justice achieved by the judicial process properly conducted. *Iustitia probatoria* is contrasted with *iustitia voluntatis*, the will to do good, which is a virtue, and *iustitia operis*, which means doing correct acts, without reference to the state of mind of the doer. *Iustitia probatoria* sits a little awkwardly in this scheme; perhaps its appearance owed something to Bishop Roger's extensive judicial activity, and his consequent interest in this aspect of the question. Eventually, Senatus works his way back to the main issue. 'You may say', he says towards the end of his *sermo*, 'that the church is sometimes deceived in its judgement, absolving the man condemned by God and condemning the man absolved by God ... but I should not have thought that this follows as a result of the saying [to Peter], which involves no contradiction, since it is not dealing with the same kind of judgement, or the judgement of the same judge, or the same kind of condemnation and absolution, for the judgement of the church is not concerned with the secret things [*occulta*] of which God is judge. And so one is not compelled to say that the church condemns the man absolved by God, since the church judges only *manifesta*.'

A short summary cannot do justice to Senatus and his arguments and careful distinctions, or indicate his place among the theologians of this period, who were much concerned with these very questions. Nothing is known of his life before he appears as a monk at Worcester; only his unusual name hints at a continental origin, and possible continental training. Bishop Roger's attitude and interests will have been influenced by his Parisian teachers and fellow students. One influence may have been that of Richard of St Victor, whose exhortations John of Salisbury hoped would carry weight with Roger during the exile of Archbishop Thomas, as noted above. Richard wrote on the role of the priest in the remission of sins, and was active in the years when Roger was studying in Paris, perhaps at St Victor itself. But even a summary shows that the bishop and the monk were debating large issues, in the light of the changing needs and opinions of their time, and that Senatus's little treatise was not simply addressed to the bishop as a patron, but answers, in a direct and personal way, the doubts which he had raised on specific questions. Mgr. Delhaye, the editor of the discussion on indulgences, suggested that the bishop was ignorant ('peu versé en droit'), and Senatus old-fashioned as compared with contemporary theologians at Paris. But this suggestion was based on confusion of Bishop Roger with Bishop Robert (1190–3), and on a misunderstanding of the bishop's question. Delhaye thought that Roger was reproving Senatus for imposing lighter penances than those laid down in the penitential canons, and that Senatus was defending himself; this would indeed have been an old-fashioned exercise at the end of the twelfth century. In fact the two were discussing a question that was only thoroughly explored by Hugh of St Cher some sixty years later.[13]

As regards the judicial duel, the questions that interested Bishop Roger were similar to those that Professor Baldwin has shown contemporary canonists debating: were duellists to be admitted to communion? was only the accuser to be rejected? did duellists fall into mortal sin? Inevitably, these problems aroused the interest of both theologians and lawyers. The lay world, too, was directly affected. In England the church was pressing its doubts and objections. In 1176 King Henry agreed that clerks should no longer be forced to take part in duels, and it was probably in 1179 that the Grand Assize enabled a defendant, lay or clerk, in a plea of land, to choose judgement by the verdict of jurors instead of by battle.[14] Nothing is known of the debates that must have preceded the agreement of 1176, or the Assize, or of the strength of the various influences that produced them. But if we consider the reasons why this once treasured Norman custom fell into disfavour, it must seem probable that the king's ecclesiastical councillors had some voice in the matter. Of these councillors those whose opinions will have been heard with most respect will have been those known as active judges as well as active pastors. The bishop of Worcester was, as we shall see, one of the most active papal judges-delegate of this time; he was travelling up and down England operating a judicial system which left little room for quasi-miraculous proofs, but depended on documents and on the evidence of sworn witnesses. The opinions and the experience of such men can hardly have failed to hasten the adoption of more rational modes of proof in the royal courts, and the rules of the church courts actually supplied details of procedure necessary for the smooth working of the new Assize.[15]

---

[13] N. Paulus, *Geschichte des Ablasses im Mittelalter vom Ursprunge bis zur Mitte des 14 Jahrhunderts*, 3 vols. (1922–3). See also L. Hödl, 'Die Geschichte der scholastischen Literatur und der Theologie der Schlüsselgewalt, I', *Beiträge zur Geschichte der Philosophie und der Theologie des Mittelalters*, xxxviii, Heft 4 (1960), and L. Ott, 'Untersuchungen zur theologischen Briefliteratur der Frühscholastik', ibid. xxxiv (1937), 539–47. None of these comments on Senatus's treatise.
[14] *Diceto*, i. 410; Glanvill, pp. 180–1. See also E. Rathbone, as cited, p. 59, n. 6.
[15] 'Excipi autem possunt iuratores ipsi eisdem modis quibus testes in curia christianitatis iuste repelluntur.' (Glanvill, p. 32.)

Senatus called his 'burdensome honour' that of 'archpriest'. This title was seldom used in England in the twelfth century, so seldom that it seems likely that Senatus himself chose to use it as a literary device, springing from his knowledge that in past centuries the archpriest had been the bishop's deputy in spiritual matters, and that still in Italy and Southern France the urban archpriest might be found in that position, heading the cathedral chapter beside a provost or dean.[16] But the bishop himself may deliberately have used the old title to give respectability to a new office, created to meet new needs. For Senatus was not merely a penitentiary. He was also required to preach. 'The word of preaching,' he says, 'which was formerly a matter of choice, is now required of me as part of the responsibility of my office.' This combination of duties must bring to mind Canon 10 of the Fourth Lateran Council (X 1.31.15), which required that suitable men should be appointed in cathedrals and other conventual churches to be coadjutors of the bishop, to preach, to hear confessions and enjoin penance, and in other things pertaining to the salvation of souls. In appointing Senatus to do just this work, Bishop Roger was anticipating by some forty years the reforming decree of 1215. Or, looking at the matter from the opposite point of view, it may be said that Pope Innocent and his advisers tried to ensure the general adoption of an arrangement devised long before by a few exceptionally zealous prelates.

The bishop did not merely require Senatus to preach, and ask his opinion on these two problems. He ordered him to write, 'quasi memoriale'. And Senatus complied; perhaps he did not need much pressing. As we have seen, he sent his opinions in writing; he sent also twenty-two sermons, with the promise of more to come when time allowed, and Lives of the Worcester saints, Oswald and Wulfstan.[17] He had hesitated for a while, he says, torn between fear and affection. But he plucked up courage, remembering the bishop's nobility of blood, drawn

---

[16] Gerald of Wales, discussing the word 'archpriest', says that some people equate it with 'dean', while others refer to the archpriest of Italian *ecclesie . . . plebane* (*Opera*, viii. 110).

[17] Senatus's Lives of Oswald and Wulfstan occur in Durham Cathedral Library MS B iv. 39. On the Life of Oswald see J. H. Raine, *Historians of the church of York and its archbishops*, ii (RS 1886), x–xi, and for the Life of Wulfstan, *Vita Wulfstani*, ed. R. R. Darlington, Camden 3rd Series xl (1928), pp. xx–xxi.

from the line of ancient kings, and his liberality of mind, burdensome to no man, at the service of all men, and love, which overcomes all things, overcame both fear and modesty. The modesty and the respect for noble birth were no doubt largely conventional; love for the generous spirit, oppressive to none, helpful to all, was no common form.

Is it a coincidence that another monastic writer, sending his work to Bishop Roger, also speaks of love as the mainspring of his action? Adam, abbot of Evesham (1161–89) wasted few words on conventional humility in the letter he addressed to the bishop in response to a request for a copy of a recent work.[18] The bishop had heard of the opusculum from 'the learned and famous Master William', to whom Adam had read it.[19] When William passed through Evesham again, on his way back from celebrations at the cathedral, he carried a message from Roger, asking that the work should be transcribed as fast as possible, and sent to him. Adam was pleased with this request because, he said, the bishop always wants to have good and holy things about him, and because his little present will help to inflame the bishop's devotion to his duty, and guide his every action. Unfortunately, the abbot's little book, like the sermons of Senatus, seems to have become separated from its covering letter, and to be lost or concealed by anonymity.[20] The covering letter itself is of some interest, since it embodies a little disquisition on love and friendship, a popular theme of the time, treated by many writers, some briefly, and some, like Ailred of Rievaulx, at considerable length.[21] Though it is naturally permeated with biblical phraseology, the letter seems to be largely original, and to contain touches that suggest genuine mutual affection beyond the conventional requirements of official

---

[18] Oxford, Jesus College MS 11, fo. 2ᵛ.
[19] Master William cannot be identified. It is tempting to think of Master William of Tonbridge, to whom Senatus addressed one of his treatises.
[20] Leland saw some of Adam's works, still preserved in his monastery, and noted: 'Adae, Eoveshamensis abbatis, ad virgines de Godestoa, *Sanctissimis et dilectissimis.* Idem de miraculo Eucharistiae ad Reynaldum, *Diu iam satisque.* Eiusdem aliquot epistolae'. (*Collectanea,* ed. Thomas Hearne (1774), iv. 160.) Was the last item Jesus College 11? The college possesses four other books from Evesham (Ker, *Libraries,* p. 81, and Idem, 'Sir John Prise', *The Library* 5th Ser. x (1955), 12.
[21] On the cult of friendship in the twelfth century see Colin Morris, *The discovery of the individual, 1050–1200* (1972), pp. 97–107, and G. Constable, *Letters and letter-collections* (Typologie des Sources . . ., ed. L. Genicot, fasc. 17, 1976), pp. 15–16.

politeness and formal rhetoric. Adam was remembered at Evesham as a great abbot, greater than his predecessors, though they had been good men, 'religiosi et valde ordinati'.[22] His respect for Roger suggests that they shared the same ideals, and his letter gives a tantalizing glimpse of the bishop taking an interest in the learned and religious life in his diocese.

The bishop's duty required him, as well as fostering the virtuous and patronizing the learned, to maintain the purity of the faith, and to condemn or recall those suspected of aberrant opinions. Heresy is seldom reported in England till the fourteenth century, but early in Roger's episcopate, a little group of strangers, variously described as *publicani* or *textores*, were discovered in the diocese of Worcester. The Tewkesbury annalist lifts his eyes from his list of deaths and elections to remark on their fate; perhaps they had settled in the neighbourhood.[23] William of Newburgh begins his account of them after mentioning Becket's election to Canterbury in June 1162, and follows it with his account of the Council of Tours in 1163.[24] They were, he says, German by race and speech; they must have been conspicuous, and probably it was not long before they were under suspicion. Gilbert Foliot's letter-collection contains two letters written in reply to a request from Bishop Roger for advice about the treatment of these 'weavers';[25] the letters seem to be alternative drafts. Roger was perhaps reporting the matter to Gilbert, and consulting him, as the acting head of the province after the flight of the archbishop in November 1164 and, as he himself was abroad till Christmas, the letters may have been written after that date.

The suspects had already been arrested and examined, and found to hold incorrect opinions on matters of faith. Gilbert approved of Roger's action. The 'weavers' had been weaving cobwebs with which they hoped to cover the whole diocese, but the Holy Spirit has resisted them through him. They had preached to the people, and on being summoned and admonished had dared to defend their opinions. Gilbert suggests that

[22] *Chron. de Evesham*, p. 102.   [23] *Ann. Mon.*, i. 49.
[24] 'Historia rerum anglicarum', in *Chron. Stephen*, i. 131–4. There seems to be no compelling reason for the date 1160, attached to this entry by the editor. See also Walter Map, *De Nugis Curialium*, tr. M. R. James (1923), p. 63.
[25] *Letters of Foliot*, pp. 207–10. See also Adrian Morey and C. N. L. Brooke, *Gilbert Foliot and his letters* (Cambridge 1965), pp. 241–3.

the heretics should be kept in solitary confinement until some secular or ecclesiastical business requires a meeting of clergy and others, at which a decision on their treatment can be taken by common consent. William of Newburgh says they were held *in publica custodia*; perhaps the bishop was able to place them, or some of them, in the sheriff's prison. If Foliot's advice was followed, they will have been visited and instructed by the bishop's most reliable clerks, and 'every means that charity can suggest' will have been used to recall them to the unity of the church, including threats and beatings of carefully regulated severity. These charitable measures were of no effect, except upon one young woman, the heretics' only convert. They were brought to a council held by the king in December 1165 or January 1166, and there condemned, not to the burning which Foliot had mentioned as one possible punishment, but to treatment equally cruel. Newburgh says that they perished miserably.

The secular clergy

Involvement with heresy was a rare and temporary experience. The lasting concern of active English bishops in this period lay elsewhere, and above all in the 'reform', and therefore in the increasingly strict control, of the parish clergy. In spite of the fragmentary nature of the evidence, there are indications that Bishop Roger was one of those who felt strongly on this subject. His strict avoidance of nepotism was not merely a kind of self-denial, rejecting the snares of earthly affection. It was also part of a larger programme, summed up in the opening lines of a papal letter addressed to the bishop early in his pontificate, probably at his own request. In November 1164, not many months after his consecration, Roger accompanied a royal embassy to the pope, which has been discussed in connection with the affairs of Archbishop Thomas and the king On 26 November, the papal letter *Inter cetera sollicitudinis* was addressed to the bishop, defining the law on clerical marriage and the inheritance of benefices, and ordering him to enforce these rules in his diocese (App. II, 61). The letter (freely translated here) begins with a statement of policy, and then turns to conditions in the diocese.

Among other matters committed to your watchful care, it is proper that your prudence should give the most exact and thorough attention to appointing and setting over the churches under your rule such ministers as know how to care properly for the Lord's house, and can usefully lead and serve his people. It has come to our notice that certain persons in your diocese, pretending to be of the ecclesiastical profession since they hold ecclesiastical benefices, contract marriage and yet presume to retain their benefices. Others, though they are sons of priests, succeed their fathers in their churches as if by hereditary right, and then, being instituted, are unlawfully promoted to holy orders. This is known to be entirely contrary to the institutes of the sacred canons. Therefore we order you on no account to allow those who marry below the subdiaconate to be separated from their wives unless both wish to turn to religion, but if they live with their wives they ought on no account to obtain benefices. Those in the subdiaconate or above who marry can and should give up the women without requiring their leave or consent; this sort of association is not to be called marriage but *contubernium*. We also command you, by the authority of this present letter, not to allow priests' sons to minister in their fathers' churches, and to remove them altogether, without right of appeal, from churches in which their fathers are known to have ministered. We also command you to summon clerks keeping mistresses, and order them most earnestly to send them away. If they refuse, you shall promptly despoil them of all ecclesiastical office and benefice, without right of appeal.

If this letter is read in isolation, it might appear as a reproof, a papal initiative prompted by the opportune appearance of the bishop at the Curia. A little reflection on the circumstances of November 1164 shows that this appearance is entirely superficial. It was only very rarely in this period, and indeed throughout the Middle Ages, that popes took the initiative in issuing such letters. There is general agreement among experts that, apart from political letters, the papal chancery seldom issued any document except upon receipt of an appeal or a petition. Of course, one person may request letters addressed to another; this is the normal procedure when commissions go out to judges-delegate, or at a later date to executors of papal provisions. Exceptionally, one man may report scandals relating to another; when the pope says that conditions in the diocese of Worcester have 'come to our hearing', this possibility must be borne in mind. But in this case there is no one obviously interested in making the report, and it is incredible that Pope Alexander should have chosen this moment to reprove this bishop. For in November 1164 the pope was in no position to risk any possible offence to a potential supporter in England.

He and his cardinals were living in poverty in France, their future dependent on the good will of the rulers and prelates of those kingdoms. For him, the Becket affair was a political disaster, requiring the utmost care and caution. In these circumstances, a bright young bishop from England, who was also the king's cousin, could probably have obtained almost any favour he asked for, and what he obtained was the letter *Inter cetera*. Possibly, like some later petitioners, he came armed with a draft of the letter he wanted.

Why did the bishop want such a statement? The law itself needed definition,[26] although the general intention of the leaders of the church had long been clear. Statements made over the preceding sixty years had been reiterated at the Lateran Council of 1139: those who marry in the subdiaconate or above shall lack (*careant*) ecclesiastical office and benefice (c. 6); such a union is no marriage (c. 7); hereditary claims to benefices are condemned (c. 16). These decrees, which seem never to have been widely known, were both less precise and less compelling than the letter to the bishop of Worcester. The command to act is less definite, and the vital restriction of appeals does not occur.

Gratian's Decretum was not helpful on this subject to a reforming prelate. A mass of relevant material is scattered through different sections of the work; it is nowhere brought together and arranged conveniently for the practical user. An expert has spoken of the 'richness and the confusion of the Decretum on this subject', and observes that 'the lack of any strict arrangement makes it difficult to extract from the Decretum a precise doctrine of ecclesiastical celibacy'.[27] The young bishop of Worcester was the first prelate to demand from Pope Alexander a new statement of the law on these matters.

The form of the statement shows that his purpose was practical, not academic. It is often stated that decretal letters are largely of two kinds, answers to requests for definition of obscure points of law, or statements made in the course of instructions to judges-delegate in particular cases. The letter *Inter cetera* is clearly related to the first category, but with this difference, that it contains an explicit command to the recipient to take action. In this respect it belongs to another large group

---

[26] M. Cheney, 'Alexander III and Roger of Worcester', p. 212.
[27] J. Gaudemet, 'Gratien et le celibat ecclésiastique', *SG*, xiii (1967), 339–70.

of papal letters, many of which contain no new or important definition of law. They are simply letters obtained by a prelate or a group of prelates who want the support of papal authority for their actions. Such letters were not, of course, entirely new, but a surprising number were issued to English addressees in the 1170s. An example is one of 1177 to Richard, bishop of Winchester, then one of the most powerful men in England. Here the process is made explicit: 'because you desire to be fortified with the authority of our precept', the pope orders him to enforce payment of tithes from earls, barons, knights and others in his diocese, without right of appeal.[28] Peter des Roches, Richard's successor, obtained seven such letters on one day from Pope Innocent III.[29] Every one of the seven contains the clause *appellatione remota*. In this important detail also, Bishop Roger was an innovator. Like Bishop Richard, he wanted to be fortified with the authority of a papal precept. And he had observed that the new habit of appeal to the pope enabled offenders to delay, if not entirely to thwart, the normal process of ecclesiastical discipline. In this new situation prelates had to defend themselves by obtaining permission from the pope to override appeals in certain cases, hence the two clauses in *Inter cetera* which empowered him to proceed, in spite of appeals to the pope by priests' sons claiming their fathers' churches, and by clergy breaking the rules of celibacy.

Reforming bishops of the 1160s and 1170s needed all the support they could get in their campaign against clerical marriage and hereditary succession to benefices, for these customs were deeply rooted and socially acceptable in England at this time.[30] Bartholomew of Exeter had tried to enforce the law against some of his clergy, and had met with flat disobedience, counter-attack and appeal to the pope.[31] Bishop

---

[28] JL 14154, ACL 4.3. X 3.30.6 is a much abbreviated text.
[29] *Calendar of Letters of Pope Innocent III concerning England and Wales*, ed. C. R. and Mary G. Cheney (1967), nos. 643–9.
[30] The monks of Christ Church, Canterbury, were prepared to accept from a priest the gift of his church, and to grant it forthwith to his son Elias, agreeing that it should descend from one heir of Elias to another, *de parente in parentem*, provided the heir was suitable (HMC 8th Report, Appendix p. 323). On the general question see C. N. L. Brooke, 'The Gregorian Reform in action: clerical celibacy in England, 1050–1200', *Cambridge Historical Journal* xii.i (1956), 1–21, and Cheney, *Becket to Langton, passim*.
[31] Morey, *Bartholomew of Exeter*, p. 134.

THE BISHOP IN HIS DIOCESE 73

Roger must have known of this, for the appeal was probably pending in the Curia at the time of the embassy, in which Bartholomew also took part. The importance of *Inter cetera* as a weapon in the campaign was quickly recognized. There is hardly an English decretal collection of this period in which it does not occur, and in 1175 it was used as the authority for a canon of the provincial council of Westminster, thus being explicitly applied to the whole province of Canterbury.

But the conciliar canon did not reproduce the instructions given to Bishop Roger in their original stringent form. The prohibition against the succession of priests' sons was now to apply only to the future; the command to eject them from benefices they already held was not repeated. Pope Alexander himself, at an unknown date, declared that a priest should not be ejected if he had been installed in his father's benefice before the council of Tours (App. II, 87), and several English prelates evidently complained that the law could not be enforced. The bishop of Hereford asserted that enforcement would involve great danger and actual bloodshed; the archbishop of York got permission to grant dispensation in suitable cases to priests' sons; even Bartholomew of Exeter was given permission to allow subdeacons to remain with their wives in certain circumstances.[32] If the surviving evidence can be trusted, Bishop Roger did not ask for any such weakening of the rules, and as we shall see, two priests' sons felt it necessary to present personal dispensations from the pope when they were involved in litigation before him about their benefices.

Only a few traces remain of Bishop Roger's efforts to enforce the rules laid down in *Inter cetera* in the diocese of Worcester, and the course of events is often obscure. Three papal letters concern a chapel, probably that of Stretton on Fosse, about which there was a dispute in his time between the son of the previous incumbent and another clerk; two other papal letters may refer to the same involved proceedings. The first (App. II, 26) is addressed to the bishop of Worcester and the prior of Kenilworth. It recounts that G., a clerk, has asserted in the pope's presence that he was canonically 'ordained' in the chapel, held it peacefully for some years, and was then ejected

[32] JL 13946, X 3.3.2 (Hereford); JL 13881, X 1.17.9 (York); JL 13904, ACL 18.13 (Exeter).

by R., a knight, unjustly and without judgement. When he brought his complaint before the bishop, the objection was raised that G.'s father had ministered in the chapel, and therefore he was unable to regain it. The pope, prompted of course by G., considers it his duty to punish 'the insolence of laymen against ecclesiastics', and orders the bishop and his fellow-judge to restore the chapel to G. There is no trace of action on this letter; perhaps it was delivered after Bishop Roger's final departure from England, or perhaps it was treated as fraudulent.

The story is elucidated and continued by a letter of Pope Lucius III to Bishop Baldwin of Worcester (App. II, 49A). This letter must have been written two years or more after the first, at the request of the opposing party. According to this account, A. had been presented to Bishop Roger for institution, but G., said to be the son of the previous minister, opposed him, saying that he himself had been 'reasonably ordained' to the chapel. The bishop then assigned the revenues to A. pending the outcome of the dispute. Much later, judges-delegate had pronounced sentence in favour of G., but Baldwin refused to execute it, as G. could not produce the original commission on which they had acted. It looks as though Bishops Roger and Baldwin were doing what they could to impede G. in his claim to his father's benefice; G. may none the less have ended his days as parson of the chapel (App. II, 93A note).

It will be observed that in this case it was not the bishop who took the initiative in removing the minister's son from a benefice. The dispute began when R. the patron presented another clerk. Patrons, and not only lay patrons, were likely to try to exploit for their own advantage the church's increasingly strict attitude to hereditary succession to benefices, and might manage to eject the incumbent and install their own candidate, as the patron of Stretton seems to have done, perhaps after buying the patronage.

A second case seems to have come to Bishop Roger's attention in a different way, but again he does not take the initiative in discovering and removing the offender. A papal commission, addressed to Archbishop Richard and the bishop of Worcester (App. II, 57), reports the complaint of Walter, a clerk. He had, he said, been presented to a benefice in the church of Wootton Wawen by the abbot of Conches, but the bishop had refused to admit him, although another person had held the benefice after his father. The commission orders the judges, if this is true, to induct Walter at once into possession of the benefice, 'as this would not infringe the apostolic decree which condemns hereditary succession in the church of God'. As in the case of the chapel of Stretton-on-Fosse, there is no sign of action on this commission, but the end of the story is revealed by two charters issued by Bishop Roger, and preserved in the cartulary of Wootton Wawen, as part of the muniments of the abbey of Conches (App. I, 11, 12). In the first, dated 25 June 1178, the bishop announces that Walter, clerk, has voluntarily renounced the portion in the church of Wootton which B., his father, held, and promised never to move a plea against the abbot and monks of Conches about it, or to support others who might do so. On 3 November in the same year, the bishop confirmed the church to Conches, declaring his wish that the monks should hold it *in proprios usus*, saving episcopal rights and a sufficient vicarage. Nothing seems to be known about the history of the church of Wootton Wawen between the gift to Conches soon after the Norman conquest, and 1178. The information provided by these texts suggests that Bishop Roger was dealing with a descendant of one of a group of priests who had served the old minster, and held portions or prebends in it by hereditary right.[33]

Bishop Roger had already had practical experience of the problem of hereditary prebends. In 1166 a complaint had been made against the transformation (in 1155) of the collegiate church of Bromfield in Herefordshire into a priory of Gloucester Abbey. One of the surviving canons was imprisoned when travelling to the exiled archbishop, who ordered the bishops of Hereford and Worcester to investigate the matter.[34] Nothing is known of the fate of the canon, or of action by the two bishops.

At Bromfield, perhaps at Stretton, and at Wootton Wawen, the new order triumphed. But efforts to remove priests' sons from their fathers' benefices were not always successful, even in the diocese of Worcester. Henry 'son of Adam the priest' was the incumbent of the chapel of Yardley, on the northern border of the diocese. We hear of him only because the chapel

---

[33] *VCH Warwicks.*, iii. 133.
[34] *MTB*, v. 402, Denton, *Free chapels*, pp. 48–9.

was the subject of litigation between the abbot and convent of Marmoutier, (who must have presented Henry or tolerated his presence), and the monks of Alcester. The bishop of Worcester was not directly involved, but he had a double interest in the case; he wished to remove the priest's son, and also to retain control of Yardley, which Marmoutier claimed as a chapel of the church of Aston, in the diocese of Coventry (App. II, nos 49B, 58B). Marmoutier won its case. A papal confirmation, addressed to the abbot and convent and Henry, their clerk, confirms a sentence of judges-delegate and records that officials of the bishop of Worcester had inducted the monks and Henry into corporal possession of the chapel. It is worth underlining the unusual address of this confirmation, which protects Henry's tenure as well as the rights of Marmoutier. Henry presumably wanted this safeguard. Bishop Roger had to content himself with having made a demonstration against a priest's son, and asserted his episcopal rights over Yardley. He or his successors could at least refuse to admit the next presentee if they judged him unsuitable.

At Painswick, much as at Yardley, litigation over the advowson drew Bishop Roger's attention to the fact that the incumbent was the son of a former minister. As part of a compromise settlement, the bishop reinstated the offender in the church, notwithstanding that his father ministered there, 'because we have received an order of the Lord Pope that this shall not prejudice him'. The implication is clear: without that order, the bishop would not have reinstated the minister's son in his father's church (App. I, 32, cf. App. II, 72). At Painswick, as at Yardley, the bishop seems to have been unable to enforce the rules against hereditary succession of benefices, perhaps because the offenders had powerful supporters.

In these two cases, the principal issue was the right to the advowson; consequently nothing is reported about enquiries into allegations against the incumbents. The church of St Mary at Droitwich was disputed by two clerks, each hoping to obtain the benefice; the question of patronage may have been involved, but it was not at this stage presented as the main issue. One party appealed to the pope, and brought an order to the bishop of Worcester to investigate his charge that his opponent was the son of the previous parson, and *in sacerdotio genitus*. A second papal letter shows that the bishop had taken action and reported back; he had enquired carefully of lawful witnesses, and found that the accused was not conceived when his father was a priest, nor was the father parson or vicar of the disputed church (App. II, 19, 60). This may not have been the end of the matter, but that is another story.[35]

In all these cases which involve accusations against men alleged to be priests' sons or inheritors of benefices, there are none in which the bishop or his subordinates have acted *ex officio* to seek out offenders. At Wootton Wawen he refused to admit a son who had been presented to his father's benefice; in all the other cases he acted as judge in disputes over the benefice or the advowson. If archdeacons and rural deans going their rounds took *ex officio* action in such cases, no trace of their doings remains. Interested parties were more likely to take the initiative. The monks of Tewkesbury, in Worcester diocese, complained to the pope that their well-endowed churches, 'collated to the support of the brethren and guests', were useless to the monastery because they were held by absentees who placed vicars in them and took the revenues. On the death of the holders, their sons were installed, sometimes because of their own importunity, sometimes at the insistence of great men or the intervention of prelates. The pope therefore granted that when the clerks or priests of those churches died, the monks might institute suitable men, with the consent of the diocesan, and that the diocesan might not refuse to admit them without good cause. The pope further declared invalid all *ordinationes* made contrary to these provisions, and forbade absolutely the admission of the sons of these clerks or priests to their fathers' benefices. Nothing seems to be known of the circumstances in which this papal letter was obtained, or the use to which it was put, though a copy was probably preserved for a while at Worcester, where it was copied in the early 1180s into *Collectio Wigorniensis*.[36]

On the little available evidence from this diocese, it looks as though in this period patrons anxious to make use of their patronage, and envious clerks seeking benefices, were the most

[35] *Worc. cart.*, p. 97 no. 181.
[36] JL 14171. The best text is Wig. 2.33, though the scribe reversed the addresses of nos. 31 and 33.

active agents in the elimination of married clergy and hereditary succession to benefices. There was, of course, nothing new or surprising about these motives. The new factors in the situation were the general change in the climate of opinion, and at Worcester the bishop's reputation, and the resulting confidence in his sympathy with action against offenders.

Monasteries, churches and patrons

At Wootton Wawen the seal was set upon the destruction of the old order by the bishop's declaration that the abbey of Conches should hold the church *in proprios usus*. A few words must be said about the meaning and implications of that phrase. It referred to an arrangement which, in its fully developed form, established the monastery as the corporate rector, taking the income of the church less a fixed portion for a vicar or vicars. This arrangement had obvious advantages for the appropriating monastery.[37] Bishop Roger gave permission to hold churches *in proprios usus* not only to Conches, but also to Gloucester, Lire, Maiden Bradley, Nostell, Saint-Évroul and Worcester Cathedral Priory. Not all these appropriations were to take effect immediately. At Maiden Bradley and Nostell (App. I, 44, 48) the change was to be made on the death of the present parson, and this might involve long delay. Nostell was involved in litigation in 1221 on the death of the parson of Newbold instituted in Bishop Roger's time.

Roger does not use the words *appropriare, appropriata*.[38] The words *in proprios usus* do not seem to have implied a fixed and invariable arrangement. At Worcester, the payment of a fixed pension by the parson of St Augustine's, Dodderhill, seems to be envisaged; this may have been an interim arrangement for the period, potentially a long one since two lives were involved, before the church could, in the words of the charter, be 'converted to the use of the monks' (App. I, 73). At Gloucester a pension of five marks from St Mary's church and the tithes of several estates are to be converted *in proprios usus*, and the vicars

---
[37] Cf. *Chron. de Bello*, p. 139.
[38] *Dictionary of medieval latin from British sources*, fasc. 1 (British Academy 1975) places the earliest use of such forms in the 1220s.

of other churches pay fixed pensions (App. I, 23). Saint-Évroul is to hold one church and various blocks of tithes *in proprios usus*; the tithes are not all in the parish of the church in question (App. I, 56).

The Lire documents are especially interesting. There are three (App. I, 38, 39, 40), each with a different object, possibly issued on different occasions. The first is a general confirmation, naming the three churches of Hanley, Feckenham and Chedworth, and reserving episcopal rights. The second concedes the same three churches *usibus monachornm Lirensium* to increase their ministrations to the poor, saving a decent living for the vicars, while the third defines the vicars' portions; they are each to receive one third of all tithes, offerings and obventions. Similar sets of documents are known from the records of other dioceses.[39]

In most cases, there are careful safeguards for the bishop's rights and for the income of the vicars. In his confirmation for Conches, the bishop reserves episcopal rights and a sufficient vicarage; in the case of Lire, as we have seen, in one charter he reserves his own rights, and in another a living for the vicars. In his confirmation for Maiden Bradley he reserves episcopal customs, in that for Nostell, *episcopalia* and *sinodalia*. In the confirmation for Saint-Évroul he reserves for himself and his successors 'our dignity and that of the church of Worcester', and confirms the church of St Peter of Rowell so long as the abbot and brethren cause it to be properly served. Only at Gloucester and Worcester is there no safeguard in the surviving charters. But even there the bishop is insisting that his approval is required; appropriation cannot be effected without episcopal authority. Three charters suggest that requests for appropriation had to be justified; at Lire and Nostell it is granted to increase funds for hospitality, at Maiden Bradley because of the sufferings of the lepers.

Though the institution is not yet fully defined, the idea of appropriation is accepted, and the bishop is even prepared, in the case of Wootton Wawen, to record that he desires it. Appropriation could help to break the grip of married clergy on family livings, and it also removed ecclesiastical patronage

---

[39] Cheney, *Becket to Langton*, p. 136 n. 4.

decisively out of lay hands. But it carried with it well-known dangers. Bishop Roger himself drew the pope's attention to the exploitation of vicars by monks, and received a clear statement of his right to intervene in support of vicars' interests (App. II, 63b). Possibly this was a result of bitter experience; a papal letter of uncertain date shows that the bishop had been involved in a brush with Kenilworth Priory as a result of his own failure to define the portion to be allotted to the vicar of Salford Priors before, rather than after, accepting him for institution. The bishop seems to have felt that this failure needed explanation; he had intended, he wrote to the pope, to discuss the vicarage with the prior (with whom he so often acted as judge-delegate), and the parties, he implies, were all respectable people, the sacristan of Kenilworth was 'a good and religious man', and Ralph, the vicar, learned and virtuous. It was a nice example of the need for strict regulation. The case helps to show what stage had been reached in the development of vicarages. Clearly no perpetual vicarage had been ordained (to use the language of a later time) at Salford Priors; the amount of the vicar's portion must have been a matter for negotiation at each institution. The course of business was not yet fixed with bureaucratic precision, nor were vicars invariably appointed for life rather than year by year, for when the dispute arose, Kenilworth tried to maintain that Ralph had been appointed for one year only. On the other hand it was assumed that the bishop had the right to intervene, and that the priory could not simply fix the vicar's portion on its own authority.

As well as claiming the right to authorize appropriations and supervise vicars and vicarages, the bishop insists on the need for episcopal control of pensions paid from churches. On this point too he obtained a useful ruling from the pope, who ruled that an action which claimed a pension could succeed only if the pension had been authorized by the diocesan (App. II, 63c). Recipients of pensions, generally though not always religious houses, had as it were to register their claims and receive charters from the bishop. The charters were carefully preserved; charters of Bishop Roger survive confirming pensions to Cirencester, Evesham, Gloucester, Lanthony (two churches), Malmesbury, and Worcester (four churches) (App. I, 10, 20, 23, 32, 34, 45, 51 and 84, 78, 79, 82).

At Wootton Wawen, Walter the clerk asserted that the benefice he claimed had been *canonice concessum*; at Stretton-on-Fosse the former minister's son asserted that he was *canonice adeptus*. These imprecise expressions were perhaps designed to conceal the fact that these claimants had not obtained their benefices in what was now, newly, the only lawful way, that is by presentation to the diocesan, admission and institution by him, and induction at his command by the appropriate officers. Where hereditary succession to benefices was normal, these formalities were superfluous; where bishops were trying to suppress hereditary succession and to assert their own authority over both clergy and patrons, the formalities became extremely important, and methods had to be devised of ensuring that they were observed. One method was to insist that rectors and vicars could produce appropriate documents from the patron and the diocesan. This was recommended by Pope Alexander to the bishop of Norwich, possibly at the bishop's suggestion; Bishop William was issuing such charters by 1168 at latest.[40] These documents, tied as they were to one man's tenure of one benefice, seldom survive from this early period. A charter of Bishop Roger, recording the admission of a vicar, is preserved in the cartulary of Cirencester Abbey, as proof of the abbey's right to receive a pension from the church in question (App. I, 10). Another, now lost, was produced by the abbot of Gloucester in the king's court in 1222. It recorded the admission of a clerk to a church on the presentation of the abbot and convent, and authorized the payment of a pension from the church to Gloucester's dependency at Stanley (App. I, 25). A third records and confirms the institution of a parson to a church which had been the subject of disputes and a complex settlement between three contenders (App. I, 83). There is nothing to show whether in these cases the incumbent received a separate charter for himself, corresponding to the later 'letters of institution'.

None of the charters or decretal letters which have been mentioned sets out fully all the steps by which a clerk became possessed of a benefice, though all the steps are mentioned in

---

[40] JL 12253, full text PL 200.929. Cf. *Reg. . . . of St Benet of Holme*, ed. J. R. West, Norfolk Record Society (1932), pp. 55–6, nos. 94–5.

one place or another. Presentation is always recorded. Admission (or reception) is recorded in the charter for Cirencester, in the lost charter for Gloucester, and in the account of the dispute over Salford Priors. The Cirencester charter says nothing of institution or induction, but the priest has obtained a right which is to be preserved *inviolabiliter*. The bishop admits the vicar of Salford Priors, and 'causes this to be announced to his chapter'; after this, assuming that the appointment is to a perpetual vicarage, the vicar cannot be removed by the patron. The papal confirmation concerning Yardley chapel is the only text concerning the diocese of Worcester in Roger's time which mentions the final stage, the induction into corporal possession. Possibly in the Salford Priors case, the bishop's notification to 'his chapter' that a vicar had been admitted, should be understood as an instruction to the rural chapter, headed by its dean, to proceed to induction on the spot. This admittedly very small sample of documents confirms that while the procedure for placing a clerk in a benefice was becoming fixed in the new form which was to endure for centuries, the terminology and the forms of documents were far from being fully established.[41]

The bishop, as this evidence shows, was playing his part in a long and laborious battle for control of the parish clergy. Canons of recent councils, decretals of recent popes, are his big guns, charters are his ammunition. He can enforce his demands for charters by refusing to recognize claims which are not supported by charters, as in the matter of claims to pensions, in which case he finds it desirable to have explicit papal backing for his demands. In addition to these weapons, he needs well-kept records in his own office, so that he can be sure about the status of churches and chapels, rectors and vicars, the names of patrons, and such matters.

Insistence on the need for written evidence may have been the cause of a slightly testy letter from Gilbert Foliot to Bishop Roger, in reply to a request for exact information about a benefice granted to an unknown Master Fromundus in Gilbert's presence. Probably the benefice had been granted when Gilbert, as bishop of Hereford, was looking after the diocese of Worcester during a vacancy. 'I too,' says Gilbert, 'want his rights to be

---

[41] Cf. *Acta Stephani Langton*, ed. K. Major, Canterbury and York Society (1950), p. xxxv, where the editor discusses letters of admission, institution and collation.

supported by ample documents, so that they cannot be overturned by falsehood'. It reads very much as though he is repeating Roger's words. But he is terribly busy, he can hardly attend to his own affairs, and he cannot recall this distant business 'with the precision you demand'. There are plenty of witnesses, he says, and the benefice is not being reclaimed; why should we sweat over superfluous things? Don't let your conscience be over-fussy at his expense, because although I remember the affair, I don't recall the details 'quas scripture forma requireret'.[42]

Bishop Roger had evidently asked some searching questions, and Gilbert regarded this with ill-concealed impatience. He may indeed have been busy on more important things; he may also, in this as in some other matters, have been a little old-fashioned. For we have to consider, why did Bishop Roger want this information? There is no sign of litigation, no trouble with the patron, and yet the bishop wants details, so that rights may be preserved in future. It looks as though he and his clerks are compiling or checking records, and this would agree with other evidence that in his time, and possibly earlier, the bishop of Worcester had his own list giving particulars of benefices in his diocese. In Bishop Baldwin's time such a list was called a *matricula*; later it may also be called a *scrutinium*. The annalist of Winchcombe Abbey, in the diocese of Worcester, reports that Baldwin found discrepancies in the *matricula* of his predecessors, and therefore held a general enquiry by means of sworn inquests and produced a new one. This gave details about patrons, parsons, vicars, tithes, chapels, pensions and endowments, 'and whether each man legally possessed what he claimed to be his'.[43] The last words suggest an intention similar to that of Bishop Roger, who wanted the rights (*iustitia*) of Master Fromundus to be properly documented.

An extract from Bishop Baldwin's *matricula* survives in the cartulary of Eynsham Abbey. It provides just the details mentioned by the Winchcombe annalist, and suggests that his words can be trusted. The extract was made *c.* 1213–38. By that time there existed yet another new survey or supplement, so

[42] *Letters of Foliot*, p. 314 no. 242.
[43] *Landboc . . . de Winchelcumba*, i. 69. On *matricula* see Cheney, *Bishops' Chanceries*, pp. 115–16.

that when Bishop Walter of Worcester in 1238 gave particulars about patronage 'secundum rotulos nostros matriculares,' there may have been several series; his words suggest that they were in the form of rolls, not loose quires or volumes.[44]

Gilbert Foliot's letter to Bishop Roger cannot be precisely dated. But it occurs in the principal manuscript of Foliot's letters in a quire which seems to contain material largely of the years 1164–8, so that there is a possibility that Roger's efforts to check or compile his *matricula* began before his departure from England in the later part of 1167.[45] If the Winchcombe chronicler can be trusted, Roger was not the first bishop of Worcester to possess a record of this type. But no other trace of a *matricula* has been noticed before his time. There seems to be no reference to a *matricula* or *scrutinium* in papal letters or episcopal charters of this period. Even when Roger confirms a pension that should surely have appeared in it, he refers only to evidence given by old men in his presence, and to the unanimous testimony of religious men (App. I, 45). It would be particularly interesting to hear of a case in which the *matricula* was used to check fraudulent assertions or cast doubt on forged or interpolated charters, but none has come to light. Of course, the mere fact of its existence should have served as a deterrent to false claims.

Lack of records, and changing notions of church government, lay behind the frequent disputes about episcopal rights over monasteries in this period. Bishop Roger could not hope to be free from these troubles. There is no record of disputes or litigation between the bishop of Worcester and the abbey of Evesham in his time, though there had been trouble under Bishop Simon in 1139, and there was to be more under Bishop Mauger. Perhaps Roger's personal relations with Abbot Adam, and the privilege which Adam obtained at Tours in 1163,[46] were sufficient to preserve peace for the time being. The privilege did not spell out in precise terms the exemption of Evesham and its dependent churches from the authority of the diocesan,

---

[44] *Cart. of Eynsham Abbey*, ed. H. E. Salter (OHS. 1907), i. 137–8. *The Chartulary... of St Werburgh, Chester*, ed. J. Tait, Chetham Soc. NS 79 (1920), i. no. 122.
[45] *Letters of Foliot*, xlv–xlvi (quire xxi).
[46] JL 10877, *Chron. Evesham*, p. 175. See also David Knowles, 'The growth of monastic exemption', *Downside Review* 1 (1932), 396–401, and G. G. Coulton, *Five centuries of religion*, ii (1927), 347–78.

but it commanded the bishops of Worcester to be content with the subjection which the monks' predecessors had shown to theirs, and it did not contain the vital words 'salva diocesani episcopi canonica iustitia'.

Acceptance of Evesham's special position did not mean that Bishop Roger was ready to accept challenges to his rights from the religious in general. He reacted sharply when Walter, abbot of Westminster, tried to institute a prior to Westminster's cell at Great Malvern. The episode is briefly described in a statement made later by Master Silvester, who was at the time one of Roger's chief clerks. Silvester testified that in the time of Bishop Roger, the abbot of Westminster instituted a prior of Malvern; 'secretly and upon his own authority, without the bishop's consent. The bishop suspended the prior, and maintained the suspension until the abbot and prior gave satisfaction for their offence in such a way that everything that had been done in connection with the institution was annulled, and the prior was then instituted by the bishop's officials at the bishop's command.' This episode must have taken place between July 1177, when the previous prior of Malvern was elected abbot of Burton, and January 1179, when the bishop left England for the last time.[47]

Bishop Roger's determination to fight for his rights at Great Malvern may have been stiffened by a recent defeat over the priory of St Oswald at Gloucester. The priory was one of the churches which were later known as royal free chapels. At this time its status was imperfectly defined, and was irksome both to the diocesan and the archbishop of Canterbury, because it had been detached from the diocese of Worcester and attached to the archbishopric of York.[48] Bishop Roger, and Archbishops Thomas and Richard, conducted a ten-year struggle against the exemption of St Oswald's, without success. The sequence of events is obscure. At an uncertain date in his exile, probably in 1166 or 1167, Archbishop Thomas wrote to Bishop Roger about the dispute between Roger and the archbishop of York, and ordered him to take no action in the matter, even at the request of the king or a cardinal, without his own prior consent. He

[47] See below, Appendix III.
[48] For the history of St Oswald's in this period, earlier accounts are superseded by Denton, *Free chapels*, pp. 51–7.

also ordered the bishop not to absolve 'the excommunicates of St Oswald and its whole *parrochia*'.⁴⁹ It sounds as though the bishop of Worcester had initiated the action. The affair will certainly have been complicated by the bitter quarrel, personal and official, between the two archbishops and King Henry's hostility to Archbishop Thomas. There is nothing to show how this phase of the dispute ended, or when and by whom the 'excommunicates of St Oswald's' were absolved. The matter never recurs in the Becket correspondence.

The dispute was renewed during Archbishop Richard's visitation of his province, begun towards the end of October 1174.⁵⁰ The visitation, the first recorded and probably the first of the kind undertaken by an archbishop of Canterbury in the twelfth century, inevitably revived the need for definition of the status of St Oswald's and of the rights of the archbishop of York. Archbishop Richard summoned the *clerici* of St Oswald's to appear before him; they refused, and were excommunicated. Both Diceto and Hoveden speak of *clerici*; perhaps the southern prelates were chiefly concerned to establish their rights over the clerks of the dependent chapels attached to St Oswald's. The archbishop of York protected his rights by an appeal to the pope, and in 1175 went over to the offensive, sending to the Council held by archbishop Richard in May at Westminster messengers, who renewed the appeal against the sentence on the clergy of St Oswald's and laid claim to the diocese of Worcester itself, along with Lincoln, Chester and Hereford. He appealed on this claim also, and Archbishop Richard appealed in his turn. It is unlikely that anyone took seriously the claim to the four dioceses, or that the bishop of Worcester had any expectation of being removed from the province of Canterbury; this was simply a move in the larger, general quarrel between the two metropolitans. In less than six months a papal legate, Hugh, cardinal-deacon of St Angelo, arrived in England at the king's request, and was promptly set to work at Winchester on negotiations between the archbishops. King Henry was able to insist that the position of St Oswald's was settled; 'by the king's advice', Archbishop Richard quit-claimed it to Archbishop

---

⁴⁹ *MTB*, vi. 193–4.
⁵⁰ *Diceto*, i. 396; *Gesta Henrici*, i. 90.

Roger of York as the king's 'demesne chapel' (*dominica capella*), and absolved the excommunicated clerks.[51]

The bishop of Worcester does not figure in the chroniclers' accounts of this dispute in the years 1174–6, but three writs issued by the king to the sheriffs and other officials of Gloucestershire, show that he was at least a dutiful supporter of Archbishop Richard, and possibly an active campaigner on his own account. Two of these writs were issued at Clarendon and witnessed by Rotrou, archbishop of Rouen; one was issued at Winchester, with Bishop Richard of Winchester as witness.[52] This last will have been issued after Richard's consecration on 6 October 1174, and before his long absence in Normandy (Michaelmas 1176 to March 1178); this writ seems likely to belong to the months between Archbishop Richard's excommunication of the clerks of St Oswald's and the settlement made late in 1175. The other two writs, though they present dating problems, deal with similar subject-matter, and may well belong to approximately the same period.[53] None of these writs mentions the archbishop of Canterbury. One of those witnessed by Rotrou refers to the dispute between the archbishop of York and the bishop of Worcester. It orders royal officials to ensure, without delay, that St Oswald's receives all its dues, and specifically that the parishioners of Sandhurst, one of its chapels, pay tithes in full; further, all who hold land in the parish of St Oswald's shall pay their dues and tithes. The second writ witnessed by Rotrou orders royal officials to do justice upon debtors of the parishioners of St Oswald's, and to cause the parishioners to have their common rights in and outside Gloucester. The third writ, witnessed by Richard of Winchester, orders royal officials to ensure that parishioners of St Oswald's pay all dues and tithes, to allow no one to injure the *capellania*, the canons or the parishioners, or to dare to avoid their communion. The parishioners are to enjoy their common rights, as agreed between the king and the archbishop of York. The details of the business are obscure, but it appears that St

---

[51] *Gesta Henrici*, i. 204.
[52] *Cal. Pat. Rolls*, 1385–9, pp. 526–7. The writs are known only from this inspeximus. Copies must have been kept at St Oswald's.
[53] Rotrou, as archbishop, is not known to have been with the king at Clarendon before the summer of 1176.

Oswald's and its clergy were suffering as a result of a sentence of excommunication pronounced, or announced, by the bishop of Worcester. The king intervenes to protect his *capellania*, giving orders to royal officials about payment of tithes and avoidance of excommunicates. The episode illustrates the hardening definition of exemption, and the helplessness of the diocesan in the area subject to a royal chapel.

It is easy to over-estimate the importance of these disputes about various forms of monastic exemption, because they bulk large in monastic chronicles and records. Placed in perspective, in this century of advance in diocesan administration, they appear as necessary test cases, by which old arrangements and traditional customs were redefined in new situations. The clashes do not prove that the bishops concerned were anti-monastic. They wanted their rights and responsibilities defined, and they had some justification for their belief that the religious life was most likely to be well conducted when it was not exempt from normal local supervision. There is practically no evidence about Bishop Roger's opinions on these questions. As we shall see, he seems to have supported Archbishop Richard at one point in his resistance to the exemption of St Augustine's, Canterbury, and he was perhaps suspected of hostility by the monks of Malmesbury, who made provision for the possibility that he would refuse to act on a commission which they obtained in the matter of their exemption from the bishop of Salisbury App. II, 79). He also complained to the pope about monastic oppression of vicars of parish churches, as we have seen. These are indications of criticism of certain legal and administrative aspects of monasticism, against which must be set his friendship with the abbot of Evesham, his learned discussions with Senatus of Worcester, and—for what it is worth—the absence of any trace of conflict with the monks of his cathedral priory.

Only these few fragmentary traces remain of some of Bishop Roger's pastoral and administrative activities in his diocese. Of some there is no trace. No charter, no chronicle, no literary reference shows him preaching, confirming children, presiding over a synod or conducting a visitation. In the first three cases we can be fairly confident that the silence of the sources arises from the fact that these things were too common to be noteworthy. Visitation presents more of a problem. The archbishops of Canterbury, from Richard onwards, visited (in the formal sense) their province occasionally, but for their contemporaries only a few ambiguous notices are to be found before the last decade of the twelfth century.[54] Ancient canons required bishops to visit their dioceses, to enquire into the state of the clergy, the ornaments and repair of churches, the morals and beliefs of the laity, the condition of monasteries; these canons were set out by Gratian (chiefly in C.10 q.1). But when the bishops of Worcester wanted to demonstrate their rights over Great Malvern, they were able, as we have seen, to produce evidence about their institution of the prior; they did not prove that they had visited the priory. English bishops of this time were by custom and economic necessity peripatetic, moving frequently from one manor to another, to say nothing of journeys for other purposes; and the manors of the see of Worcester were well spread over the diocese.[55] In the course of his residence in each and his travels from one to another a zealous bishop could combine convenience and pastoral care. That Bishop Roger, like his contemporaries, travelled in his diocese and made sporadic descents on notorious offenders, goes almost without saying. It is improbable, however, that he visited either the monasteries or the parishes of his diocese in the systematic and formal way desiderated, but seldom realized, in later times.

It might be supposed that an interest in monastic discipline, connected with visitation, prompted Bishop Roger's enquiry to Pope Alexander as to whether monks might accuse their abbot and receive payment from the revenues of their house to cover expenses arising from the accusation (App. II, 64). The pope's answer to this question was issued between September 1171 and September 1172; if the query did indeed arise from the bishop's practical experience of visitation, it shows that he visited, in the technical sense, in the early years of his pontificate, before his absence of 1167–72. But the query more probably arose from his experience as a judge-delegate. Just this problem must have arisen when the monks of St Augustine's, Canterbury, accused Clarembald, their abbot-elect, before the pope, and the pope commissioned the bishop of Worcester and others to investigate and take action. Their sentence was published in

[54] Cheney, *Becket to Langton*, pp. 139–41.
[55] Haines, *Bishopric of Worcester*, p. 75.

1173; the early stages of this case might have prompted the bishop's question.

We have said that there is no reference to the diocesan (or any other) synod among materials relating to Bishop Roger, though there is evidence that in some English dioceses of this time the synod was a regular and expected event. Roger's contemporary, Richard Peche of Coventry, speaks casually of his clergy gathering for a synod 'as is customary'; the occasion is recorded only because the bishop issued a charter about some judicial business which was settled there.[56] Similarly a synod of the diocese of Canterbury is recorded because an appeal was made from its judgement to that of the pope (App. II, 3). We are justified in assuming that synods met in the diocese of Worcester in Roger's time, but every detail remains obscure. None of his charters mentions judicial business brought before a synod, nor is there any reference to cases taken from it by appeal to a higher court.

The judge

Where then, and how, did Bishop Roger deal with litigation arising in his diocese? There is noticeably less evidence about his activity as judge-ordinary than as judge-delegate, and what there is, is less detailed. The bishop's charters, like those of his contemporaries, seldom describe the past history of the matter when announcing judgements or settlements; indeed their very terseness made them ineffective as legal instruments, and reveals them to be products of a society that still instinctively favoured the spoken rather than the written word.

It is not always stated in these charters that litigation has taken place. For example, the bishop confirms a *transactio* between the houses of Evesham and Kenilworth, at the request of Abbot Adam and Prior Robert (App. I, 21). The terms are already set out in a chirograph. The five witnesses of the bishop's charter are all more or less regular members of his household; they include Master Silvester and Samson, two of his chief clerks, and Simon, archdeacon of Worcester. The very word *transactio* suggests previous litigation, probably before the

---

[56] Cheney, *Becket to Langton*, p. 186 and *passim*.

bishop, but no details are recorded. Similarly John Fruschelu, in *presentia nostra constitutus*, at an unspecified place, concedes that his chapel of Littleton is subject to the church of Dumbleton (App. I, 1). The abbot of Abingdon agrees that there shall be services in the chapel three times a week. We are left to assume that the parties have been contending about their rights before the bishop, and that the dispute has ended with the submission of John Fruschelu. But again nothing whatever is revealed in the charter about the nature of John's claim or the course of the proceedings. Robert and Hawisia Foliot his wife, *constituti in presentia nostra*, confirm her father's gift of a church to Lanthony Priory (App. I, 33); possibly there has been litigation, but once more there are no details. The original grant to Lanthony was read aloud before Richard and his wife *in communi audientia*. It is tempting to see in this phrase the beginning of the usage that in the next century labelled the bishop's personal, peripatetic court his *audientia*, but in this case the writer may only have meant 'in public'. Certainly it would be unwise to suppose that at this date the word must denote a session of a formal tribunal. In two of these cases the words *in presentia nostra constituti* suggest formality, and show that the parties had appeared in person before the bishop, but stop short of saying that he was acting as judge. It remains possible that in some cases there had been no litigation, and the parties were simply following the new fashion of putting an amicable agreement into writing, and having it recorded by higher authority.

Other charters apparently arising from litigation in the diocese are a little, but only a little, more informative. Almost without exception, they refer to proceedings in the bishop's presence. There is no mention of a separate court, with its own name, its own officials, or a fixed seat; the court is where the bishop is. For example, there is a dispute between Richard, a knight, and the abbot of Evesham about the advowson of the chapel of *Westona* (App. I, 20). It is terminated on 6 September 1176 or 1177, at Fladbury, where the bishops of Worcester have a manor. Richard, *in presentia nostra constitutus* in the parish church, renounces the advowson and whatever right he had seemed to have. The witnesses include Samson, the bishop's clerk, Robert, the bishop's chaplain, Robert 'Monachus', parson of Cleeve, all frequent witnesses of his documents, the priest and clerk of Fladbury, two *magistri* described as 'of Evesham', perhaps acting for the abbot, and the abbot's seneschal. Nothing is recorded about the earlier stages of the affair, though the opening words of the charter make it certain that there have been formal legal proceedings.

Similarly, nothing is known of the proceedings that lie behind a composition made in the bishop's presence on 16 May 1177 in the church of St Peter, the parish church at Winchcombe. The parties are the churches of Tewkesbury and Beckford, the abbey and a parish church whose rector was Master Silvester, the bishop's clerk. Unfortunately, the composition is known only from a summary in an inventory of Tewkesbury muniments, which does not recite the charter in full or list witnesses. The settlement is detailed and far-seeing; payment of tithes will vary according to the abbey's method of exploiting its land. But where both parties soberly desired agreement, there was no need for the elaborate procedures of the learned law, with its time-consuming and expensive formalities. In one case, which will be discussed in more detail later, the abbess of Fontevrault renounces litigation 'quia servum Dei non oportet litigare', agreeing to accept whatever was arranged by the bishop and three named laymen, with the advice of friends. Informality rules; these persons are not named as arbiters, and the resulting settlement is described both as a *concordia* and a *transactio*.[57] This is not because the bishop and his *iurisperiti* have never heard of the formal canonical process of arbitration. The bishop has been an arbiter himself in a delegated case some six years earlier (App. I, 41), and made use of arbiters in 1173 to settle his dispute with Osney Abbey about the church of Bibury (App. I, 51, n.2). Perhaps we should say that the *iurisperiti*, and the Roman-canonical procedure on which they thrive, have not yet taken control of the bishop's court; forms of action matter less than they will do in fifty years' time, decisions (however they are reached) are still recorded in the old manner, briefly and with a minimum of technicality, relying for the future as much upon the evidence of witnesses as upon the words of the charter.

[57] *Worc. cart.*, pp. 88–9 nos. 162–4.

A group of Worcester documents concerns a series of related disputes between the cathedral priory and a local nobleman, Osbert FitzHugh. They show the bishop apparently hearing cases, or at least arranging the solemn final settlement, in the crypt of his cathedral before the altar of St Peter, on 9 April 1175, a few days before Easter. One of the disputes concerned the church of All Saints, Worcester. The bishop's charter announces 'querelam que vertebatur inter . . . monachos Wigorn' et illustrem virum Osbertum filium Hugonis super iure advocationis et patronatus ecclesie Omnium Sanctorum in Wigorn' hunc finem sortitam fuisse' (App. I, 79). Osbert obtains, or retains, the advowson of All Saints; the monks are awarded a small compensation in the form of an annual pension of half a mark, and possibly by having the parson presented to them, and by them to the bishop.[58]

On the same day, in the same place, Osbert formally in the bishop's presence recognized the validity of his father's charter confirming his grandfather's gift to the cathedral of Boraston and the church of Dodderhill, and a saltpit in Droitwich. This time it is Osbert and his brother who receive compensation; they are to present to the church during their lifetimes, presenting to the prior, not directly to the bishop. The bishop's charter, alone of his charters for Worcester, survives in the original, and therefore the full list of witnesses, omitted by the cartulary-maker, is for once preserved. Those present before the bishop, on that final day in the cathedral crypt, as well as Osbert FitzHugh and his brother, included the subprior, chamberlain and cantor of Worcester, two of the bishop's chief clerks, Master Silvester and Master Moses, Adam son of Edwin, another of his clerks, a Master Godfrey, Walter of All Saints, parson of one of the disputed churches and also rural dean (App. I, 80), and a couple of eminent laymen, both tenants of the bishop, Hugh Poer and Robert de Luci. Hugh was probably also involved in a related dispute, as will appear. Master Godfrey was not one of the bishop's regular clerks, though he witnesses another of Roger's charters concerning the cathedral (App. I, 84). Possibly he was the prior's nephew, and was employed by the

[58] This last proviso may be a fraudulent insertion in the cartulary copy of the bishop's charter; it does not appear in Osbert's charter, which explicitly mentions presentation by him to the bishop (*Worc. cart.*, p. 95 no. 177).

monks.[59] Neither this list nor the list of witnesses to the settlement at Fladbury suggest a strictly constituted court. Those present, beside the parties and others involved, are either the bishop's chief clerks or persons available locally, and their function is simply that of witness.

A third dispute, involving Osbert FitzHugh and the cathedral, may have been ended on the same occasion (App. I, 80, 81). The bishop's charter announcing the settlement is a little more informative than the two which have just been examined. It refers explicitly to legal proceedings in the bishop's presence (*cum in presentia nostra questio orta esset*) between Ralph, prior of Worcester, and Osbert FitzHugh about the church of All Saints and the church of St Clements, both in Worcester. The prior of Worcester stated that St Clements was in no way subject to All Saints, of which, as we have seen, Osbert was claiming, or had already obtained, the advowson. Osbert formally stated (*in iure confessus est*), that he claimed no rights over St Clements for himself, and Hugh Poer 'who asserted that he is the *dominus fundi*' and Richard of Grafton, perhaps a sub-tenant, conceded to the cathedral the rights they had claimed. Walter, parson of All Saints, was present and raised no protest. All those concerned with the possible subjection of St Clements to All Saints are thus brought face to face, and all accept its independence, and 'this being done in the bishop's presence and with the witness of many men', the bishop makes All Saints church free, so that it shall be the *dominica capella* of the monks.

Taken separately, the documents seem to show the bishop sitting in judgement on three cases of dispute over advowson. Taken together, they suggest a negotiated settlement, from which the element of judgement is absent. The bishop does indeed persuade Osbert FitzHugh to respect the rule which he had urged upon the pope himself, that 'what has once been reasonably decreed, and confirmed by episcopal and royal authority, especially when it is granted to a religious house' shall not be 'overturned and invalidated at the whim of a layman at the succession of each new lord' (App. I, 34, and below p. 191). The bishop's persuasion was no mere exercise in sweet reasonableness. It was backed by a threat, implicit or explicit,

---

[59] *Worc. cart.*, p. 113 no. 213.

for in case of necessity he might excommunicate Osbert, and lay an interdict on his lands. Bartholomew of Exeter had taken this action when Joel of Vautort tried to seize the patronage of a church granted by an ancestor to the canons of Plympton, giving rise to a case in which Bishop Roger acted as judge-delegate (App. II, 52); Bishop Robert Foliot of Hereford was using the same weapons at about this time against another west-country nobleman, Hugh Parvus of Moreton, in a dispute about the patronage of two churches in Worcester diocese (App. II, 90A). By coming to terms, Osbert saved himself from the trouble which Joel and Hugh brought upon themselves, and obtained some compensation; the monks of Worcester were spared labour and expense, and the bishop had the satisfaction of keeping disputes about advowson out of the secular court.

In the case of St Augustine's church, Dodderhill, Osbert's recognition of his father's grant cannot have been lightly given, for it involved him in some embarrassment. Nearly twenty years earlier he had granted the church to the nunnery founded by himself and his mother at Westwood near Worcester, as a cell of the abbey of Fontevrault. Now, the abbess of Fontevrault protested, saying that Osbert's grant to Westwood had been confirmed by Bishop Alfred. Further compromise was necessary. At the petition of the king, the monks granted an estate to the nuns, and freedom from tithes on their lands in the parish of Dodderhill. The agreement was made in Bishop Roger's presence on 4 November 1178.[60] Osbert was thus relieved of any obligation to provide the nuns with other benefits to replace his lost grant.

The case illustrates very clearly the shift of opinion about lay rights over churches. Bishop Alfred had, it seems, been prepared to accept Osbert's right to resume his father's gift to Worcester, and by implication to acquiesce in the view that the advowson of a church belonged automatically to the lord for the time being of the fee in which it lay, the *dominus fundi*, who could overturn and invalidate (as Bishop Roger put it) his predecessor's grants. In the 1170s, English bishops, or at least those who were leaders of opinion in the church, were not prepared to accept this view. Moving in step with canonist

[60] Ibid., pp. 88–9 nos. 162, 164.

theory,[61] they acted on the assumption that the rights of lay patrons of churches ought to be severely restricted, particularly at two points. First, advowson should not be tied like a house or a tree to one piece of ground, but could be given away permanently, under ecclesiastical control, preferably into ecclesiastical hands. And second, the advocate should be entitled to present a clerk to a bishop, but not to name and install him in a benefice on his own sole authority, like a lord enfeoffing a life tenant. Laymen were quite well aware of this change of attitude; significantly, Archbishop Thomas, shortly before his death, had been accused before the king of having 'obtained a certain privilege from the pope, for himself and the bishops, destroying the advowson of earls and barons, and even of the king'.[62] The bishops of the 1170s were more circumspect than Thomas. They recognized that strict enforcement of the new canonist theory might be impossible, and would certainly cause resentment among their lay friends and benefactors, who had power to help or harm the church. Bishop Roger, himself a noble among the noblest, must have understood the attitude of the nobility, even if he did not sympathize with it, and have appreciated the need to act in each case so as to minimize the affront caused by application of the new rules.

As we have seen, Bishop Roger's notifications of decisions and settlements made before him in diocesan matters are terse, and seldom reveal the details of the claims put forward by the parties or the proofs by which they supported their case. Sometimes it is clear that a document was the decisive factor, as when Osbert FitzHugh handles and ratifies his father's charter, or Robert and Hawisia Foliot his wife hear and ratify her father's charter for Lanthony. Sometimes oral testimony is decisive; the bishop confirms the pension claimed by Malmesbury Abbey from Shipton church after many men of ripe age have given evidence in his presence. But there is nothing to show how the old men gave their evidence, where they met the bishop, and whether they were examined singly or collectively. On one occasion, and one only, the bishop announces the result of a plea which was settled by the collective verdict of jurors. In his

---

[61] Cf. P. Landau, *Ius Patronatus*.
[62] *MTB*, iii. 128. The accusation reveals the fears of contemporary laymen, whose opinions on these questions are seldom recorded.

presence, by the oath of lawful men, it was recognized (*recognitum*) that a hide of land called *Herdewicha* in Hartlebury belonged to the demesne of the church of Hartlebury, and Absalon, who held it, resigned it into the hand of the prior of Worcester, receiving it back for life at a rent of six pence a year (App. I, 85). The form of words suggests a collective statement on a matter of fact. Possibly the crux of the dispute was the precise nature of Absalon's tenure, hereditary or of limited duration. In ordering or allowing a sworn inquest to decide a plea concerning land, Bishop Roger was no innovator. Professor van Caenegem has shown that similar procedures were used up and down England in this century, in circumstances so diverse that they defy all attempt at classification.[63]

The number of cases settled by the bishop as Ordinary in his diocese seems very low. Comparison with the situation in the diocese of London, as revealed by Gilbert Foliot's letter-collection, suggests that this low figure is partly the result of destruction of evidence. But even if the known cases should be multiplied by some arbitrary figure, perhaps doubled or trebled, even taking account of some five and a half years' absence from England, the total still seems small for an episcopate of fifteen years, or sixteen and a half from the time of his election.

Is it possible that litigants who in earlier times were content to accept the decision of the bishop's synod or the archdeacon's chapter (or to endure injury without hope of justice), and in later times would have appeared before well-regulated local courts, were in this period particularly prone to go, if they could, to the highest court, that is to the pope himself? That this may have been so is suggested by the number of cases in which papal judges-delegate heard cases arising in Worcester diocese, or the bishop himself received commissions, instructions and requests following appeals or petitions from his subjects to the pope. Judges-delegate were commissioned to hear disputes about the churches of Moreton Valence and Whaddon, and Bibury, the chapel of Yardley and the vicarage of Salford Priors. A proposed chapel at *Bram* (possibly in Worcester diocese) was the subject of an appeal or petition. Bishop Roger, as judge-delegate, investigated the status of the incumbent of

---

[63] R. van Caenegem, *Writs*, part I, especially pp. 72–4.

St Mary's, Droitwich, and adjudicated in a dispute over the church of Rowell. With another judge he heard cases concerning tithes of Woolverley, the patronage of Snitterfield, the patronage and the incumbent of Painswick, the alleged ejection of a priest from his benefice, a claim to a portion in the church of Wootton and Wawen. Would these litigants have gone to the trouble and expense of an appeal if they had been confident of obtaining efficient and prompt justice in the diocese? This question will be considered in more detail in connection with the bishop's general activity as judge-delegate; seen from the point of view of the diocese, the evidence supports the suggestion that the local courts of the church in England were at this time in the midst of a process of change and unsettlement. The synod was ceasing to be acceptable as a court; it met infrequently and it could not satisfy the new demand for procedural regularity and legal erudition. But an alternative system was not yet fully established. There was no court meeting at fixed times in fixed places, under an official appointed for the purpose, so that litigants could be spared the trouble and cost of following the bishop in his constant travels, though some bishops were already appointing deputies who would regularly hear cases on their behalf.[64] Appeals to the pope, and commissions to papal judges-delegate, seem to have diminished in number as acceptable local courts became established.[65]

On the basis of this small body of evidence, the central court of the diocese of Worcester in Bishop Roger's time appears as an amorphous institution, of which the one essential characteristic is its absolute dependence on the person, or the *ad hoc* authority, of the bishop. Evidence relating to other dioceses seems to confirm the scanty information from Worcester. Even at Canterbury, it was only in the middle of the thirteenth century that a permanent court was established with a fixed seat.[66]

---

[64] The Council of Tours, 1163, *c.* 7 condemned the custom of appointing deans or archpriests to judge cases in place of the bishop, *sub annuo pretio*, that is for an annual payment to the bishop, the deputy recouping himself from the profits of the court. Appointment of salaried employees did not involve simony, and was not condemned.
[65] On this question see Colin Morris, 'From synod to consistory: the bishops' courts in England, 1150–1250', *Journal of Ecclesiastical History* xxii (1971), 115–23.
[66] M. M. Morgan, 'Early Canterbury jurisdiction', *EHR* lx (1945), 398; Brian Woodcock, *Medieval ecclesiastical courts in the diocese of Canterbury* (1952), pp. 7–8.

The bishop's staff and household

To assist him in the central administration of the diocese, the bishop depended chiefly on a small group of men in frequent, if not constant, attendance upon himself. Apart from the learned Senatus, whose duties were pastoral and spiritual in character, Bishop Roger seems to have made little use of monks for this purpose. Even the prior of the cathedral monastery had little place in diocesan administration in normal times, though Ralph, prior of Worcester at Roger's accession, had been in office since 1146, and must have been a venerable and well-known figure. He could have known the bishop as a boy, and must have helped to organize his election; he had already worked with three bishops of Worcester. He accompanied Roger to the council which met at Oxford early in 1167, and must have been among those summoned to the council of Westminster in 1175. But he witnesses only three of the bishop's charters, all of which could have been issued at Worcester. In one of these the priory was closely concerned; one records the gift of a church in the diocese to Lanthony Priory, a matter in which the cathedral monastery, as the bishop's chapter, had some official interest; one records a judgement of the bishop in a case arising in the diocese of Hereford. Only this last case dealt with matters in which the church of Worcester had no concern, and here the prior's function was probably simply that of a witness to the bishop's act (App. I, 51, 30, 63).

But in the abnormal conditions of Bishop Roger's long absence from 1167 to 1172 the records of arrangements made about churches in the diocese show the prior playing the chief part, often with one of the two archdeacons. Between 1167 and ?1175 the prior and the archdeacon of Worcester announced that they had instituted a parson to the church of Newbold Pacey, 'by authority of the Lord Roger, bishop of Worcester'.[67] Between 1167 and about the end of July 1169 the same pair answered an enquiry from Bishop Hilary of Chichester (d. 13 July 1169) about action taken by Bishop Roger on an occasion when they had been present (App. I, 16). By order of the bishop, the prior, 'who was at that time acting for the bishop in ecclesiastical business', and the archdeacon of Gloucester set

---

[67] BL MS Cotton Vespasian E. xix (Nostell cart.) fo. 114ʳ. Cf. App. I, 48.

their seals to an agreement between the abbeys of Tewkesbury and Holy Trinity, Caen;[68] although the bishop's clerk Master Silvester witnessed the agreement he evidently had no commission to act for his absent employer. Another *transactio* was announced by the same pair, the prior and archdeacon, 'cum vices domini Rogeri Wigornensis episcopi gereremus'.[69] There is a strong probability that all these cases belong to the period of the bishop's exile, and it is noteworthy that a generation later the prior and archdeacon of Worcester were said to claim the right to exercise the bishop's jurisdiction when the see was vacant.[70]

Until nearly the end of his pontificate, Bishop Roger could count on the presence and service of both the archdeacons of his diocese. Two archdeacons of Worcester, Master Godfrey (1144–67) and Master Simon Luvel (1167–89) were both resident working officials, as was Matthew, archdeacon of Gloucester (*c.* 1158–1178). Matthew witnesses only two of the bishop's surviving charters (App. I, 3, 22); he may have been an old man in the 1170s, and he was probably less likely to be in attendance on the bishop than his colleague with his base in the cathedral city. Before Roger's time, probably when the see of Worcester was vacant, Gilbert Foliot and Archbishop Thomas were in correspondence with him on diocesan business, and he consulted Gilbert about a tricky matrimonial case that had come before him.[71] Master Godfrey had been archdeacon of Worcester, possibly with some interruption, for almost twenty years at the time of Roger's election. Gilbert Foliot was prepared to tell Pope Eugenius that Godfrey was a distinguished and virtuous man, admirably learned in sacred and secular literature, who carried out his duties with wisdom and discretion. He was of sufficient stature to be appointed to act as papal judge-delegate with Gilbert, *c.* 1161.[72] Godfrey's successor,

[68] Caen, Arch. dép. Calvados, original charter of Abbot Fromund and the convent of Tewkesbury, uncatalogued. Copy in BN MS lat. 5650 fo. 36ᵛ, partial transcript in PRO, PRO 31/8/140B/3, p. 257 no. 86. Original noted by Lechaudé d'Anisy, *Mémoires de la Société d'Antiquaires de Normandie* viii (1835), 177. *Cal. Docs. France*, p. 144 no. 431.
[69] PRO 164/20 (Godstow cart.) fo. 27ᵛ. Cf. *The English register of Godstow nunnery*, Early English Text Society, Original Ser. 129 (1905), i. 131.
[70] *Chron. Evesham*, p. 227.
[71] *Letters of Foliot*, pp. 162, 309; *Cirencester cart.*, ii. 371.
[72] *Letters of Foliot*, pp. 396, 488, 73, 394.

THE BISHOP IN HIS DIOCESE

Master Simon Luvel, was appointed by Bishop Roger, probably not long before his exile. He may have been in the bishop's service before his appointment, since he witnesses one of his charters without any title (App. I, 29). In this charter, and in a letter from John of Salisbury, he is called *magister* (above, p. 31); elsewhere he is not so described. John, as we have seen, wrote to Simon as to an old friend, who would be in touch with Bishop Roger. Simon was a frequent witness of Roger's charters in the 1170s; indeed he was among the most constant of the bishop's attendants, accompanying him to the council held at Oxford early in 1167, to Westminster in 1176, and to Newbury, Salisbury and Bath when the bishop was acting as judge-delegate. His usefulness was not limited to diocesan business; on one occasion he is found acting in the bishop's place as subdelegate to hear a case committed to the bishop (App. II, 102). Before he became archdeacon of Worcester, Simon was already a canon of Exeter, and was in the confidence of Bishop Bartholomew. He carried a message from that bishop to the pope, about the priest of Veryan, said to be the son of the last parson, and *in sacerdotio genitus*,[73] and returned with instructions about the offending priest and a general order to act in similar cases. His links with Bartholomew, Roger and John of Salisbury suggest a group of men with the same vision of the church and its needs.

By contrast with these three archdeacons, William of Northolt, Matthew's successor in the archdeaconry of Gloucester, had been a clerk of Archbishop Theobald, and is regularly to be found, both before and after he became archdeacon, in the company of Archbishop Richard. He was a canon of St Paul's, and perhaps a protégé of Gilbert Foliot, who wrote to Bishop Roger urging him to fulfil a promise to William.[74] Perhaps Roger was having second thoughts about appointing a man who would seldom perform his duties in person, or give his bishop the benefit of his learning and ability. William was at least serving the church, if not the church of Worcester, unlike so many archdeacons whose time was devoted to the king's service. He was himself bishop of Worcester from 1186 to 1190.

---

[73] Morey, *Bartholomew of Exeter*, pp. 92, 138.
[74] *Letters of Foliot*, p. 310.

THE BISHOP IN HIS DIOCESE

The separation of bishop and chapter, the rise of the non-resident archdeacon, the determined efforts of bishops to govern more effectively, combined to produce a situation in which bishops had to maintain their own clerical and administrative staff, and to experiment with the creation of new offices. Bishop Roger's staff are not well known, because so many of his charters are preserved only in cartularies which commonly omit the witness lists. From the surviving lists and from a few other mentions, a small group of men emerges, who seem to be the bishop's senior, or his most regular, attendants. Master Simon Luvel, archdeacon of Worcester, we have met already. Master Silvester, too, has been mentioned more than once. He was presumably already a responsible, if not a senior, clerk in 1165, when he was sent to report on the flying crucifix of Stanway. He remained continuously in Roger's service, served his successor, Baldwin of Ford, and followed Baldwin to Canterbury. He may be identical with the Master Silvester who was a canon of Chichester by about 1190, archdeacon in 1197, and still in office in 1213.[75] If so, he must have been a bright young man when he came first to serve the young bishop of Worcester. It will be convenient to examine in the next chapter the suggestion that his was the guiding hand in the formation of the collection of decretals of Pope Alexander, which is known, because of its obvious Worcester connections, as *Collectio Wigorniensis*. For the present, it need only be said that the suggestion is attractive, without being conclusively proved.

Beside Silvester stands Master Moses, an almost equally frequent witness of the bishop's acts. He was probably in Roger's service before the end of 1167 at latest (App. I, 29). Possibly he was an older man, for he generally appears before Silvester in charters witnessed by both. Moses and Silvester are invariably called *magister* in witness lists, and it is tempting to assume that this indicates some sort of higher education, though there is nothing to show where this might have been received, or in what faculty. Indeed it is uncertain what precise sense, if any, attached to the title in the 1170s, and hard to believe that all the *magistri* who appear in England in the later twelfth century had formally incepted at a university, as would be the

---

[75] H. Mayr-Harting, *The Acta of the bishops of Chichester, 1075–1207*, Canterbury and York Society (1964), p. 213.

case fifty years later. The most that can be said with certainty is that the appearance of *magistri* in the bishop's familia, in this as in other dioceses, indicates the need for well-educated men to staff the growing diocesan bureaucracy.

Samson, generally styled *clericus*, is another conspicuously regular witness. He was already in Bishop Roger's service by March 1165, when he accompanied the bishop to Bath (App. I, 72). On that occasion Samson and Archdeacon Godfrey were the only Worcester witnesses; probably they were the senior members of the bishop's party. His is the last name in a list of 'men of great authority' present at the publication of a judicial sentence (App. I, 50). There, and in another text (App. I, 35), he is called *magister*; in each case there is some reason for thinking that the document in question may not have been drawn up in the bishop's office. The possibility must be considered that the title was here used by a draughtsman who was not familiar with the members of the bishop's household. Or perhaps Samson earned his title by a period of absence for study in the schools, for he appears regularly as *magister* in the witness-lists of Archbishop Baldwin's charters.

Canon law and long established custom required a bishop to have chaplains in constant attendance. Bishop Roger's chaplains, Gilbert and Robert, are accordingly to be found as frequent witnesses of his charters, often appearing together. Gilbert's first appearance is probably before February 1167 (App. I, 7). He is the only member of the bishop's staff who can be proved to have been with him in France in 1167-72 (App. I, 7). He was not a monk, for we shall see shortly that he was parson of two churches in Berkshire. Robert, the other chaplain, witnesses no dated charter before March 1176. He is once called Robert of Upton, and is not identical with Robert Monk (*monacus*), once called parson of Cleeve (App. I, 20), who also witnesses frequently in the 1170s. This second Robert is unlikely to have been a monk; *monacus* must be a patronymic or a nickname. It appears therefore that Bishop Roger did not employ monks of his cathedral as his chaplains.

These seven men, Archdeacon Simon of Worcester, the *magistri* Moses and Silvester, Samson the clerk, the chaplains Gilbert and Robert, and Robert Monk seem to have been the bishop's regular attendants when he was in England. During the bishop's 'exile', Silvester and Simon were certainly in England; Roger's clerks were evidently not expelled and deprived of their benefices, unlike those of Archbishop Thomas. Gilbert the chaplain was with him in France, and Robert Monk may have been there also (App. I, 38).

A few others, either less eminent or less often with the bishop, are described as his clerks. Adam, son of Edwin the reeve of Gloucester, witnesses only twice, but was called 'our clerk' by the bishop when instituted as parson of St Augustine's, Dodderhill, in November 1178 (App. I, 83). Peter of Withington witnesses once in 1178; Peter, parson of Withington, was a clerk of Bishop Baldwin,[76] and may have served his predecessor. William of Gloucester witnesses twice and is named among 'our clerks' (App. I, 1, 59), and William, clerk of Trun, witnesses twice, perhaps both times in Normandy (App. I, 7, 38), but is not called 'our clerk'. Ranulfus (or Radulfus) Gansellus witnesses once among 'our clerks' and twice without description (App. I, 51, 3, 33), and Alured witnesses once among the bishop's clerks. This material must obviously be treated with caution; we cannot hope to define the position of these almost unknown clerics, or to understand why the draughtsman sometimes did, and sometimes did not, describe them as the bishop's clerks.

On several occasions, a clerk named Baldwin appears with the bishop of Worcester. It is hard to say how many men are involved, or what was their connection with him. Badduinus and Master Baldwin appear together in 1173 (App. I, 69), and Master Baldwin possibly in 1175 (App. I, 82); there are also Master Baldwin of *Dredon* and Master Baldwin Exoniensis (App. I, 1, 29). Baldwin de sancto Genesio appears at Bath in 1165, not explicitly in Roger's train, and again in 1173 (App. I, 72, 60). Assuming perhaps arbitrarily, that Badduinus was the chaplain of some benefice near Warwick, and that Baldwin was the archdeacon of Exeter, two other individuals seem to emerge; Master Baldwin who perhaps took his name from the bishop's manor of Bredon, and Baldwin from St Gennys in Cornwall, or possibly from Saint-Genix in Savoy. Either of these could be the B. who carried a petition from the bishop to the pope

---

[76] *Landboc de Winchelcumba*, i. 70–1.

(App. II, 58), or the unsuccessful claimant to the archdeaconry of Bath *c.* 1167, called *magister* by the pope.[77]

All these men, apparently, could be described as the bishop's *officiales*. There is no reference in the texts relating to Bishop Roger to an Official, in the singular. It is only in the episcopate of William of Northolt (1186–90) that we meet Thomas, *dictus officialis*. In Worcester, as in most English dioceses, this was a development of the closing years of the century.[78]

Bishop Roger could not reward his *officiales* by making them canons of his cathedral, and there were at this time no collegiate churches in his diocese to provide prebends for his nominees. Very little evidence survives to show how they were provided for. Pope Alexander made occasional pronouncements condemning pluralism, generally at the prompting of a clerk who wanted a benefice. There is nothing to suggest that Bishop Roger, or any of his English contemporaries, adopted this policy. Master Simon, the archdeacon, was a canon of Exeter, and may have succeeded to the lands and rights held of the bishop by Archdeacon Godfrey, and noted at many points in the Red Book of Worcester (below, p. 109). Simon may also, in Roger's later years, have held the church of Claverdon, of which the advowson was given to the bishop by William, earl of Warwick in 1176 or 1177.[79] In later times, the church was attached to the archdeaconry, and provided, or helped to provide, an income for the archdeacon, and thus relieved the bishop of the need to maintain him from the episcopal estates.

Master Silvester was rector of Beckford, with its chapel of Aston (App. I, 68). This was a substantial benefice; it was valued in 1291 at £27 13*s.* 4*d.*, with a vicarage worth £6 13*s.* 4*d.* in addition.[80] The church was in the gift of the abbot of

---

[77] Above, p. 32. For Saint-Genix compare Delisle, *Recueil*, ii. 3.

[78] Cheney, *Becket to Langton*, pp. 147–8, and for Thomas, *Landboc de Winchelcumba*, i. 70–1.

[79] Liber Ruber of Worcester (deposited in Hereford and Worcester Record Office) fo. 135ʳ, cf. Haines, *Bishopric of Worcester*, p. 31 n. 4. The church was not necessarily vacant at the time of the gift.

[80] *Taxatio . . . pape Nicholai IV*, London, Record Commission 1802 (cited as *TPN*), p. 223b. The valuations of 1291 are cited for purposes of comparison, without entering into the question of the relationship between the valuation and the actual income of the benefice. Earlier in the thirteenth century it was assumed that a benefice with an annual income of five marks (£3. 6*s.* 8*d.*) could support one resident priest.

Cormeilles; presumably the abbot, or the prior of Newent (a cell of Cormeilles), chose to accommodate the bishop's clerk. Similarly Osbert, abbot of Lire (1166–77), presented Gilbert, the bishop's chaplain, to the churches of Swallowfield and Sinningfield in Berkshire. The two churches produced a substantial revenue: in 1291 they were valued together at £20 a year, plus a pension of £2 to Lire (TPN p. 188b).[81]

Robert the chaplain, *de Upton*, was perhaps parson of Upton on Severn, of which the bishop was patron. It was not as rich as Beckford or Swallowfield, but was worth at least a comfortable £12 a year in 1291 (TPN p. 216b). Peter was parson of Withington, also in the bishop's gift, and worth as much as Gilbert's two churches (TPN p. 224a). Robert Monk's church of Cleeve was worth twice as much, and must have been one of the plums in the patronage of the bishop; in 1291 it was valued at £40 a year (TPN p. 224a). Upton, Withington and Cleeve were all churches on the bishop's estates. No wonder Bishop Roger made a determined effort, involving at least two missions to the pope, to regain the patronage of Bibury and its chapels, valued (with one chapel) in 1291 at £33 13s. 4d. plus portions valued at another £10 (TPN p. 222a). The church, on the bishop's manor of Bibury, had been granted to Osney *reclamante capitulo* by Bishop John of Pagham (App. I, 50; App. II, 36).

One man, whom Bishop Roger himself described as his *familiaris* (App. I, 17), does not appear as a witness to his charters issued as diocesan, or indeed, with a solitary and explicable exception (App. I, 50), to his acts as judge-delegate. This is Master David of London, a lawyer of some distinction. David was obviously not a member of the bishop's *familia*, in the sense in which that expression might be applied to Archdeacon Simon, or Master Moses and Master Silvester. The evidence suggests that it was a common interest in intellectual pursuits, and especially in the law, that drew the two men together; David's association with the bishop, and its possible significance, will therefore be considered below, in connection with Roger's contribution to the 'new law' of the church.

[81] BL MS Egerton 3667 (Carisbrooke cart.) fo. 26ᵛ. Possibly the presentation was made *c.* 1166, when jurors 'recognized' that Swallowfield belonged to Lire (van Caenegem, *Writs*, pp. 286–7).

As well as these clerical officials, the bishop needed employees to deal with secular business, such as the care of his houses in the diocese and his property in London, the management of his estates, the fulfilment of his obligations to the king, and all the ensuing record-keeping. These men occasionally appear as witnesses; thus we hear of Robert the Marshal, Galfridus Blund, bailiff of the bishop's soke in London, and Matthew *de camera*, perhaps the chamberlain of the bishop's house at Alvechurch (App. I, 2, 1, 64). On a lower level, Roger Cook (or the cook) was still receiving sixty shillings a year from the revenues of the bishopric in 1196 of the gift of Bishop Roger.[82] Herbert Hostiarius held land in the bishop's manor at Bredon, *per Rogerum episcopum*; he must have been appointed in Roger's early years, before the end of 1167 at latest.[83] The names of four more chamberlains are recorded, each probably in charge of one episcopal residence, Roger at Kempsey, Osmund at Fladbury, Stephen at Hartlebury and Stephen (probably not the same man) at Wick Episcopi. The same source provides the name of Herlo, the constable, and of Algar and G. the stewards.[84]

Of these secular officials little is known. Were they clerks or literate laymen? Did they have their own clerks? The marshal and the constable must have been responsible for the bishop's knights, and the fulfilment of his military obligations to the king and, since the bishops of Worcester were involved in running disputes with the king and with their own military tenants, they will have been well aware of the need for precise information on these matters.[85] The stewards and the chamberlains of the manors were responsible for estate and household management; they too needed a mass of detailed information about tenants' holdings and liabilities. Many of these officials must have been involved in a major effort, made early in Roger's episcopate, to provide an up-to-date record on these subjects.

The Red Book of Worcester

The results, perhaps not the complete results, of this effort have been preserved by a series of chances. Late in the next century,

---

[82] *The Chancellor's Roll, 8 Richard I*, Pipe Roll Soc., NS 7 (1930), p. 208.
[83] *Red Book of Worcester*, p. 109. For the date see below, p. 109.
[84] Ibid., pp. 82, 145, 205, 58, 149, 36, 38.
[85] Chew, *Ecclesiastical tenants-in-chief*, pp. 17–22.

the bishop of Worcester was Godfrey Giffard, an able administrator who had risen to be the king's chancellor. Godfrey had a survey made of the lands of the see, the services of his tenants, his rents and such matters, and to the text of this survey there were appended, manor by manor, first a copy of a survey made some twenty years earlier, and secondly a copy of a survey so old that Giffard's clerks called it briefly 'Domesday'. Presumably this was the earliest survey they could find; perhaps they were influenced, in their choice of title, by its concern with hides and gelds, which will have reminded experts of the king's Domesday Book, with its similar preoccupation. Giffard's volume is now lost, like so much else from the muniments of Worcester. But it was copied early in the eighteenth century by the Worcester historian William Thomas, and his transcript has at last been printed, more than 200 years after his death.[86]

Giffard was also interested in knights' fees, because of their financial implications in his own time. On this subject too there must have been a search for old evidence, for following the surveys there are copies of documents of many periods relating to tenants of the see who held by military service. This part of the Red Book was described by Thomas as 'part of another old register', which suggests that leaves or a quire from another book were bound in with the surveys. But possibly this material was also copied in Giffard's time, for it is followed by statements relating to his own activities.

The contents of the book fall, therefore, into two distinct parts, the surveys of estates on the one hand, and on the other the lists, jottings and miscellanea relating to knights' fees. Here we shall be concerned only with the twelfth-century material to be found in each part. As regards the surveys, Thomas opined that the 'Domesday' was compiled in the time of Bishop Baldwin. The modern editor at first accepted his view, and printed the various sections under the headings 'Blockley in 1182', 'Ripple in 1182' and so on. But Thomas was wrong. There are no references in it to land held 'per Baldwinum episcopum', but there are grants by Bishop Roger; these in turn are few compared with the references to earlier bishops, running back as far

---

[86] Thomas noted that the first page of the Red Book was numbered 78; part must already have been missing. There is no 'Domesday' survey for the bishop's manor of Bibury.

as Theulf, appointed in 1113. This alone would suggest a date early in Roger's episcopate. The half dozen references to Archdeacon Godfrey make it certain that the Domesday survey was made before his death in 1167 (or at latest 24 March 1168). It was in 1166 that the king demanded from all tenants-in-chief details of their own military tenants. The need to provide exact information on this subject could have inspired the bishop and his officials to conduct a survey, and to extend the scope of their enquiries to cover all tenures, and also liability to gelds. But it is noticeable that the bishop's reply to the king is not cast in the form demanded. Henry had asked his tenants to state how many knights each had holding fees established before the death of King Henry I, how many had been enfeoffed since, and how many were 'super dominium'[87] (a phrase variously interpreted at the time and still much discussed). The bishop of Worcester classified his military tenants in three groups, but not the three listed by the king: he reported his knights 'anciently enfeoffed', those enfeoffed in the time of Bishop Samson (1096–1112), and those enfeoffed of the domain by Bishop Theulf (1115–23).[88] This arrangement by bishops may reflect that underlying the Red Book of Worcester, in which tenants are recorded as holding 'per Simonem episcopum', 'per episcopum Iohannem' and so on; if this is so, the Worcester survey had already been made when the king's enquiry was received, and was drawn upon to provide the bishop's reply. This argument is, however, not quite conclusive, for the bishop had other reasons also for reporting to the king in the form that has been noted. Like his predecessors and successors, he refused to admit any liability to the king for military service and related burdens, beyond the bishopric's traditional *servitium debitum* of fifty knights, and this service should have been provided by the tenants 'anciently enfeoffed'. Even when he was in exile in 1168, the see of Worcester paid on this basis the 'aid' demanded for the marriage of his cousin's eldest daughter, and refused to take into account the knights enfeoffed by Bishops Samson and Theulf.[89] Bishop Roger did not allow his personal contempt for riches to injure the rights of his church.

[87] *Red Book of the Exchequer*, i. 248.
[88] Ibid., i. 300–1.
[89] Chew, *Ecclesiastical tenants-in-chief*, pp. 17–36.

The survey shows, for each manor, the number of hides and liability to gelds; it then lists the tenants, roughly in descending order. Military service is never recorded, which perhaps suggests that this was being noted simultaneously in a separate place. The services of the humbler men and women are recorded in great detail, and show how arrangements had been made to provide for the lord's every need, not merely for his necessary agricultural work. Whether all these services were actually performed by the persons named is another question. The editor suggests that the 'Domesday' survey may represent a statement of services drawn up with a view to valuation and commutation, and observes that there had been two such valuations of the priory's estates by 1240. It seems a little hazardous to envisage similar methods and intentions in the 1160s, but the possibility remains. One pointer in the opposite direction is provided by the Red Book itself, since it notes that when the bishop is in residence in his manor of Hampton (Lucy) certain lands pay twelve pence instead of providing lights for the hall, the chamber, the clerks' chamber, the *dispensa*, the buttery, the stable, the brewery, the steward's lodging and one other as required. This obligation had been commuted, and the fact was duly noted.

There is no clue to the method by which the survey was made. Under Bishop's Cleeve it is noted that the hundred witnesses that Nigel ought to carry the bishop's messages.[90] This is exceptional, and perhaps indicates the settlement of a dispute brought to the hundred court. Under Kempsey it is noted that G. and Ks (according to Thomas) found certain stock in the manor; possibly G. is the steward, who has been mentioned already; possibly each steward was responsible for surveying the manor under his care.

The Red Book reveals little about Roger's doings in his diocese, though it provides the single glimpse of him acting as a feudal lord, receiving the homage of one of his military tenants.[91] It has more to say of Bishop Simon, who is seen dedicating a church here, a cemetery there, baptizing the son of a local nobleman elsewhere; each occasion is recorded

---

[90] *Red Book of Worcester*, p. 351.
[91] Ibid., p. 441. A note made after Roger's time shows that Aytrop Hasteng did homage to him for half a knight's fee in Flecknoe.

because on each he gave away or let out land from the episcopal estates. There are no such entries for Roger, perhaps because the survey was made soon after his consecration, more probably because he was chary of alienating land. His involvement with transactions made in his name may often have been purely formal, but one may have aroused his interest. The survey records that in Bishop's Cleeve Girold held assart land for one mark a year, 'per Rogerum episcopum'. Roger was sufficiently concerned about the letting of assarts on his manors to address an enquiry on the legal aspect of the matter to the pope some years later (App. II, 8b, and below, p. 182).

The survey itself may be a monument to Bishop Roger's initiative. For it is not impossible that this was the first attempt to record in writing the facts about the lands of the bishopric, for the benefit of the bishop. Godfrey Giffard's clerks, searching for old evidence, presumably found nothing earlier. Some religious houses had already caused surveys to be made of their estates, and it is highly probable that surveys were made of which all trace is lost. But even the archbishopric of Canterbury had no large-scale survey of its manors before the time of Stephen Langton, and Abbot Samson of Bury, according to his biographer, received nothing in writing at the time of his election about the administration of the abbey except a small sheet (*scedula*) which listed the knights of St Edmund, the names of the manors, and the order in which one food-farm followed another.[92] Samson, taking possession of his estates in 1182, was promptly involved in disputes, and this caused him to have enquiries made in each manor about the annual rents of the free men, the names of the villeins, and the services of each, and to have everything written down. Bishop Roger, enthroned on 4 February 1165, may have had similar experiences, and reacted in the same way.

Conclusion

It cannot be proved that Roger's 'Domesday' survey of his estates had no predecessor, but it is the first of which we have positive evidence. The same must be said of the *matricula* of the

---

[92] F. R. H. Du Boulay, *The Lordship of Canterbury* (1966), pp. 10–11. *Jocelin of Brakelond*, pp. 28–9, incorrectly translated.

churches of the diocese. But beside these possible indications of a capable and inventive mind at work, there stand a number of others that have been noted in the course of this chapter. On four distinct points he has been observed anticipating by some forty years the legislation of the Lateran Council of 1215; he appoints a learned man to act as confessor and preacher, he takes a critical interest in the judicial duel, and in grants of indulgences, and he draws the pope's attention to the exploitation of vicars of parish churches. He was also apparently the first English bishop to observe the usefulness of a specific papal warrant for his campaign against inheritance of benefices and clerical marriage. He may also, though here the evidence is scanty, have been among those bishops who were ceasing to deal with litigation in the diocesan synod, and were turning instead towards the new system in which professional lawyers, trained in the learned law, administered justice in specially constituted courts. In a lesser field, it will appear that he was one of the first English bishops to use the developed form of the Inspeximus, that 'neat diplomatic instrument', which was later adopted by the royal chancery, where it became the invariable form of confirmation.[93] This last is a small matter, but again it suggests the alert mind, observing new needs, adopting new solutions. This is not to say that the bishop initiated every change that took place in the diocese in his time. He had picked capable men to serve him; we can be sure that they made their contribution, though we cannot assess its scale. But the variety of the evidence suggests that it was indeed the bishop who provided the driving and unifying force. The following chapters, dealing with Bishop Roger's work as a papal judge-delegate, and his influence on some of Pope Alexander's legal pronouncements, will provide some further evidence to the same effect.

---

[93] Below, p. 231; Cheney, *Bishops' chanceries*, pp. 90–6. Bishop Roger's charter (App. I, 75) is the more significant since Archbishop Theobald's inspeximus for Rochester, cited there (pp. 93–4), has suspicious features.

4
THE JUDGE-DELEGATE

The sources

This chapter is devoted to the evidence relating to Roger of Worcester's activity as a papal judge-delegate in the years 1163 to 1179, and tries to place it in its historical setting. The early history of the office of judge-delegate would require treatment on a European scale, and cannot be attempted here, nor will it be possible to enter into all the minutiae of procedure. Happily there is available a lucid and fully-documented account of procedure before judges-delegate in England in the first half of the thirteenth century,[1] which can be taken as a guide for the England of the 1170s, if not of the 1160s. There were indeed many refinements of law and procedure in the intervening years, but as we shall see, the basic framework of the 'roman-canonical'[2] process was established in Bishop Roger's time, and was taken for granted by pope, judge, lawyer and litigant. We therefore turn directly to the bishop's judicial work, not as Ordinary in his diocese, but as the pope's delegate, in which capacity he heard lawsuits arising all over the province of Canterbury, occasionally in the province of York, and once or twice in Normandy, probably during the period of his exile in 1167–72.

Material for the study of this aspect of the bishop's work is inevitably less abundant than that relating to similar activity in the years after 1198. After that date the papal registers provide a massive bulk of evidence; at the same time, documents drawn up in the course of litigation tended steadily to grow longer, fuller and more precise. But for the period from about 1170 at latest, in spite of the loss of the papal registers and many local records, the papal judge-delegate can be observed

---

[1] Jane E. Sayers, *Papal judges delegate in the province of Canterbury 1198–1254* (Oxford 1971).
[2] On the expression 'roman-canonical' see for example K. W. Nörr, 'Päpstliche Dekretalen und römisch-kanonischer Zivilprozess', in *Studien zur europäischen Rechtsgeschichte*, ed. Walter Wilhelm (1972), pp. 53–65.

at work in England, through the use of papal letters preserved in what was substantially a new sort of legal text, the so-called decretal collection, of which more must be said in the next chapter. More than two-thirds of the cases delegated to Bishop Roger would be unknown but for a text found in a decretal collection. For the period before *c.* 1170 a comparable study would have to be based almost entirely on the cartularies and the original deeds, relatively few in England, which survived the Reformation and the vicissitudes of religious corporations thereafter (to say nothing of 'normal' attrition by war, fire, negligence and the deliberate destruction of records of no permanent value to the owners). The surviving texts for the early period usually record only a sentence or other final settlement; the commission on which the judge-delegate acted is seldom copied, and the course of the case is seldom described. Some light is thrown on the development of appeals to the pope, and on the ensuing delegation of cases to local judges, by the collection of letters made by John Salisbury in his years as clerk to Archbishop Theobald; but even taking this source into account, it may be said that Roger of Worcester and his contemporaries are the first generation of papal judges-delegate whose activity in England can be studied in any detail.

Though fuller than for earlier decades, the sources still have many limitations, which must be noted at the outset, and borne in mind throughout the following enquiry. Of all courts that of the judge-delegate was least likely to preserve records. It was an ephemeral thing; it met, did its work, and dissolved. It was left to the parties to preserve the sealed documents with which a case would normally end, and any other texts that might be useful in the future, including perhaps the original commission on which the judges had acted. As a result, all but a minute fragment of the extensive 'paper work' of Bishop Roger's cases is lost. The abbey of St Bertin possessed an original commission; Christ Church, Canterbury, probably had another; Saint-Évroul had an original citation (App. II, 6, 46i; App. I, 57), Luffield a letter of proxy, Worcester Cathedral another letter from a litigant.[3] The abbey of Bury St Edmunds evidently obtained copies of documents issued by Bishop Roger

---

[3] *Luffield charters*, p. 38; *Worc. cart.*, p. 88.

THE JUDGE-DELEGATE 115

and his fellow-judge in the course of a case, and this may already have been common practice; what is remarkable is that they were copied into a cartulary, and so were preserved (App. I, 4, 5, 6). Much can be learned about the way in which cases were theoretically supposed to be handled, from the writings of contemporary canonists, particularly the *ordines iudiciarii*. But while these texts may elucidate surviving records, it would be unwise to assume that the course of litigation always, or even often, precisely followed the paper models.[4] Here we shall be concerned entirely with the actual conduct of cases by the bishop of Worcester.

Much of the evidence must therefore be drawn from the bishop's charters announcing the end of delegated cases. But these are normally, like his charters arising from diocesan business, extremely terse. The commission on which the judges had acted is only once recited, on an occasion when the senior judge was Gilbert Foliot; possibly he or one of his clerks (was it the Bologna-trained Master David, who was present?) insisted on this advanced formula, and on the unusually full account of the case (App. I, 50). In most cases the past history of the dispute, the origin of the claimant's alleged right, the course taken in litigation before the bishop as judge-delegate, are all passed over in silence. Surviving commissions may tell only part of a long story. Of those preserved in decretal collections, some are abbreviated, with or without warning. Others are not the first commission issued in the case in question, but were copied because they dealt with some nice point of law or procedure thrown up in the course of litigation, so that the original *narratio facti*, or statement of the case, is often missing. The fullest accounts of actual cases are likely to be contained in reports to the pope, sent when confirmation was requested for a sentence or other settlement, or when a case was returned to the Curia upon a fresh appeal, or when a special problem had arisen, such as the appearance of a second commission possibly obtained by fraud. Few such reports survived unless the sender made a collection of his letters, as Gilbert Foliot, Arnulf of Lisieux, and John of Salisbury did. A report on one of Bishop Roger's cases is preserved among the later letters of John of

[4] Cf. the observations of R. H. Helmholz, *Marriage litigation in medieval England* (1974), p. 139 and *passim*.

Salisbury, who may have drafted this long and well-written piece (App. I, 8). Occasionally the substance of a report might be incorporated in a later papal letter, as occurred in the second commission to Bishop Roger about the church of Burbage, which rehearses the earlier history of the case as the bishop had reported it (App. II, 62).

The background

Before turning to the detailed evidence offered by these reports, charters and papal letters, it will be as well to notice the words of the one contemporary who had something to say about the work of Roger of Worcester as a papal judge-delegate. When Archbishop Stephen Langton had come at last to take possession of the see of Canterbury, Gerald of Wales, now an old man, offered him a present. It was a version of Gerald's Life of St Remigius of Lincoln and those of his successors, brought up to date for the occasion, and to it were appended sketches of the six most important bishops of his time, to serve as uplifting examples for the archbishop's contemplation. The sketches consist simply of 'a few things worthy to be remembered' about each man, and they were arranged in three pairs, Henry of Winchester and Archbishop Thomas of Canterbury, Bartholomew of Exeter and Roger of Worcester, Archbishop Baldwin and Hugh of Lincoln, the last soon to be canonized.[5] The first and last pairs included the canonized martyr, a second saint, and Bishop Henry, who as the king's brother and the papal legate had been for many years a man of outstanding influence in the church. Why did Gerald place Bartholomew and Roger in this distinguished company?

In contrast to the other bishops about whom he was writing Gerald stressed in these two cases 'zeal for ecclesiastical justice' and activity in hearing lawsuits that had been taken to the

---

[5] Vita sancti Remigii, in *Giraldi opera*, vii. 57–67; see above p. 1. According to the editor, the first version of the Vita was written *c*. 1198. Of the sketches, the account of St Hugh was written before his death in Nov. 1200. The section on Roger of Worcester begins abruptly, without the linking passage or phrase with which Gerald introduced the second member of each of the other pairs. Possibly something was omitted at this point from the single surviving text, Corpus Christi College, Cambridge, MS 425. This may be the copy presented to Langton; it has conventional portraits of the bishops.

Curia by appeal, and then committed for decision to judges-delegate in England. This zeal and this activity were not attributes that would in most periods have qualified a man for inclusion among the six most eminent bishops of half a century. But Gerald had lived through those times, and he had some specialized knowledge of the subject; had he not lectured in Paris *in causis decretalibus*?[6] He knew that precisely during the pontificate of Alexander III these were matters of particular importance in the life of the church, in its administrative and political, if not in its pastoral and spiritual, aspect.

The reason for this unusual situation was basically simple, and is too well known to require long discussion here. During the hundred years before the election of Pope Alexander in 1159, the Latin Church had been struggling to free itself from lay control. It had developed elaborate and passionately held theories justifying distinction between ecclesiastical and secular matters, clerical separatism, and the exemption of churchmen and church property from the judgement of laymen. The attempt to withdraw the church from lay judgement might have led to greater autonomy in the provinces; when King William I of England ordered that *episcopales leges* should be dealt with in future by the bishop and not by the hundred court, he was, it may be supposed, envisaging a simple transfer of business from a local mixed court to a local ecclesiastical court. But the claim to separation and exemption for the church was accompanied by ever more sharply defined assertions by the papacy, the central government of the church, of its absolute powers, its right and duty to lead, to control and to judge all its subjects. At first the claim was translated into practice only in matters of exceptional importance (*causae maiores*). Pope Paschal II, writing to King Henry I of England and his bishops, emphasized the right of the Roman Church to hear *causae maiores*, but significantly he also complained to both king and bishops that 'you withdraw from the oppressed the right of appeal to the apostolic see, although it is laid down by councils and by the decrees of the holy fathers that all the oppressed may appeal to the Roman Church'.[7]

[6] *Giraldi opera*, i. 45.
[7] *Eadmeri historia novorum in Anglia*, ed. M. Rule (RS 1884), p. 232, JE 6453. Cf. Brett, *English church*, pp. 36–7.

The general right to hear appeals from the oppressed was a potent weapon in the hands of popes determined to exercise greater control over the provinces. It made the decisions of every local prelate, every local court, subject to review and reversal, and made any and every attack on a cleric or on church property a potential political issue. The idea of appeal to Rome was, as Pope Paschal asserted, no new thing. But the swift establishment of the general right of the pope to hear all appeals, great and small, and the rapid increase in the number of such appeals from all over western Europe, owed much to a new factor, the intensive study of Roman law, first in Italy and then in northern centres. Students of Roman law found before them a model, sanctified by antiquity and Roman associations, and explicitly approved by the canons, of a developed, centralized system of law, complete in all its parts, and important among those parts was an elaborate system of appeals. Such a system was quite foreign to the customary law of the northern, Germanic, peoples; an acute observer in England noted its civilian origin.[8] It threatened to breach the autonomy not only of local church courts and local prelates, but also of secular courts and secular rulers, and secular rulers were likely to try to protect themselves. At Clarendon in 1164 the claim was made that, according to the custom of Henry I and the king's other ancestors, no appeals in ecclesiastical matters should be 'taken further' than the archbishop, unless the case had been notified to the king, and the king had given his assent; in effect, Henry II asserted that his grandfather had operated what may be described as a licensing system, giving, and by implication claiming the right to refuse, permission to appeal to the pope. Very little evidence seems to be available about Henry I's practice in this matter, but his grandson's claim is not likely to be based on pure fiction. Apart from a few *causes célèbres*, appeals seem to have been few until the closing years of the reign.[9]

The reign of Stephen saw a change. Appeals were becoming more common throughout western Europe, and the king's right

---

[8] *Appellatio . . . de iure civili est* (William FitzStephen, *MTB* iii. 94). Gervase of Canterbury links *appellationes antea inauditae* with the coming to England of the civil law and its teachers. (*Gervas. Cant.* ii. 384–5.)

[9] Brett, *English church*, pp. 50–7; cf. H. Böhmer, *Kirche und Staat in England und in der Normandie im XI und XII Jahrhundert* (Leipzig 1899), pp. 299–310.

to the throne was challenged; his supporters and those of his rival were soon stating their cases before the pope. Nothing is heard of the system of royal licensing. Appeals are mentioned in a matter-of-fact way in letters of Gilbert Foliot which belong to this period, and in the Life of Robert Béthune, bishop of Hereford (d. 1148), where the author, a canon of Lanthony Secunda, observes that all who brought their cases back from the Lord Pope to be heard in England rejoiced to have the upright Robert as their judge.[10] Both the canon and the chronicler of Abingdon Abbey make it clear that for churches and churchmen the king's weakness was a disaster. The chronicler observes that in those days royal letters were of little use, and therefore Abbot Ingulph turned to the pope, and obtained a privilege, with confirmation of possessions, from Eugenius III.[11]

The chronicler Henry archdeacon of Huntingdon, regarded the increase in appeals as the result of the deliberate policy of Henry, bishop of Winchester, who had brutally (*crudeliter*) introduced them into England.[12] The chronicler was an old man; his attitude may be contrasted with that of the canon of Lanthony, and may point to a difference of opinion on this subject between the 'religious' and some of the senior secular clergy. The seculars saw their control over their subjects diminished by appeals, and themselves exposed to malicious, often entirely mendacious, accusations. Paschal II had accused the bishops of England, as well as the king, of 'withdrawing from the oppressed the right of appeal'. When strong government returned to England, a suspicion again arose at the Curia that the hierarchy did not view appeals with enthusiasm. Pope Adrian, writing in 1156 to Archbishop Theobald, accused him roundly of conspiring with the king to bury appeals.[13] This letter was written at the prompting of the monks of St Augustine's, then in dispute with their archbishop; the accusation may have been quite unjustified. It illustrates nicely the way in which a prelate might be slandered by a litigious subject. Sir

---

[10] H. Wharton, *Anglia sacra* (1691), ii. 311. On the Life see the unpublished study and edition by B. Parkinson, B.Litt. thesis, Oxford 1951.
[11] *Chron. de Abingdon*, ii. 190.
[12] *Historia anglorum*, ed. T. Arnold (RS 1879), p. 282.
[13] *Hist. S. Augustini*, pp. 411–13, JL 10128.

Richard Southern has suggested that the pope may at this time have instructed his friend, John of Salisbury, to use his influence at Canterbury in support of appeals. John was soon, by his own account, in trouble with the secular authorities for 'diminishing the royal majesty', and was held responsible 'if anyone invokes the Roman name' or 'claims a shadow of liberty in celebrating elections or hearing ecclesiastical causes'.[14] These words suggest that some years before the dispute between the king and Archbishop Thomas appeals to Rome were among the matters which Henry II and his advisers saw as affecting royal rights, matters in which royal power had been reduced since the days of his grandfather and which he was determined to restore to the former situation. His attitude is understandable, since, as we have seen, recourse to the pope was associated in men's minds with the inability of a king to maintain order and to protect his subjects. The licensing system operated once more, as Richard of Anstey's story demonstrates, though the evidence does not show whether all appellants obtained licences.[15]

So it was already clear, by the time Bartholomew and Roger were elected to their bishoprics, in 1161 and 1163, that appeals to Rome were causing friction between the church and the royal government, and that there were perhaps some differences of opinion on the subject within the church in England. The pope was now Alexander III, perhaps a canonist by training, certainly keenly interested in the legal and judicial system of the church, and well aware of the key place which the appeal now occupied in that system. He asserted his opinion in an early mandate to England: it was his duty, he said, to ensure that no man should be compelled to suffer for lack of justice, and that every man should through papal sollicitude obtain all his rights.[16]

[14] R. W. Southern, *Medieval humanism* (Oxford 1970), pp. 245–6. *Letters of John of Salisbury*, i. 32, no. 19 (=PL 199, ep. 115), and for the dating pp. 257–8.
[15] The case of Richard of Anstey has been much discussed, and the account of his long lawsuit, with its statement of his costs, several times printed, most recently by P. Barnes, in *A medieval miscellany for D. M. Stenton*, Pipe Roll Soc., NS 36 (1962), pp. 1–24. See also *Letters of John of Salisbury*, i. 227–37, 267–71, and Cheney, *Becket to Langton*, pp. 54–8.
[16] Alexander's opinions are discussed by B. Smalley, *The Becket conflict and the schools* (Oxford 1972), pp. 138–59. The mandate is JL 11839; for the date see M. G. Cheney, 'The recognition of Pope Alexander III', *EHR*, lxxxiv (1969), 474–97.

To maintain what was now regarded at Rome as his normal and proper right, the pope needed allies in England, allies who would defend the free flow of appeals against interference, allies who would respect appeals from their own and inferior courts (for the papacy accepted no restriction as to the stage at which its judgement might be invoked), and allies who would act efficiently and honestly as papal delegates in hearing cases which could not be ended at Rome. With the increase in the number of appeals, the importance of the quality of the available judges-delegate increased also. The press of business alone made it desirable to remove cases from the Curia; the pope had to admit that overwork might cause mistakes. And with the increase in the number of cases, there came inevitably a change in the character of lawsuits and of litigants. The Curia no longer had to deal almost exclusively with great men and with a few great questions about which it had some previous knowledge, such as the relations of the archbishops of Canterbury and York, or the subjection of the Scottish church to an English archbishop. By the 1160s the typical case might concern possession or occupation of a parish church (App. II, 16, 95, 127), the endowments of a small priory (App. II, 10), or internal trouble in a monastery (App. II, 100). Often the pope had to admit that he could not discover the truth (e.g. App. II, 74), often cases could not be settled at Rome without almost certain injustice, for only the rich could afford to transport witnesses and documents over long distances, and both witnesses and documents might perish in the process.

Delegation of cases to local judges, armed with temporary papal authority overriding all other jurisdictions, had become by the 1160s an essential adjunct of the system of appeals, and the availability and quality of those judges became at the same time a matter of importance to the head of the church. The judge-delegate was also useful from the financial point of view. He received no salary; he and his clerks were maintained by their ordinary revenues and benefices. The papacy in the twelfth century was in the unusual position of a ruler operating an extensive judicial system without having to devise means of paying its judiciary and ancillary staff, other than a relatively small number at the Curia itself.

These judges-delegate were seldom mere investigators, taking evidence on the spot and forwarding it to the Curia for decision. They were normally required to take full responsibility, which might involve many sessions spread over months or years, and to pronounce sentence or arrange a settlement. Some prelates wished to escape this new burden. As early as 1141 a bishop of Laon had obtained exemption from this work, and others may have sought the same privilege.[17] Some prelates could not be relied on to do this work well; there were complaints of delays, partiality, high-handed behaviour, disregard of the rules of procedure. At all times, the attraction of the appeal to the pope depended for the litigant in the last resort on the quality of the judge who would eventually hear his case. The same factor would be decisive in upholding the reputation of the Curia as the refuge of the oppressed.

But the quality of the available judges was of particularly critical importance in the pontificate of Alexander III, because of the point which had been reached in the development of the law and procedure relating to appeals, delegations and papal rescripts.[18] At the time of his election, innumerable problems, large and small, lacked authoritative definition. In the next twenty years that definition was to a great extent provided, as a result of trial and error, and comments and questions from the recipients of papal mandates. Much of the new law was the product of interaction between the Curia and judges-delegate, a subject which will be discussed in more detail in the next chapter. As the law developed, ever greater responsibility was laid upon those delegates. The natural tendency of the Curia was to issue very precise and detailed instructions; this was the nearest substitute for immediate judgement by the pope. Such commissions *sub certa forma* limited very severely the exercise of discretion by the recipients. They might help to avoid partiality or the effect of inexpertise in the judges, but they were often issued when only one party had been heard, and so were liable to cause confusion, delay, expense and actual injustice, as seems to have happened in a case committed to Bishop Roger and the

[17] E. Müller, 'Der Bericht des Abtes Hariulf von Oudenburg über seine Prozessverhandlungen an der Kurie im Jahre 1141', *Neues Archiv*, xlviii (1930), 111–12. Apart from this well-known case, no example of this privilege seems to be recorded until the 1180s.
[18] This was noted by R. von Heckel, 'Das Aufkommen der ständigen Prokuratoren an der päpstlichen Kurie im 13 Jahrhundert', *Studi e Testi*, xxxviii (1924), 294–5.

abbot of St Albans (App. II, 48). This was unsatisfactory, and still more unsatisfactory was the effect such mandates might produce upon judges, for some clearly contented themselves with executing the mandate, overriding all protests, and leaving the injured party to reopen the case later if he was sufficiently determined and had the necessary resources. Arnulf, bishop of Lisieux, for example, had to complain to the pope that he had been cited to appear before judges-delegate who were entirely ignorant of the law, and had stated that they would simply carry out 'quod eis prima facie velle littera videtur'.[19]

So the pope had to spell out the rule that delegates are expected to act on commissions according to law and reason. 'We were not writing to an illiterate', he says in exasperation to no less a prelate than the archbishop of Reims, who has acted on a commission with slavish precision and total lack of legal propriety; to a group of English judges he says sharply, 'We were not writing to idiots, but to discreet persons, and it is your duty to discern what the law [*ratio*] requires.'[20] The 'idiots' had overridden a peremptory exception; they should have known that this was not permissible. Guiding principles were formulated on the basis of this sort of experience. In 1175 the pope enunciated the rule that the instructions contained in a commission must always be understood to include the words 'si preces veritati nitantur', even if no such words appear. Judges were told that they might ignore the *certa forma* if it was obtained by fraud; they must ignore a second mandate in a case if it did not mention the first; they should not act upon dubious commissions but refer suspected forgeries to the pope, and so on.[21] In short, it had become evident that however detailed and precise a commission might appear to be, however much the Curia might discuss the case and come to the very brink of a decision, yet it was always necessary for the judge-delegate to conduct careful enquiries to discover the truth, and to know the law and act according to its rules. The tendency of the time, therefore, was to rely increasingly on the discretion and legal

---

[19] *Letters of Arnulf*, p. 209.
[20] 'Non scripsimus homini illiterato' (Martène and Durand, *Ampl. coll.*, ii. 871); 'Non scripsimus idiotis' (JL 13984, X 2.13.3, Holtzmann and Kemp, pp. 40–1).
[21] JL 14317 to the archbishop of Canterbury; for the date see Duggan, *Decretal collections*, p. 162. JL 13950 to the bishop of Hereford. JL 14156 to the bishop of Winchester. JL 12253 to the bishop of Norwich.

knowledge of the local judge, and gradually the *certa forma* became less common, though the Curia was always tempted to lay down the law upon insufficient evidence. The typical commission of the end of the century orders judges to hear a case and end it *fine canonico* or *fine debito*, without further instructions. In these circumstances, Gerald of Wales was well justified in including two famous judges-delegate in his group of great bishops, and his assertion about Pope Alexander's high opinion of them becomes entirely credible.

Bishop Roger as judge-delegate

The pope himself stated his views on the importance of this work in a letter to Bishop Roger which confirms and adds to the information given by Gerald. It refers first to petitions carried by B., the bishop's messenger, which are granted as far as possible; presumably B. carried back other letters on these matters. Alexander then urges the bishop to continue to devote himself to his duty with vigilance and constancy; 'and to give to the lawsuits of the poor, committed to him by the apostolic see, that care and diligence which becomes a wise and discreet man, and one no less eminent for his courage than for the nobility of his blood. For we do not believe that you could do anything more pleasing or more acceptable to God than working to bring justice in all matters to the poor and others, without fear or favour of any man'. (App. II, 58.) It would be interesting to know whether this statement was prompted by one of the petitions carried by B. the bishop's messenger. Had the bishop asked for some relief from the endless stream of commissions, or suggested that constant occupation with lawsuits was not the work most pleasing to God? The biographer of St Hugh of Lincoln records that Hugh wished to resign his bishopric, so that he should not have to spend almost every day deciding lawsuits, and that he regarded work as a judge-delegate as a cross to be borne as a matter of obedience. He expected at the Last Judgement no reward for spending his time in this way, but only hoped for forgiveness.[22] The pope's letter to Roger is at once a reassurance and a statement of policy; no other work is more necessary, and this is the work

---

[22] *Magna vita Hugonis*, pp. 299, 301.

specially required of a wise man, and one distinguished for courage and nobility. Every word was carefully chosen, even the reference to courage and nobility. These are not in normal times the most necessary attributes of a judge, but they made the bishop a particularly useful papal delegate in the 1160s and 1170s, when there was conflict, violent or suppressed, between the developing legal systems of church and state in England. His courage was exploited by the pope when there was tricky work to be done,[23] and his close relationship to the king probably gave him some degree of immunity from harassment by royal officials.

The pope's letter was copied in a contemporary hand on to a blank flyleaf at the end of a commentary on the Lamentations of Jeremiah by William of Malmesbury. The book, which belonged to Worcester cathedral priory in the fifteenth century, may already have found a home there, or it may have been the bishop's personal property. Certainly he was the individual most likely to wish for the preservation of the papal letter. As the years went by, and his time and energy were consumed with the hearing of delegated cases, he may have comforted himself with the statement of the Vicar of Christ, that there was nothing he could do which would be more acceptable to God.

Though it was printed by J. A. Giles and Canon Robertson in their editions of material relating to Archbishop Thomas, this letter occurs in none of the collections of documents put together by the archbishop's party or by his opponents. The single copy stands alone, in a book with Worcester associations, suggesting that this was a personal matter, which had no direct connection with the archbishop and his affairs.

The copyist omitted the dating clause of the letter, and there are few clues to show when it was written. Evidently the bishop had been some time in office; he was pressed to continue his good work. The reference to his petitions may be connected with his known petition for authority to establish a monastery at Keynsham. This petition was granted by the pope in a letter of 16 March 1167, of which the text was also copied on to a blank flyleaf, this time of an eleventh-century *Moralia* of Gregory I (App. II, 46ii). The circumstances of that time would

[23] E.g. App. II, no. 64 orders Bishop Roger to forbid the bishop-elect of Lincoln, the king's son, to appoint to an archdeaconry.

suit the terms of the papal letter, and the pope's insistence on the importance of this form of judicial work. At Clarendon in January 1164 King Henry had forced the English bishops to recognize his right to license appeals and to control the course of business in ecclesiastical courts. Later, he was accused of preventing appeals altogether; in November 1167 papal legates were told that he had now relaxed his *interdictum*.[24] If the undated letter to Bishop Roger was written in March 1167, at the same time as the letter about Keynsham, it becomes easier to understand the pope's assertions about the importance of the work of the judge-delegate, and the implied need for courage on the part of the recipient of a papal commission.

Alternatively, the papal letter might belong to the second half of 1172. In the settlement negotiated with King Henry after the murder of the archbishop, only one of the royal rights defined at Clarendon was explicitly renounced by the king, and this was the right to regulate and control appeals. This, it must be assumed, was the only point on which the pope's agents had been told to insist absolutely. Having obtained this concession the pope will have been anxious to exploit it; at this time, as in 1167, he needed capable and willing men to act as judges-delegate. We have, however, no knowledge of a petition from the bishop of Worcester to the pope at that time, so that, on the present very scanty evidence, the spring of 1167 seems the most probable date.

In his account of the bishops of Exeter and Worcester, Gerald of Wales stressed the sheer quantity of delegated litigation handled by them, 'almost all the cases' sent by Alexander III for hearing in England. The statement reflects the reputation left by these two men, but it is very obviously incorrect. The surviving evidence shows that almost every bishop in England acted sometimes as a judge-delegate of Pope Alexander, some of them very often, and that some abbots and priors were active in this work, notably Adam of Evesham, Simon of St Albans, Baldwin of Ford, and Robert of Kenilworth, the name of whose house baffled so many continental scribes. But the nature of the evidence makes it difficult to form a reliable estimate of the amount of litigation handled by any one judge in proportion to the total.

[24] *MTB*, vi. 272.

Many cases must be quite unknown to us. The decretal collections, from which more than half the evidence comes, normally record only commissions that contained useful statements of law, and chanced to come to the notice of a collector. Keepers of archives and cartulary-makers were concerned above all to preserve title-deeds, nearly always those of corporate bodies, cathedrals, collegiate churches, monasteries. In many lawsuits only one party was anxious to record the outcome; if the archives of the victor have perished, the record of the case is probably lost with them. Of documents concerning cases won by individual secular clerks, and by laymen, few traces remain in English sources. An occasional reference to an early case in later records (e.g. App. I, 52) confirms the evidence of the decretal collections which show that such men also appealed to Rome, and that they, or their representatives, were appearing in the Curia beside bishops, abbots and priors, and that many of their cases were heard and terminated in England. If conditions in England resembled those of France, we should have to conclude that the known cases of appeals and delegations in this period form only a small fraction of the whole. A collection has survived of papal letters to Henry, successively bishop of Beauvais (1149) and archbishop of Reims (1162), who died in 1175.[25] It contains over five hundred letters, of which, at a cursory inspection, some three-quarters concern litigation. Of this large number of letters, only two found a place in decretal collections; most of the cases would be unknown but for Archbishop Henry's register. Should it be assumed that if a similar register were to be found of letters to Archbishop Richard, or to Bishop Roger himself, it would reveal a similar proportion of known to unknown cases? It is hard to accept such a hypothesis, and in the next chapter some evidence to the contrary will be discussed in connection with the formation of the early decretal collections. But the survival of Archbishop Henry's register points a warning: we are much more likely to underestimate than to overestimate the number of appeals to the pope and commissions to judges-delegate in this period.

---

[25] Arras, Bibliothèque municipale, MS 964, printed Martène and Durand, *Ampl. coll.*, ii. 624–1011. The 'register' contains a few non-papal letters also. I have not seen the MS.

The great majority of Bishop Roger's cases is known only from texts preserved in decretal collections, and these texts present many problems. The material was collected by lawyers for lawyers, for use in court and classroom. The names of individual litigants, churches and even judges were of minor importance, and as the collections grew in bulk and were copied more often it became common to abbreviate the addresses as much as possible. Names were reduced to such forms as Wig', Wint', Vig', Norwic' (often written norWic'), Ram', Rem', Exon', Lexov', and then hopelessly confused. Almost every important letter of Pope Alexander to a bishop of Worcester or Winchester is found in some collection with address to the other, while the titles of the bishops of Norwich and Bisceglie (Vigiliensis) may be confused with either. If pressed for space or time, a scribe might copy only the name of one judge, but leave the plural form of a commission to show that there were several addressees, or the formula *discretioni vestre* to show that one or more of them was not a bishop.

An additional difficulty in considering the activity of an individual judge is the problem of distinguishing between successive holders of the same office. Most papal letters of this period carried (in suitable cases) a personal address, often in the form of a bare initial, thus *R. episcopo Wigorniensi*. But inevitably questions were soon raised about the validity of commissions to judges-delegate addressed to a prelate who was succeeded by another before the termination of the case, or even before the commission was presented (e.g. App. II, 58B). Perhaps such questions were the cause of the appearance or the increased use of the gemipunctus instead of the name or initial in addresses, thus, . . *episcopo Wigorniensi*, which enabled the Curia to address the holder of an office without specifying an individual.[26] Scribes copying decretal collections were apt to omit names and initials even when these had been present in the exemplar; the advent of the gemipunctus meant that even in the original and the register copy (if any) the personal name

---

[26] A. Giry, *Manuel de diplomatique* (Paris 1894, reprint 1925), p. 535, suggests that the gemipunctus was used from the end of the twelfth century. A cursory examination of texts printed in the Papsturkunden series shows that it was not uncommon in the 1170s, and appears occasionally in the 1160s. The papal letter mentioned above (App. II, no. 58B of 1173 x 1176) refers expressly to an earlier letter addressed not to persons but to places, i.e. to the unnamed heads of specified monasteries.

was missing. We have texts of many letters which were apparently addressed in this way 'to the bishop of Worcester' in the time of Alexander III, when there were three bishops. The dating of these letters is discussed in more detail in Appendix II; for the present purpose it has been assumed that Alexander sent no judicial commissions to Bishop Alfred (d. 31 July 1160), and only a few, perhaps five or six in addition to those which carry his name, to Baldwin.

Even when it is possible to be reasonably sure about the identity of the recipient of a papal mandate, reliance on the evidence of decretal collections presents another problem. The decretal collectors, being concerned only to assemble useful legal definitions, were not interested in the subsequent history of the case. Some commissions may never have been presented, or arrived too late (e.g. App. II, 17). Some arrived, but were suppressed because conditions had changed in the three months or so since the messenger set out. Sometimes the knowledge that a commission had been obtained may have been enough to bring about a settlement out of court. The cartulary of Malton Priory records an agreement made in 1173 between two parties about tithes, 'about which they should have come to court before the Lord Bishop of Worcester on a writ of the Lord Pope' (App. II, 93, n.). Similarly, a commission to the bishop of Worcester and prior of Pentney may have led to a settlement without a judgement (App. II, 70). This process is illustrated by documents (App. I, 57–8) concerning a dispute between the Norman abbey of Saint-Évroul and the priory of Bermondsey, for which the papal commission is lost. The bishops of Worcester and Hereford (Robert Foliot) write to the prior and monks of Bermondsey, ordering them, by papal authority, to urge the earl of Leicester to satisfy the monks of Saint-Évroul about the church of Widford. If he does not, the prior and monks must appear at Cricklade on a stated date to answer 'according to the form of the apostolic mandate which is already sufficiently known to you'. The summons is peremptory, in the technical sense; there must have been earlier letters or summonses. But before the formal opening of proceedings, *ante litis ingressum*, the earl, whose father's reshuffling of his benefactions had caused the trouble, 'with liberal munificence removed all cause for complaint'.

It is possible, therefore, to form a rough, but certainly inexact, estimate of the number of commissions addressed to any one prelate as judge-delegate, but in the great majority of cases there is no evidence to show whether action was taken on the commission, or how, or whether, or at what stage the case ended. So, in estimating the extent of Bishop Roger's judicial work, we have to deal in impressions and not in statistics.

On the basis of this imperfect evidence, it may be said that the bishop was commissioned to act as papal judge-delegate in perhaps a hundred cases of which some trace remains. No detailed examination has been made for other contemporary bishops. Bartholomew of Exeter, according to his biographer, received some seventy papal letters, some of which are not commissions.[27] Surprisingly, only eight *acta* were found of Bartholomew as judge-delegate, while for Roger the figure is thirty-five. These figures may be compared with those that can be derived from the modern edition of the letters and charters of Gilbert Foliot, bishop of London. The editors list thirty-eight decretals and other papal mandates addressed to him, not all of which are commissions, and print thirty documents issued by him as judge-delegate.[28] Of the commissions of which the texts are preserved, one is addressed to Gilbert jointly with Bartholomew, ten with Bishop Roger. No other names recur so often in the decretal collections, with the possible exception of Adam, abbot of Evesham, who acted as Roger's colleague on at least eleven occasions. The number of cases heard by Bartholomew and Gilbert could probably be increased by a closer look at the material, but on the present evidence it appears that Roger acted more frequently than either, and during a shorter period. For Bartholomew was bishop of Exeter from 1161 to 1181, and Gilbert was bishop of London from 1162 to 1187, long after the death of Pope Alexander. Roger was bishop of Worcester from his election in March 1163 till August 1179, during which time he was out of England for some five years and probably also from January 1179 till his death. Bartholomew and Roger acted together as judges in some twenty-three

[27] Morey, *Bartholomew*, p. 44.
[28] *Letters of Foliot, passim*. The thirty-eight papal letters listed on pp. 526–9 represent thirty-six documents (no. 28 is part of no. 31, and no. 30 is a short version of no. 12), of which one (no. 10) was not addressed to Gilbert. The editors note that 'about forty of his letters and *acta* deal with delegated cases'.

cases; this is nearly a quarter of those in which Roger was judge, and more than a quarter of Bartholomew's cases. These figures show why the two men were linked in the mind of Gerald of Wales, and explain, if they do not justify, his large assertions about their judicial activity. They also perhaps demonstrate some prejudice on his part against Gilbert Foliot.

It will be noticed that in this period a case might be delegated to two judges, or even to one, rather than to three, as became normal later. On this point the charter evidence confirms that of the decretal collections, which might otherwise be suspected of omitting the names of some addressees. Bishop Roger's charters show him acting with one other judge in some sixteen cases, and alone in five. He may even act alone as judge-delegate to hear a case arising in his own diocese, a point to be remembered when we consider the reasons which prompted litigants to appeal. If one of the appointed delegates was absent, the fact was noted in the announcement of the sentence or settlement. Commissions often allowed one or two judges to proceed in the unavoidable absence of a colleague; in the case of one judge, he might be ordered to associate wise and learned men with himself.

Where Bishop Roger had colleagues, they were often from the same part of the country. Nearly two-thirds of his cases can be accounted for in this way: his fellow judges being Bartholomew of Exeter, the two Roberts of Hereford, the abbots of Evesham, Ford and Cirencester, the prior of Kenilworth, the dean of Hereford, the archdeacon of Exeter, and John of Salisbury, treasurer of Exeter. The only frequent colleagues from further afield are the bishop of London, the archbishop of Canterbury and the abbot of St Albans. Litigants were themselves responsible for delivering citations and commissions; it was therefore convenient to choose judges from the same area.

In view of the five-year break in Bishop Roger's judicial activity in England, one might hope to be able to form some estimate of the number of cases heard before the end of 1167, and the number that fall in the later period, after his return. Such an estimate would have a special interest as illustrating the effect, if any, of the settlement of Avranches of 1172 upon the flow of appeals to Rome. Unfortunately, the deficiencies of the sources make it impossible to form any but the most tentative conclusions. The commissions preserved in decretal collections commonly lack their dating clauses and, though a few can be dated fairly precisely, and many more approximately, yet the majority remain uncertain. Many of the bishop's decisions were undated (some dates may have been omitted by later copyists), and none is dated before 16 October 1173. It cannot however be assumed that all undated judgements were issued before that date. The earliest commission of which a trace survives was issued while Roger and Robert of Melun were both still bishops-elect, that is before 22 December 1163 (App. II, 101). We may assign to 1164 the case between Bartholomew of Exeter and the clergy of the archdeaconry of Barnstaple; a decision in a case concerning Daventry can be placed with certainty early in 1167, and Roger's involvement in one stage of the dispute about Pentney priory must belong to 1166 or 1167 (App. II, 31, 108, 10). To the early years, before March 1167, must belong a case concerning the church of Gamlingay (App. II, 124), known only because a letter survives in which Nigel, bishop of Ely (d. 30 May 1169), informed Robert of Hereford and Roger of Worcester that proceedings had already taken place, and ended after enquiries in his synod. A dispute between William, bishop of Norwich, and some of his monks, must also fall before the death of Robert of Melun (App. II, 100). A letter preserved among the correspondence of Archbishop Thomas mentions a dispute over the church of Harlington, and a commission to Hilary, bishop of Chichester (d. 13 July 1169), and the bishop of Worcester (App. II, 95). This too must belong to the early years. Even if the cases concerning Luffield, St Andrew's, Northampton, Osney and Worcester, for which undated judgements of Bishop Roger survive, are also allotted to the early period, these cases form only a minute fraction of the total, while there are some forty cases at least in which there is some serious reason for thinking that they fall in the period after 1172. The contrast is striking, even when the fifty or so undatable cases are remembered, for it is very unlikely that all these fall in the earlier period. This, of course, is exactly what the general history of the time, and the personal history of the bishop, would lead us to expect.

But if the nature of the evidence is considered, the contrast is less dramatic. The commissions certainly addressed to the bishop of Worcester before *c.* 1172 are known, with one exception (App. II, 31), from cartularies and letter collections. But the mass of cases, some certainly and many probably, belonging to the 1170s, is known, and generally only known, from the decretal collections. If we consider cases committed to Bishop Roger after 1172, which are known from non-decretal sources—that is, from the same type of sources as provided information for the period before 1172—we shall find at a rough count some twenty which certainly fall after that date, to compare with the nine which certainly fall before it. The number has doubled, but the period is longer, six years and perhaps three months against four and a half years, and the bishop is no longer a youthful newcomer, but an experienced, respected and senior prelate. The impression of a prodigious, manifold increase may be illusory, and arises chiefly from the availability of a new type of source. This situation prompts further questions about the date of the decretal collections and the means by which their compilers gathered material, questions which will be explored further in the next chapter.

Gerald of Wales asserted that Pope Alexander sent numerous commissions to Roger and Bartholomew of Exeter because of his high opinion of their probity, suggesting by his words that in the choice of these bishops as judges the decisive voice was that of the pope, rather than the litigants. It is difficult to test this assertion, for there survive from Alexander's time no accounts, official or otherwise, of procedure at the Curia in such matters. An account of proceedings in 1141 suggests that at that date the pope, with the assisting cardinals, expected to name at least one judge. After yielding to the litigant, Abbot Hariulf of Oudenburg, over two judges, Pope Innocent II is alleged to have said that he himself ought to have the choice of at least one. The form of words suggests that it was only by special favour that the abbot had had his way over the choice of two :'tibi nostro concessu duorum electio data est, minus non decet quam ut vel unius electio nobis tribuatur'.[29]

Like Abbot Hariulf, most litigants will have had some opinion about the judges-delegate before whom they would wish to plead, or whom they would, if possible, avoid. St Hugh

[29] See above, p. 122, n. 17.

of Lincoln, according to his biographer, was the choice of honest litigants without special power or influence; men of middling or low status, who were confident in the merits of their case, wished to appear before him, for under the examination of that most just judge truth and equity overcame those who relied on their strength or on subterfuges.[30] The biographer's story is consistent with Pope Alexander's words to Bishop Roger, stressing the importance of the judge-delegate's work in bringing justice to the poor and others, without fear or favour of any man. The dishonest litigant, of course, will also try to choose the judges, and will select those likely to be biased in his favour. Master Ralph de Alta Ripa, summoned to appear before the bishop of Worcester and a colleague, went to the pope and obtained a fresh commission to the bishop of London, his uncle and patron, and the bishop of Norwich, to whom he was apparently also related (App. II, 49). Clearly on this occasion, Master Ralph managed to influence the choice of both judges. The case was eventually returned to the first pair, because the other party had sufficient stamina and resources to 'refuse' the hostile judges and make yet another journey to the Curia.[31]

As soon as evidence becomes more copious, it shows the petitioner at the Curia suggesting the judges-delegate to whom his case should be committed.[32] It is to be expected that this will already have been normal procedure in the time of Alexander III, and this expectation is confirmed by casual references to commissions addressed to judges-delegate at the suggestion of a litigant (e.g. App. II, 80). But occasionally a commission will include words which suggest that the pope has himself chosen the judges because of his special confidence in them. This was not a matter of common form; the number of such commissions forms a small fraction of the total. If commissions are examined in which these expressions of trust occur, it will be found that they all concerned cases which involved special problems and required special care. One such commission concerned Clarembald, abbot-elect of St Augustine's, Canterbury,

[30] *Magna vita Hugonis*, p. 299.
[31] On the canonical procedure of *recusatio* see Linda Fowler, '*Recusatio iudicis* in civilian and canonist thought', *SG*, xv. (1972), 717–86.
[32] Sayers, *Papal judges*, p. 109.

accused by his monks of dilapidations, breach of the customs of the house, scandalous living and a string of other offences (App. II, 33). Clarembald had been the king's choice as abbot, and he had been a declared opponent of the murdered archbishop; he had been a member of a royal embassy to the pope which presented the king's case and defended his actions. It was said that some of the party that went with the archbishop's murderers had set out from his house on the fatal day, and returned to it afterwards. The report (App. I, 8), sent by the judges to the pope, shows that Clarembald's fate was seen as exemplary, and a step towards the punishment of the assassins themselves. The pope committed the case to the bishops of Exeter and Worcester (by name: *B. Exon' et R. Wigorn' episcopis*, there were to be no substitutes) and the abbot of Faversham, *de quorum prudentia et honestate plurimum confidimus*, with the command to set aside all favour or fear.

A similar expression of confidence occurs in the commission by which Pope Alexander delegated a case involving conflict of jurisdiction with the secular court to Bishop Roger and another judge (or judges), 'quia ... de vestra discretione et honestate confidimus'. A little dossier of documents on this case must have been preserved at Worcester, and from it three commissions, which occur nowhere else, were copied into Collectio Wigorniensis (App. II, 27, 68A, 2). The earliest ordered Roger and Robert, prior of Kenilworth, to investigate the complaint of Master Hugh, that although he had canonically obtained the church of Whittlesea, O., *nepos* of the last incumbent, had been intruded into it, against the wish of the monks of Thorney. The judges decided for Hugh; he was put in possession, and the archbishop of Canterbury was ordered to enforce the sentence. But a third commission shows that O. then sued Hugh and his witnesses in the secular court, 'contrary to ecclesiastical liberty', and that they suffered serious losses. The bishop of Worcester and the unknown judge(s) were ordered to absolve Hugh from O.'s claim to possession. When O. had restored the losses, he might plead before the addressees as to right, but if he took Hugh before the secular court again they were to impose perpetual silence on him. The case may have involved patronage; this is suggested by the reference to the wish of the monks of Thorney. The Thorney cartulary contains no trace of a judgement. But the final commission shows how the pope wished this awkward case to be handled, and that he entrusted it deliberately to the bishop of Worcester.

The same suggestion of deliberate choice of judges appears in the commission entrusting to the archbishop and Bishop Roger (by name: R. Cantuar' et R. Wigorn') the dispute between Joel of Vautort and the canons of Plympton about the church of Sutton. 'Since neither party had come prepared to deal with the case', says the pope, 'we could not bring it to a fitting end, and decided to commit it to you, having faith in your prudence and uprightness' (App. II, 37). This case certainly concerned patronage; it was also probably complicated by the fact that Joel's messenger had arrived first at the Curia, and obtained a commission to the archbishop by suggesting that Joel had appealed to the pope from the judgement of the bishop of Exeter, placing himself and his possessions under the protection of St Peter, and that the bishop, disregarding the appeal, had laid an interdict on all the churches on his lands. In this case a surviving document shows that the ecclesiastical judges were able to act, and to give their sentence in favour of the canons of Plympton, who preserved a copy of it (App. I, 53).

In another case the special choice of judges seems to be associated with the emergence of a special problem and reference to Rome for a second time. On this occasion the problem was legal and procedural. A dispute over tithes had been committed to Bartholomew of Exeter, who had adjudged possession to one party. The other party asserted that he had offered a silver vase as a pledge that he would give satisfaction, and demanded that the judge should at once proceed to the question of right. He then appealed to the pope, presumably because Bartholomew would not accept this demand. The pope now commits the case to the bishop of Worcester and the abbot of Evesham, 'having full trust in your prudence and honesty' (App. II, 39). On another occasion the pope commits a case to the bishop of Worcester and others unknown, in whom he has full confidence, with the consent of the parties, one of whom seems to have had the king's support in his claim to the disputed benefice; the case was further complicated because a commission had been issued to other judges when only one party had appeared in the Curia (App. II, 75). Similarly, the consent of the parties is recorded when the pope committed a dispute over the church of Bungay to Bishops Bartholomew and Roger and the abbot of Bury (App. II, 88). In both cases, the form of words suggests that the pope selects or suggests certain judges, and the parties accept them. Similar expressions of confidence occur in similar circumstances in commissions to other judges; for example, a dispute about the chapel of Yardley was committed to one set of judges, referred back to Rome on a second appeal, and committed to Gilbert Foliot and Simon, abbot of St Alban's, 'de quorum prudentia et honestate confidimus' (App. II, 49B).

These instances make it clear that in politically sensitive cases, or in cases that had not been settled by the first commission, the pope was likely to take charge of the choice of judges, and to ensure that they were selected from a small group of trustworthy and experienced men. The same situation can be observed later in the century. St Hugh's biographer remarks that the popes of his time delegated to him all the most difficult and troublesome cases that were heard in England by apostolic authority, and during the pontificate of Innocent III a few favoured judges heard the great majority of important cases concerning England.[33] If cases committed to Bishop Roger are examined with this fact in mind, it will quickly become apparent that, in addition to those that have just been mentioned, very many of them concerned great men, great institutions, great issues, or cases that other judges-delegate had been unable to settle. Some of these notable cases will now be studied in a little more detail, as illustrations of this general statement.

Among cases which had long defied settlement, one of the oldest was the dispute between the cathedral priory of Durham and the abbey of St Albans about the church of Tynemouth. The church had been seized *c.* 1090 by Roger de Mowbray, and granted by him to St Albans. Durham had never ceased to demand the return of the church, but its muniments were few, and as time passed few witnesses remained who could testify to Durham's rights. The pope committed the case to Bartholomew of Exeter and other judges, but the prior of Durham appealed again, and fresh judges were appointed — Roger of Worcester,

[33] *Magna vita Hugonis*, p. 299; C. R. Cheney, *Pope Innocent III and England* (1976), p. 27.

Robert dean of York, and John treasurer of Exeter, the same John of Salisbury who had composed Archbishop Theobald's reports on appeals to the pope fifteen or more years earlier. The bishop and John succeeded in arranging a compromise, by which Durham finally recognized the right of St Albans, but obtained substantial compensation (App. I, 18). Representatives of the ancient churches of St Frideswide's, Oxford, and Wimborne, Dorset, also appeared in separate cases before the bishop and a colleague to plead long-standing claims. St Frideswide's had been trying for thirty years to obtain, or regain, the church of St Mary Magdalen outside the north gate, but its case was hopeless since Pope Eugenius had long since given judgement to the contrary (App. I, 50). Wimborne was claiming tithes of whose history there survives a full and curious account, sent by Robert, earl of Leicester, to the pope; in this case again a compromise was arranged (App. I, 42). A compromise was also made before Bishops Bartholomew and Roger in a dispute involving St Albans and the church of Luton; in their notification of the *transactio* a long tale of violence, illegality and conflict is passed over in discreet silence (App. I, 54). In addition to these longstanding disputes, Bishop Roger was commissioned to hear numerous cases of more recent origin which other judges-delegate had failed to settle (App. II, 5, 6, 12, 35, 44, 75, 77, 78, 87).

Alongside these protracted cases, others may be observed which dealt with important matters of policy and principle. One case committed to Bartholomew and Roger turned on the new rule of legitimation by subsequent marriage (App. II, 22) and also, as we shall see, involved a possible conflict of jurisdiction. Another turned upon the method of calculating tithes, which affected the chief source of income of every parish church. The question was: may expenses of production, especially labourers' wages, be deducted before tithes are paid? The pope rules that they may not, and instructs the two bishops to enforce his ruling, which becomes the law of the church (App. II, 34). Two cases concern Cistercian privileges relating to tithe-paying, and another similarly concerns the Hospitallers (App. II, 51, 85, 76). The thorny issue of monastic exemption arises in the case of Malmesbury Abbey; the bishops of London and Worcester were commissioned in 1174 to investigate, not to decide upon, the abbey's claims, and if necessary to protect the abbot and the bishop of Llandaff, who had given him benediction. On this occasion the pope seems to have had less faith than usual in his delegates, for the commission allows one judge to act alone if the other cannot or will not act—a most exceptional proviso (App. II, 79). The dispute between Bartholomew of Exeter and some clergy of the archdeaconry of Barnstaple has already been noticed more than once; it must be mentioned again, briefly, in the present connection. This case arose from Bartholomew's attempt, in the early years of his pontificate, to enforce the rules of clerical celibacy in his diocese. It was a test case, which other bishops and clergy would observe with keen interest. Roger of Worcester, only a few months consecrated, was named as a judge, together with the eminent Henry of Blois, bishop of Winchester, and the theologian, Robert of Melun, bishop of Hereford (App. II, 31). Unfortunately there is no trace of a sentence.

Disputed jurisdiction

Important as these cases were for the church, another large group of disputes made even greater demands on the papal judge-delegate. These were cases involving, in various ways and various combinations, royal interests, royal officials, possible infringement of royal rights as defined at Clarendon in 1164, or other conflict of jurisdiction. Bishop Roger was often commissioned to hear such cases; examination of some examples will show what sort of problems he encountered, and will also throw some light on the large question of disputed jurisdiction in the 1160s and 1170s.

Of these cases an early example (the earliest datable) was the protracted dispute between the earl of Norfolk and the canons of Pentney. In this case, King Henry, the exiled archbishop, the bishop of London, and the bishop of Norwich as diocesan were all interested, and all directly involved. Henry of Winchester and Roger of Worcester were commissioned in 1167 to hear one stage of the dispute, which seems to have turned upon the rights of the founder of Pentney over lands granted to it. The commission (App. II, 10) envisaged the excommunication of the earl in circumstances which might constitute a breach of the rule, defined at Clarendon, that no tenant-in-chief or royal official might be excommunicated, or their land laid under interdict, until the case had been brought before the king. Presumably it was felt at the Curia that, if any judges could bring this awkward case to a satisfactory conclusion, it was these two bishops of princely status, discretion, and undoubted loyalty. But there is no record of action taken by them.

The king's objection to the excommunication of his officials, clerical as well as lay, put the papal delegate at a disadvantage in dealing with cases involving this large and influential group of men (quite apart from the abnormal risk in such cases of intimidation of the opposing party and his witnesses), since excommunication and interdict were the principal sanctions of the papal delegate, as of other ecclesiastical judges. This situation may account for the length of some cases in which royal officials were involved. One of these men, and one of the more eminent, was Nicholas de Sigillo, archdeacon of Huntingdon. He was defendant in a complex dispute over the church of Buckworth (App. II, 17). N., a royal chaplain, perhaps the same man, was the defendant in a protracted dispute concerning the chapel of Sutton (App. II, 5); he had already obtained a commission by fraud, before Bishop Roger was instructed to hear the case. In a dispute over the church of Holy Cross, Bungay, the plaintiff was a clerk of the earl of Norfolk and the defendant was Wimer, priest and *capellanus*, the same Wimer *capellanus regis*, who was sheriff or under-sheriff of Norfolk for seventeen years (App. II, 24, 59, 88). In this puzzling case, the outcome of which is unknown, the bishops of Exeter and Worcester were three times commissioned as judges. The king was alleged to be involved, in some way not specified, in a case committed to Gilbert Foliot and Bishop Roger (by name: G. London' et R. Wigorn' episcopis), in which an old clerk claimed that he had been forced to resign his church *metu regio cooperante*. Two commissions had been issued already. Only the third survives, which unfortunately gives few details, and the outcome is again unknown (App. II, 67).

Royal policy, rather than royal intervention, may have been a factor in a case of which the origin lay in the period of the archbishop's exile. The bishop of Worcester and the prior of Kenilworth were commissioned to act upon the complaint of a clerk that he had been ejected from the church of St Hippolytus of Dinsley when it was seized by Richard de Lovetot, and that he had not dared to protest. The judges were ordered to restore him, to obtain repayment of lost income, and to prevent his being disturbed in future without process of law, *citra formam iuris* (App. II, 23). This last unusual responsibility seems to prolong indefinitely the authority of the papal delegates as protectors of the suppliant. Did its appearance indicate special papal interest in the case, or a curial effort to devise a method of protecting litigants, or a momentary aberration on the part of the draughtsman? No judgement survives, as is to be expected in a case between a secular clerk and a layman.

Cases in which the royal government might deny the church's right to jurisdiction presented perhaps the most delicate problems of all in this period of conflict, and require special consideration. The king's fatal quarrel with Archbishop Thomas had been sparked by the problem of procedure in the trial of 'criminous clerks'. Very few such cases were committed to judges-delegate in this period, if the surviving evidence can be trusted, but one, concerning a clerk suspected of murder, was committed to the bishops of London and Worcester (App. II, 86). The papal letter assumes that the matter will be dealt with by the ecclesiastical court, and reveals nothing about the means by which it had come to the pope's attention. 'It has been made known to us,' he says, that G., a clerk, is suspected of a murderous attack on Willelmus Sarracenus, and 'wishing to ensure that an innocent man is not condemned or a guilty one left unpunished', the pope outlines the procedure to be followed and the punishment to be inflicted unless innocence can be established. The letter presents several problems; it occurs only in a few decretal collections of English origin or English associations, and its date is unknown. Possibly it was issued after the negotiations of 1175–6, in which the papal legate, Hugh Pierleoni, agreed that clerks accused of forest offences should be tried by secular courts, and the king accepted that other clergy could be claimed by the church courts. However that may be, it is interesting in the present connection that these two bishops were entrusted with the execution of the pope's orders in this matter, which had so large a bearing on the question of the exemption of the clergy from lay judgement.

Even disputes about tithes might arouse the interest of the

king's court and lead to conflict over jurisdiction. Some such conflict had already taken place when an obscure case was committed to the bishops of Exeter and Worcester (App. II, 35). The abbot of Ramsey, the previous judge-delegate, had not acted, 'because of the king's justices'. Possibly the conflict arose because the tithes formed a substantial part of the endowment of a church. Such cases were later claimed by the king's courts as affecting the rights of patrons, and were being heard by them in the middle of the thirteenth century.[34] The early history of this development seems to be unknown. Though the details of the case defy elucidation, and its end is not recorded, the commission is of some interest, since it shows the pope entrusting a tricky problem to two of his best judges, in the hope that they may be able to defend the interests of the church.

Jurisdiction in disputes over patronage was claimed for the secular court at Clarendon, and was not, like control of appeals, renounced in 1172, nor yet, like trial of criminous clerks, the subject of a later settlement. Yet commissions were issued to judges-delegate by Alexander III in such cases, sometimes with specific instructions to prevent the matter from being taken to the lay court. For example, the bishops of Worcester and Hereford were ordered to use the threat of anathema to force a lay lord to plead about patronage before themselves or the diocesan bishop, and not before a secular judge (App. II, 68, 1175 × 1179). The outcome of the case is unknown, but the commission must have reached the bishop of Worcester, from whose records it was copied into *Collectio Wigorniensis*. This was not an isolated case. Bartholomew of Exeter and Bishop Roger received similar orders to enforce the church's claim to jurisdiction in a dispute about the church of Isham. It was alleged that a layman had granted the patronage to the priory of Huntingdon, and had then himself presented a clerk. The bishops were ordered to remove the clerk, and to use ecclesiastical censures against any person resisting the execution of the mandate. Again the date of the commission is unknown, but it probably reached the bishop of Exeter, the senior judge, and was preserved among his archives, since it appears with other Exeter material in *Collectio Alcobacensis Prima* (App. II, 47).[35]

---

[34] Norma Adams, 'The judicial conflict over tithes', *EHR*, lii (1937), 1–22.
[35] On *Coll. Alcobacensis* I see below, pp. 203–6.

The same instruction to use ecclesiastical censures to force a case of patronage into the church court appears in a commission from which most of the detail has been omitted by the copyist (App. II, 16). Yet another commission, of which only a fragment is preserved, orders Bishops Bartholomew and Roger to hear a question of patronage, if this should be raised (App. II, 82).

In some cases the issue of patronage probably lay just under the surface of what appears as simple litigation between two clerks over a benefice. For example, the church of St Mary, Droitwich, disputed in Roger's time between two clerks, was in 1203 the subject of litigation in the king's court about patronage; and a dispute between two clerks, William of Careville and Adam, terminated by the bishop as judge-delegate, is known only from the record of proceedings in the king's court in 1221 about possession of the advowson (App. II, 19, App. I, 52). Similarly, later litigation about patronage suggests that this may have been the crucial issue in the dispute about the church of Buckworth, which has been mentioned already. The first papal letter, committing this case to the bishop of Worcester and the abbot of St Albans, has not survived; we know only that the judges were accused by one party of acting less diligently than was proper, which raises the suspicion that there was some difficulty about the execution of the commission.

The cases of patronage which have so far been mentioned are known only from decretal collections, which preserved the papal mandates but were not concerned with subsequent action. On the evidence of these cases, it might be argued that although conclusions can be drawn about the attitude of the Curia to such cases, and about its selection of suitable judges, there is no proof that the papal delegates actually heard and terminated any case. But sentences preserved in English archives show that cases explicitly concerning patronage were, in this period (or part of it), heard by ecclesiastical judges, including judges-delegate.[36] Bishop Roger's charters include several decisions in such cases; in two instances a papal commission is also preserved in decretal collections. One of these is the dispute between Joel

---

[36] Compare J. W. Gray, 'The ius presentandi in England from the Council of Clarendon to Bracton', *EHR*, lxvii (1952), 481–509, and Cheney, *Becket to Langton*, pp. 108–11.

of Vautort and the canons of Plympton which has been mentioned already. The commission delegating the case to the archbishop of Canterbury and Bishop Roger refers explicitly to 'the case in which the said knight claims the right of patronage'. Joel did not appear before the judges, but they heard the case and gave sentence against him, on the ground that the same claim has been made by his grandfather and quashed by Bishop William of Exeter (App. II, 37; App. I, 53).

Both mandate and sentence are preserved in a case concerning the church of Painswick. The commission describes the circumstances as they were related to the pope in a written appeal by the prior and canons of Lanthony (App. II, 72). The church had been given to them by Hugh de Lacy, earl of Hereford, and subsequently Roger, earl of Hereford, who had married Cecilia, Hugh's granddaughter and heiress, 'recognized' the gift in the presence of John, bishop of Worcester (1151–7). The bishop invested the brethren, who for some time enjoyed peaceful possession, and the church of *Wyca* appears in a privilege of 1152 for Lanthony.[37] But Cecilia and Roger were later divorced, and she took as her second husband William of Poitou, and on his death a third, Walter of Mayenne. Both of these claimed that Earl Roger's recognition of the gift was invalidated by the divorce, and diverted the revenues of the church from the priory to Roger the priest, who may have been presented or intruded by William. The papal letter does not actually order the bishop to hear a case of patronage, though it refers to advowson, and to patrons and advocates; it orders him to cause the canons of Lanthony to possess the church, and to prevent advocates making such changes in his diocese in future, by means of excommunication. The bishop's response is not recorded, but later, one cannot tell how much later, Walter of Mayenne and the countess informed him and Archdeacon Matthew that they had granted the church to Lanthony 'because we know that they had it by the gift of Hugh de Lacy'. Nothing is said of proceedings in the royal or the ecclesiastical court; the letter is witnessed by the archbishop of Canterbury, which suggests that the case was discussed, if not judged, at some general gathering of great men.[38] Then, perhaps at the

[37] *PUE*, i. 295, no. 53.
[38] PRO C/115/K2 6683 A 1 (Lanthony cart.), section 16 no. 1.

same time, perhaps later, the bishops of Exeter and Worcester, as judges-delegate, announce that the dispute between the canons of Lanthony and Roger the priest has been ended by a composition made in their presence (App. I, 31, 32).

The form of the judges' announcement suggests the possibility that a procedure was being followed, somewhat similar to that described by Glanvill, by which the victor in a suit of advowson in the king's court could sue the clerk presented earlier by the loser in the ecclesiastical court. But the Lanthony cartularies, which preserve many documents about the church, preserve no record of secular proceedings. However that may be, the bishop of Worcester succeeded in inducing Walter of Mayenne and his wife to restore the church, with or without litigation, following the complaint of the canons to the pope. Although this case is better documented than most, there are still baffling gaps in the evidence, which illustrate the difficulty of reconstructing the course of litigation, and of forming a clear opinion about the procedure likely to be followed in such cases at this time.

Roger of Worcester and Robert, prior of Kenilworth, were certainly commissioned by Pope Alexander to hear a dispute between the canons of Darley and William, earl Ferrers, about the church of Uttoxeter. The ensuing composition makes it clear that the advowson was at issue. The earl, in spite of his father's grant, his own confirmation, and confirmations by two successive bishops of Coventry, retained the patronage, consoling the canons with the prospect of a pension of two marks a year.[39] It is not clear that the canons had ever presented, in other words, that they had possession of the advowson, as possession was understood in the king's court. This point, the essential matter in the royal assize *De ultima presentatione*, seems not to be explicitly defined in ecclesiastical records of the 1170s, though possession of the advowson, according to the custom of England, figures prominently in an important ruling addressed to the abbot of St Albans (X 3.38.19 of 1173 × 1176). Other laymen gained, or retained, patronage of churches by settlements made before the bishop of Worcester and his fellow judges-delegate (App. I, 69, 49, 46). In each of these cases, as

[39] *Darley cart.*, ii. 574–5.

at Uttoxeter, the loser, a religious house, is consoled with a pension. In a second case concerning Darley Abbey, also delegated to the bishop and the prior of Kenilworth, the position was reversed: the abbey obtained, or retained, the church of Crich, but renounced any claim to the manor (App. I, 13). Exceptionally, a dispute over the church of Dodford, delegated to Bishop Roger and Simon, abbot of St Albans, before *c.* January 1176, ended by one party giving up its claim, sympathizing with the poverty of the other, and to spare expense to both (App. I, 43). In addition to these cases, an abstract of charters from Harrold Priory includes an otherwise unknown sentence issued by Bishop Roger in favour of the priory, *super iure et proprietate ecclesie parochialis de Braunfeld*, and a record of later proceedings in the king's court shows that Bishop Roger and Adam, abbot of Evesham, acting as judges-delegate, forced or persuaded Hugh Poer to ratify his father's gift of a church to Daventry Priory (App. II, 27, 107).

None of these cases, in which patronage was either possibly or certainly involved, appears to belong to the 1160s. All the dated or datable cases fall in 1173 × 1178. Some, if the full story were known, might be found to deal with matters which lay outside the area claimed for the king's court by the time of 'Glanvill' (*c.* 1187–9). But the number will still be sufficient to support the view that cases of patronage were heard, and often heard, in ecclesiastical courts in this period. The litigants were not always churchmen, who were under some obligation, or some pressure, to avoid the secular court; some laymen were also content to appear before the bishop acting as papal delegate, just as others appeared before him in his diocese. Even so great a man as the earl of Leicester meets the demands of Saint-Évroul after an appeal to the pope; presumably the abbey would not have appealed if less expensive and less offensive methods had not been tried without result. Occasionally laymen seem to have appealed to the pope in cases of patronage. Bishop Roger wrote to the pope *c.* 1174 about Gilbert of Muntfichet, who was trying to obtain the patronage of two churches by means of a papal rescript (App. I, 24), and one of the claimants to the church of *Waltona* must originally have done the same (App. II, 16). We hear obscurely of resistance and opposition, but some laymen were forced to accept the decision of judges-delegate; beside Joel of Vautort we may place Hugh of Moreton, who in 1177 had to renounce his claim, *tam de proprietate quam de possessione*, to two churches in Worcester diocese, which had been given by his father to Hereford Cathedral (App. I, 28), and Walter of Mayenne and the Countess Cecilia who, after long resistance, ratify her grandfather's gift of Painswick church to Lanthony, after the prior's appeal to the pope.

The general history of jurisdiction in cases of patronage in the period between the Constitutions of Clarendon and 1179 cannot be written on the basis of a study of one bishop. It presents many problems, some highly technical, which can only be solved, or at least clarified, when a serious attempt has been made to assemble a substantial number of cases, and to subject them to detailed examination, both as regards terminology and the precise course and form of each suit.

The evidence relating to Bishop Roger provides some useful material for a wider enquiry, particularly because a number of the cases are dated or datable, and all must fall before his final departure from England early in 1179. It prompts many questions which cannot at present be answered with any confidence. Was Roger commissioned more often than other papal delegates to hear cases which fell in the area claimed by the king's court? How energetically were the king and his servants prosecuting that claim before Roger's departure? Did that departure, soon followed by his death, have any effect in this matter? Certainly it removed the one bishop closely associated in men's minds with Thomas Becket and his death in the cause of ecclesiastical liberty and jurisdiction, the one bishop whose opposition might have been carried to the point of confrontation.

This was not simply a matter of the bishop's general reputation. Precisely on the matter of patronage, it can be shown that he held views hostile to the traditional rights of landholders over churches on their estates. In a letter to the pope, written in 1174 (App. I, 24), he expressed the opinion that patrons should not be allowed to withdraw or redistribute gifts made to churches, and confirmed by episcopal and royal authority. It is even possible that one of the objects of the new royal possessory procedure, *De ultima presentatione*, was to offer at least a partial defence against this new attitude, by giving patrons and their heirs a chance to withdraw gifts of patronage, up to the moment when the recipient had obtained possession by actually presenting a clerk to the benefice in question. Bishop Roger must have been known as a leader in the movement to reduce the powers of patrons, and to destroy the old assumption that the local lord, the *dominus fundi*, was free to appoint clergy and make arrangements about parish churches, including the revocation of a predecessor's grants.

The cases that have been examined must prompt the question whether the Church sometimes tried to evade the king's claims by representing disputes over patronage as disputes between a monastic patron and a clerk. The cases concerning the churches of Painswick and Holcot are each described in this way. And how are we to interpret the fact that some of these cases are concluded at the king's court, though not by the king's court? Hugh of Moreton's case and the dispute over the church of Widford were ended at Westminster in 1176 and 1177; the dispute over Painswick may have ended on a similar occasion, when a great noble and the archbishop of Canterbury were to be found together. The Holcot case was ended in January 1177 in the king's chapel at Windsor, the king being out of England. Whatever answers may be given eventually to these questions, the evidence relating to cases heard by Roger of Worcester as judge-delegate and as diocesan seems to point to the conclusion that the decisive struggle over jurisdiction in the matter of patronage took place after he had left the country for the last time *c.* January 1179. The appearance of the royal assize *De ultima presentatione* is fairly securely dated *c.*1180, and the first heavy fine for holding a plea of advowson in the church court appears in 1184.[40] The deaths of Bishop Roger in August 1179, and of Pope Alexander in August 1181, may have been as important in the timing of these developments as the much quoted canon of the Lateran council (X 3.38.3), allowing bishops to collate to benefices vacant for more than three months.

Leaving the question of patronage, it may be noted that Bishop Roger was at least once involved as judge-delegate in another type of case falling in the disputed borderland between ecclesiastical and secular jurisdiction. While the church made

---

[40] Van Caenegem, *Writs*, p. 333; Cheney, *Becket to Langton*, p. 110.

no claim to hear cases relating to lay fee, the secular court made no claim to pronounce upon the validity of a marriage. But upon the validity of a marriage might depend the legitimacy of an heir to lay fee, and the success or failure of the claim to land. Therefore the state was tempted to reach back, and assert an interest in legitimacy, and did in England establish its own rules; at the same time the church was tempted to reach beyond the validity of marriage to its consequences. A commission addressed to the bishops of Exeter and Worcester on 5 July 1177 illustrates this process. Herbert has complained, so the papal mandate runs, that his wife's uncle is trying to disinherit her because she was born before the *desponsatio* of her mother, though later her father took the mother as his wife. The judges are ordered, if the father lawfully married the mother, to declare the daughter legitimate and, further, to forbid her uncle to disturb her about her inheritance, and to lay ecclesiastical censures upon him if he disobeys this prohibition (App. II, 22). Quite apart from the question, will the king's court accept the church's definition of legitimacy? there is here the further question: is not the church overstepping its rights in issuing these orders about inheritance? It has not been possible to identify Herbert and his wife, or to discover whether the bishops executed the papal mandate. But in the next year the king reacted sharply to a commission to other judges, also dealing with a question of legitimacy and also intruding, though in a different way, upon a related question of lay fee. The pope felt compelled to issue new instructions, 'bearing in mind that judgement about such possessions belongs to the king, so he says, and not to ecclesiastical authority'. He ordered the judges to hear only the question of legitimacy.[41]

Cases concerning land, quite apart from questions of legitimacy and inheritance, were occasionally heard by the bishop of Worcester as judge-delegate. One was a dispute between the bishop of Salisbury and a tenant (App. I, 60); another commission covered three separate claims by the monks of Christ Church, Canterbury, against various knights who professed to hold manors by hereditary right *sub firma perpetua* (App. II, 45). It might be supposed that these were not cases that would fall within the area claimed by the secular courts,

[41] X 4.17.7; Diceto, i. 427, *sub anno* 1178, dated 1 Oct.

though one of the Canterbury cases was ended there in 1241. The bishop presided in 1175 as judge-delegate over two settlements between monasteries and laymen in disputes over land, but little information is given about the nature of the claims (App. I, 13, 37).

To sum up: a pattern seems to emerge from the evidence of these cases, obscure though they are at many points. In the first three years after the settlement of Avranches, nothing is heard of conflicts over jurisdiction. It may be supposed that King Henry proceeded cautiously during and immediately after the rebellion of his sons, the more so since the Young King may have been trying to obtain papal support by promising concessions to the church (below, p. 214). In 1175–6, King Henry was able to drive a bargain in the matter of clerks accused of crimes, yielding on the general principle, but retaining jurisdiction over those accused of forest offences. In 1178 he forced the pope to accept that ecclesiastical judges hearing legitimacy and marriage cases might take no action involving lay fee. In 1179–80 the major attack began on the matter of patronage. The disputed areas were isolated and dealt with one by one, in contrast to the method tried in 1164, and with, from the royal standpoint, much better results.

This interpretation of the evidence conflicts with the common assumption that the king's 'ancestral customs' as defined at Clarendon in 1164 are to be regarded as legislation, and as legislation that was continuously in force from that date. A distinction must be made: the definition was one thing, the promise of the bishops of England to observe the customs so defined, was another. It was not for nothing that the king and his supporters at Clarendon bullied the bishops and threatened them with physical violence in order to extract the promise, not for nothing that the bishops refused to the end to set their seals to it. As part of the hard-fought settlement of 1172, Henry released them from the promise, and undertook not to demand it in future, as the papal legates reported to their correspondents: 'relaxavit episcopos de promissione quam ei fecerunt de consuetudinibus conservandis, et promisit quod non exiget in futurum'.[42] This amounted to a return to the *status quo ante bellum*; in theory the church was free to compete for control of

[42] *MTB*, vii. 522, 523.

the disputed ground. It follows that the prelates of England who were the chief papal judges-delegate in the 1170s were not simply assisting in the development of the new legal and judicial system of the church as an internal, ecclesiastical, matter; they were also in the front line of the second phase of the struggle with King Henry over the effective boundaries between the power of the king and the power of the church. Maitland, feeling towards the same view, said in a discussion of jurisdiction over patronage cases that 'the struggle must have been sharp while it lasted';[43] it was for this reason that Pope Alexander stressed the courage required of a judge-delegate, and often urged judges to act 'setting aside all fear or favour'. These were no empty words.

Undisputed jurisdiction

Cases falling in the area of disputed jurisdiction form perhaps about a fifth of the total number in which Bishop Roger is known to have acted as a papal delegate. The vast majority concerned purely ecclesiastical matters. To put the picture of his activity into better perspective, it will be as well to look at it now from a different point of view, concentrating on this much larger group of disputes. We must consider what were the subjects of these cases, who were the litigants, why they had appealed to the pope and how their cases were handled. Once again, it must be stressed that the surviving evidence provides only partial answers to these questions.

The first question presents the fewest difficulties, since the principal issue is normally well-defined by the commission to the judge or judges. Exceptional cases are few, varied and easily identified. Among them are the proceedings against the abbess of Amesbury and her nuns, the dispute over Tynemouth Priory, disputes over diocesan boundaries, monastic exemption, burial rights (App. II, 98, 18, 25, 41, 21). There are three marriage cases, and three accusations against the heads of religious houses by their monks (App. II, 3, 22, 74, 14, 33, 100). Eighteen cases concern tithes; among these some, as we have seen, deal with major issues of principle, others are simply competing

[43] F. W. Maitland, *Roman canon law in the church of England* (1898), p. 62.

claims for the same dues. But a clear majority of all cases concern parish churches and chapels, some fifty-eight out of a total of about a hundred. Perhaps this is not surprising; churches provided churchmen with their means of living, well or poorly as the case might be, and patronage was a piece of property carrying with it both financial and less tangible assets. Even in settled times, there would have been motives for disputes, and these were not settled times. During Stephen's reign, churches and chapels had changed hands along with the estates in which they lay, and neither side in the civil war was in a strong position to do justice upon private acts of dispossession. Other disturbance of property rights brought similar problems for the church, notably the confiscation of the English lands of the king of Scots in 1174. In the 1160s, all the archbishop's clerks, relatives and adherents had been deprived of their benefices, in theory only temporarily, but some had difficulty in regaining them in 1170, and we do not know how many were restored without dispute after the settlement of 1172.

At the same time the church itself caused a major upheaval by its assault on hereditary succession to benefices; many churches, chapels, and prebends, which had formerly descended peacefully from father to son, were now, as it were, thrown into the ring, and new uncertainties were created by the transformation of lay ownership of churches into patronage, by the new insistence on episcopal control of gifts of churches to religious houses, and by the development of strict procedures for the admission of clergy to benefices. New offices and new methods were needed to operate this new control and supervision, and these did not spring up overnight; they were developed by trial and error over many years. An example of a dispute caused by this attempt at control, without first providing the necessary system and the necessary bureaucracy, is provided by the litigation between the vicar of Salford Priors and Kenilworth Priory (App. II, 49c), which has been discussed in connection with Bishop Roger's diocesan activities. Fifty years earlier, the bishop would very probably never have heard of the appointment; fifty years later a permanent vicarage would very probably have been ordained. In the 1170s, the bishop and the priory both assumed that the vicar must be presented to him for institution, but no system had been established to ensure, as a matter of routine, that the vicar's income was fixed before institution took place; hence the dispute. While these changes were taking place, there was great scope for collision between old customs and new methods, and genuine doubt about many points of detail, and therefore fertile ground for litigation.

Of these cases concerning churches, we have seen already that some certainly and some probably concern the advowson. Some, on the other hand, certainly do not concern the advowson: A sues B because B was instituted to A's benefice upon a false report of A's death (App. II, 48); A sues B for non-payment of a pension (App. II, 71); A says he was properly instituted and the archbishop claims that he was not (App. II, 7). Many concern priests' sons and hereditary succession to benefices (App. II, 19, 26, 27, 57, 69, 72, 77, 83, 87), though this is not necessarily the only or the principal issue. But in many cases it is not clear what was the basis for the claims of either party (App. II, 5, 12, 17, 19, 23, 24, 95, 96, 101, 117, 122). If we consider the dispute over the church—or chapel—of Potton, we shall have great difficulty in discovering exactly why Hugh the parson of Sandy thought he had a right to Potton, or exactly who was his opponent, although two papal commissions and a sentence are preserved (App. I, 47; App. II, 12 and 84). From the more informative of the two surviving commissions, and it is a long one, we hear a great deal about comings and goings to the Curia, but of the principal cause we only learn that Hugh says he was violently dispossessed and has sworn to renounce his claim, and that Th., clerk of the king of Scots, holds the church. The notification issued by Bishop Roger as judge-delegate informs the children of Holy Church that Hugh has withdrawn his charge of violent dispossession and renounced his plea against the prior and monks of St Andrew's, Northampton, who are not mentioned in the papal letters, while Th., the clerk, is never mentioned by the bishop. With this case we may compare a dispute over the church of Burbage; again two papal letters survive in decretal collections, and Bishop Roger's sentence is preserved. The sentence reveals more than usual about the course of proceedings before the bishop as judge-delegate but, as in the Potton case, we are left guessing about the nature of the claimant's alleged right (App. I, 62; App. II, 54, 69B). These are relatively well-documented cases. Many others are known only from a single decretal, a single charter, or some other even less instructive scrap of evidence, so that, although we can point to a large number of disputes about parish churches and chapels, we can only discover the legal issues involved in a small proportion of them.

We have asked, who were the litigants? As the Potton case has shown, this is not always obvious. Most litigants are ecclesiastics, but in the very numerous disputes over churches laymen may be directly concerned, as when the canons of St Paul's, Bedford, sue 'him who was said to detain the church of Holcot', but end by making a settlement with the lay patron. It is in patronage cases that laymen appear most often, which gives point to the royal claim to judge these cases. They appear in the few matrimonial cases, and cases concerning land, also occasionally as delinquents who eject clergy from benefices, fail to pay tithes properly, or to bury a relative in the parish churchyard, or to deliver to a church the gift intended by a testator (App. II, 34, 23, 24, 21). Once a monastic house is sued for debt, perhaps by an Italian money-lender (App. II, 20). One layman goes to the pope for permission to establish a chapel (App. II, 90). Among the clergy, monastic houses are not as conspicuous as might be expected, though the exempt orders and the great exempt houses sue and are sued at the Curia, as also the would-be exempt, such as Malmesbury. In some disputes between religious houses and secular clerks, it is not clear which party initiated the appeal. Setting these aside, it appears that there are some twenty-seven cases (possibly thirty-one) initiated by religious houses, and twenty-four in which they are defendants. In eleven of these, both parties are religious. But there are fifty cases which seem to be initiated by seculars, and forty in which they are defendants, of which cases twenty-nine are between seculars. Even though, in some disputes between seculars, a religious house probably stood behind one of the parties (App. II, 12, 27, 49B, 81, 88), these figures are a little surprising, and all the more so since nearly a quarter of the total number of cases is known only from texts preserved in the cartularies of religious houses.

Of these secular clergy, many were men of some consequence. Bishops are involved in eight or nine cases, cathedral dignitaries, including archdeacons, in six or seven. Some other litigants are well-known figures, or serve great men; three serve the king, one the king of Scots, one the earl of Norfolk, one the justiciar, Richard de Lucy; there is a member of the Lucy family, and a nephew of Robert Pullus, late chancellor of the Roman Church. It cannot be assumed that absence of a title means poverty or humble status. Wimer, called priest or chaplain, was the sheriff of Norfolk. Ralph de Alta Ripa was a nephew of Gilbert Foliot; his connection with the bishop of London was mentioned only because his opponent feared that he would not get a fair hearing. It is more than likely that other litigants, such as the six almost unknown *magistri*, had powerful patrons of whom we are not aware. Even the cases that have been mentioned here approach half the total in which secular clergy were involved; only once is a commission to Bishop Roger explicitly issued on behalf of a poor clerk (App. II, 93), while four concern cases of hardship and misfortune, assuming that the stories told to the pope were true.

Why did these litigants, laymen, monks and secular clergy, appeal to the pope? Possibly there was in this period a higher proportion than in later times of sinners avoiding correction and scoundrels evading justice, because rules designed to prevent abuse of the appeal system were only in process of formation. For instance, it was probably only in or after 1175 that the pope authorized English bishops to proceed against certain notorious offenders in spite of appeals, and throughout the 1170s he was issuing a stream of rulings designed to prevent and punish fraud and unjustified delay.[44] But these improvements were very recent; the forger and the delinquent still hoped to profit by recourse to the distant, omni-competent but all too fallible Curia.

Of the *bona fide* litigants, some had no choice in the matter; the law itself now compelled them to take their case to Rome. A priest, whose village had been destroyed by a Cistercian abbey, had no hope of a remedy except from the pope, who had given the order its privileges (App. II, 51); the bishop of Worcester himself, trying to reclaim a church granted away by a predecessor, had to refer to the pope although the grant was undoubtedly bad in law, because a pope had confirmed it (App. II, 36). For those who had a choice, the immediate

[44] Below, p. 219–20, above, p. 123.

standstill produced by an appeal was clearly a major attraction. The local judge could not proceed to a decision, the execution of a sentence was suspended, those contemplating violence might be deterred, for the appellant placed his person and property under the protection of the Roman Church. Any action against him while the appeal was pending was an affront to the dignity of that church, a matter for urgent enquiry and official indignation. Action taken against an appellant will regularly be countermanded. Even the respected bishop of Exeter, trying to enforce the rules of clerical celibacy in his diocese, is firmly ordered to reinstate a vicar deposed while at the Curia, and to remove the man he had instituted in the vicar's benefices (App. II, 31; cf. 69, 75, 78). This standstill was likely to be valued particularly by an individual whose marriage was being questioned, or by a subject who considered himself oppressed by a superior (App. II, 3, 74, 78, 7).

A local procedure was evolved in this period to make the protection of the appellant more effective. If he was disturbed in any way, he could apply to the archbishop of Canterbury, whose right to act on such occasions was approved by Pope Alexander in an undated letter to Archbishop Richard.[45] The germ of this early tuitorial procedure may perhaps be seen in two of Bishop Roger's cases, in which litigants obtained mandates to the archbishop, alleging that action had been taken against them after appeal (App. II, 58A, 86A). In the dispute over the exemption of Malmesbury Abbey, the bishop of Salisbury complained to the archbishop that his existing rights had been ignored after appeal, whereupon the archbishop investigated the complaint and punished the offenders, without reference to Rome.[46] This action was probably taking place while messengers from the abbey were fetching a mandate instructing the bishops of London and Worcester to take the first steps upon the principal issue (App. II, 79).

---

[45] JL 13809, X 2.28.17, ACL 10.23. This mandate, *Cum teneamur*, may be the papal authority alleged by later archbishops for their right to hear tuitorial appeals from all in their province. It was interpreted in this sense in the rubric (from a lost MS) in ACL: 'Quod si cuius possessio post appellationem fuerit turbata, archiepiscopus potest emendare'.

[46] On the case see David Knowles, 'The growth of monastic exemption', *Downside Review* 1 (1932), 228–31. The archbishop's report to the pope, preserved among the letters of Peter of Blois, is printed in PL 200.1456–9.

Though this may seem surprising, desire for prompt action may also have prompted appeals; it certainly did so in the case of the knight Richard of Anstey.[47] For the litigant who wished to plead before a higher authority than a rural dean or vice-archdeacon, the long journey to Rome had to be compared with the difficulty of tracking down and engaging the attention of the appropriate bishop. Perhaps the habit of appeal to the pope was strengthened by the many long episcopal vacancies of this period. The archbishopric was effectively vacant from December 1170 for about three and a half years (to say nothing of the six years of Thomas's exile) till Richard returned to England in August 1174, bringing with him the newly consecrated bishop of Bath, whose see had been vacant for nearly eight years. In October 1174 bishops were consecrated to four sees, of which Hereford had been vacant for seven and a half years, Ely for five and a half, Chichester for five and Winchester for three. Of the new bishops, three were royal servants, busy on the king's affairs in England and France, and not normally accessible to their subjects. The great see of Lincoln had no confirmed bishop-elect till July 1175, after eight and a half years; here too the elect was often out of England, often attending the king, and he was never consecrated. The vacancy at Norwich, of nearly two years, seems short by comparison with these. This situation may have tipped the balance in many cases, and induced litigants to take the road to Rome.

Once at the Curia, a commission could be obtained urging the appointed judges to act swiftly, *diligentius*, *maturius*, or *cum omni studio*, or if the worst came to the worst, bringing a rebuke for delay (App. II, 4, 17). Or a time-limit might be imposed, within which the judges must act, and after which their authority expired; this was a two-edged weapon, not apparently much favoured by English litigants in this period. Among Bishop Roger's cases, it will be seen that on one occasion the archbishop of Canterbury was instructed to act if the appointed judges, the bishop and a colleague, did not proceed within forty days; on another the bishop and a colleague took over a case in which the previous judge had not acted within the allotted time (App. II, 17, 35). Unfortunately, the evidence is never sufficient

---

[47] See above, p. 120, n. 15.

to show how long a time elapsed between the issue of a commission to Bishop Roger and the end of the case; where there is a dated judgement, we cannot be sure of the date of the mandate, and vice versa. In the dispute over Tynemouth Priory, a commission seems likely to have been issued after 15 January 1174, and the judges' notification of the settlement is dated 12 November of the same year (App. II, 18; App. I, 11). On this occasion both parties may have been prepared to end their long quarrel by compromise. Where one party was determined to cause as much delay as possible, a much longer time could pass before a decision. One of Bishop Roger's sentences records that two years had passed between the early and the final stages of the case; the delay seems to have been due to the plaintiff, who was given every possible opportunity to state his case (App. I, 62). In another case, when there was a delay of nearly a year, one party complained to the pope and obtained a mandate reproving the judges for their *tepiditas*, and threatening punishment (App. II, 4). Even in this case, the plaintiffs had been promptly put back into possession of the church from which they had been violently ejected. The distinction between possession and right was firmly established, and the judge-delegate, with his extensive powers, could probably move as fast as the king's court in dealing with violent dispossession.

Immediate protection, influence on the choice of judges, reasonably prompt action, judges with authority to give orders to the highest prelates and cut across diocesan and provincial boundaries, all these attracted the potential appellant. In addition, the sentence or composition was made under papal authority, and—at the cost of another long journey—the further safeguard of papal confirmation could be obtained. For example, Bishop Roger wrote to ask for confirmation of a composition made before him concerning the bishop of Salisbury; the canons of Osney obtained confirmation of a sentence pronounced by Gilbert Foliot and Bishop Roger; the abbot and convent of Marmoutier obtained confirmation of a sentence concerning a chapel in Worcester diocese (App. I, 61; App. II, 50 n, 58B). As a last security, the confirmation might, like other letters of grace, be enregistered in the papal chancery at the request of the impetrant, at a time when no ecclesiastical court in England kept any permanent record of its decisions.

Another compelling motive for appeals has been touched upon in an earlier chapter.[48] There was no satisfactory local alternative. No English diocese at this time had a formally constituted diocesan court, with permanent officials and regular places and times of meeting. In these circumstances, appeal to the pope, generally followed by a commission to local judges-delegate, opened the door not only to the highest court, not only to an impartial court, but to a new and more sophisticated kind of court, which was providing a training in new methods for English judges and lawyers, and to some extent a model for the episcopal courts of the future.

There were then many reasons for appeals to the pope, and many of these were not merely reasons for appealing in the modern sense of taking a case from a lower to a higher court, they were reasons for taking cases to the pope as to a court of first instance. The habit of bypassing all lesser ecclesiastical jurisdictions must already have taken hold in England by 1164, when King Henry at Clarendon required the bishops to accept both his right to authorize or forbid appeals to the pope, and an invariable course of cases from the hearing of the archdeacon to the bishop, and from the bishop to the archbishop, before there was any question of taking the matter further. In 1172 the king accepted that appeals should be made freely to the Roman Church; this acceptance carried with it the end of his attempt to regulate the course of ecclesiastical business in ecclesiastical courts, and there seems to have been a rush of first instance cases to the Curia in the following decades. In nine-tenths of the cases in which Bishop Roger acted as a papal delegate, there is no trace of earlier proceedings in England before archdeacons, bishops or archbishops. The few certain or probable appeals from lower jurisdiction are quickly enumerated. Twice he heard appeals that had been made in the archbishop's synod, both in matrimonial cases (App. II, 3, 74); there was also one appeal from the bishop himself in a matrimonial case, and possibly one other (App. II. 8, 29). One case certainly proceeded from the bishop of Exeter, acting *ex officio*, to Archbishop Thomas, and from his hearing to that of the pope (App. II, 31); is it a coincidence that this took place

[48] Above, p. 97, and compare R. C. van Caenegem, *The birth of the English Common Law* (Cambridge 1973), p. 23.

in 1164? The dispute between Joel of Vautort and the canons of Plympton had also been before Bartholomew, and a dispute over the church of Preston Capes had been, at some time, before the archdeacon of Northampton (App. II, 37, 28). Of course, the terseness and general inadequacy of the sources may conceal other appeals from local hearings. Three commissions of Pope Alexander relate to a dispute about the church of Whittlesea, and none mentions that there had been proceedings in England before the appeal to the pope. But the cartulary of Thorney Abbey, which possessed the patronage, contains a copy of a report required in earlier (possibly much earlier) proceedings about the church before the archbishop (App. II, 27, n.3). There may be other cases in which there were earlier proceedings, but the available evidence strongly suggests that a high proportion of cases was taken to the pope was taken as to the Universal Ordinary, and this high proportion underlines the attractions of the Curia for litigants in ecclesiastical cases in the second half of the twelfth century.

We have asked how litigants were treated, who obtained commissions addressed to Bishop Roger and his fellow judges-delegate. To answer this question, evidence must be selected which shows what actually took place when the bishop, with or without a colleague, acted on papal commissions. The evidence is limited, for in more than half of Bishop Roger's cases there is no surviving trace of action. Moreover no one case is fully documented, so that information has to be assembled from shreds of evidence supplied from many cases, over many years, but chiefly from 1172 to 1178. This evidence, fragmentary though it is, makes it abundantly clear that the basic 'roman-canonical' procedure is taken for granted, and therefore mentioned only casually, or when some unusual problem arises. Thus the public reading of the judges' commission is mentioned once only, because on that occasion the defendant alleged that it was forged (App. II, 49). Similarly, the citations or *edicta* summoning the parties will be mentioned only when one fails to appear, as in the patronage case between Joel of Vautort and the canons of Plympton, in which the judges record that 'die igitur et loco partibus constituto, cum iamdictum Iohelem quarto edicto peremptorio citassemus, ipse nec venit nec pro se responsalem destinavit' (App. I, 53). Bishop Roger's judgement in a dispute over the church of Burbage notes that Alan of Hurstbourne neither came nor sent a *responsalis*, in spite of 'plurima edicta peremptoria per ampliora quam canones et leges indulgeant intervalla' (App. II, 62). This notice reveals, almost casually, the background of legal expertise against which the bishop acts. In these cases, the earlier, non-peremptory summonses are assumed, but they are mentioned explicitly in Bishop Roger's report to the pope about the proceedings between the monks of Bury St Edmunds and Thomas, dean of Colchester. Thomas failed to appear in response to two non-peremptory summonses, nor did he send a *responsalis* or a sufficient excuse. The bishop only mentions the matter in his report because he wishes to put to the pope his views on suitable punishment for such non-appearance (App. I, 6 and below, p. 189). The appointment of a proxy by the abbot and convent of Saint-Évroul is mentioned in a charter concerning their church of Rowell, perhaps because on another occasion they had accused the bishop of proceeding when they were not properly represented (App. I, 62; App. II, 44A).

Judges could attempt to force one party to appear in court by putting the other in possession *causa rei servandae*, making use of a procedure adapted from the civil law by canonists. The bishop and his colleagues several times adopt this procedure (e.g. App. II, 48, 49). A single copy survives of a letter in which the judges announce their decision on this point to the diocesan, and carefully request him to put one party into 'the kind of possession we have indicated' (App. I, 4). It went without saying that this action did not transform that party into the true possessor (cf. App. II, 2, 35).

The *litis contestatio* is seldom mentioned, but the bishop refers to it in passing in his sentence about the church of Burbage (App. I, 62). The statements of the parties are heard, and this is commonly noted, *allegationibus hinc inde auditis* (e.g. App. I, 54). These will be copied and will be sent to the pope if there is a further appeal, along with the attestations of witnesses (App. II, 89). In the Burbage case more information than usual is provided about the production of witnesses at different stages in the case, about the copying of sworn evidence, and the possibility of disputing that evidence and objecting to the witnesses (App. II, 62). The swearing-in of witnesses according to the proper form is mentioned in the judges' report on the case of Clarembald, abbot-elect of St Augustine's, Canterbury (App. I, 8). The *exceptio* is mentioned only once, in a sentence issued in 1166 × 1167; the bishop reports that one party 'transactionis exceptionem opposuit' (App. I, 16). In many cases the parties make a settlement and there is no sentence; Bishop Roger's cases show some seventeen settlements as against nine sentences. This may be achieved by choosing arbiters (App. I, 41, 51), and may take place *ante litis ingressum* (App. I, 58). Such settlements may involve a future payment to be made *nomine transactionis* (App. I, 54); the draughtsman is distinguishing this kind of settlement, binding individuals, from one made *nomine ecclesie*, binding an undying institution.

These scattered references could no doubt be much extended by a more thorough and expert search. But they suffice to show what was in the minds of English judges-delegate in the time of Alexander III, when they report that they have acted *rite* or *ordine iudiciario*. They may make mistakes; what judge does not? Bishop Roger was twice accused of acting incorrectly in the conduct of a case (App. II, 45, 69B). It is difficult to tell whether the accusations were justified, but in the first of those cases the pope himself, though ordering an investigation, expresses disbelief. He expects his delegates in England, like his delegates elsewhere, to know and follow the rules of procedure, as they are understood by the developing legal science of the time.

Possession, right and restitution

Because of the stress laid by English legal historians on the development, in just this period, of possessory procedures in the English royal courts, a brief reference must be made to the treatment of possession and disturbance of possession by Bishop Roger and his fellow-judges-delegate. The evidence seems to belong entirely to the 1170s, but it would be dangerous, for reasons already stated, to draw hasty conclusions from this fact. The situation in the 1160s requires further investigation, based on a wider range of material. The evidence relating to Bishop Roger shows a firmly established distinction between possession and right, *possessio* and *proprietas*. This distinction appears as part of the accepted framework within which judicial action is taken and decisions made. It is assumed that possession must be protected, and that, where it is said to have been disturbed, the matter must be separately investigated, before any hearing on the question of right. The best documented case is the dispute between Osney Abbey and St Frideswide's Priory over the church of St Mary Magdalen outside Oxford.[49] This dispute had been taken before Pope Eugenius; his sentence, issued on 6 February 1152, says nothing about *possessio* or *proprietas* but adjudges the church to Osney. Later, perhaps in the 1160s, certainly before about July 1173, Osney obtained a commission to judges-delegate on a complaint of violent dispossession; these judges decided that Osney had 'the most complete proofs both of right and of lawful possession'; the abbey was put once more into corporal possession. But they were again dispossessed, again appealed to the pope, and obtained a commission to the bishops of London and Worcester, ordering them to investigate the charge of violent dispossession, to restore possession to Osney if the charge is proved, and then to hear the principal *causa*, always provided that, if Pope Eugenius had settled the matter 'nulla de proprietate questione reservata', the judges shall impose silence on St Frideswide's 'tam de proprietate quam de possessione' (App. II, 52). Osney was apparently put promptly back into possession, but the hearing on right was delayed until yet another commission was obtained to the same judges ordering them to act more diligently, and also to restore to the abbey revenues lost as the result of dispossession (App. II, 4).

The distinction between possession and right is spelt out equally clearly in a papal commission, the last of three, about the church of Whittlesea, though in this case no final judgement survives. Master Hugh had complained that he had been violently dispossessed of the church by a clerk O., and had regained possession before the bishop of Worcester and prior of Kenilworth. O. then sued Hugh and his witnesses in the lay court, causing them great losses. Hugh went again to the pope and obtained a fresh commission, ordering the bishop and a colleague to declare Hugh the 'true possessor', and to absolve him from any claim by O. on the matter of possession. When O.

[49] *Oseney cart.*, ii. 216–34.

has made good all the losses, he may plead on the matter of right (App. II, 2).

The commissions to Bishop Roger and his colleagues in these two cases attracted little attention from canonists. But they noted another, which ruled that the victor in the matter of possession must be put into corporal possession of the disputed object before the hearing on the matter of right, and yet another which spelt out the rule that the possessor may lawfully repel force with force (App. II, 39, 86A). They were also interested in a ruling addressed to the bishop and a colleague in the course of the long dispute over the church of Potton. The claimant asserted that he had been violently dispossessed; his opponent said that he had renounced the church of his free will. The pope rules that the charge of violent dispossession must be heard first, observing that renunciation after dispossession is unlikely to be spontaneous; the bishop duly investigated the charge (App. I, 47). Dispossession is not always violent, but may be effected *sine iudicio*. Bishop Roger was ordered to investigate the claim of the dean of Lincoln that he was despoiled thus of a prebend at Hereford, and the claim of a clerk who was despoiled of his church when a false rumour of his death caused the patron to present another clerk (App. II, 75, 48). These cases are, of course, only a small sample of those that could be used to illustrate the operation of the distinction between possession and right, and the interest of the canonists in the protection of possession, in the time of Alexander III. The sample is too small to allow comparison between developments in the law and practice of the church, and similar developments in English secular law, but it is perhaps large enough to suggest that there is room for further enquiry in this field.

Conclusion

In examining Bishop Roger's delegated cases, we have touched lightly on many large questions, each of which deserves more extended treatment. The bishop's part in the development of the canon law, and of procedure in ecclesiastical courts, will be studied in more detail in the next chapter. So far as his practical work as a papal judge-delegate is concerned, some firm conclusions and some interesting possibilities have emerged from the present study of his activity. The evidence shows that almost from the time of his election he was acting as a judge in cases taken by appeal to the Curia and returned for hearing in England, and that within a year or two he was being commissioned, generally with others, sometimes alone, to hear politically delicate cases, or cases that other judges had failed to terminate. In the 1170s, for which there is more material than for earlier times, Roger emerges as possibly the most-employed judge-delegate in the province of Canterbury, and this means the most-employed in England. The decretal collections, from which much of this material is drawn, are of course biased in favour of cases that interested lawyers, but this in itself underlines the quality, if not the quantity, of Roger's work; it was to him that so many of these tricky cases were committed. His activity, coupled with his personal eminence and reputation, gave much-needed support to the church in this time of conflict; it was for this reason that Pope Alexander III urged him to continue this work and stressed its importance. It has been noticed that nearly a quarter of Bishop Roger's delegated cases may fall in the area of jurisdiction disputed between the royal and the ecclesiastical courts, with a preponderance of patronage cases; whether his work had any effect on the outcome or the timing of the dispute, is a question that cannot be answered, but should not be forgotten. Certainly he, and the other members of the select group of senior judges, had some responsibility for the rapid increase in appeals to the pope (both appeals from lesser jurisdictions and recourse in the first instance), which is a marked feature of the pontificate of Alexander III.

5
THE BISHOP AND THE LAW

PART I BISHOP ROGER AND THE MAKING OF NEW LAW

Introduction

In the last chapter some questions were discussed which arise in connection with Bishop Roger's activity as a papal judge-delegate. But he was more than a faithful executor of papal commissions. Scattered through the decretal collections, from those of the 1170s to the great authoritative collection of 1234, there are letters or parts of letters addressed to him by Pope Alexander, giving rulings on a variety of legal and procedural topics, letters which are not commissions, but replies to questions of principle raised by the bishop. In addition there are a few letters dealing with questions of principle arising from individual cases, in which it is certain or probable that the bishop had asked for a ruling from the pope. These letters raise questions about the respective contributions of the bishop (and other bishops) and the pope to the development of the canon law; there is also other material, limited in extent but not negligible, which throws some light on this problem. A study of Bishop Roger would be incomplete without an attempt to assemble this evidence, to notice the topics that interested him, and to offer a few comments on his part in the formation of the 'new law'.[1]

By the time of Pope Alexander's death in 1181, it must already have been clear to all who were concerned with the law of the western church that a rapid development, a change so dramatic as to appear as a revolution, had taken place in his pontificate. Beside the accumulated mass of the old law, with its venerable, confusing, often inapplicable and sometimes (in spite of Gratian's efforts) contradictory statements, there were now in circulation hundreds of pronouncements, all dealing with current problems in up-to-date terms, all carrying the

[1] Part I of this chapter expands and revises an essay on a similar theme: M. Cheney, 'Alexander III and Roger of Worcester'.

authority of recent popes, particularly Alexander himself. The way had been prepared for this development by the intellectual and political movements of the last half century; a combination of personal and political factors brought it to a head. Pope Alexander's training, interests and attitude were obviously of major importance.[2] Much of his early life is obscure, but there is no doubt that he had lectured at Bologna *in sacra pagina* at a time when the study of law and the study of theology were still closely linked, and experts have long accepted his authorship of a commentary on Gratian's Decretum; this commentary included a section on matrimonial law, which circulated separately, and enjoyed some popularity, to judge by the number of surviving texts.[3] Alexander's utterances as pope make it clear that his view of the church was strongly coloured by notions of jurisdiction, of legal and judicial, as opposed to moral and spiritual, authority. He frequently stressed his position at the apex of a judicial system, the duty of all churchmen to lay their legal problems at his feet for solution, and his own right to ensure that 'all men receive the fullness of justice',[4] in other words to his right to receive appeals from any person, at any time, from any place, on any ecclesiastical matter.

The increase in appeals has been discussed in the last chapter; in the present context one additional observation must be made. Increased litigation brought to the Curia not only litigants, but a swelling band of experts, curial officials, proctors and advocates, who will, as in later times, have kept a sharp watch for pronouncements of the reigning pope, as a guide to curial opinion and in order to improve their own expertise and the service they could offer to their clients. These pronouncements were contained in papal letters addressed to recipients all over Pope Alexander's obedience; they might be noted by experts at the Curia, or in the provinces, or by both simultaneously. As we shall see, there seems to have been greater activity in some

---

[2] On Alexander's attitudes see Beryl Smalley, *The Becket conflict and the schools* (Oxford 1973), pp. 138–59. The slender evidence about Alexander's training and writings is emphasized by John T. Noonan, 'Who was Rolandus?', in *Law, Church, and Society*, ed. K. Pennington and Robert Somerville (University of Pennsylvania 1977), pp. 21–48.
[3] Cf. *Repert.*, pp. 127–8, and S. Kuttner in *BMCL*, NS iii (1973), 62 n. 2.
[4] JL 11839; the arenga is printed in translation in *EHR* lxxxiv (1969), 497. Compare for example JL 14350.

provinces than others in noting and circulating useful rulings, and thus in forming the earliest collections of Pope Alexander's decretals; I shall return to this point in the second part of this chapter. Already a small number of important statements, made by popes from Innocent II to Adrian IV, had found their way into circulation, and appear in little appendices to older canonical collections.[5] It was not long before Pope Alexander's statements were circulating also. Small collections may have been formed in England *c.* 1174 × 1175 (below, p. 201), and collections of much greater length were copied in England, France and Italy, which show no knowledge of the Lateran Council of March 1179. Attention was perhaps first concentrated on Alexander III's general legal definitions, but increasingly even his less formal statements, made in connection with individual cases, were also copied, circulated and studied.[6] In common parlance the word *decretalis*, or *decretalis epistola*, was used to cover both replies to abstract legal problems submitted to the pope, and commissions to judges-delegate, or indeed any papal letter that contained a useful statement of law. More precise definitions appear in learned works, but the pope himself was prepared to use the word *decretalis* to mean simply a papal mandate.[7] For the purpose of this chapter 'decretal' will mean a papal letter preserved by lawyers for its legal interest. This is a convenient rather than a scientific definition, and occasionally it leaves room for doubt. For example, five commissions about a dispute over a church at Bungay appear in a decretal collection (*coll. Florianensis*, cc. 168–72); they were possibly of personal, rather than academic, interest to the man who first copied them. Should they be classed as decretals? In spite of such problems, this definition is useful, since it emphasizes the process of selection that determined which papal

[5] *Repert.*, p. 273.
[6] This is a tentative suggestion, requiring further examination. It is based on the observations first, that many of these definitions preserve their dating clauses, perhaps indicating that they circulated at an early date in the collecting process, before excision of legally irrelevant matter became habitual, and second, that in what seem to be the earliest collections, the bulk of the material is of this sort. For example see *Coll. Wigorn. alt.* Duggan, *Collections*, pp. 152–4.
[7] Cf. JL 13870, X 2.28.15, to the bishop of Durham. For an account of canonists' discussions and definitions of *decretales*, see J. Hanenburg, 'Decretals and decretal collections in the second half of the twelfth century', *Revue d'hist. de droit*, xxxiv (1966), 552–99. See also Fransen, *Les décrétales*, p. 7.

statements would, and which would not, have quasi-legislative effect.

These decretals of Pope Alexander, collected, sifted, retouched, dissected and arranged during five decades by some of the best brains of the time, formed the solid foundation of the collection produced by Raymond of Peñafort and sent by Pope Gregory IX in 1234 to Bologna with the order that it alone should be used in future, both in court and classroom. The user of that comprehensive, systematic collection must admire the range and precision of Pope Alexander's rulings, and the clarity of vision with which he observes the problems of remote areas and issues appropriate orders. But the very efficiency, the comprehensive, systematic arrangement, of the *Liber Extra* conceals the true nature of Alexander's legislative, or quasi-legislative, activity. There is no evidence that he ever contemplated a systematic, comprehensive revision of the law, or that any overall plan guided and stimulated his work in this field. He did not, as far as we know, attempt to control the use or the circulation of his pronouncements, to distinguish the genuine from the false, the correct from the corrupt or altered text, to separate statements of general application from those of only local or temporary validity, or even to ensure that later and better opinions superseded earlier and less good rulings. No official collection of them was published in his time. Instead of being the conscious architect of a new body of law, he appears on close inspection as a judge and, one might almost say, a legal consultant;[8] in both capacities, his pronouncements were normally made in response to a stimulus from the provinces.

It was this stimulus, in the form of a request for a ruling, or an appeal, that caused the pope and the lawyers of his circle to direct their attention to a particular problem. This is true of almost every general definition of the law, and even of Alexander's conciliar decrees, other than those directly affecting the pope or the Curia. It is also commonly true of legal statements

---

[8] If this seems an absurd description of a supreme legislator, it should be remembered that the lawyers who collected and examined papal pronouncements in this period rejected some, cut or altered others, and also included a few which, as the glosses show, were ignored, and known to be ignored, in practice. Fransen, *Les décrétales*, p. 35, goes so far as to say, 'les collections de décrétales ne sont rien d'autre que des recueils de jurisprudence choisie'.

and procedural instructions incorporated in commissions to judges-delegate; these, as we shall see, were often inserted at the request of the litigant, occasionally at the request of a judge. It is also true of the rulings addressed in the 1170s to the archbishop of Canterbury and his suffragans, many of which followed application to the pope by the archbishop after his provincial council in 1175.[9]

Papal pronouncements elicited by bishop Roger

This view of Pope Alexander's legal achievement rests partly on the insecure basis of the argument from silence. But it can be tested by examining his rulings addressed to Roger of Worcester, taking this bishop as an example, as one of several whose names appear very frequently in the decretal collections, and most conspicuously in the earliest collections, which consist only, or largely, of decretals of Alexander III. Rulings dealing with matters of principle will be considered first; commissions and other evidence bearing on this question will then be examined for any additional information they can provide.

There are four or five decretals of the first type addressed to Bishop Roger, and one possibly addressed to him.[10] They contain the pope's replies on some twenty distinct problems, and almost all these replies were of sufficient importance and precision to be selected for inclusion in the Decretals of 1234. The series begins not many months after the bishop's consecration, with the letter *Inter cetera solicitudinis* (App. II, 61) of 26 November 1164, dealing with clerical marriage and hereditary succession to benefices. This letter has been discussed in connection with Bishop Roger's work in his diocese (above, p. 69) and that discussion need not be repeated here, but a few points must be stressed for their bearing on the present enquiry. Although the letter makes no reference to an approach or petition from the bishop, it is almost certainly the result of a request made by him on the occasion of a short visit to the pope at Sens. The bishop assumed, as the pope assumed, that the continued existence of married clergy, holding benefices in the

---

[9] M. Cheney, 'Council of Westminster', *passim*.
[10] JL 14136, 1 Comp. 4.1.3 (App. II, 29 below) replies to a question on matrimonial law posed by the bishop of either Winchester or Worcester.

diocese of Worcester, was 'entirely contrary to the provisions of the sacred canons'; it was the bishop who realized that the older authorities did not form a sufficient basis for the enforcement of the canons in England in 1164. He was perhaps the first prelate who was both sufficiently interested in the enforcement of clerical celibacy, and sufficiently aware of the deficiencies of the existing law, to apply to the pope for a fresh ruling on the subject. He obtained from Alexander a crisp statement of the law, with an explicit order to enforce it in his diocese, and permission to override appeals in certain cases. *Inter cetera* is one of the earliest of the hundreds of decretal letters issued by Pope Alexander (always remembering the many undated letters); it is therefore in all probability one of the early examples of a movement of opinion in the church in England, which led increasingly to recourse to the pope as a means not only of settling legal uncertainties, but also of overcoming obstacles to the enforcement of the law. In this movement of opinion Roger was a leader, one of those whose example was followed by other English prelates, occasionally even in the difficult 1160s, and conspicuously in the 1170s and onwards.[11]

Inter cetera, though addressed in personal terms to a single bishop, ordering him to enforce the law in his diocese, passed into almost all the decretal collections up to Compilatio I, and the last section of it appears as X 1.17.3. The other sections, though they continued to circulate for some thirty years, were superseded by later decisions of Alexander III, many of which arose in their turn from further experience of reform and law-enforcement in England. This letter offers an example of the new law in the making. The pope does not move unprompted. He gives the bishop of Worcester the authority for which he asks; later he issues other letters modifying and refining the law

[11] Two letters to Bartholomew of Exeter may belong to the 1160s. One, Coll. I Alc. c. 77 (Morey, *Bartholomew of Exeter*, p. 133 no. 8) was probably issued before Simon Luvel became archdeacon of Worcester in 1167. A second, JL 13909+ 13916 + 13903, is referred in one collection to the register of the sixth year, Sept. 1164–Sept. 1165, but there are few genuine references to Pope Alexander's registers before 1167–8 (Holtzmann, 'Die Register', pp. 51–2). William bishop of Norwich received an important decretal letter, JL 12253 + 14356, before his death in Jan. 1174. Bishops had, of course, consulted popes before Alexander. Innocent II replied to Henry of Winchester about the divorce that led to the Anstey case (JL 8274), and Eugenius III replied in Nov. 1146 to five questions asked by Jocelin of Salisbury (Loewenfeld, *Epistolae pontificum*, p. 103).

and the rules governing the enforcement of the law. These later letters are sometimes issued in connection with a particular case (e.g. App. II, 87), sometimes at the request of individual prelates, occasionally at the request of a group of bishops, such as the suffragans of Canterbury and their archbishop. His various pronouncements circulate side by side for twenty or thirty years. Eventually it is not the pope, but the lawyers and scholars working on his rulings, who reduce them to order in systematic lawbooks.

The next dated letter of Alexander III to Bishop Roger, dealing with general legal questions, belongs in all probability to the period of the bishop's self-imposed exile. The pope responds to questions raised by Roger on the basis of his experience as diocesan and as judge-delegate in the four years before he left England as a gesture of support for his exiled archbishop. This long letter *Meminimus nos ex parte tua* may originally have been issued as two distinct documents, both despatched from Benevento in 1167 × 1169 (App. II, 63 and 91). Since they cannot be far separated in date, and it is uncertain which is the older, they may be treated as one for the present purpose. Unlike *Inter cetera*, which deals with related aspects of one problem, *Meminimus* replies to questions on a variety of unconnected topics. It provided nine chapters of *Extra* and in addition two of Compilatio I; in one decretal collection it is divided into no less than fourteen sections. It is worth noting at once that, in dealing with the bishop's questions, the pope never suggests that he should have known the answer already, or been able to deduce it for himself. This will not surprise those familiar with the decretals of the later twelfth century, but because of some old controversies in England on this point, it must be clearly stated. Pope Alexander was quite prepared to tell a correspondent that he should have known the answer to his own question: *scire debes*, he says to the dean of Chichester, who has raised a point of procedure relating to a boundary dispute.[12] But such occasions are extremely rare.

One group of problems dealt with in this letter arose, like *Inter cetera*, from the bishop's concern with the parish clergy of his diocese, and has therefore been discussed briefly in that

---

[12] JL 13845, X 2.19.3 with incorrect address and other variants.

connection.[13] Roger had complained 'about monks who exploit vicars of parish churches to such an extent that they cannot live decently or offer hospitality'. The pope's reply instructs the bishop not to admit a vicar presented by monks, unless enough of the benefice is assigned, in the bishop's presence, to the vicar to allow him to meet episcopal claims (*iura episcopalia ... persolvere*) and have a suitable and sufficient amount for himself (App. II, 63b). This instruction, like those of *Inter cetera*, was probably suggested by the bishop himself, because he wanted the support of papal authority for his work in his diocese. The pope met his problem by placing two restrictions on the right of monastic rectors to take for their own use the revenues of parish churches. The vicar must not be reduced to unseemly poverty, and the church must be able to make its contribution to the central organization of the diocese through its payment of episcopal dues. And the bishop shall decide whether these conditions have been met, since he is authorized to refuse to admit a fit clerk, presented by the true patron or corporate rector, unless a portion, which he judges suitable, has been assigned to the vicar. This was a new right, which had not before been explicitly defined. The bishop, taking his problems to the pope, has provoked the making of a new rule, required by the new conditions of his time. He was not the first bishop to observe the need to define a vicar's portion, but he was apparently the first to ask for a papal ruling on the matter.

It was, of course, only a first step. The new rule seems to envisage a fresh round of bargaining before each institution. But a portion once assigned and approved in the bishop's presence will have tended to become fixed and permanent, so that the rule was an important step towards the decision of Pope Innocent III that a perpetual vicarage was a benefice with a permanent endowment (X 1.3.27), and the decree (c. 32) of the Lateran Council of 1215, which required that a suitable portion of the revenues of all churches should be allotted to the resident priest.

But the new rule was not enough for Bishop Roger. He also obtained power to deal with underpaid vicars to whom his predecessors, or even he himself, had already committed the

---

[13] Above, p. 80.

cure of souls. The papal letter authorizes him to remove them, unless a sufficient *sustentatio* is assigned to them by the monks. Was this another draconian measure suggested by Bishop Roger? It amounted, like the order to remove priests' sons from benefices, to something very like retrospective legislation, and attracted the attention of a contemporary, who wrote one of the sparse glosses in Gilbert Foliot's decretal collection: 'Nota: sacerdotibus curam animarum auferre in penam monachorum'.[14] There seems to be no evidence that Roger or any of his episcopal contemporaries ever deposed a vicar or sequestrated a benefice in order to enforce the payment of a better *sustentatio* to a vicar, and this passage was omitted from the Decretals of 1234.

In addition to the question of vicarages, Bishop Roger raised the question of pensions paid or received from churches without the bishop's knowledge. The pope's reply (X 3.39.8) is not very lucid; the number of variant readings in early texts suggests that contemporaries found it unsatisfactory. But at least it contained a clear statement that 'simple priests and clerks cannot on their own authority bind their churches to make payments, especially after their own demise', thus making the consent of a superior essential for the establishment of a permanent right or liability. Possibly the full extent of this problem as it existed in England was not at that time appreciated at the Curia.

The bishops of the province of Canterbury returned to the matter in 1175, with a proposal that clerks should be forbidden to pay pensions secretly from their churches, in order that others should succeed them. No provincial canon was issued on this subject, probably because no existing canon or decree could be found to provide the required authority for it. A collective approach was then made to the pope, who addressed to the archbishop and his suffragans a letter (JL 13816) much longer, fuller, and more precise than the ruling sent to Bishop Roger, but building upon it. The new letter assumes that pensions paid from churches require the sanction of the diocesan, and orders bishops to take action without deferring to appeals against offenders who agreed to pay unauthorized pensions in order to

[14] Oxford, Bodl. MS E Mus. 249 fo. 123^r. Gloss to Coll. Belverensis 1.10b, cf. Duggan, *Collections*, p. 155.

obtain a benefice, or in order that their relatives might succeed them. The procedure is the procedure followed by Bishop Roger in 1164; the local problem is put to the pope, and a papal letter obtained containing a fresh statement of the law and an order to enforce it, with permission to override appeals in certain cases. Each time, it is local initiative that prompts the pope to issue a new formulation of the law. The motive behind this initiative is the desire of 'progressive' elements in the local church to have the authority of the pope behind them when attacking long-established local custom. For, in this matter of pensions, they were attacking local custom, no less than in the matter of clerical marriage and inheritance of benefices.

Returning to *Meminimus*, it will be noticed at once that the sections dealing with parish churches and the parish clergy form only a small part of the whole. Several sections deal with problems arising in connection with appeals and delegated jurisdiction. One of them shows that Bishop Roger had raised the question of appeals to the pope on very small matters. Such appeals had been admitted by the civil law (Cod. 7. 62. 20); the bishop would hardly have raised the matter if he had not hoped for some serious discussion of the possibility of restricting appeals on trivial questions and matters of small value. Some of the motives for this approach are obvious. As diocesan he will have found such appeals tiresome and frustrating; as judge-delegate he will have resented the trouble and expense involved in acting on commissions in these cases. And perhaps in these cases the advantage of the rich over the poor was most obvious, and the powerful litigant was most often to be seen oppressing the weak and the friendless.[15] King Henry II was said to have forbidden appeals, 'for the benefit of poor clerks', at about the same time that Bishop Roger was raising this question at Rome.[16] Was this a coincidence? Was the bishop trying to counter this particular criticism of the appeal system? Here, as so often, we suffer from having only one side of the correspondence; we do not know what the bishop proposed or what reasons

---

[15] Compare the story told by Caesarius of Heisterbach about a poor priest, who appeared before Pope Innocent III to defend his title to his one church against the claim of a rich pluralist. His success qualifies as a miracle. *Dialogus miraculorum*, ed. Joseph Strange (1851), I. 381, Dist. 6 cap. 29.
[16] M. Cheney, 'Alexander III and Roger of Worcester', p. 215.

he put forward. The idea of restricting appeals was not unreasonable. Some twenty years later Pope Gregory VIII issued a general constitution (JL 16056) forbidding appeals on small matters, and defining an alternative procedure. The elderly pope, who had been a cardinal since 1156, could have remembered the discussion on Bishop Roger's proposal. Pope Alexander, however, replied sharply, 'We wish you to understand that it is necessary to defer to appeals made upon trivial questions of any sort and any size, no less than to those concerning greater matters' (X 2.28.11). Though the Curia pronounces upon a problem only at the request of a correspondent, it will not, of course, invariably give the correspondent the answer he hopes for.

Two sections of *Meminimus* concern the interpretation of the words *appellatione remota* in commissions to judges-delegate. One is cast in personal form: 'If a case has been committed to you *appellatione remota*, and the defendant sets out for the apostolic see after the citation has been delivered, you may nonetheless proceed with the hearing *secundum iuris formam*, but if he sets out before citation, this does not apply' (X 2.28.9).[17] This ruling was evidently abused. The bishop of Durham found it necessary to ask for a further statement, and Pope Alexander defined the judges' right to proceed in certain circumstances, 'because the decretal letter by which such (fraudulent and malicious) appellants had seemed to be protected, was not made by us to cause injustice to anyone, but to remove injustice' (X 2. 28.15. The gloss cross-refers to the appropriate section of *Meminimus*). Again, the law is being refined on the basis of a dialogue between the pope and his delegates; the latter learn by hard experience the problems that need attention; the pope provides, or tries to provide, solutions.

In the second of these two sections, the ruling is expressed in general terms. The bishop has asked whether sentence must be deferred because of an appeal made, 'as often happens', upon a related question (*super incidenti questione*), although the case was committed *appellatione remota*. The pope rules that where a dispute arises on an *exceptio*, and this gives rise to an appeal, the judge-delegate must suspend his hearing on this point and, if

---

[17] The translation is based on early texts of the letter, such as Belverensis 1.10e, printed in *Gilberti epistolae*, ii. 99. The text of X has been reworked at the end.

the principal issue cannot be settled without it, decision on this too must be suspended; only if the defendant appeals on the basis of a falsehood can the judge proceed to a decision (X 2.28.10). This ruling was important because, as the bishop had discovered, judges-delegate were often faced with this problem, which could not be avoided when the Curia issued commissions at the petition of one party in the absence of the other.

As a result, this is one of the rare definitions of Pope Alexander III which can be proved to have been cited in the courts at an early date. There are two references to it in the 'register' of Master David of London.[18] One occurs in a report to Pope Alexander from Thomas, prior of Dunstable, who records that in the course of a protracted dispute before judges-delegate between William, a clerk, and the nuns of Ickleton about the church of Fowlmere, William has appealed, and proves that his appeal must be admitted 'on the authority of a certain decretal letter of yours to the Lord Bishop of Worcester, in which decretal letter it is stated that where an appeal is interposed *super incidenti questione*, the hearing of the principal matter must be suspended'. This report must be dated 1174 × 1179.[19] The second reference occurs in a report to Alexander from the bishop of London upon a case committed to him *appellatione remota*. The case is returned to the pope, because there has been an appeal *super incidenti questione*, and the bishop judges that such an appeal must be admitted. Though this report cannot be dated more closely than 1162 × 1181, and though there is no explicit mention of the decretal, its appearance in Master David's 'register' immediately before the letter of the prior of Dunstable must suggest that David had an interest in both cases, perhaps acting as advocate and using the ruling of the decretal in both for the benefit of his clients. Practical necessity in the courts caused the bishop to ask his question, and practical necessity in the courts caused it to be noted, circulated and put into effect.

---

[18] Liverani, *Spicilegium*, pp. 762, 640; better edition of the second report in *Letters of Foliot*, pp. 319–21. On Master David's register, Vat. lat. 6024 fos. 140–54, see Z. N. Brooke, 'The register of Master David'. This article is indispensable for users of Liverani's edition, which has many errors, and rearranges the letters according to the supposed authors.

[19] The former archdeacon of Poitiers is now bishop of Winchester (cons. 6 Oct. 1174), and Bishop Roger is living.

Just how quickly these rulings became known, in England and elsewhere, is a nice question. In 1177, Richard, bishop of Winchester, put to the pope just the same problem about the appeal on a *questio incidens*, and received a reply giving the same ruling in different words (1 Comp. 2.20.34, JL 15152). The bishop of Winchester and his clerks presumably did not know of the ruling given to Bishop Roger. Another question also arises: would the pope and his legal experts have drafted a fresh statement, if they had remembered the existence of the earlier one?

Still dealing with the process of appeal and delegation, a further section of *Meminimus* defines the effect of the insertion of a time-limit in a commission to judges-delegate (1 Comp. 1.21.12). A very similar ruling had been addressed in 1165 to William, bishop-elect of Chartres (X 1.29.4); it must be supposed that Bishop Roger did not know of it, and again the question arises, whether the earlier ruling was remembered, or recorded in writing, at the Curia.

Diocesan administration and judicial appeals by no means exhaust the topics touched upon in this letter. Two sections concern matrimonial problems. One turns on the precise point at which a promise to become a monk becomes binding and so invalidates a subsequent marriage (X 4.6.3). Another concerns 'a parishioner of yours', who has committed incest (1 Comp. 4.20.6). In this second enquiry, the bishop was drawing attention to a tricky point of law, and Pope Alexander's ruling did not satisfy Pope Innocent III, who deliberately took a different line from that expressed 'a quodam predecessore nostro . . . in simili casu' (X 4.13.6). The difference of opinion between the popes underlines the acumen of the bishop of Worcester, who first raised the issue.

Three final sections of *Meminimus* concern the validity of grants and charters. One deals with grants made by 'an abbot of your diocese' which are later denounced by some of the convent. Here the pope instructs the bishop, in effect, to use his own judgement, taking into account the size of the grant and local custom, always provided that custom does not clearly (*manifeste*) run counter to the canons (X 3.24.3). Grants made by the heads of religious houses, without the formal consent of the whole convent, were a not uncommon cause of disputes; the bishop of Worcester may have had a personal interest in the matter because of its bearing on his attempt to reclaim the church of his episcopal manor of Bibury, granted irregularly by Bishop John of Pagham to Osney Abbey (App. II, 36). A further section declared that a grant made to a monastery cannot be rescinded even if a condition stated in the grant was not fulfilled, unless the grant spelled out that failure to meet the condition would involve cancellation (X 4.5.9). The final section ruled, in more cautious terms than usual, upon the evidential value of charters (*scripta autentica*) of which the witnesses are dead. 'It does not seem to us,' the pope says, 'that they have any force, unless by chance they have been drawn up by a notary (*per manum publicam*) ... or have an authentic seal by which they can be tested' (X 2.22.2). The bishop had put his finger on a problem common throughout Europe, in this period of transition from Germanic to Roman, or romanized, law. Pope Alexander's ruling was quoted by Innocent III in connection with an Italian case.[20] The pope evidently knew that it would only be 'by chance' that the bishop of Worcester would encounter a notarial act in England, where the authentic seal took the place of the notarial instrument. It would be interesting to know whether the pope or the bishop imported into the discussion the reference to the deed drawn up *per manum publicam*.

Meminimus was issued in September 1167 × 1169. Just as *Inter cetera* seems to be among the earliest decretals of its kind, and indeed of any kind, addressed to an English prelate by Alexander III, so *Meminimus* is among the earliest of the 'multiple-subject' decretals, which dealt with a group of unrelated legal and procedural problems. So many decretals are undated that precision is impossible, but the evidence suggests that, while Italian prelates were eliciting such decretals in the 1160s,[21] very few were addressed to English prelates, or to any prelates north of the Alps, before *Meminimus*. By contrast, there are at least some thirteen such decretals addressed to English prelates by Pope Alexander in or after 1171; together,

[20] H. Bresslau, *Handbuch der Urkundenlehre* (Berlin 2nd ed. 1912–31, reprint 1958), i. 656–8.
[21] For letters to Italian recipients see W. Holtzmann, 'Kanonistische Ergänzungen zur Italia Pontificia', *QFIAB*, xxxvii, xxxviii (1956–7), also printed separately with different pagination (1959). For letters to English prelates see above, p. 171, n. 11.

these letters account for some one hundred chapters of the new law. The bishop of Worcester, perhaps again in common with Bartholomew of Exeter, seems in this matter also to have been in the forefront of a movement of some importance in the history of the canon law.

Two further decretals, each replying to two unrelated questions, were addressed by Pope Alexander to Bishop Roger, in answer to his requests for definition of the law. One of these (App. II, 54), like *Meminimus*, belongs to the long period of Roger's absence from his diocese, according to the entry in the lost manuscript of the *Appendix Concilii Lateranensis*. The editions deriving from this lost text give this letter the inscription *Idem Wigornien' episcopo in 12 libro Registr'*, which should indicate the register of Alexander's twelfth year, 20 September 1170 to 19 September 1171. The bishop himself visited the pope before Easter 1171, as one of the group sent to negotiate for the king after the murder of the archbishop, but the decretal makes it clear that he did not put his questions personally. 'This question,' it says, 'was laid before us on your behalf', just as *Meminimus* begins, 'We remember that we received the following question on your behalf' (*ex parte tua*). The bishop had asked whether monks might bring complaints against their abbot. The pope replies that, although monks may not bring complaints against other persons, they may bring an accusation against their abbot unless there is some reasonable and obvious impediment, and, since they have nothing of their own, their necessary expenses must be allowed by the monastery.

The bishop's question may have been prompted by the beginning of proceedings against the abbot-elect of St Augustine's, Canterbury (App. II, 33). The problem was not uncommon. Accusations were made later against the abbot of Malmesbury (App. II, 14) and, at an uncertain date, against the bishop of Norwich, himself a monk, by the monks of his cathedral priory (App. II, 101). The second question concerned the status of papal confirmations, and to this the pope's answer was sharp and clear. 'We wish you to understand,' he says, 'that judgement may not be given against the terms of confirmations by the Roman pontiffs, unless a fresh mandate has been obtained, or it is certain that the confirmation was obtained by fraud.' The significance of this ruling (X 2.30.2) has perhaps been insufficiently stressed. By this date, all major religious houses and corporations, and very many minor ones, had obtained at least one papal confirmation of their possessions; the ruling meant that any claim to property or rights named in a confirmation had to be taken for judgement by papal authority. The effect of the ruling can be observed in the story of the bishop's efforts (mentioned above) to reclaim the church of Bibury, which had been named in a papal privilege for the abbey of Osney (App. II, 36).

The second of the two-part decretals, *Ad aures nostras* (App. II, 8), addressed to Bishop Roger, has no dating clause and no register-reference in any of the surviving collections. It was very probably issued before 1175, since it occurs in two collections which contain no material certainly later than the summer of 1174,[22] and since, as will shortly appear, it was perhaps issued before the Council of Westminster of May 1175. Both sections of this letter reply in personal form to the bishop's questions. The first deals with a matrimonial problem. A subject of the bishop has put away his wife and 'joined to himself' a relative of hers. When the first woman brought a complaint against him, the existence of the marriage was proved by witnesses. But the man, wishing to remain with the second woman, appealed to the pope. The bishop does not seem to have deferred to the appeal; nothing suggests that the man has appeared before the pope. Instead, the pope instructs the bishop on the action to be taken. If the two women are very closely related, 'you shall separate him from both, all right of appeal and contradiction being denied, and cause him to remain for ever without hope of marriage. If it is proved that they are related only in the third degree or less closely, you shall compel him to leave the second woman, and having imposed fit penance for his action, you shall bind him to receive the first woman as his wife and to treat her in future with marital affection.' It will be observed that only in the first situation was the right of appeal withdrawn. This may have been the aspect of the matter that particularly interested the bishop. At the time of the provincial council of Westminster, a proposal was made that appeals should not be allowed in cases where men had left their wives for other women,

---

[22] Below, pp. 201–2.

and tried to protect themselves against correction by this means. The proposal seems to have been referred to the pope, and accepted by him in a decretal addressed to the archbishop of Canterbury and his suffragans (JL 13823). It seems unlikely that the bishop would have written, and the pope replied as he did, after that acceptance.

In the second part of this letter, the pope defines the bishop's right to let newly cleared land on his episcopal estates to hereditary rent-paying tenants, normally those who had cleared the land, or their descendants (X 3.13.7). This apparently simple question touched on the larger issue of a prelate's right to alienate, in one way or another, the property of his bishopric. The crux of the matter lay in the words *hereditario iure*. Churches in England had been leasing land for centuries, sometimes for as long a term as three lives,[23] but a fully hereditary tenure constituted, in effect, a permanent leasehold, and therefore fell under the ancient ban on alienation of church property, in which, using the terms of the civil law, *emphyteusis perpetuum contractum* was specifically condemned. Bartholomew of Exeter had occasion to consult the pope on a related problem, because some canons of Exeter had let church lands in perpetuity. Pope Alexander authorized him to have the leases revoked; their impropriety is assumed without discussion.[24] Archbishop Thomas had made enemies, even before his dispute with the king, because he assumed that it was his right and duty to reclaim lands let by his predecessors. Perhaps this episode prompted the bishop of Worcester to ask for clarification of the law, at least as regards essarts, in which he had a particular interest as his estates contained large areas of woodland. The survey of his estates made *c.* 1167 shows that he had already let assarts for money rents, but does not show whether they were let *hereditario iure*.[25]

In addition to these letters, in which the pope replied to questions posed by the bishop, there is one (App. II, 36), probably issued in 1172 or 1173, which replies not to a request for a legal definition but to a lost letter of complaint from the

---

[23] R. V. Lennard, *Rural England, 1086–1135* (Oxford 1959), p. 159.
[24] X 3.13.9 = JL 17624, wrongly ascribed to Pope Celestine III.
[25] For Archbishop Thomas, *MTB*, iii. 250–2. For Bishop Roger, *Red Book of Worcester*, p. 357.

bishop about the pope's handling of the dispute, which has been mentioned already, between Worcester Cathedral and Osney Abbey about the church of Bibury. The greater part of the papal letter consists of an account of the past history of the case and a request to the bishop to give up the church 'divino intuitu et pro reverentia beati Petri'. Such a request was regarded by contemporary canonists as tantamount to a command, but the pope admitted that 'according to the rigour of the law' the grant made by Roger's predecessor to Osney, and confirmed by Pope Eugenius, was invalid if it was made despite the opposition of his chapter. This pronouncement soon found a place in decretal collections; its swift appearance illustrates the way in which collectors seized upon every scrap of useful material in their efforts to build up a new law-book out of recent papal pronouncements, and the various pressures that stimulated definition of the law. It may be significant that a papal letter of great interest to the bishop of Worcester and his clerks found its way quickly into collections of Pope Alexander's rulings. This point must be considered later in this chapter, when other evidence is discussed which bears on the question of the bishop's possible share in the formation of decretal collections.

Very few papal letters to Bishop Roger appear to have been prompted by a request by him for a ruling on a point of law or procedure arising in the course of a case committed to him as judge-delegate. One such ruling, issued in 1177, dealt with the case, surely most exceptional, of two clerks who had both been properly instituted to the same benefice at the presentation of the abbess of St Mary's, Winchester (App. II, 30). Master Nicholas had been presented by the abbess, 'the convent not objecting'; Master Herbert had been presented later, with the assent of the convent. The pope's ruling on the case joined his letter concerning Bibury to form the nucleus of a *titulus* in the systematic collections: 'De his que fiunt a prelato sine consensu capituli'.

Two further mandates may perhaps have arisen from requests for instructions about the handling of cases in progress. Each was addressed to the bishop of Worcester as one of a pair of judges-delegate; neither makes it clear how the matter had come to the pope's notice. Each is concerned with a case on the borderline between ecclesiastical and secular jurisdiction—one with the procedure to be followed in dealing with a clerk suspected of murder, and one with a dispute over patronage, which had already been taken to a royal court. The first mandate (App. II, 86) cannot be dated more closely than to the period of Roger's episcopate. Its assumption that the case will be dealt with by the church may possibly mean that it belongs to the period after the settlement between the king and the papal legate, Hugh Pierleone, in 1176, when the church established its right to deal with clerks accused of crimes other than forest offences. The procedure that lay behind the issuing of this letter is obscure; there is no reference to an earlier commission, or to a request from the bishops for instructions, nor yet to a complaint by an interested party. The two bishops may have asked for advice, and so elicited this ruling, knowing that it would be convenient to cite a papal decision in the event of a clash with the lay power. The ruling was copied only in Anglo-Norman decretal collections, and one or two that are closely related to them; it was not received into Compilatio I or *Extra*. It must have had some local importance for a limited time, but it made no contribution to the definitive form of the law.

The second mandate (App. II, 68) has been mentioned already in connection with disputed jurisdiction in patronage cases. Here again, the judges may have consulted the pope, in order to be sure of papal support in any clash of jurisdiction. This mandate had even less effect on the final formulation of the law than the letter on the case of the suspected murderer. It must have been preserved at Worcester, and copied there into *collectio Wigorniensis*, but it is found in no other surviving collection. In spite of the many uncertainties surrounding these two papal letters, the interesting possibility seems to arise from them that English bishops in the 1170s were determined not to make the same mistake as Archbishop Thomas. There was to be no local crusade for ecclesiastical liberty and jurisdiction; whatever steps they took in that direction, they would take only with the explicit support of the pope, and at his order.

These few letters provide almost the only evidence to show Bishop Roger voluntarily consulting the pope about a case in progress. One or two others might at first seem to arise from such action, but on investigation they can be shown to concern matters that had by their nature to be referred to the Curia, such as forgery of a papal commission (App. II, 84) or the issue of conflicting commissions to different sets of judges, ordering them to deal with the same case (App. II, 49, 62).

Papal pronouncements addressed to bishop Roger at the request of litigants

Many commissions addressed to the bishop of Worcester, as to other judges, do, of course, contain instructions on procedure or, less often, definitions of the law. This is why they were preserved by the decretal collectors, and are consequently known to us. But it must never be assumed that these instructions and definitions were issued at the request of the judge-delegate, unless this is explicitly stated for, in almost all cases, the involvement of the judge began only when the litigant appeared and presented the commission. Nor should it be assumed that the instructions and definitions were inserted spontaneously by the Curia. In many commissions it is obvious, and in some it is actually stated, that the insertion has been made at the request of the litigant or his representative, because it will operate to his advantage. The bishops of Exeter and Worcester received a commission ordering them to send clerks to the homes of witnesses, if any are old or ill, or if Nicholas, being poor, cannot afford to transport them to the judges' presence (App. II, 81). It is a safe assumption that Nicholas prompted this instruction, and that this statement, which passed in an altered form into the decretals of 1234, was formulated for the benefit of a priest's son, whose father had paid a fourfold increase in the pension due from his church, so that his son might succeed him, evading the canons against hereditary succession. In another case, the same bishops were instructed that witnesses, lay or clerical, named by a litigant, should, if necessary, be compelled to give evidence (App. II, 92). Nothing is known of the circumstances in which this order (if genuine) was issued; it must be assumed that it was formulated at the request of the litigant in special conditions which justified the use of compulsion, e.g. intimidation of witnesses by the other party. Similarly the bishop of Worcester and the archbishop of Canterbury were politely instructed (*non lateat prudentia vestra*) that canons of Plympton should not be excluded from giving evidence in a case concerning their church merely because they were canons, unless there was some other lawful impediment (App. II, 37). The pope assumes that the judges are competent to decide what constitutes a lawful impediment; the instruction was obviously added to the end of the long commission at the prompting of the *nuntius* of the canons. In the course of the dispute between St Albans and Durham over Tynemouth Priory, St Albans seems twice to have obtained supplementary mandates to judges-delegate on points of procedure. One instructed the bishop of Worcester and his fellow judges to ensure that the monks of Durham entered upon the case with the authority and consent of their bishop, so that if St Albans won the bishop would not be able to reopen the matter (App. II, 18). At an earlier stage, the bishop of Exeter and his colleagues had been ordered to receive monks of St Albans to give evidence; the problem was very similar to that in the Plympton case. But on this occasion the wording of the mandate suggests that the pope, or the draughtsman, regarded the instruction as superfluous and perhaps offensive, and therefore took the trouble to explain to the judges that the instruction was sent at the request of the abbot and monks of St Albans, 'although we know that you are endowed with such learning and discretion that you would have no doubt as to what witnesses you ought to admit'.[26]

In all these cases it is certain or highly probable that instructions on procedural matters, some of which passed into the authoritative *Liber Extra*, were formulated at the request of litigants. The same is probably true of an important ruling on tithe-law, contained in a commission to the bishops of Exeter and Worcester (App. II, 34, and p. 138 above). There is no suggestion that the judges have been involved in the case before, or that the erring villagers were *parrochiani* of either bishop. The commission must have been obtained by the parson of Horton, and the rule defined for his benefit.

It has been necessary to insist at some length that papal statements on law and procedure in commissions addressed to the bishop of Worcester were only on relatively few occasions

[26] *PUE*, iii. 338 no. 203.

elicited by a request from him for a ruling on a point upon which he felt uncertain. This necessity arises because the influences that lay behind Pope Alexander's pronouncements were more subtle and more varied than a superficial study might suggest, and because only a close examination of each text reveals the subjects on which the recipients of the pope's letters had themselves drawn attention to problems of law or procedure arising in the course of a case. Common sense would suggest that messengers were not lightly despatched in the middle of a case on a journey that could hardly take less than three months and might well take six, and on a few occasions the bishop of Worcester is to be observed solving his problems by other means. In his early days, he settles a difficulty by consulting his fellow bishops, who happen to be meeting conveniently nearby (App. I, 16). On another occasion he takes the law into his own hands, granting longer delays than the 'laws and the canons' allow, and does not consider it necessary to justify himself when reporting on the case to the pope (App. II, 62). On a case concerning the abbey of Bury St Edmund, he consults *iurisperiti* on the propriety of awarding costs against a defendant who has ignored the first, non-peremptory, citations, and takes action accordingly (App. I, 6).

A request for a papal ruling

This last case proved to be a particularly intractable one, and the question of costs was only the beginning of the judges' problems. By a lucky chance, some of the cause papers must have been deposited at, or copied for, the abbey, and were later entered into a cartulary, long after they can have been of any practical use. Among them is a copy of a report to the pope from Bishop Roger (App. I, 6), the single survivor of many that he must have sent when cases were removed from his hearing by a fresh appeal to Rome. The report and the related documents are interesting for the light they throw on relations between pope and bishop, and the way in which information and questions on legal matters reached the Curia.

To explain the situation, the case must be very briefly described. The abbot and convent of Bury were suing Thomas, dean of Colchester, to recover pensions alleged to be due to the abbey from two churches. They had obtained a commission to Bishop Roger and Simon, abbot of St Albans, ordering them to remove Thomas from the churches if he would not obey the judges. As we have seen, Thomas did not respond to the first citations, and was condemned to pay the monks' costs. The bishop then arranged for the churches to be sequestrated, but after a few days Thomas's brother William intervened and the sequestration was interrupted. William asserted that he, not Thomas, was parson of the two churches, and appealed, claiming the usual protection, while Thomas claimed that he himself was both patron and William's vicar, appealing to both pope and king. Thomas then appeared before the judges, appealed and departed, though appeal was forbidden in the commission. An attempt to put the monks in possession *causa custodie* (in another text *causa rei servande*) was thwarted by William *manu armata* (App. I, 5, 6). When the diocesan tried to hold an enquiry in the local chapter, Thomas appealed again, and proceedings were suspended. The bishop had felt competent to settle the award of costs against the defendant for non-appearance, but now a more serious problem had arisen. Proceedings had been opened against one man, generally accepted as the parson, but, when the judges-delegate began to take action against him, another man claimed that he was the parson, and that the action constituted an injury to himself, against which he appealed. Was the appeal valid? Who should punish such fraud, the delegates or the Ordinary? On these questions the opinion of the higher judge was required. At the same time the brethren of Bury may have felt it necessary to send a representative to appear before the pope at the term appointed by their opponents; the bishop's report may have been designed to serve two purposes, to support the abbey's case and to convey his questions.

Since he has to describe the course of the case, the bishop reports his decision in the matter of costs, and the reasons for it. He wished, he says, 'to meet by a new remedy the subterfuges which are frequently practised in our parts owing to the malice of litigants'. His words underline the fact that he is making an innovation; he is searching for a *new* remedy. He has consulted legal experts, asking them by what right (or on what authority, *qua ratione*) is it possible to punish the contempt of persons cited by apostolic authority, who fail to appear in court before the peremptory edict? The experts agreed that such persons should be condemned to pay expenses, 'so that they may not appear to ignore with impunity citations made by apostolic authority'. Bishop Roger supports this opinion with a statement of his own view: 'unless a penalty is inflicted for contempt, their impunity will make others think it a matter of no importance to show contempt for the first and second citations, and to weary ourselves and the plaintiffs to no purpose'. On this point, the bishop does not ask the pope for a ruling, but informs him about local conditions and local opinions, in the confident manner of one expert addressing another on a subject of concern to both.

But on the intervention of the third party, his appeal, and the respective duties of the diocesan and the judge-delegate, a ruling from the pope was to be desired, and the bishop asks for a suitable rescript, distilling from his account of the case the question of principle that it has revealed.

> In this way (he says) our jurisdiction has been eluded, and the rights of the brethren of St Edmund remain in suspense. Therefore, Holy Father, lest we should be wearied yet longer in acting upon your mandates, by the perversity of such malignant men, will you please instruct us by a rescript *sub certa forma* whether action should be taken by delegated authority or by the judge ordinary, to repress the presumption of those who do not claim to be parsons or *domini* before the beginning of proceedings about a church or possession, and who do not assert their claim even when proceedings are begun in their presence, or to their knowledge, against a third party. Then, when the third party is about to receive an unfavourable sentence, or has already lost possession by judgement, then at last they assert that they are parsons or *domini*, and protect themselves by appeal, so that he who triumphs by judgement cannot be put in possession, and the sentence pronounced by apostolic authority cannot be duly enforced.

Here the single text of the report ends; it can hardly have been despatched to the pope without at least some respectful conclusion. No reply has been identified. It is typical of the fragmentary state of the evidence that in this solitary case, where the text survives of a letter from Bishop Roger to Pope Alexander asking for a ruling, the pope's reply is lost. Possibly the report was not dispatched. However that may be, the bishop's letter lifts for a moment the veil of obscurity which conceals the antecedents of most of Alexander's decretals. Here the whole process is laid out; the commission, the early difficulties, the consultation between the judge and his legal advisers, the further problems, and finally the appeal to Rome. This appeal, if prosecuted, removes the case to the Curia, and makes it necessary to report the early stages of the case; at the same time it provides the opportunity to stress the problems that have arisen, and to ask for a definition that will regulate such problems in future.

Contacts with the pope

Bishop Roger's other reports to the pope will have conveyed similar information, and sometimes similar requests; a much employed judge-delegate was in a favourable position to present his own view of the needs and conditions of the church in his area. The extent of this correspondence should not be underestimated. Even the fragmentary surviving evidence preserves two further reports from the bishop (App. I, 16, 61), and references to at least six others, of which the text is lost, but which formed the basis for action by the Curia in the next stage of the case.[27]

Only a part, and not necessarily the major part, of the bishop's contact with the pope arose from his work as judge-delegate and from his desire for rulings on legal and procedural problems. As diocesan, he must also have sent a steady flow of letters, for various purposes, addressed to the head of the church. These letters, like the reports on delegated cases, provided the Curia with information on local conditions, and enabled the writer to express his own opinions. Sometimes he writes because his own interests are affected, as in the dispute over Bibury church, and in connection with litigation between third parties about a chapel in his diocese which is alleged to be dependent on a church in the diocese of Coventry (App. II, 49B). Sometimes he writes about appeals arising in the diocese, as in the case of a vicar who demanded a larger portion (App. II, 49C), or a case in which one of his subjects is involved, as when the abbey of Gloucester is sued by a lay nobleman about the patronage of churches in another diocese (App. I, 24). This last case is a nice example of the way in which routine business enabled a bishop to express his own views. The letter in question

---

[27] App. II, 49, 55, 60, 62, 84, also *Oseney cart.*, ii. 226.

was written in 1173 in support of the abbey, which was defending its right to the patronage of two churches, claimed by the owner of the estate in which they lay. They had been given long ago to the abbey, as the bishop explained, before the father of the present lord received the estate from the king; but in spite of the lapse of time and the change of ownership, the present lord felt, as many others felt at this time, that the churches were an integral, inseparable, part of the estate, and that the previous holder had no power to grant them away for ever. He had pursued his claim in the ecclesiastical courts, and had now taken the case by appeal to the pope himself. So the abbey obtained a letter of support from its diocesan, among others, and preserved a copy of it in its archives. The bishop reported the facts, enclosed copies of relevant charters, and then issued a warning.

Let your judgement, Holy Father, weigh carefully, whether at every change of individual lords, which happens very often in human life, that which is known to have been once reasonably ordained, and strengthened with episcopal and royal confirmation, ought to be overthrown and invalidated at the will of a layman, particularly when the grant has been made to a religious house.

About two years later, Pope Alexander issued a commission to Bishop Roger about a case concerning the priory of Lanthony, in which just the same principle was at stake. In this commission the pope enunciates the rule that 'it seems entirely absurd, and ought to be entirely eliminated from the church of God, that at each individual change of patrons according to human condition, the ordinations of churches should be changed' (App. II, 72). The similar sentiments and the rather similar phrases of the bishop's letter to the pope, and the pope's letter to the bishop, must attract attention. Perhaps Roger had written in support of Lanthony in terms resembling those of his earlier support for Gloucester; at any rate, the coincidence serves as a reminder that in many matters, and particularly matters concerning local custom of landholding and property rights, the considered opinion of the local prelate formed the essential basis for wise judgement in the Curia. The coincidence also suggests that a ruling, which passed into the Decretals of 1234 and became the law of the church, may have been prompted by an opinion expressed by Bishop Roger.

This short examination of decretals addressed to Bishop Roger has hardly touched the interest of these texts for the history of canonistic doctrines, but it suffices to illustrate the process of stimulus from the province and response from the centre which underlay the formulation by Pope Alexander of the statements which were used to form a substantial part of the new, post-Gratian, law of the church. In this process, the bishop was remarkable because of the number of important rulings issued in answer to his requests, and because of the early date of some of these decretals; this evidence suggests that he was more alert than most of his contemporaries in England to the deficiencies of the existing law, and more inclined to refer to the pope for definition of legal uncertainties. It also suggests that he was more seriously concerned than many of his fellow-bishops about the customary non-enforcement of the reforming canons of the preceding century, many of which had made little impact in England. Here, too, he led and others followed. It has been shown that frequent employment as a papal judge-delegate will have given him numerous opportunities to discover the weak points in the law, and in the rules relating to delegated jurisdiction, and also frequent opportunities to supply general information about English conditions, and opinions about English needs. At the same time this employment accounts for the numerous commissions addressed to him, which were preserved because they contained useful statements on legal matters. Though Bishop Roger was outstanding in these respects, and perhaps especially influential because of his noble birth and royal connections, his singularity must not be exaggerated. At most points his colleague, Bartholomew of Exeter, is to be found pursuing the same policies, and exercising similar influence, though he does not seem to have acted quite so often as a judge, or begun to refer legal problems to the pope quite so early in his episcopate. It may be assumed that there was collaboration and mutual influence between these two men who had many experiences and many friends in common, but on this subtle personal matter no certain information can be found in the surviving sources.

Even deeper obscurity surrounds the relationship between Archbishop Richard and these two, though Dr Duggan drew attention to the number of papal letters addressed to him, and suggested that the three might be pursuing a common policy.²⁸ Richard took up energetically the work of reform barely begun by Archbishop Thomas, and pursued by Bishops Roger and Bartholomew from 1164 onwards. He also took up the policy of requesting papal rulings to support local reforms, to an extent unheard of among archbishops of Canterbury in the past, and seldom equalled in the future.²⁹ At the same time, letters on reform apparently ceased to be requested by the bishops of Exeter and Worcester individually, which may indicate that they were now acting in concert with the archbishop. Perhaps they took the view that papal letters giving orders for the whole province of Canterbury were likely to have greater impact than letters addressed to individual prelates.

PART II: THE 'ENGLISH' CONTRIBUTION

The problems

Lack of evidence makes it impossible to pursue the question of influence further, to discover who led, who followed, how many prelates were involved, and the extent to which a consistent and concerted policy was being followed. But the obvious influence of these men on the formulation of Pope Alexander's decretals prompts some further questions. Roger, Bartholomew, Richard, and in the 1170s many of their Anglo-Norman colleagues, elicited many papal rulings, received many commissions as judges-delegate. By what process did these rulings and commissions come to be circulated, collected, and eventually to form a large part of the new law? More specifically, did Anglo-Norman prelates and lawyers, such as these bishops and their clerks, have any hand in the process? And how did it come about that more than half (363 out of 713) of Pope Alexander's surviving decretals—his statements preserved for their legal interest—seem to have been addressed to English prelates?[30]

---

[28] Duggan, *Collections*, pp. 149–50.
[29] Fifteen such rulings are listed in JL between nos. 13802 and 13823 inclusive, and this is not the total.
[30] The figures are given by Holtzmann and Kemp, pp. xvi–xvii, and Duggan, *Collections*, p. 7.

It must be said at once that at the present time these questions cannot be answered with any precision, in spite of much patient labour by many scholars. Nothing is known about the part played by any individual in collecting and arranging the pronouncements of Pope Alexander, before the early thirteenth century, with the single exception of Bernard of Pavia. Bernard completed his Breviarium (later called Compilatio I) early in the 1190s. His fame arose from the use of the Breviarium as a text for teaching at Bologna, and the adoption of his method and arrangement by Peter of Benevento in 1210 for his compilation of decretals of Pope Innocent III; it was only at that time that what had been fluid, experimental and variable hardened into a fixed form, decisive for the future. But Bernard used the large decretal collections assembled by earlier workers; it was the arrangement, not the content, of his book that was original. Already in those earlier collections the massive 'English' contribution to the new law was evident; the origin and significance of that contribution must be studied primarily on the basis of those earlier collections.

On the formation of those collections, the literary sources are silent. This is not surprising, for the habit of copying and passing on important papal rulings was an old one; what was new was the accelerating growth in the number of recent decretals in circulation, and the accelerating shift in emphasis from the old law to the new. These changes roused baffled alarm in conservative minds. In the 1190s Stephen, bishop of Tournai, complained to the reigning pope about the 'impenetrable forest of decretals', supposedly of Pope Alexander, which were being cited in the courts while the older canons were despised and rejected; he suspected that some were concocted by 'advocates and hirelings in their chambers'.[31] Stephen did not take part in the new movement; he did not, it seems, ask for rulings from the pope, nor are commissions addressed to him preserved in decretal collections. In these respects he presents a sharp contrast to Archbishop Richard of Canterbury and Bishops Bartholomew and Roger. He shows too a distrust of the decretal collections; the material they contain may be produced fraudulently by advocates. Perhaps it is significant that he thinks of

[31] PL 211 col. 516–17, ep. 251; J. Desilve, *Lettres d'Étienne de Tournai*, p. 345, ep. 274.

advocates in this connection. Perhaps too it is significant that the decretalists of Bologna, who in the thirteenth century sometimes remark on the work of their predecessors, have nothing to say about anyone before Bernard of Pavia. Was this because the early stages of the collecting process were not centred on Bologna, but took place to a large extent elsewhere?

The silence of the literary sources on the subjects of this enquiry forces the enquirer to use other evidence. The first line of approach must be on the basis of general considerations: who wanted Pope Alexander's legal and procedural rulings? and why? Who wanted and needed collections of those rulings? These considerations can be illustrated from the material relating to Bishop Roger. The second line of approach is through the canonistic writings of the period, including the decretal collections themselves. Here two problems arise. As regards the collections, the surviving texts are probably only a small fraction of those that once existed, so that the chain of development and filtration is obscure at the most critical points. Even the surviving collections have not yet all been edited or analysed in print. As regards the other canonist writings, including the glosses to the collections themselves, many await thorough study and modern editions; as this laborious and highly technical work proceeds, new light may be thrown upon the history of the collections and perhaps on their makers. In these conditions and in the present context, all that can usefully be attempted will be to bring together such evidence on Bishop Roger and his circle as seems to have a bearing on the matter, and to draw attention to a few relevant points arising from examination of some early decretal collections, especially those which seem to have some connection with him or with Worcester.

Reforms and the making of law

We have seen that the bishop was one of a group of active and influential churchmen—the *potiores* of his time, in the words of Giraldus—who were determined to promote reforms in the church in England. The desired reforms were many and various, but broadly speaking they had two main objectives, improvement of the quality of the parish clergy, and reduction of lay control over the churchmen and spiritual matters. Pursuit of the first objective led to the drive to enforce the canons on clerical celibacy and inheritance of benefices, and also to enlarge the powers of bishops over their clerical subjects. Pursuit of the second led to the attempt to limit and control the exercise of patronage, to resist the claims of the royal courts in matters of jurisdiction, and to offer an acceptable and efficient alternative jurisdiction under the authority of the papacy.

These special interests of English prelates are reflected in the distribution of Pope Alexander's decretals to English addressees. If we take as a basis for enquiry the so-called *Appendix Concilii Lateranensis*, an early systematic decretal collection,[32] with undeniable English connections if not certain English origin, it will be found that there is a marked concentration of 'English' decretals in precisely these areas. In Part 18, on married clergy, eleven out of fifteen chapters go to English addressees; in Part 19, on priests' sons, all ten; on patronage, twenty-five out of twenty-six; on vicars, possibly all six; on benefices all five; on legitimacy, all five. On appeals, the preponderance is not quite so marked, since twenty out of thirty-two go to England; but on judges-delegate there are eighteen out of twenty-two; on the interpretation of rescripts all nine, on sentences all five, on exceptions all three, on spoliation (the ecclesiastical parallel to disseisin), six out of nine (five of these were addressed to the bishop of Worcester). By contrast, on burial rights one chapter out of five goes to England, on usury four out of ten, on simony, six out of eighteen, and in the two marriage sections, three out of ten and sixteen out of thirty-three. These figures have been produced without a complete check on the textual history of every decretal, but the margin of error is probably quite small; there is no reason to mistrust the picture the figures present, and its indication of the subjects that most interested English prelates and lawyers in the time of Pope Alexander.

Because the interests of these prelates were primarily active, pastoral and judicial and not academic, Gratian's Decretum, which they knew, did not meet their needs as it met the didactic

---

[32] Systematic, for this purpose, means arranged according to subject-matter. On this collection see Duggan, *Collections, passim*, and Holtzmann, *Studies*, pp. 141–59. The first version was probably produced *c.* 1185. It contains a few decretals of Pope Lucius III.

needs of the jurists and canonists of Bologna. The prelates did not want to weigh the conflicting decisions of past centuries, still less did they want to hear old opinions quoted, which ran counter to modern fashions; did not the Decretum contain a list of popes who were sons of priests, even of popes? The active pastors needed unambiguous, authoritative statements on current problems, couched in modern legal language, and they were apparently prepared to send their clerks away at intervals on the long journey to the Curia with requests for such statements. Can it be doubted that they were keenly interested in the replies? And can it be doubted that, as the number of statements increased, every English prelate was compelled to take account of them and to be informed of their words? This necessity is nicely illustrated by a letter of Gilbert Foliot: one claimant to a church accuses the other of being a priest's son, trying to succeed his father 'contra sacros canones et decretales epistolas que pre manibus aput multos habentur'.[33] A judge faced with such an assertion, an advocate defending a client, had to possess those decretal letters in order to do his work.

Some decretal collections

And English churchmen did indeed equip themselves with these new, essential texts. There are decretal collections, sometimes more than one apiece, connected with Worcester, London, Rochester, Lincoln, Durham, Canterbury probably, Exeter possibly, others with Bridlington Priory, Fountains Abbey, Pershore Abbey, and possibly Bury St Edmunds, and another half dozen of unknown English provenance. All these were produced before the end of the century, and some much earlier.[34] These are the chance survivors of a type of manuscript particularly liable to destruction. They were very soon out of date, and after 1234 they were useless for all practical purposes. That so many survive gives some inkling of the number that may once have existed.[35] Only two collections can be associated

---

[33] *Letters of Foliot*, p. 320; Liverani, *Spicilegium*, pp. 639–40.
[34] On these collections see Duggan, *Collections, passim*; on the possible link with Bury, ibid., p. 116.
[35] Cf. N. R. Ker, 'The migration of MSS from English medieval libraries', *Transactions of the Bibliographical Society, The Library*, 4th Ser. xxiii no. 1 (1942) especially pp. 6–7 on losses of legal MSS.

with individuals. One is the so-called *Belverensis*, preserved in the principal manuscript of the letters of Gilbert Foliot. The other is *Wigorniensis*, which perhaps belonged to Bishop Baldwin, and was taken by him to Canterbury; to this we shall return shortly. No collection can be directly associated with Bishop Roger, but there are several which will repay a brief examination, because of their possible connection with him or with Worcester.

The most doubtful case can be disposed of at once. The collection known as *Regalis* (BL MS Royal 15 B iv, fos. 107–118) forms part of a miscellaneous volume which belonged to Worcester Cathedral at the end of the Middle Ages, by which time the present contents had been bound up together.[36] The decretal collection was compiled at earliest *c.*1181 and could, on palaeographical grounds, have been written at any time in the next twenty years, though it has no items later than Pope Alexander's time.[37] Apart from its provenance, there are two slight indications of a possible link with Bishop Roger, or with papers left at Worcester after his death. The first is the appearance of Pope Alexander's confirmation of the sentence concerning a chapel in Worcester diocese, in which Roger had been interested (App. II, 58B), with the address in the full original form, and the date. This is doubly notable, since most of the addresses in the collection are shortened and many corrupt, and the dating clause is omitted in all other cases. The second is the inclusion of the full text of a long commission to Archbishop Richard and Bishop Roger, which commonly appears in a severely abbreviated form (App. II, 37). But this full text also appears in one collection of the Italian group (Cusana, c. 39), so that it would be dangerous to dogmatize about the source from which either collector obtained this item.

Two decretal collections are more certainly connected with Worcester. *Collectio Wigorniensis* (BL Royal MS 10 A II) was compiled, like *Regalis*, after Bishop Roger's time.[38] It consists of a neat, efficient transcript of a substantial older collection of decretals of Alexander III, including many to non-English addressees. In this older collection, the material had been arranged roughly according to subject, in seven books or *partes*. Into his transcript of this collection, the compiler of *Wigorniensis*

[36] Ker, *Libraries*, p. 108.   [37] Duggan, *Collections*, pp. 81–4.   [38] Ibid., pp. 95–8.

inserted copies of additional letters, almost all of which were addressed to Bishop Roger, or concerned him as diocesan or judge-delegate. Papal letters to Baldwin, as bishop of Worcester, were added at the end of the little codex and, later still, letters issued when he was archbishop of Canterbury were added on the blank leaves at the beginning and end. There are, according to the editor, 274 items, divided into 429 sections. The basic collection in seven books cannot have been completed before *c.*April 1181 at earliest, since it included a letter of 23 January of that year, and it was probably not compiled at Worcester; it could have been lent to Baldwin or one of his clerks, just as chronicles were often lent by one monastery or author to another, and returned when the borrower had made his copy. *Wigorniensis* itself was evidently compiled at Worcester, where its compiler had under his hand papal letters addressed to, or concerning, Bishop Roger, and was probably completed before Baldwin was translated to Canterbury in December 1184.

It has been suggested that the compiler was Master Silvester, who served Roger and Baldwin at Worcester and moved with Baldwin to Canterbury, and the suggestion is attractive though it cannot be regarded as proved beyond possibility of doubt.[39] The basis for the suggestion is the hypothesis that the collection will have been compiled by a senior clerk who successively served Roger at Worcester, Baldwin at Worcester, and Baldwin as archbishop. (The last stage in this progress does not seem to be essential to the argument, since the Canterbury letters are clearly additions.) Master Silvester, Simon archdeacon of Worcester, Samson, and Peter of Withington all transferred from Roger's service to Baldwin's and, though Silvester and Simon were probably the senior members of the group, too little is known of them, and of their relations with Baldwin, to make the authorship of the collection certain, or absolutely to rule out the activity of an outside expert. Whoever was the compiler of *Wigorniensis* he had learnt his trade in a good school, for the collection is an efficient, if not an original, work. The new division of the material into books, according to subject matter, was recognized as a useful innovation, rubrics were provided to indicate the contents of the longer letters, and the

---

[39] H. M. R. E. Mayr-Harting, 'Master Silvester and the compilation of the early English decretal collections', *SCH*, ii (1965), 186–96.

books and capitula were numbered. This numbering was another innovation, providing the means for a system of quick and easy reference, and it may have been the Worcester compiler's own idea; it does not seem to have been tried outside England till a later date. *Wigorniensis* shows that someone working at Worcester, probably one of Bishop Roger's former clerks, was well abreast of the canonical developments of his time, unlike, for example, the compiler of *Collectio Claustroneoburgensis*, who used the same basic collection but entirely ignored the division into books, and failed to number the items or to provide rubrics.

The other collection from Worcester, known as *Wigorniensis Altera* (BL MS Royal 11 B II, fos. 97–102), provides an almost startling contrast, and seems to belong to a more primitive stage of development. It consists of only ten decretals, presented as twelve items, and was never completed; the initials and inscriptions are often missing. It occupies six folios of a volume of undoubted Worcester provenance, which was already in the possession of the cathedral priory in the thirteenth century.[40] The volume contains miscellaneous works, chiefly legal and theological; none, if they have been correctly identified by the cataloguer, is later than Bishop Roger's time. The decretal collection seems to be the latest item. The canonistic material consists of Paucapalea's Summa on the Decretum of Gratian, and part of the Stroma of Rolandus, both composed before *c.*1148, and a collection, otherwise unknown, of extracts from the Decretum concerning penance and excommunication, brought together 'so that they shall not escape the searcher'. The theology includes work of Hugh of St Victor (d. 1141), and Odo, bishop of Cambrai (d. 1113).[41] Both the theological and the legal works would have seemed a little old-fashioned in the 1170s, but perhaps would have been suitable for a student twenty years earlier. A small coincidence—it may be no more —should be mentioned. One of the theological items is the *Expositio in canonem missae* ascribed to Odo, bishop of Cambrai (PL 160.1054), of which the preface begins (on fo. 181^v), 'Presumptionis argui timeo, quod ausus sum rem difficilem

---

[40] Ker, *Libraries*, p. 208; Duggan, *Collections*, pp. 69–70, 152–4.
[41] On the canonistic material see *Repert.*, pp. 126, 128, 240, 283; on the contents as a whole, Warner and Gilson, *Catalogue*, ii. 343–4.

contingere ...'. These words seem to be echoed in a letter of Bishop Roger to the pope in favour of Master David of London (App. I, 17), which begins 'Presumptionis argui non timemus, cum id a serenitate vestra petere decrevimus quod hinc placere debeat ex honestate, hinc offensam non incurrat ex rei facilitate'. Possibly the form of the letter reflects the remembered words of the treatise. If so, the link between the bishop and the volume, and the early decretal collection, may be closer than has been suspected, and the collection of extracts on penance would take on a new significance, connected with the bishop's known interest in this subject.

Of the ten letters in *Wigorniensis Altera*, four were addressed to Roger, and one each to Bartholomew of Exeter, William of Norwich, Geoffrey archdeacon of Lincoln, Roger, archbishop of York, and the archbishops of Reims and (probably) Sens. The last two are additions, so that we have eight 'English' letters, followed by two addressed to French prelates, which might have come to hand later. Of this little collection, four out of ten, or four out of eight if the 'French' letters are excluded, were addressed to Bishop Roger, and one each to the other recipients. This could indicate that the collector was working at Worcester, using and adding to locally received material. Certainly someone, presumably at Worcester, was particularly interested in *Meminimus*, which occurs here in a form found nowhere else, its various sections having been rearranged, possibly to bring together the sections on appeals. It may be significant that the collection contains Pope Alexander's letter to Bishop Roger about the church of Bibury (App. II, 36), while the parallel letter committing the case to Bartholomew of Exeter, which probably contained the same statement of law, has not been preserved. Nor does it contain the letter of 1165 x 1166, answering questions put by Bartholomew to the pope.[42] None of the ten letters in *Wigorniensis Altera* is certainly later in date than June 1173; of the two that are otherwise undatable, one has been described as an early opinion of Pope Alexander.[43] The first eight letters, and one of the additions,

---

[42] See above, p. 171, n. 11.
[43] Fraternitatem tuam, JL 13873 = Wig. alt. c.10, is discussed by G. Constable, *Monastic tithes from their origins to the twelfth century* (Cambridge 1964), pp. 295-304. The remaining letter in Wig. alt. is App. II, no. 8 below.

appear in a different order in the first group of Gilbert Foliot's decretals (Belv. c. 9–18); could this little group of important texts have been assembled as part of the preparations for the Council of Westminster in 1175, at which two of the items were taken as the basis for provincial canons? Whatever the collector's motives may have been, the collection perhaps had influence beyond the English circle in which it was composed, for the *Belverensis* group appears again in almost the same order, in the midst of one of the early 'Italian' collections, *Collectio Florianensis*, cc. 94–102,[44] and more confusedly in other related collections (*Duacensis, Cusana, Berolinensis I*). It looks as though there was in circulation a little collection of Pope Alexander's decretals, all addressed to English or North French prelates, which became embedded, like a fossil in later rock, in the Italian collections.

Professor Walther Holtzmann, a great student of these decretal collections, noted the parallel between *Belverensis* 9–18 and *Florianensis* 94–102, and suggested that a collection like *Florianensis* must have been carried to England, perhaps from Bologna, and there left its traces. But is it likely that a small part of a collection (*Florianensis* has 172 items) would be extracted, and precisely the earliest items? Is it not much more likely that a little collection was formed in England and carried to Italy? Certainly somebody, perhaps an advocate, perhaps a litigant, perhaps a student, provided *Florianensis* (or its exemplar) with a tailpiece of five letters of 1174–6 concerning an otherwise unknown dispute over the church of Holy Cross at Bungay in Suffolk. This apparently minor question, concerning the history of a very small decretal collection, touches upon a crux in the history of the new law. Was Italy, and more particularly the great centre of legal study at Bologna, from the beginning the chief source from which knowledge of Pope Alexander's decretals was spread through Europe? Should it be accepted that prelates like Bishop Roger, and clerks like his *magistri*, received and acted upon papal letters in England, but made no collections of such letters till they received collections from Italy? This question must be squarely faced, since it is certain

---

[44] On *Flor.* see Holtzmann, *Studies*, pp. 68–88.

that later in the century canonists were obtaining material from the papal registers.[45]

In this connection, some useful evidence is supplied by a decretal collection known as *Alcobacensis I*, which belonged to the Cistercian abbey of Alcobaça in Portugal. The collection has been discussed briefly by Dr Duggan, and more fully by Professor Holtzmann.[46] To appreciate its interest for our enquiry, its structure must first be understood in its broad outline, ignoring minor complexities. It began with the canons of the Third Lateran Council; then followed decretals, which fall into distinct parts. These parts must originally have been distinct collections, which were copied out one after the other. The first collection is now incomplete at the beginning, but its surviving part shows close similarity to two other texts, collections from Tortosa and Eberbach, which were described long ago by Professor Holtzmann.[47]

It is with the second collection that we are now concerned. It begins with chapter 50, at which point the similarity just mentioned comes to an end, and the decretals begin to carry full addresses in the form used in original papal letters.[48] With the exception of one letter to the archbishop of Rouen, all the letters (nos. 50–125) in the second collection were sent to England. The full addresses suggest an early stage in decretal collecting, and possible derivation from the originals received by the addressees, since a short form had long been usual in canonical collections, and the papal registers gave only the briefest indication of the addressee: *episcopo Wigorn'* or the like. This impression is reinforced by the general correctness of the place and personal names—the latter commonly reduced to initials—even though there are plenty of indications that the scribe was not familiar with English places and persons. While Canterbury and Worcester may appear in slightly garbled forms, Kenilworth, that bugbear of continental copyists, is

---

[45] Holtzmann, 'Die Register', *passim*.
[46] C. Duggan, 'English decretals in continental primitive collections, with special reference to the primitive collection of Alcobaça', *SG*, xiv (1967), 51–72; Holtzmann, *Studies*, pp. 33–50.
[47] *ZRG*, xvi (1927), 33–77, and xvii (1928), 548–55.
[48] The full form is used, with a few exceptions, up to c.85, after which either the scribe decided to save time by adopting the short inscription normal in canonical collections, or he was drawing on yet another distinct source.

rendered precisely in its correct spelling, which again suggests that not many copies lay between the originals and the present form of the collection from Alcobaça.

Dr Duggan has drawn attention to the high proportion, in *Alcobacensis* as a whole, of papal letters addressed to Archbishop Richard, Bartholomew of Exeter and Roger of Worcester, and to the blocks of consecutive letters to the first two. He suggested that the collection drew in some way upon their archives. The group of letters to Bartholomew is particularly striking. Chapters 73–85 are addressed to him, alone or with others, with one exception: c. 84 (JL 12412) is addressed to the Cistercians in England, reproving them for holding patronage of churches. This letter could have interested, and been impetrated by, any English bishop, including Bartholomew; indeed we know that the subject interested some English bishops, since it was raised at the council of Westminster.[49] Two letters, c. 76 and c. 77, are found nowhere else; they never passed into the main stream of decretal collections.[50] Their appearance here supports the suggestion that this part of *Alcobacensis* drew upon the archives of the recipients of Pope Alexander's letters, and that not many copyings intervened between it and the originals.

The concentration of letters to Bishop Roger is at first sight less striking. At the beginning of the second part of *Alcobacensis* there are twenty-three letters, chapters 50–72, of which eleven are addressed to him, alone or with others, and two have general addresses; of these two he might well have possessed a copy. This accounts for chapters 52, 53, 54, 55, 56, 60, 61, 63, 64, 65, 66, 68, 71.[51] Examination of the other letters reveals that chapter 50 (JL 14158), addressed to Richard, bishop of Winchester, concerns the church of Coughton, Warwickshire, in the diocese of Worcester, and that chapter 67 (JL 14171) is

---

[49] M. Cheney, 'Council of Westminster', p. 65.
[50] Morey, *Bartholomew of Exeter*, pp. 134, 133.
[51] The chapters addressed to Bishop Roger appear in App. II as follows:

    1 Alc. 52 = no. 57   1 Alc. 61 = no. 26
          53 = no. 50   63 = no. 75
          54 = no. 53   (64 = JL 13961 + 13963)
          55 = no. 70   65 = no. 23
          56 = no. 47   66 = no. 7
          60 = no. 19   (68 = JL 13743)
                               71 = no. 51

addressed to the abbot and brethren of Tewkesbury, also in Worcester diocese. It concerns the bishop, and inheritance of benefices, and has been discussed already (above, p. 77). Further, chapters 51, 57, 58, 70, and 72 all concern cases in which Bishop Roger had been involved; they appear in Appendix II as numbers 93A, 86A, 49B, 17, and 28. Twenty of the twenty-three letters are thus accounted for. The remaining three do not concern the bishop as judge or as diocesan. Chapter 59 (JL 13995), addressed to the bishop of London, deals with the case of a priest's son, ordained by that bishop to his father's benefice. Chapter 62 (JL 13955), addressed to Robert, bishop of Hereford and Baldwin, abbot of Ford, deals with a priest of Exeter diocese, attempting to succeed his father, and chapter 69 (JL 13946), addressed to Robert of Hereford alone, answers three questions posed by him, of which the last concerned the treatment of married clergy in his diocese; the pope allows the bishop to leave them in their benefices, *sub dissimulatione propter multitudinem*. These three letters might perhaps have been inserted among the others in the course of transcribing and enlarging the collection. This sort of process is often to be observed in later collections, in which additions, written in margins, on odd sheets, or over erasures, are brought into the text at the next transcription. But this supposition leaves out of account the similar subject-matter of the letters, and cuts across the evidence provided by the full addresses and the accurate spellings, which show that in this case few copyings had taken place. Is it not at least equally likely that the bishop who in 1164 had elicited the decretal *Inter cetera solicitudinis*, about clerical marriage and inheritance of benefices, took the trouble to obtain copies of other papal letters on the same subject? Be that as it may, the arrangement of the other twenty letters points inescapably to one conclusion. Groups of consecutive letters addressed to individual prelates might be accounted for by supposing that a collector was trying out a scheme of arrangement by recipients, a scheme which was perhaps used in one early collection.[52] But these twenty letters must have been taken from Bishop Roger's office, for there, and only there, would letters addressed to him and letters to other addressees concerning his diocese and cases in which he had acted as judge,

[52] Collectio Parisiensis I (Friedberg, *Canones-Sammlungen*, pp. 45–63).

all be found together. The arrangement of these letters implies that his office acted as a centre of collecting activity, assembling papal letters from various sources to serve as records of diocesan and delegated cases; and further, if the letters on clerical marriage and inheritance of benefices are accepted as part of this group, it implies that he and his clerks were reaching out beyond the useful record of individual cases, to papal letters of general legal interest. In this activity the bishop himself appears as the keystone on which these various interests converge, diocesan administration, delegated jurisdiction, and reform of the clergy by enforcement of neglected rules.

The rest of this second part of *Alcobacensis* offers no such clear-cut picture, and many problems remain. The twenty 'Worcester' letters in Bishop Roger's group must be a small selection from the very much larger number of which he may have had texts because they were addressed to him, or concerned his diocese, his interests, or his delegated cases. There is no obvious principle of selection. None of the decretals is here which answer questions put by the bishop to the pope; two were in the first part of the collection and one occurs later, not in the compact group. Neither the date nor the compiler of the second, 'English', part of *Alcobacensis* can be discovered with any certainty. Of the date, it can be said that many of the letters belong to the period 1175–9; all were issued before Pope Alexander's death in 1181, and probably none was issued after the time of the Lateran Council of March 1179. Walther Holtzmann opined,[53] on rather slight evidence, that the text which underlies the first part of *Alcobacensis* had been obtained at the Council. Both parts might equally well have been obtained through contact between students of law at Bologna, Paris, or lesser centres, for in these places clerks of many nations habitually met and inevitably discussed Pope Alexander's pronouncements, texts of which must have been available for consideration.

Master David of London

As to the author, or compiler, of the second part, the leading position of the letters concerning Bishop Roger, and the number

---

[53] Holtzmann, *Studies*, p. 12.

of them, might possibly indicate a compiler attached to his household, or an independent *iurisperitus* who was in the bishop's favour and had access to his files of papal letters. In this connection a few words must be said about Master David of London, who may have been in just this situation, though only a few slight traces remain of the relationship between the two men, and nothing further can be proved about the compiler of the second part of *Alcobacensis I*. One of these shreds of evidence points to a common interest in intellectual pursuits; after the archbishop's murder, when David and the bishop had returned to France from the Curia, where both had been acting on behalf of the king, David sent a servant to Tours to borrow from Roger 'certain Sentences of Master Robert', perhaps works of Roger's teacher, Robert of Melun. Further, Master David certainly knew the decretal *Meminimus*, of 1167 x 1169, since the section on appeals *ex incidenti questione* is twice referred to in his letter-collection. Bishop Roger himself acknowledged David as his *familiaris* (App. I, 17); at about the same time, Gilbert Foliot referred to David as his own *quondam domesticus*, now Roger's *familiaris*, implying that David had transferred his loyalty from himself to the bishop of Worcester.[54] At that time David was certainly in contact with Bishop Roger, from whom he obtained a letter of recommendation to Pope Alexander against Gilbert on account over a dispute between them about the payment of a pension. Roger's letter commends David's learning and his devotion to the pope; David, he says, 'personam vestram digno extollens preconio, acta vestra magnificavit' (App. I, 17). Was David, the lawyer, known as an admirer of the pope's legal achievements? He needed no introduction to Alexander, for in 1171 the pope himself had commended David to King Henry, and had tried, perhaps imprudently, to provide him to the next vacant prebend in Lincoln Cathedral, observing that David's learning made him worthy of a bishopric. There were at the time six vacant sees in England, but David never obtained a bishopric.

[54] On the loan of the Sentences, see p. 10 n. 24 above. *Magister David Londoniensis* gave to Merton Priory a collection of theological and logical texts, now BL Royal 9 E xii. Sir Richard Southern kindly drew my attention to this volume, which must be taken into account in any consideration of David's intellectual interests outside the field of canon law. On the appeal *ex incidenti* see p. 176 above; for Foliot's letter see *Letters of Foliot*, p. 312. See also PL 200.737–8.

David's letter-collection shows that he was a dedicated professional lawyer who had studied at Clermont, Paris and Bologna over many years, and had visited the Curia on a number of occasions, starting perhaps with the negotiations for the canonization of King Edward the Confessor in 1160-1, and continuing in the 1170s. It shows too that Bishop Arnulf of Lisieux was an old acquaintance, possibly a patron; indeed the survival of David's collection, in a manuscript containing also letters of Arnulf and of John of Salisbury, may be some pointer to the circles in which he moved and was respected. Closer study of this manuscript may reveal more about Master David's legal work and about the various phases of his life. The only trace of his writing seems to be a few glosses, possibly of the 1180s, which have long been tentatively ascribed to him.[55] But even the little that is now known of him is of some interest for the present enquiry, since it provides an example of an independent legal expert, working largely in England but with continental training and contacts, who could have had a hand in the formation of the decretal collections that were assembled and circulated in England and the north of France from the 1170s onwards. No evidence exists which enables us to ascribe a surviving collection to him, and yet it is permissible to remember the two small and apparently early collections from Worcester and London, and to consider the possible connection between them and the learned David, *domesticus* of the bishop of London, *familiaris* of Roger of Worcester. That Bishop Roger counted David among his *familiares* is some indication of the bishop's interests, though it is impossible to estimate the extent of David's influence, as compared with that of other legal experts, whose lives and connections are even less well known than his, because nothing survives of their personal correspondence.

Conclusion

The evidence about Bishop Roger is too patchy and incomplete to provide definite solutions to the problem of the contribution made by him and his English contemporaries to the formation of the decretal collections of the later twelfth century. But in

[55] Kuttner and Rathbone, 'Anglo-Norman canonists', p. 286.

spite of its defects, it provides information which confirms some received opinions, and at the same time suggests that others ought to be modified. The central question, to which many others are linked, concerns the much debated problem of the significance of the large number of Pope Alexander's decretals addressed to recipients in England. That 'English' clerks were zealous in collecting these decretals, and others, seems to be abundantly proved by the surviving texts, though none of the collectors can be identified. That these clerks made extensive, but not of course exclusive, use of locally received material—the sealed originals or copies preserved in the archives of English prelates—seems certain; *Collectio Alcobacensis I* reveals more clearly than other early collections the process of copying blocks of papal letters obtained in this way. Further, this evidence suggests that the influence of a very few prelates, Roger of Worcester among them, may have been even greater than could be deduced from a simple listing of the addressees of papal letters, since close examination of the texts shows that papal letters addressed to others may have been copied by a collector from his archives. Thus far, the conclusions put forward by Dr Duggan, on the basis of a general study of English decretal collections, are confirmed by a detailed study of a limited area.

On the other hand, it seems necessary to modify the further conclusion that the number of Pope Alexander's surviving decretals addressed to English prelates and dignitaries 'merely reflects the relative influence of the canonists in the various countries in providing the raw material for the professional collections'.[56] This conclusion implies that Pope Alexander's legal pronouncements of all sorts were more evenly distributed to the various provinces of the Catholic Church than is now apparent, and that many of those addressed, for example, to recipients in the south of France or Spain have disappeared. Those addressed to England, and especially the province of Canterbury, survived in decretal collections and now seem relatively numerous (according to this view) because English

---

[56] Duggan, *Collections*, pp. 144–5. Compare the present writer's opinion expressed in 1941, 'English prelates were among the leaders in Europe of canonist opinion in their efforts to build up a more complete body of law, by asking for rulings and recording them for the benefit of posterity', *EHR*, lvi (1941), 187.

clerks copied pronouncements in which they were interested, whereas clerks in other areas did not trouble to assemble this raw material, out of which were formed the 'professional' (mostly Bolognese) collections of the early thirteenth century.

That clerks in other areas, with the significant exception of northern Italy, were indeed less energetic in this respect seems certain,[57] and yet this is not the whole story. The evidence relating to Bishop Roger suggests a chain of cause and effect more subtle and more complicated, in which the reforming zeal of some English prelates, the stimulus of local, secular, legal and judicial innovation, and the pressure of conflict with the king, were all important links. These factors produced a special situation in England, in which some influential prelates had special motives for eliciting legal rulings from the pope. Many of these rulings contained explicit references to local English conditions, to difficulties, abuses, evil customs 'in your diocese', or 'in your province', or *in partibus vestris*. It will not have been immediately obvious to lawyers and teachers in other regions that these rulings would be of general application and lasting importance, even assuming that they might have learned of their existence. But in England, as we have seen, it was necessary for all churchmen to take note of them, to possess texts; in other words, the number of important rulings elicited by English prelates must itself have acted as a spur to the formation in England of collections of Pope Alexander's decretals. Once awareness of this need was aroused, every visit to court and council, every episcopal consecration and funeral, every session of papal judges-delegate, became a potential centre for the exchange and discussion of papal rulings. Further, once the collecting habit was established, capable advocates and teachers—Master David and his like—quickly extended the range of their material, copying papal letters of all kinds, chiefly commissions to judges-delegate, but also occasional privileges, confirmations and semi-personal letters which

---

[57] Clearly no one with access to the official papers of Archbishop Henry of Rheims (above p. 127) chose to use that substantial collection of letters in order to compile a handbook of Pope Alexander's legal rulings, though there were many that could have been used. E.g. no. 317 declares that commissions to judges-delegate should always be deemed to include the proviso *si ita est*, or similar words. A similar ruling addressed to the archbishop of Canterbury is X 1.3.2; the letter to Archbishop Henry does not appear in decretal collections.

seemed to have some possible legal interest; important papal letters to continental addressees would, of course, also be included.

This sequence suggests a distinction which has not been made in the past, and which has some interesting implications. The number of Pope Alexander's general rulings addressed to English recipients, at their own request, reflects the problems and preoccupations of the leaders of the English Church in his time; these problems and preoccupations were not common to all areas. It is therefore possible, and even probable, that the apparently high proportion of Alexander's general rulings addressed to England does indeed bear some relation to the proportion originally directed by him to this, as opposed to other, provinces of the church. But the apparently high proportion of papal letters of other sorts, notably commissions to judges-delegate, addressed to England, may well reflect the swift establishment in England of the habit of collecting papal pronouncements of legal interest, of which, in the nature of things, the first to be obtained will have been those directed to the same region. The preponderance, in the early decretal collections, of commissions concerning English cases will accordingly reflect the activity of English collectors, and does not necessarily indicate that Pope Alexander sent more commissions to judges-delegate in that area than to judges in other comparable areas.

These conclusions will have to be re-examined when the new *Regesta Decretalium* is available, and when the stately series of *Papsturkunden* produces its desired objective, a new *Regesta Pontificum* for the twelfth century. But in the meantime, they serve to throw some light on a larger question of historical interpretation. The preponderance of Pope Alexander's surviving decretals addressed to England is seen to arise from two distinct, though related, sources. The first was the pressure of some English churchmen for reform and for papal support, pressures observed by Professor Z. N. Brooke, who stressed the unreformed state of the English clergy, and by Professor Foreville, who noted the wish for support, evident in many applications by English prelates to Pope Alexander III.[58] The

[58] Z. N. Brooke, 'The effect of Becket's murder on papal authority in England', *Cambridge Historical Journal*, ii (1928), 213–29; Foreville, *Église et royauté*, pp. 390–1.

second source was the activity of English canonists and legal practitioners, who assembled and studied Alexander's pronouncements before they were assembled in such quantity or studied with such intensity in other places. This aspect of the matter was stressed by Dr Duggan, on the basis of his detailed studies of English decretal collections. These different points of view had seemed to conflict, but, as so often happens, on closer inspection they are seen to blend into a single complex picture, reflecting faithfully the variety of motive and circumstance that underlies the surviving traces of men's doings in the past.

6
THE LATER YEARS, 1172–1179

It has been convenient to discuss in separate chapters Bishop Roger's work in his diocese, his activity as a papal judge-delegate and his place in the development of the new canon law, ranging in each over the whole period of his episcopate. These were his chosen, or imposed, fields of special interest, and in them, if the surviving evidence can be trusted, his life's work was chiefly done. In this chapter a few points will be discussed which concern the bishop's later years, but fall outside those special fields.

In the second chapter it was suggested that Roger probably returned to his life and work in England only after the final ceremonies of reconciliation between King Henry and the church at Avranches on 27 September 1172. After, as before, that time evidence about his movements is sparse and irregular. In the winter of 1172/3, Gilbert Foliot, who was conducting the business of the election to the vacant archbishopric of Canterbury, reported to the king that he had obtained the approval of all the suffragans for each of the three candidates put forward in succession by Henry.[1] Foliot was adept at glossing over awkward facts, but his words imply that Roger was in England and had been consulted. The bishops held discussions about elections late in 1172, in February 1173 and in April when six bishops were elected. Finally on 3 June at Westminster Richard, prior of Dover, was elected archbishop, after prolonged disputes between the suffragans and the monks of Christ Church, Canterbury, about their respective rights. Richard's consecration was fixed for 10 June. On 8 June the suffragans met at Canterbury, but proceedings were halted by a notice served on the prior, stating that the Young King, now in open rebellion, had appealed to the pope against all the elections, because they had been made without his consent. Notice of the appeal was also given to the papal legates, who were still in France, and to the bishops of London, Exeter and

[1] *Letters of Foliot*, pp. 291–5; Foreville, *Église et royauté*, pp. 373–84.

Worcester.² Gilbert was dean of the province, but the bishops of Norwich, Rochester, St David's, St Asaph and Coventry were all senior by consecration to Bartholomew and Roger; why were these two specially notified? It seems unlikely that all five senior bishops were infirm, and that none of them came to Canterbury for the great occasion. Possibly the Young King was already posing as a defender of ecclesiastical liberties, and hoped that these two bishops would be sympathetic; more prosaically, he may have reckoned that they would be more punctilious than the rest in deferring to his extra-judicial appeal.³ Gervase, who will have observed these proceedings, noted that there was a difference of opinion among the bishops on this point, and Gilbert Foliot, reporting to the pope, hints that he would have ignored the appeal as 'suspect for many reasons'. In the event, the appeal was respected, and the consecrations deferred 'out of reverence for the papal majesty'. Richard of Dover and Reginald, elect of Bath, set out for the Curia, and waited long for a judgement. The pope watched the fate of the rebellion before committing himself; Gervase asserts that the decision for Richard was taken after a rumour had been put about of reconciliation between King Henry and his son. Reginald, reporting to King Henry from Italy, expressed the hope that Richard would be given authority to deal with the other bishops-elect, and the archbishop did indeed consecrate Reginald on the way home.⁴

But the archbishop was not given unfettered freedom to deal with all those who had not appeared before the pope. One of these was John of Greenford, elect of Chichester. The Young King had appealed against all the elections on general grounds, and in addition, as the pope noted in a letter to John, 'objections were made to each of you' (App. II, 32). In John's case, it was objected that he was the son of a canon, on which matter the pope gave him a dispensation. It was also objected that he

---

² *Letters of Foliot*, pp. 295–6; *Gervas. Cant.*, i. 245.
³ The Young King's attempt to pose as a defender of the rights of the church is revealed in a letter to the pope, preserved in BN lat. 14874 fos. 116ʳ–121, from St Victor of Paris, printed *Recueil des historiens de France*, xvi. 644–8. On the authenticity of the letter see Foreville, *Église et royauté*, pp. 378–84. The carefully limited concessions proposed would tend to support Professor Foreville's view that the letter is genuine.
⁴ *Gervas. Cant.*, i. 247; *Gesta Henrici*, i. 68–70.

had an eye defect, and on this point the archbishop was ordered to take a decision, acting with the advice of his suffragans, particularly the bishops of Exeter and Worcester. It must be assumed that the bishops advised in John's favour. The papal letter survives only because it was preserved in decretal collections as authority for the opinion that a man could become a bishop in spite of an eye defect, so long as this did not constitute a major deformity.

Archbishop Richard consecrated four bishops, including John of Chichester, on 6 October 1174. One awkward case remained; that of Geoffrey, the king's son, elected to the great see of Lincoln, who was both illegitimate and well below the age normally regarded as proper for election to a bishopric. He too, as Ralph de Diceto records, eventually received a dispensation from the pope, both as regards his age and his birth, and on 9 July 1175 at Woodstock his election was confirmed by the archbishop and the bishops of London and Worcester.[5] According to the latest canonical opinion, it was an archbishop's right and duty to confirm the elections of his suffragans;[6] Diceto's precise statement raises the possibility that in this case, as in that of John of Chichester, the pope had required Richard to act with the advice of named suffragans, of whom again Roger of Worcester was one.

In the light of these two cases, a statement of the satirist, Nigel, called Wireker, which might otherwise be dismissed as a literary fable, deserves a moment's attention. Nigel, in his *Tractatus contra curiales et officiales clericos* (*c.*1193), naturally devotes some space to episcopal elections, and to the acceptance by the church of bishops named by the king from among his servants. To this general acceptance Nigel cites one exception, Roger of Worcester, who, being summoned to Canterbury for the consecration of a bishop, wrote to Archbishop Richard and his suffragans saying that he did not and would not consent or subscribe to that election, and would not be present, 'and you know why'. So, says Nigel, this one man, famous for holy living, faith and nobility, chose to incur blame among men rather than to sin against God and his conscience.[7] If Nigel's facts are

---

[5] *Diceto*, i. 401.   [6] Robert L. Benson, *The Bishop-elect* (Princeton 1968), *passim*.
[7] T. Wright, *Anglo-latin satirical poets and epigrammatists of the twelfth century* (RS 1872), i. 198.

correct, the bishop in question cannot have been John of Norwich, consecrated at Lambeth in December 1175, or Peter, bishop of St David's, consecrated in Bishop Roger's presence in November 1176. It must have been to one of the group of 'king's men' elected in 1173 that Roger objected. Of those the most likely was perhaps Geoffrey Ridel, elect of Ely, the *archidiabolus* of Becket's correspondence, with whom Roger had clashed because of his failure to observe his excommunication by the exiled archbishop. Before his consecration, Geoffrey had to clear himself on oath of complicity in the archbishop's murder, and of breach of the rules of celibacy, both matters of special interest to Roger.

It would be unwise to put much faith in the details supplied by the satirist, though he was a monk of Canterbury and had the means of knowing the truth. But the story shows that Roger acquired notoriety for a protest against the election of a *curialis*. The incident would have been particularly noteworthy to contemporaries if, in this case also, the pope had instructed the archbishop to act with the advice of the bishop of Worcester.

As well as bishoprics, many abbeys and priories in England were vacant at the time of the settlement at Avranches. An undated letter of Pope Alexander, instructing religious of the province of Canterbury to elect new pastors, is preserved in two decretal collections, those associated with Canterbury and Worcester.[8] The appearance of this text in *Collectio Wigorniensis* suggests that Bishop Roger may have interested himself in these elections also, since much of the otherwise unknown material in the collection came from his archives.

When the disputed episcopal elections were settled, and a start made with the selection of heads for the vacant religious houses, the leaders of the church in the province of Canterbury could turn, or return, to the normal preoccupations that had been disturbed by the dispute of 1163–72. Some of the new bishops were royal servants, who continued, after their elections as before, to serve the king and lead his government. Bishop Roger, after 1172 as before, was no *curialis*. Perhaps the nearest he came to direct service to the king was in the matter of the nuns of Amesbury, whom the king wished to remove and replace with nuns of Fontevrault. Even here, Bishop Roger,

---

[8] *Coll. Cantuar.* 1.6; Duggan, *Collections,* p. 163; *Coll. Wigorn.* 2.9.

with Bartholomew of Exeter, acted on a papal mandate, and not directly on the orders of the king, though the mandate was issued at the king's prompting. The text is lost, but some of the content can be reconstructed from a papal letter to the abbess and nuns of Fontevrault, of 15 September 1176 (or possibly 1174), telling them of the king's intentions, and instructing them to be ready to take possession. The letter to Fontevrault says simply that the king wishes to 'commend' the house to Fontevrault, and intends greatly to increase its endowments; the present nuns should therefore 'ascend the ladder of the virtues'. What exactly was in the draughtsman's mind as he shaped that equivocal phrase? The nuns of Fontevrault are informed that the archbishop of Canterbury, and the bishops of London, Exeter and Worcester, or any three or two of them, have been ordered to go to Amesbury and 'advise and induce' the nuns to accept the transfer; any who cannot be induced are to be placed in other monasteries and well treated. Nothing is said of accusations against them. But according to the *Gesta Henrici*, the king sent the bishops of Exeter and Worcester to Amesbury on 22 January 1177, and by papal mandate they deposed the abbess because of her evil life, and dispersed those nuns who were 'disgraced by rumour of shameful ways, all, that is, except those, who abandoning the error of their vileness, wished to remain in the service of God in the Order of Fontevrault'. The ceremonial installation of nuns of Fontevrault took place in the king's presence on 22 May. Bishop Roger's name is conspicuous by its absence from the long list of prelates who attended at the king's command. The terms of the papal letter to Fontevrault suggest that the pope may not have been fully informed about the business, and Roger of Hoveden states that the nuns of Amesbury, so far from being kindly treated, were placed in close custody. It is a pity that no report to the pope from the prelates survives, such as was by chance preserved in the case of the abbot-elect of St Augustine's, Canterbury.[9]

Bishop Roger never appears as a royal judge, administrator or ambassador, and his attestations of royal charters are rare. It is the more remarkable that he was with the king at Westminster in July 1174, when the kingdom was torn by rebellion,

---

[9] The papal letter is *PUF*, v. 251–2, no. 160. See also *Gesta Henrici*, i. 135, 165; *Hoveden*, ii. 118–19; *Giraldi opera*, viii. 170, and *VCH Wilts.*, iii. 243–4.

treachery and civil war. Gilbert Foliot and Roger head the witnesses to a royal grant, dated at Westminster, for the lepers of Harbledown, near Canterbury; if this charter has been correctly dated, Gilbert must have come with the king from his famous act of penance at the tomb of the murdered archbishop. Possibly Roger had also been at Canterbury, though he is not mentioned in accounts of the proceedings. Nearly three years later, an exceptionally impressive state occasion also brought Bishop Roger to court. He was one of the eleven bishops who witnessed King Henry's award, dated 13 March 1177, in the dispute between the kings of Castile and Navarre.[10]

Apart from these unusual occasions, it was at ecclesiastical councils, or meetings when ecclesiastical business was expected, that Roger is recorded in attendance on the king.[11] From the point of view of the internal development of the church in England, the most important of these gatherings was the council which met at Westminster in May 1175, in the presence of King Henry and the Young King. The suffragans of Canterbury were required to attend on 11 May; the final meeting and promulgation of decrees took place a week later. Nothing is recorded of the genesis of this meeting, and very little about its proceedings.[12] The archbishop's summons asked his suffragans to collect information in their dioceses about matters needing reform, and to report them for consideration; he also ordered them to cite abbots, archdeacons, priors and deans of conventual churches. There is no full list of those who attended, and therefore nothing to show how many of the abbots and others of Worcester diocese responded to their bishop's citation. As to Roger himself, the *Gesta Henrici* names him among the bishops present, while Gervase of Canterbury states that he was absent through illness.[13] Roger issued a sentence as judge-delegate at Lambeth on 26 June, and was with the king at Woodstock about

---

[10] Eyton, *Itinerary*, p. 181 (July 1174), p. 211 (March 1177).
[11] Chroniclers sometimes note the presence of unnamed bishops with the king, e.g. in Oct. 1175 and Jan. 1176 (*Gesta Henrici*, i. 101, 107) when there is no evidence of Bishop Roger's whereabouts.
[12] Pending the appearance of *Councils and Synods*, I, see C. R. Cheney, 'Legislation of the medieval English Church', *EHR* l (1935), 385–8. For the decrees see *Gesta Henrici*, ii. 85–9, and for the summons, *Letters of Foliot*, p. 306.
[13] *Gesta Henrici*, i. 84; *Gervas. Cant.*, i. 251.

a fortnight later, so that any illness—if such there was—was temporary.

The archbishop required his suffragans to report matters needing correction, and a list survives, incorporated in a slightly later decretal collection, of the problems, or some of the problems, that were reported.[14] It consists simply of thirty-seven terse propositions; there is nothing to show precisely the stage at which it was produced, or which prelate, or prelates, had put forward the various items. Twenty-two of these propositions, and part of another, are covered by canons of the council. Another seven or eight seem to have been held back for reference to the pope; they were dealt with in papal letters addressed to the archbishop of Canterbury and his suffragans. A few must have been rejected, perhaps by the council, perhaps by the pope, at least for the time being.

Some of the propositions concern problems in which, as we have seen already, Bishop Roger was certainly interested. The third, fourth and fifth dealt with clerical celibacy, clerical marriage as an impediment to holding a benefice, and hereditary succession to churches. These were the subjects covered by the decretal *Inter cetera solicitudinis*, addressed to the bishop more than ten years before. A single conciliar decree covers the three subjects; it was explicitly based on the decretal and consists of a summary of its provisions, with one important difference. Where the bishop had obtained a general order to remove priests' sons from their father's benefices, the decree only forbids hereditary succession to benefices in future.

Another proposition (no. 28) raised the matter of unauthorized pensions from parish churches and chapels, about which Bishop Roger had written to the pope some years earlier (App. II, 63c, and above, p. 174). The proposition makes clear the link between control of pensions and control of institutions: 'pensiones aliis non faciant clerici in ecclesiis occulte ut alii eisdem succedant'. No decree was issued on this subject, perhaps because what the proposer (or proposers) really wanted was permission to override appeals in dealing with offenders. The problem was referred to the pope, who responded with a decretal letter (JL 13816) to the archbishop and his suffragans,

---

[14] On this list (Wilkins, *Concilia*, i. 474–5, from BL Claudius A iv fos. 191^v–192^r) see M. Cheney, 'Council of Westminster'.

defining the bishop's right to depose both clerks who had promised to pay increased pensions in order to get a benefice, and those who promised higher pensions to monastic patrons, on the understanding that their sons or nephews would eventually be presented to their benefices.

A further proposition (no. 22) raised another subject on which Bishop Roger consulted the pope (App. II, 8, and above, p. 181): 'uxorati relictis uxoribus aliis adherentes, cum corripiuntur, non appellent'. Here the intention is quite explicit; appeals to the pope have been used to thwart local proceedings, and local prelates consequently need the right to override such appeals. Again there is no conciliar decree, for only the pope can grant this right, but again the matter was referred to the pope, and the right—carefully defined—was granted by a decretal addressed to the archbishop and suffragans (JL 13823).

Bishop Roger's known interest in these questions must suggest, though it does not prove, that it was he who brought them before the council; at the same time it must be supposed that other prelates shared his concern, and that the problems were sufficiently widespread to warrant attack by decree or decretal. Several other propositions tackle problems that arose in cases in which Roger was involved, generally as judge; any of these cases might have stimulated an active prelate to bring a problem up for discussion.[15] That a man of Roger's temperament and occupations will have been deeply interested in the council and its aftermath there can be no doubt, and his position as one of the senior bishops of the province will have given his opinions added authority on this occasion. At the time of the council, the archbishop of Canterbury and five suffragans had been in office only for a short time, and the election to Lincoln was not yet confirmed, the 'elect' being a young prince shortly to be sent discreetly to study abroad. Norwich was vacant. There remained the obscure Richard Peche of Coventry, two Welsh bishops (one of whom was deposed at the council), Gilbert Foliot, an able, senior, man in a key position,

---

[15] No. 1, on presentation and institution, compare App. II, 7. No. 2 (first part) on Cistercian tithe-exemption, compare App. II, 51. No. 7, on the need for the tonsure, compare App. II, 50. No. 16, on ordination in another diocese, compare App. II, 94. No. 21, on monks holding farms, compare App. II, 70. No. 33, on payment of costs by defeated litigants, compare App. I, 6. No. 35, on child marriages, compare App. II, 74.

Bartholomew of Exeter, and Roger of Worcester. Of these only the last two had come through the strain of the Becket affair with reputations enhanced rather than tarnished, and these two were now regularly travelling the country as papal judges-delegate, seeing and hearing much of the general condition of the church and the clergy, and corresponding with the pope. Their opinions can hardly have failed to carry great weight at this time. It would not be surprising if the moving spirits behind the reforming activities of the council were the archbishop, Bartholomew, Roger, and possibly Gilbert Foliot, though the extensive remains of his correspondence show no trace of the subject.

Less than a year later, a second council should have taken place. The papal legate, Hugh Pierleoni, summoned the prelates of both English provinces to meet at Westminster at mid-Lent (14 March), to hear the *mandata et precepta* of the pope.[16] Were these mandates and precepts replies to the questions referred to Pope Alexander after the provincial council of 1175? The legate's council never took place, being broken up by a riot at the start, in which the two archbishops and their supporters fought for the seat at the legate's right hand. Roger of Worcester was present; Gerald of Wales records the quip with which he turned the king's anger with the Canterbury party into laughter at the expense of York (above, pp. 2–3), and he made use of the meeting to conduct some unrelated business (App. I, 58).

A still greater council of the church was yet to come. Just as the archbishop of Canterbury had celebrated the end of a long period of stress by assembling the prelates of his province at Westminster in 1175, so Pope Alexander celebrated the end of the long papal schism by presiding over a gathering of prelates of the catholic world at the Lateran palace in Rome in March 1179. The summonses went out in September 1178 (e.g. JL 13097); papal messengers came to the British Isles, as to other regions of the Catholic Church, to order *in vi obedientiae* (according to the *Gesta Henrici*) all archbishops, bishops and abbots to attend. In England, the papal subdeacon Albert visited the greater churches, carrying the pope's letter; presumably he included Worcester in his travels. Diceto's account

---

[16] *Gesta Henrici*, i. 112–14.

of his doings suggests that prelates negotiated with him about attendance, and that the old and the sick were excused, while some bought exemption from the journey, *clandestinis pactionibus*. According to the *Gesta*, others, 'who did not wish to behave in this way', set out in person.[17]

The fragmentary list of bishops who attended the council names only four from England, and the same four are named by Hoveden: Bath, Hereford, Norwich and Durham.[18] But the Annals of Tewkesbury record that Archbishop Richard and Bishop Roger of Worcester crossed the sea to go to the Roman council, and Gervase of Canterbury says that the archbishop set out, but turned back after reaching Paris.[19] The statement of the Tewkesbury annalist about Bishop Roger seems likely to be accurate, though there is no direct evidence to support it, except the bishop's otherwise inexplicable death at Tours. The annalist is likely to have been well informed about his own bishop, and his statement about the archbishop is supported, as we have seen, by Gervase. At the end of 1178 the bishop disappears from English sources. There is no document issued by him, no litigation before him, that is dated after November of that year. He was with the archbishop at Winchester when the king held his Christmas court there, for they witnessed Henry's solemn confirmation of the establishment of regular canons at Waltham Holy Cross, and also the similar confirmation for Fontevrault, relating to Amesbury, which probably was issued on the same occasion.[20]

---

[17] Ibid., i. 209–10; *Diceto*, i. 429–30.

[18] R. Foreville, *Latran I, II, III et Latran IV* (Hist. des conciles oecuméniques, vol. 6, Paris 1965), p. 390; *Gesta Henrici*, i. 206; *Hoveden*, ii. 171.

[19] *Ann. Mon.*, i. 52, s.a. 1178; *Gervas. Cant.*, i. 276. Gervase relates the journey to the conflict over the exemption of St Augustine's, Canterbury. The details of his story present some chronological difficulties.

[20] For the Waltham charter, see Eyton, *Itinerary*, p. 224, and *Cartae Antiquae 11–20* (Pipe Roll Society, NS 33 (1960), pp. 38–41 no. 357. The Fontevrault charter is known only from an inspeximus made a century later (*Cal. Charter Rolls*, ii, 1257–1300, p. 157; Delisle, *Recueil*, ii. 113–16). The charter, as it now stands, contains a reference to 1179, which caused Berger, editing Delisle's work, to admit as a possible date Apr. 1179, when King Henry again held court at Winchester. This court, however, broke up on 10 April at latest, and the charter is witnessed by two bishops who attended the Lateran Council, of which the final session was held on 19 Mar. It is almost impossible that the bishops were back in England in time for the Easter court, Easter falling on 1 Apr. The reference to 1179 must arise from a later insertion or a copying error. The Fontevrault charter therefore provides no compelling evidence for supposing that Bishop Roger was in England in Apr. 1179.

Archbishop Richard and Bishop Roger must have left England very early in 1179, for they had to be in Rome on 5 March, and the journey commonly took about six weeks. The words of the Tewkesbury annalist suggest that they were traveling together. It may be supposed that these two prelates were among those who did not attempt to evade their duty to obey the call to the council, and that both will have been keenly interested in the prospect of reforms to be proposed by Pope Alexander III. They had also a more immediate common interest, arising from the affair of the abbot-elect of St Augustine's, Canterbury.

The abbot-elect had refused to swear obedience to the archbishop in return for benediction; the archbishop had therefore refused to bless him. After prolonged dispute, which the pope heard at Rome, Alexander ruled in favour of the elect, in April 1178. He instructed the archbishop to bless the abbot without receiving profession of obedience, and ordered the bishop of Worcester in peremptory terms to administer the benediction if the archbishop failed to do so within thirty days of receiving the mandate (App. II, 43). But both archbishop and bishop continued stubbornly to disobey the pope's orders. According to the chronicler of St Augustine's, the archbishop misrepresented the case to the king, and suborned the bishop, who after many delays alleged that he was forbidden by the king to give the benediction.[21] There was evidently much discussion and manoeuvring during the second half of 1178; the archbishop and Bishop Roger will have set out with some anxiety for their meeting with the pope whose orders they had disobeyed.

Bishop Roger died at the abbey of Marmoutier, near Tours, on 9 August 1179. Nothing is recorded of his movements between his departure from England and his death. The archbishop turned back from Paris, we do not know why; the bishop did not return with him. That Roger went on to Rome, and attended the council, seems improbable, in view of the evidence

---

[21] On this phase of the dispute over the exemption of St Augustine's, Canterbury, see David Knowles, 'The growth of monastic exemption II', *Downside Review* 1 (1932), 411–14. The chief sources are Thorn's chronicle, in Twysden, *Scriptores X*, col. 1824–5, *Gesta Henrici*, i. 209, *Hoveden*, ii. 149, and the papal letters JL 13039–40, 13293–4.

provided by Hoveden and the list of participants.[22] What became of him? The chronicle of Robert of Torigni, abbot of Mont St Michel, notes under the year 1179 that the bishops of Worcester and Evreux, and the abbot of Bec, all died *catartico impediente*.[23] The chronicler's words hint at an epidemic of some kind. Bartholomew, archbishop of Tours, also set out for the council, but turned back from Paris, being too ill to proceed.[24] This combination of circumstances suggests the possibility—it can be no more—that Bishop Roger also fell ill at Paris, and was induced to accompany the archbishop towards a familiar refuge at Tours.

King Henry, perhaps at the prompting of the monks of Worcester, wrote to the monks of Marmoutier, ordering them to give up his cousin's body for burial elsewhere. A copy of the reply of the abbot and convent has survived, in a manuscript which has some connection with the abbey of Pershore, in the diocese of Worcester.[25] The monks describe their alarm on hearing the king's letter read in their chapter, and declare their conviction that it will be a disaster for their house if they do as he asks, and allow Bishop Roger's body, 'the treasure divinely given', to be carried away. They can hardly think of anything more impossible; it cannot be extorted from them by the destruction of their house, perpetual exile or the shedding of

[22] The only hint to the contrary occurs in the two late thirteenth-century MSS of what Stubbs called the 'intermediate compilation', which served as a source for 'Walter of Coventry'. Here the mention of the council is followed by the note that Roger, bishop of Worcester, died at Tours on the way home (*Memoriale fratris Walteri de Coventria*, ed. William Stubbs, i (RS 1872), 309 and xxxviii–xl.
[23] *Chron. Stephen*, iv. 287.
[24] Letters of Stephen of Tournai, PL 211, col. 341 no. 40 (ed. Desilve, no. 49).
[25] Oxford, St John's College, MS 96 fo. 151, mentioned in *Historians of the church of York and its archbishops*, ed. J. Raine, ii. (RS 1886), ix–x. H. dei gratia excellentissimo Anglorum regi et duci Normannorum et Aquitanorum et comiti Andegavorum, fratres capituli Maioris Monasterii et eorum humilis minister H. salutem et orationes. Lectis in capitulo nostro altitudinis vestre litteris, excellentissime regum, contritum est cor nostrum in medio nostri, contremuerunt omnia ossa nostra [cf. Jer. 23:9]. Ex his nimirum monasterii nostri pendere exitium, salve pace vestra, non ambigimus, si indultum nobis celitus thesaurum nobilem, domini Rogerii pie recordationis Wig' quondam episcopi venerabile corpus, patiamur ut petit vestra nobilitas asportari. Unde quoniam apud nos fere nihil hac re impossibilius quippe quia nec ipsa monasterii nostri eversio nec perpetui exilii inflicta asperitas sed nec proprii sanguinis generalis effusio posset extorquere quod exigitur, clementie vestre genibus provoluti omnimoda devotione deposcimus quatenus de cetero repellendo non pigeat eos qui suggerunt quod et Martini titulis et divinis dispositionibus defunctique desiderio noscitur obviare.

their blood. They beg the king to repel those who have made this suggestion, derogatory to the rights of St Martin, and contrary to divine providence and the wish of the dead man. These bold words, with their unmistakable allusions to the Becket affair, had the desired effect. The bishop's body remained undisturbed, presumably in the great church of St Martin, which was entirely demolished after the Revolution.

The monks' assertion about the bishop's wish, though it comes from a biased source, may yet have reflected the truth. For Marmoutier at this time was no simple monastery of merely local eminence. It was the head, if not of an order, at least of a widespread ring of dependencies, and it enjoyed something of the reputation that belonged to Cluny and Cîteaux in their great days. Soon after Roger's death, Guibert, later abbot of Gembloux, spent a year there, and wrote a treatise in its praise. He describes the round of services, the cupboards filled with books, the spiritual refreshment and instruction offered daily in chapter by 'magistri et sacri tractatores eloquii', the seemly, orderly life, down to the clean straw beds and the lights burning at night in dark places. Guibert left the monks of Marmoutier with regret, but comforted, 'for I shall not be separated from their spiritual company, and when the Lord gives me rest, I hope and pray that—not by my own merits, which are nothing, but by the prayers of my defender the most blessed Martin, which can do great things—I may be joined with them for ever'.[26] The same thoughts perhaps urged Bishop Roger towards Marmoutier on his last journey.

Roger was remembered at the Norman abbey of Lire, where his name occurs among the obits of 9 August, and at Osney, according to the terms of the composition made when he and the monks of Worcester confirmed Bishop John's gift of the church of Bibury (App. I, 51). Earl William of Gloucester, in his brother's memory, granted to the monks of Worcester freedom from tolls on their food and clothing bought at Bristol, and at Sainte-Barbe in Normandy the canons had a little extra refreshment on his anniversary, paid for, at his request, out of

---

[26] E. Martène and F. Durand, *Thesaurus novus anecdotorum* (1717), i. 606–18. See also *Analecta Bollandiana* iii (1884), 243–57.

the revenues of the church of St Peter of Breuil, which he had been instrumental in obtaining for them.[27]

Roger of Worcester was probably under fifty years old when he died; he had been a bishop for a little over sixteen years from the time of his election, of which some five and a half years were spent outside England. Any attempt to assess the achievements of those sixteen years, and the significance of his work, is beset with pitfalls, and any summary statement is liable to mislead. Yet from the mist of uncertainties about his life and motives, one or two points stand out clearly. He was certainly one of those who battled for the reform of the parochial ministry of the church in England, and one of those who were convinced that this reform could be accomplished only, or chiefly, by a three-pronged attack on hereditary succession to benefices, on clerical marriage, and on the concept of private, independent control of parish benefices, such as had been freely exercised in the past by 'owners' of parish churches and chapels. The constant pressure of an able, somewhat puritanical, and yet aristocratic bishop must have added immeasurably to the force of the campaign. Secondly, Roger was one of the principal papal judges-delegate of the 1170s, and therefore one of those who re-established the appeal to Rome as an accepted and much employed part of the legal system of England, after the disruptive conflict of 1164–72, a development which also brought added force and speed to the romanization of procedure in the internal courts of the English church. Thirdly, he was conspicuous among those prelates to whom Pope Alexander III addressed his pronouncements on legal and procedural matters; this bishop's perception of problems needing definition, of administrative and procedural difficulties, led to the formulation of a considerable number of papal rulings that were decisive for the future law of the church. Though in these ways he was outstanding, Roger was both a leader and a follower of movements of opinion in England and in the wider area of Catholic Europe, seldom isolated, but almost always one of a group of men, bishops and others, with similar aims and similar concerns.

[27] *Recueil des historiens de France*, xxiii. 473 (Lire). *Oseney cart.*, i. xxiv: hic pro Rogero, Willelmo, Iohanne episcopis. *Worc. cart.*, p. 29 no. 49. For Sainte-Barbe see above, p. 53.

For the rest, perhaps the chief outcome of this close study of one very imperfectly-known individual is the destruction of some well-worn stereotypes. For Roger was a princely bishop who despised riches, and gave his life to the church; he was a loyal subject of King Henry II, but was yet prepared to oppose him, at some personal risk, on matters of principle. He was also a loyal agent of the pope, devoting time to judicial work, possibly at the expense of more spiritual and intellectual interests, and yet he was apparently prepared to disobey a papal order of which he disapproved. Herbert of Bosham and Gerald of Wales stress his conventional virtues, his good life, and yet Gerald could not suppress his recollection of the bishop of Worcester's tendency to jokes and wisecracks. If in the attempt to penetrate the mist of time, the shreds of evidence about him have been overstrained or misinterpreted, his own bold words of defence may be quoted: this is nothing to what might have been said, if the wine had not run out.

APPENDIX I

ACTA OF BISHOP ROGER, WITH SOME RELATED DOCUMENTS

INTRODUCTION

Appendix I includes some seventy-one complete or probably complete texts of documents issued by Bishop Roger; there are none issued by him as bishop-elect. In addition there are an incomplete text (58), three probably composed by his clerks but cast in impersonal form as records of litigation before him (9, 68, 14A), and two issued by parties to lawsuits heard by him (26, 28A); as we shall see, these last were perhaps written by his clerks. A few lost charters are noted. This collection is far from being a complete record of all traces of documents issuing from the bishop's office, or bearing his name. Not included is his profession of obedience to Archbishop Thomas (which was almost certainly written by the archbishop's clerks), his return of knight's fees of 1166, references in papal letters to lost correspondence with the pope, references to letters to the archbishops and Gilbert Foliot, and letters issued in the course of judicial work, even those whose existence is implied by the recipients' answers (cf. App. II, 122–6).

Documents issued in the bishop's name, and now lost, must far outnumber the survivors; this is particularly evident in connection with his work as papal judge-delegate. A sentence or notice of a settlement survives in about one-third of the possible cases (not all will have proceeded to this stage), while citations, letters requesting evidence, mandates to the diocesan or archdeacon, letters excusing the bishop from attendance, have almost all perished. Surviving texts of all kinds come largely from monastic archives, which themselves have suffered immense losses. Worcester cathedral itself now possesses only the merest handful of early originals, among them only one of the thirteen granted to Worcester by Bishop Roger, and known from the fine thirteenth-century cartulary. Here and elsewhere there has been loss of another kind; cartulary-makers saved time and parchment by omitting witness lists,

1   Salisbury Chapter Records, Press iv, C 3 Potterne 16 and 21 (see pp. 231 and 293)

II Bishop Roger's seal, PRO E/329/399 (see pp. 229)

APPENDIX I

often copying at most the first one or two names, and so depriving the historian of precious evidence about the bishop's household and entourage, and an aid to the dating of undated documents. In all, forty-three documents have the full witness-list, and four have abbreviated lists.

The surviving documents include no personal letters. The nearest approach is the recommendation of Master David of London to the pope (17), which contemporaries would have called *commendaticiae*. The rest fall broadly into two groups, forty-one issued by the bishop as diocesan, and thirty-four issued by him as judge-delegate. There are a few uncertain cases (e.g. 7, 26), and one exception (36), a family matter.

The documents

A few brief remarks are made here on the diplomatic of Bishop Roger's acta, to draw attention to some points of interest; these remarks may be seen as footnotes to the standard work on English episcopal acta of this period: C. R. Cheney, *English Bishops' Chanceries 1100–1250*.

Only twelve originals survive of acta of Bishop Roger. The shape of these documents varies considerably, though all are of modest size. Most are wider, some much wider, than they are long, but the handsome judicial notification for Durham (18) is almost square, while a confirmation for Bordesley (2) has attracted attention because of its long, narrow shape.

Four originals retain their seals (2, 3, 18, 19); there is also a drawing in Sir Christopher Hatton's Book of Seals of the seal once attached to no. 64, and a cast of unknown origin in the British Museum.[1] The pointed oval seal, about 80 × 50 mm. max., appears to be the same in all cases, though different coloured wax is used on different occasions. It shows the bishop in mitre and mass vestments, his right hand raised in blessing, his left holding his crozier, with the legend ROGERUS DEI GRATI[A] WIGORNENSIS EPC (the final *A* of *gratia* is never visible). The little counterseal is a classical gem, with

---

[1] W. de Gray Birch, *Catalogue of seals in the Department of Manuscripts in the British Museum* (1887), i. 359 no. 2275.

the legend SIGILLUM ROGERI.² It may have been the seal used by Roger before his election.

Sealing was *sur double queue*, with the single exception of no. 57. Sometimes the parchment tag seems to have been passed through a single slit through the fold and body of the document, but no. 28 and the two parts of the chirograph preserved at Salisbury (60) have the more secure system of triple slits, with the lowest at the very point of the fold. The prevalence of sealing *sur double queue* reflects the character of the surviving documents; all were in some sense title-deeds, intended to have lasting validity. No. 57, the exception to the rule, was a citation; it serves as a reminder that documents of temporary importance may regularly have been sealed *sur simple queue*.

The handwriting of these originals is very varied; it would be hard to prove that any two were written by the same scribe, with the possible exception of two small documents written in a quick, informal hand (57, 19). All but one are written in what may loosely be called charter hands, but some are conspicuously different from the general run. No. 7 was issued by Bishop Roger and Daniel prior of Sainte-Barbe; it was probably written by a Norman scribe. No. 64 for Southwark is unusual in many respects, including its irregular and rather untidy script. Alone of all our texts it uses the first person singular, and transposes the normal *dei gratia*. The only witness connected with Roger is the bailiff of the bishop's soke in London; all the rest are Exeter men, headed by their bishop, who is called *magister* (again very unusual). The seal seems to be genuine, and it is hard to imagine a forger producing so crude a text; was it written by the bailiff's clerk? Obviously the charter had an unusual origin, about which it would be easy, but fruitless, to speculate.

No. 55, preserved in the archives of Saint-Évroul, also attracts immediate attention. It is written in a fine large upright bookhand, a type of script used in no other charter

---

² The gem is perhaps work of Roman date, and of no great merit. It shows two works of the fifth century B.C. by the Athenian sculptor Pheidias: Left, an Athena, probably the Athena Promachos; Right, the Zeus of Olympia. Mr A. G. Woodhead of Corpus Christi College, Cambridge kindly identified the figures from a photograph of the seal attached to no. 2.

APPENDIX I 231

in the bishop's name. But it reappears in two charters issued, not by the bishop, but by two litigants in two separate cases with which he was concerned (26, 28A). These two documents are very similar in appearance. Each is about twice as wide as it is deep, in each the writing almost entirely fills the available space, leaving only very narrow margins; each is very clearly ruled. The two may well be written by the same practised hand. Bishop Roger's clerks, Master Moses and Master Silvester, are the only witnesses common to both documents; possibly one of them wrote the texts, though on general grounds it seems more likely that an unknown professional scribe was employed. Whoever wrote the documents, their appearance suggests that the bishop's clerks might produce charters for parties to lawsuits with which he was concerned, a fact which might be surmised but could not be proved unless the original survived. A script both more impressive, and easier to read, than the normal may have been thought suitable for this purpose. These two charters and Roger's twelve originals may therefore have been written by twelve different scribes, or ten if the Norman charter and the Southwark oddity are eliminated. Whether all these scribes were in any sense members of the bishop's household is an open question.

Four of the originals are notifications issued by Bishop Roger as papal judge-delegate, announcing the sentence or settlement by which a case was ended. Three of these are in chirograph form (18, 37, 60); of no. 60, very exceptionally, both parts survive. None of the three mentions in the text that the chirograph form was being used; many texts known only from copies may have been prepared in this way.

In their internal structure, their forms and formulae, Bishop Roger's charters are almost all characteristic texts of their time; the forms can be matched in dozens of contemporary documents. Nos. 75 and 77 are exceptions to this rule. They are noteworthy as early examples of the inspeximus form of confirmation, which was only just coming into use. The bishop of Worcester and his clerks, if not the inventors of the form, were among the first to adopt this useful innovation.

Though in general the forms are in common use, they are far from being standardized or invariable. Indeed they vary so much that there is no document in this collection, with the possible exception of no. 64, that can be identified as a forgery because of its departure from the usual formulae. Even the form of the bishop's name varies. In originals we find R, R with various abbreviation marks, Rog' (most often), and Rogerus in full once. In thirty cases the bishop's name follows the general address (*Universis sancte matris ecclesie filiis* or the like), while in thirty-one cases it precedes it. There seem to be preferred forms which recur frequently; the general address just cited occurs some thirty-eight times, but twenty-two texts have a variety of other addresses. The bishop's title is *dei gratia Wigorn' episcopus* in thirty-eight cases (not the same thirty-eight), but in twenty-seven many different forms appear. Two letters to the bishop of London, written at different stages of the same case, use different forms and a different greeting (4, 5). In one charter for Wootton Wawen the bishop's title is *Wygorn' episcopus*, in another, issued only a few months later, it is *Wigorn' ecclesie dictus minister*; in one his name stands before the address, in the other after it, though in other respects the address and greeting are identical (12, 13). The variations, though sometimes slight, and sometimes perhaps due to later copyists, are sufficiently numerous to remind the reader of the constant possibility of external writing, particularly by clerks or scribes employed by beneficiaries. Just as the bishop's clerks composed and copied documents issued in other men's names, and bearing other men's seals, so the bishop was probably ready to have his seal affixed to charters written by other men's clerks. In such cases it must be assumed that these clerks were responsible for details, while important points were settled in discussion beforehand.

Documents issued by two or three judges-delegate must commonly have been issued in this way. The senior judge and his clerks were perhaps normally responsible for issuing the announcement of the sentence or settlement, and for citations etc. issued in the course of proceedings. It will be observed that no. 50, issued by Gilbert Foliot and Bishop Roger, differs from all other notifications made by Bishop Roger in incorporating the full text of two papal commissions. No. 8, issued jointly by Bartholomew of Exeter, Roger, and the abbot of Faversham, is preserved among the letters of John of Salisbury, and was presumably composed by him; as Treasurer of Exeter he will have carried out this work for his bishop, who was the senior judge. This very slight evidence raises the possibility that no. 53 was drafted and written by Archbishop Richard's clerks, and no. 31 by clerks employed by Bishop Bartholomew. Similarly, documents issued by Roger jointly with junior prelates, such as Robert Foliot of Hereford, or Adam abbot of Evesham, were probably the work of Roger's clerks (15, 18, 37, 49, 60, 61, 69, 74). Some of the variations in script, formulae and arrangement must have arisen in this way, but not all; the bishop's own clerks could and did introduce variations, as in nos. 4 and 5, mentioned above.

Only twenty-three documents carry a date of some kind. Of these, some give the day and month in the Roman manner, with the year of incarnation, some have the year only. The year begins on 25 March. The first dated document in the collection is no. 72, a notification in impersonal form of the settlement of a lengthy dispute at Wells. The earliest which is formally an act of Bishop Roger is a notification as judge-delegate, dated 16 October 1173 (61). Occasionally it is made clear that the date is that on which a charter was written (32) or that of the event recorded (30, 58, 83). Occasionally a date is fixed by reference to an event such as the legatine council at Westminster in March 1176, which points to a possible date without naming a precise day. Most dated documents arise from litigation, but not all such documents are dated, and some diocesan business is dated (13, 83). The evidence, though rather slight, points to an increasing tendency in the 1170s to add dates to formal documents.

This edition

The model provided by the British Academy's series of *English Episcopal Acta* has been followed as far as possible. Originals have been printed in full. Other texts are printed if previously unpublished, or if published in scarce books, or if an existing edition was not satisfactory for the present purpose. Other documents are calendared, but witness-lists, where available, are printed in full.

As regards orthography, the usual problems of editors of medieval texts have been met as follows.

c and *t*, often hard to distinguish even in originals, have been 'normalized', e.g. *reverentia, cautio*, except where an original clearly reads *reverencia, caucio* etc.

v and *u* are 'normalized' throughout, e.g. *vester, universis*.

Capital letters are used as far as possible according to modern conventions.

Punctuation of originals is reproduced as exactly as is possible without the use of special type; no attempt has been made to reproduce the punctuation of cartulary copies.

Abbreviations have been extended rather sparingly, especially in dealing with adjectival forms of place-names. There is some doubt about the preferred form for Worcester in this period, and some evidence that *Wigornensis* (as on the bishop's seal) was being replaced by *Wigorniensis*; *Wygorn'* has also to be reckoned with. The form has therefore been reproduced as it is found, generally without extension.

ACTA OF BISHOP ROGER

1. Abingdon Abbey

23 Aug. 1164 x *c.* 1 Jan. 1179. *Notification that John Fruschelu has conceded that his chapel of* Lutletona *is subject to the church of* Dumbleton.

B = Chatsworth House, Derbyshire, MS 71 (Abingdon cart.) fo. 61^v. s.xiv med.

C = Bodl. MS Lyell 15 (Abingdon cart.) fo. 60^r. s.xiii ex.

Universis fidelibus et filiis sancte matris ecclesie R. dei gratia Wigorn' ecclesie minister salutem. Ad universorum referimus

APPENDIX I

notitiam quod Iohannes Fruschelu in presentia nostra constitutus concessit quod capella sua de Lutletona[a] adiacet in perpetuum ecclesie de Dumeltone, et hoc in manu nostra idem Iohannes firmavit fide interposita, et abbas de Abendona consessit quod in memorata capella fiat servitium ter in ebdomada et omnibus festivitatibus celebrandis. Testibus[b] magistro Bald' de Dredona, magistro Fulc', Willelmo de Gloec', Samsone clerico, Galfrido de Dumeltone, Matheo camerario, Waltero de Bath'.

a Littletun C.   b Hiis testibus (*witnesses omitted*) C.

The charter could possibly have been issued by Bishop Robert (5 May 1191–?27 June 1193). The appearance of Samson, Bishop Roger's clerk from at least March 1165, and of Matthew the chamberlain, point to the earlier bishop, but neither of the *magistri* witness other charters of Roger, unless Master Baldwin of *Dredona* is identical with the Master Baldwin of no. 82. *Lutletona* has not been identified. William Frusselu held half a knight's fee in *Luctone*, in Gloucestershire, c.1211–12 (*Red Book of the Exchequer*, ii. 604).

Bedford, St Paul's, *see* **Newnham, no. 46.**

2. Bordesley Abbey

24 Sept. 1178 at Alvechurch. *Notification that Walter son of William of Stanes has confirmed his father's gift of Osmerley to the monastery of Bordesley, to be held in fee farm for four marks yearly of himself and his heirs.*

A = PRO E/329/399 (formerly Ancient Deeds B.S. 399). Endorsed: Osemereley. (s.xiii); . R. Wigorn' episcopi. (s.xii/xiii). Approx. 128 × 265 + 10 mm. Sealed *double queue*; green wax seal with counterseal (see p. 229 and Plate II).

Pd from A, T. Madox, *Formulare Anglicanum* (1702), p. 2 no. 5.

R' dei gratia Wig' . episcopus . omnibus sancte matris ecclesie filiis ? salutem. Universitati vestre notum fieri volumus . quod Walterus filius Willelmi de Stanes . inpresentia nostra iuramento dato concessit . et confirmavit donationem illam quam pater eius Willelmus dedit . et carta sua confirmavit monasterio sancte Marie de Bordesleya et monachis ibidem deo servientibus . scilicet totam terram de Osmerl' cum omnibus que ad eandem terram pertinent . in bosco et plano .

in pratis . et pascuis . et molendinis . et aquis . et extra . et cum omni libertate haie eiusdem terre Osmerl' . in feudofirma tenendam de eo et heredibus suis libere et quiete ab omni seculari servicio inperpetuum pro .iiii. marcis. argenti . post decessum matris sue . ei et heredibus suis duobus terminis annuatim reddendis . scilicet invigilia sancti Iohannis baptiste .ii. marcis . et innatali domini .ii. marcis . et ipse Walterus et heredes sui si aliquis de terra predicta monachis de Bordesleya calumpniam fecerit ⁚ omnia predicta contra omnes homines eisdem monachis sicut hereditatem suam warantizabunt. Tali conditione quod supradicti monachi .iiii. m' . terre vel redditus equipollentes si eos adquirere poterint ⁚ sepedicto Waltero vel heredibus suis[a] pro .iiii. marcis. superius dictis assignabunt . unde eos legittime paccare possint. Terram vero supradictam de Osmerl' et haiam et omnia ad eas pertinentia absque alio redditu et consuetudine seculari . libere et integre et honorifice idem Walterus a se et heredibus suis inperpetuum eisdem monachis possidendam concessit . et pro hac concessione .ii. marcas ab eis se recepisse cognovit. Dixit autem se hoc fecisse pro anima patris sui . et antecessorum suorum et pro salute sua et heredum suorum . et pro fraternitate ecclesie de Bordesleya. Hec autem omnia fideliter tenenda et observanda inpresentia Augustini Watreford' episcopi et nostra . idem Walterus tactis sacrosanctis ewangeliis iuravit et christianitatem suam super hac concessione fideliter tenenda ⁚ apud nos interposuit . apud Alveivecherche .viii. kal' Octobris . anno ab incarnatione domini .m⁰ . c⁰. lxxviii. Testibus . Gilleberto et Roberto capellanis. Willelmo clerico de Habendona. Willelmo dicto episcopo de Cadem'. Roberto monacho. Teodelino clerico. Osberto et Iohanne clericis . Watreford' episcopi. Roberto de Parco. Galfrido de Warnestan. Waltero de Wpeton'. Roberto Trian. Roberto filio Willelmi filii Henrici. Matheo de Camera. Henrico de Cliva. Roberto Marescallo. Henrico de Cadem'. Radulfo de Wiltona. Rogero de Lond'.

[a] suis *repeated and deleted.*

Osmerley no longer exists. It was in the forest of Feckenham, cf. *VCH Worcs.*, ii. 152, under Osmaresley. The unusual shape of this long, narrow, document is noted in Cheney, *Bishops' chanceries*, p. 46.

3. Bristol Abbey

23 Aug. 1164 x Dec. 1174. *Notification that the churches of Berkeley Hernesse (Berkeley, Wotton-under-edge, Beverstone, Almondesbury, Ashleworth and Cromhall) have been granted to St Augustine's, Bristol.*

A = Berkeley Castle, Trustees of the Berkeley Estates, Mun. no. 17. Endorsed: .R. episcopus Wig' de ecclesiis de Berkel' (s.xiii in., centre foot); R' marny (s.xiv, centre top); Skildemor(?) (s.xiv, at foot, left, parallel with side of document). Approx. 115 × 125 + 17 mm. Sealed *double queue* through three slits in fold; green wax seal with counterseal, damaged, in bag.

B = Ibid. no. 158, in inspeximus of Bishop William of Worcester (not collated).

Abstract in I. H. Jeayes, *Descriptive catalogue of the charters at Berkeley Castle* (1892), p. 11 from A, p. 56 from B.

R. dei gratia Wigorn' episcopus omnibus ad quos littere iste pervenerint salutem et caritatem. Quoniam ea que a nobis canonice gesta sunt ad posterorum volumus extendi cognitionem universitati vestre duximus intimandum nos ecclesie beati Augustini de Bristoll' intuitu religionis que in ea a prima fundatione cooperante Domino noscitur floruisse ecclesias de Berkelehernesse cum omni integritate concessisse ac dedisse. scilicet ecclesiam de Berkelai . et de Wtton' . et de Beverstana . et de Almodesberi . et de Aisseleswrde . et de Cromhala . singulis cum suis pertinentiis . et canonicos eiusdem ecclesie de eis investivisse . Quod ut ratum et inconvulsum permaneat presentis scripti et sigilli nostri testimonio roboravimus. His testibus Matheo archidiacono . Clemente Lanton' priore . Rand' Gansel . Nicholao decano . Augustino capellano . Daniele capellano et multis aliis.

> The charter is not found in the abbey cartulary. Its final date is fixed by the death of Clement, prior of Lanthony, before the end of 1174. On the complex history of these churches, and competing claims of the abbeys of Bristol, Gloucester and Reading, see B. R. Kemp, 'The churches of Berkeley Hernesse', *Trans. of the Bristol and Gloucester Arch. Soc.* lxx (1968), 96–100. Robert Marny, notary public (d. 1349), was employed by Bishop Wolstan of Worcester (R. M. Haines, *A calendar of the register of Wolfstan de Bransford* (HMC 1966), p. v).

4. Abbey of Bury St Edmunds

1172 × 1177. *Request to the bishop of London to place the monks of Bury in possession* causa rei servande *of the churches of Holy Trinity, Colchester, and Berechurch, in the course of litigation between the monks and Thomas dean of Colchester.*

B = BL MS Lansdowne 416 (cart. of Infirmary of Bury) fo. 46^r. *c.* 1425.

Venerabili fratri et amico in domino carissimo G. dei gratia London' episcopo R. dei gratia Wigorn' ecclesie minister et S. abbas sancti Albani salutem et sincere dilectionis affectum. Commisit nobis dominus papa causam que vertitur inter abbatem et monachos sancti Edmundi et Thomam decanum de Colcestr' super ecclesia sancte Trinitatis de Colcestr' et alia que Birdescherche dicitur cognoscendam et fine debito terminandam. Nos vero predictos abbatem et monachos sancti Edmundi adiudicavimus mittendos in possessionem predictarum ecclesiarum causa rei servande. Vobis igitur de cuius prudencia plurimum confidimus auctoritate qua utimur rei huius execucionem duximus committendam adeo ut predictos fratres in possessionem ecclesiarum qualem prediximus introducatis. Valete.

> Nos. 4, 5, and 6 concern a protracted case heard by Bishop Roger and Simon abbot of St Albans as papal judges-delegate. Simon was elected *c.*21 May 1167, at most a few months before Roger left England for some five years; the case must belong to the 1170s. No. 6 must have been composed before the bishop's final departure *c.*1 Jan. 1179; no. 5 must have been issued at least six months before no. 6, and no. 4 at least six months before no. 5. Probably the intervals were much longer. The commission on which the judges acted is lost, but is summarized in no. 6 (cf. App. II, 103).

5. Abbey of Bury St Edmunds

1173 × summer 1178. *Order to the bishop of London to excommunicate Thomas priest of Colchester and others who forcibly resisted the execution of a previous order (no. 4), unless they desist at the bishop's warning.*

B = BL MS Lansdowne 416 (cart. of the Infirmary of Bury) fo. 46^v. s.xv in.

APPENDIX I

Venerabili fratri et amico in domino carissimo G. dei gratia London' episcopo R. eadem gratia Wigorn' ecclesie dictus episcopus et Simon divina largitione abbas sancti Albani salutem et sincere dilectionis plenitudinem. Ex transmissa dilectorum fratrum nostrorum abbatis et monachorum beati Edmundi insinuatione accepimus quod Thomas presbiter de Colcestr' et quidam alii inconsulti caloris homines executioni sententie nostre ob manifestam contumaciam memorati Thome contra ipsum promulgate necnon executori cui eiusdem executionis officium iniunxit vestra serenitas in summe sedis iniuriam et contemptum resistere non verentur, et ne prefati fratres in possessionem ecclesiarum super quibus habetur in domini pape rescripto mentio rei servande gratia mittantur pertinaciter contradicunt. Ne igitur tante presumptionis impunitas effrenate mentis hominibus prestat audaciam et consimilia perpetrandi fiat exemplum, experientie vestre auctoritate apostolica mandare compellimur ut tam in prenominatum Thomam quam in alios quicunque date sentenție qualibet temeritate duxerint executioni resistendum, excommunicationis sententiam maturius promulgetis nisi ad vestram commonitionem a sua pertinacia desistant, eosque tamquam auctoritatis apostolice contemptores ab omnibus sicut excommunicatos cautius evitari faciatis. Valete.

See also no. 4 for discussion of dating, and no. 6.

6. Abbey of Bury St Edmunds

Late 1173 x c.1 Jan. 1179. *Report to the pope on the execution of a commission to Bishop Roger and Simon abbot of St Albans, to hear the complaint of the monks of Bury that the parson of Holy Trinity and Berechurch, Colchester, fails to pay the pension due from the churches. The bishop summoned Thomas, thought to be parson of the churches, but he did not appear; the bishop on the advice of learned men condemned him to pay the expenses of the monks in coming to two hearings, hoping by this new remedy to counter the wiles of those who scorn to appear before the peremptory summons and waste the litigants' and judges' time. Master Raymond, vice-archdeacon, was ordered to sequestrate the churches, but the priest placed in them was prevented from acting by Thomas's brother William. Thomas then appeared in court, appealed and refused to plead. The judges ordered the bishop of*

London to put the monks in possession cause custodie *(no. 4), but William claimed that he was parson, resisted the executors with armed force, and himself appealed (no. 5). The bishop of London enquired in full chapter whether William was considered to be parson before the start of proceedings, upon which Thomas claimed that he was injured by the enquiry and appealed again, thus eluding the jurisdiction of the judges. The bishop of Worcester asks the pope to state whether the judge-delegate or the Ordinary should take action against those who claim to be parsons or owners only when a third person is about to suffer an adverse sentence or has actually lost possession by judgement, with the result that the victor cannot be put in possession, and a sentence pronounced by papal authority cannot be executed.*

B =BL MS Lansdowne 416 (cart. of Infirmary of Bury) fo. 46^v. s.xv in.

Pd from B, *PUE*, iii. 372–4 no. 243.

> For the date see nos. 4 and 5. No reply is known; possibly the report was not despatched. Abbot Simon later announced that Thomas and his brother had renounced the rights they claimed in the churches, and the pope confirmed them to Bury (ibid., fo. 46^r, and 51^v pd. *PUE*, iii. 391 no. 260). This was not the end of the case; twenty years later Abbot Samson of Bury 'conceded' to Thomas, dean of Colchester, the advowson of the two churches *hereditabiliter* (ibid., fo. 47^v, pd. in *The Kalendar of Abbot Samson* ed. R. H. C. Davis, Camden 3rd ser. 74 (1954), pp. 161–2 no. 149). Bury did not get any pension. On this case see above pp. 189–90, and M. Cheney, 'Alexander III and Roger of Worcester', pp. 220–2.

7. Caen, Abbey of St Étienne

? June 1171 x ?Mar. 1172. *Notification with Daniel prior of Sainte-Barbe-en-Auge, that Richard of* Chinchebouuilla *has renounced the rights he had claimed in the church of Bretteville l'Orgueilleuse in favour of the monks of St Étienne of Caen, on condition that they give him two bushels of barley a year for life.*

A = Caen, Arch. dép. du Calvados, H 1854 (2). Endorsed: .D. (large single letter); concordia de ecclesia de Bretteville (s.xiii). Approx. 135 × 153 + 25 mm. Sealed *double queue*; two tags remain, seals lost.

Partial transcript from A, PRO, PRO 31/8/140B part I p. 180, s.xix.

Summary from A, *Mémoires de la Soc. des Antiquaires de Normandie*, vii (1834), 3 (describing the bishop of Worcester as bishop of York).

R. dei gratia Wigorn' episcopus. Daniel prior sancte Barbare omnibus ad quos presens carta pervenerit ? salutem. Notum facimus universitati vestre quod Ricardus de Chinchebouuilla abiuravit in presencia nostra quicquid iuris se dicebat habere in ecclesia de Brettevilla Orgelosa . et eam cum omnibus pertinenciis suis ecclesie sancti Stephani Cadomi omnino dimisit . ea tamen condicione ? quod Willelmus abbas sancti Stephani et monachi predicto Ricardo duos modios ordei annuatim persolvendos in elemosinam concesserunt et assignaverunt ? quamdiu in seculari habitu vixerit. Ita quod idem Ricardus xiiii. sextarios percipiet apud Billeium ad mensuram de Billeio . et ad eamdem mensuram reliquos .x. percipiet apud Iz' . inter augustum et feriam prati. Post obitum vero predicti Ricardi . vel eius conversionem in habitum religionis ? illi duo modii soluti et quieti remanebunt abbati et monachis Cadomi. Si vero contigerit quod aliquis contra eos predictam ecclesiam cum suis pertinenciis forte obtinuerit ? non reddent ulterius predicto Ricardo duos predictos modios ordei . salvis tamen et sibi redditis cartis suis et munimentis ? que eis in composicione facta reddidit . et ipsi in eisdem cartis et munimentis conservandis ? eamdem curam et diligenciam quam et suis adhibebunt. Et idem Ricardus cum monachis stabit cum eorum expensis contra omnes homines de eadem ecclesia . excepto fratre suo . et cum nullo stabit contra eos . nec cum fratre suo nec cum alio. Et hanc composicionem sigillorum nostrorum munimine testificamur. His testibus . Iohanne archidiacono Sagiensi . Alexandro . Hugone de sancto Petro . Reginaldo . Simone . canonicis sancte Barbare . Gilleberto capellano . Willelmo de Trum.

> Other charters in *liasse* H 1854 show that several settlements relating to this church were made *anno ab incarnatione* 1171, cf. *Cal. Docs. France*, p. 161 no. 456. No. 7 is therefore assigned to that year. Bishop Roger was at Tusculum at Easter; he is not likely to have reached Normandy before *c.*1 June. Eyton places related proceedings in June/July 1171; Delisle dates them 1171 x 1173 (*Itinerary*, p. 158, *Recueil*, i. 578). The *feria prati* was the fair of St Denis (9 Oct.) at Caen (A. Giry, *Manuel de diplomatique* (Paris 1925), i. 266). H 1854 (3) records that this *conventio* was made 'coram Rogero episcopo Wigorn' apud sanctam Barbaram, presentibus Alveredo abbate sancti Petri super Divam,

Daniele priore sancte Barbare, Iohanne archidiacono Sagiensi, Willelmo de Trun'. The words suggest that Roger, and only Roger, was acting as judge.

8. Canterbury, Abbey of St Augustine

c. June 1173. *Report, with Bartholomew bishop of Exeter and Clarembald abbot of Faversham, to Pope Alexander III on the execution of a commission (App. II, 33) to investigate complaints against Clarembald abbot-elect of St Augustine's, Canterbury, and to remove him if the condition of the house cannot otherwise be reformed, appeal being forbidden. The judges came to Canterbury, and took evidence from the convent and from sworn witnesses, the elect having fled. His offences are many and notorious; his private life is unspeakable, and also notorious. They have accordingly deposed him, and ask the pope to confirm their act. They have also, considering the compulsion under which the monks acted* (pensantes ... necessitatis articulos), *granted such absolution as is lawful to those who communicated with Clarembald's servants, who went from his lodging to the murder of St Thomas, and returned to it afterwards. They demand severe punishment for the murderers, and warn that whoever supports this man will be considered an enemy of God and a disturber of the Church.*

Pd with translation, *Letters of John of Salisbury*, ii. 786 no. 322, cf. p. xlvi for further remarks on dating. Also *Joannis Sarisberiensis... opera*, ed. J. A. Giles (1848), ii. 268–73, no. 310, and PL 199 cols. 365–8.

> At Michaelmas 1174 the abbey seems to have been in the king's hands for a year and a quarter (*PR 20 Henry II* p. 1), which suggests that Clarembald was deposed *c.*June 1173 (though Diceto, i. 354 notes the event between entries for 12 Feb. and 2 Mar.). No. 8 was probably composed soon afterwards by John of Salisbury. The pope sent confirmations to the judges and to the convent, JL 12706, 12707, of 25 and 26 May 1174, 1175, or 1176 (*Hist. S. Augustini* pp. 414, 413).

9. Carisbrooke Priory

Aug. 1164 x *c.*1 Jan. 1179. *Record in impersonal form of a composition made before Roger bishop of Worcester and Robert prior of Kenilworth, judges-delegate, about the vicarage of Newchurch (Isle of Wight), between the monks of Lire and Jocelin de Insula their clerk.*

B = BL MS Egerton 3667 (Carisbrooke cart.) fo. 71ᵛ. s.xiii med.

C = Évreux, Arch. dép. de l'Eure, H 590, Titres de Lire vol. iv fo. 327 no. 31, French summary, s.xviii.

Controversia que inter monachos Lire et Iocelinum de Insula clericum eorum vertebatur super ecclesia eorum de Niwecherch' in hunc modum amicabili compositione terminata est. Idem siquidem Iocelinus medietatem vicarie quam totam ad se iure spectare dicebat refutavit et monachis omnino quietam clamavit cum medietate omnium que ad ministrationem altaris eiusdem ecclesie pertinent. Alteram vero medietatem eiusdem vicarie et dimidium totius ecclesie de Niwecherche tam in decimis quam in aliis obventionibus que de iure parochiali eidem debentur ecclesie sepedictus Iocelinus tenebit tota vita sua de predictis monachis nomine monasterii Lire, reddendo eis annuam pensionem uno anno x s. et altero anno xiii s. ut semper pensio biennii ad summam excrescat xxiii sol'. Hanc itaque compositionem ex parte monachorum in verbo veritatis ex parte Iocelini fidei illatione firmatam, Rogerus dei gratia Wigorn' episcopus et frater Robertus dictus prior de Kenildeworda quibus a domino papa prescripte cause est delegata cognitio, auctoritate statuunt apostolica firmam et inconcussam permanere et utriusque parti precludunt omnem aditum reclamandi.

Cf. no. 14, the undated record in impersonal form which accompanied no. 13.

10. Cirencester Abbey

23 Aug. 1164 x 27 Dec. 1176. *Notification that Jordan, priest, has been received as perpetual vicar of Preston, at the presentation of Andrew abbot of Cirencester with the consent of the convent. Jordan shall pay a yearly pension of forty shillings. 'Testibus Osberto, Waldrico, Willelmo, canonicis Cyr', magistro Petro, Roberto monacho, Galerando de Cricklade.'*

B = Bodl. (loan from Lord Vestey) Cirencester cart. (Reg. A) fo. 111ʳ. s.xiii med.

Pd from B, *The Cartulary of Cirencester Abbey*, ed. C. D. Ross (London 1964), ii. 338–9.

The final date is fixed by the death of Abbot Andrew.

11. Conches, St Peter's Abbey

25 June 1178 at Alvechurch. *Notification that Walter, clerk, has renounced the portion in the church of Wootton Wawen which his father had held, and has sworn not to trouble the abbot and monks of Conches about it.*

B = Évreux, Arch. dép. de l'Eure, II F 2463 (Wootton Wawen cart.) fo. 30^r. s.xv.

Universis sancte matris ecclesie filiis Rog' dei gratia Wigorn' ecclesie dictus minister salutem in domino perpetuam. Ad omnium cognitionem referatur Valterum clericum in nostra[a] presentia constitutum proprio motu et spontanea ut nobis videbatur voluntate portionem ecclesie de Wotton' quam B. pater suus[b] tenuerat et quam Roger frater ipsius ad se spectare proposuerat, cum universis ad eamdem portionem spectantibus tactis sacrosanctis euuangeliis imperpetuum abiurasse et quod nec per se nec per alium abbati nec monachis de Castellione super ipsa portione questionem movebit aut questionem moturis auxilium seu consilium prestabit[c] iuramento adiecisse. Quod ne posteris[d] sit dubium hoc in scripti[e] seriem redigi decrevimus et redactum sigilli nostri inpressione muniri curavimus. Facta est autem abiuratio aput Alvichechirche anno verbi incarnati millesimo c^{mo} septuagesimo octavo vii kal' Iulii. Test'[f] Guilleberto capellano nostro, Alduyno et Stephano monachis Bordesle et Thoma monacho Castellionis, Iordano clerico de Warwik, magistro Sil',[g] Petro de Stodleya, Valtero Cumin[h] milite, Hugone de Londinton', Godwino de Warwik, Amfrido de Bereford.

    a vestra B.   b meus B.   c prestabat B.   d nec poteritis B.   e scripte B.   f et B.   g fil' B.   h Cunin B.

    No. 11 is preceded in the cartulary (fo. 29^{r-v}) by a notification dated 25 April 1178 of Baldwin abbot of Ford, as papal judge-delegate, that Walter's brother, Roger, had renounced his claim to half the church, in return for 30 shillings a year from the abbot of Conches. App. II, 57 is a papal commission to the archbishop and Bishop Roger concerning Walter's claim.

12. Conches, St Peter's Abbey

3 Nov. 1178 at Worcester. *Confirmation of the gift of Robert of Stafford of the church of Wootton Wawen to the church of Conches,*

APPENDIX I

with permission to hold it in proprios usus, *reserving episcopal rights and a sufficient vicarage.*

A = Cambridge, King's College Mun. now lost.

B = Bodl. MS Dugdale 12, pp. 361–2, transcript of A, dated 17 June 1649.

C = Évreux, Arch. dép. de l'Eure, II F 2463 (Wootton Wawen cart.) fo. 23^v. s.xv.

D = Ibid., fo. 24^r, in inspeximus of Bishop William of Worcester.

E = BN MS lat. 12777, p. 723, transcript of C, not collated.

Pd presumably from B, W. Dugdale, *Antiquities of Warwickshire* (1656), p. 599 (2nd ed. p. 371).

Printed here from B with select variants from C,D.

Rogerus dei gratia Wigorniensis^a episcopus universis sancte matris ecclesie filiis salutem. Que viris ecclesiasticis et maxime religiosis in diocesi nostra pietatis intuitu sunt collata, ne fraude vel dolo malignantium imposterum valeant perturbari, munimento scripture debent commendari et ea episcopali ut^b decet auctoritate confirmari. Proinde ecclesiam de Wottona cum omnibus pertinentiis suis quam Robertus de Stafforde concessit et carta sua quam inspeximus ecclesie sancti Petri Castellionis et monachis ibidem Deo servientibus confirmavit, episcopali auctoritate et presentis scripti serie predictis monachis et ecclesie dignum duximus roborare. Volumus itaque quod prefati monachi supradictam ecclesiam de Wottona cum terris et decimis et obventionibus et omnibus aliis ad eandem^c ecclesiam pertinentibus in proprios usus libere et quiete habeant et inperpetuum possideant salvo tamen iure episcopali et vicaria competenti et sufficienti. Et ut hec^d predicti^e Roberti donatio et nostra pariter confirmatio futuris temporibus rata et inconcussa permaneat, eandem^c ecclesiam sepedictis^f monachis sicut superius dictum est presentis scripti attestatione et sigilli nostri impressione confirmamus.^{g} Testibus magistro Rogero sacrista de Warwik,^{h} magistro Moyse,^{j} magistro Silvestro, Gilberto et Roberto Aluered (*sic*) capellanis, Roberto monacho et Guillelmo^j scriptore de Legrec'.^{k} Facta est autem hec confirmatio apud Wygorn' anno ab incarnatione domini millesimo c^{mo} lxx^{mo} viii^o iii^o non' Novembris.

a Wigorniensis B, Wygorn' CD.   b *om.* ut CD.   c eamdem CD.
d *om.* hec BC, hec D.   e predicti CD, predicta B.   f sepedictis CD.
g D *ends here.*   h *om.* magistro *and* Warwik C.
j C *omits all between* Moyse *and* scriptore.   k Legrec' C, Warwik *deleted* B.

Robert of Stafford's gift was a confirmation of grants by his father and grandfather. He granted the church of Wootton to Conches *sine aliquo participe*, and his charter was witnessed by (among others) Walter, *clericus*, perhaps the Walter of no. 12, Walter's two brothers and Roger Bachelere, perhaps his uncle. Cf. no. 12, App. II, 57 and p. 74 above.

13. Darley Abbey

23 Aug. or 22 Sept. 1175 at Worcester. *Notification as papal judge-delegate of the settlement of the case between Albinus abbot of Darley and Hubert son of Ralph about the manor of Crich. Robert prior of Kenilworth, the second judge, was absent. Hubert granted certain estates to the canons, and part of a wood; he also granted the church of Crich, as his father had given it, and as the canons held it on the Purification after the capture of the king of Scots (2 Feb. 1175). For these concessions the convent renounced the rights they had claimed in the manor of Crich. Papal privileges and confirmations of the king or the bishop of Coventry shall not on this point prejudice Hubert or his heirs. (Witnesses omitted.)*

B = BL MS Cotton Titus C. ix (Darley cart.) fos. 148^v–149^r. s.xiii ex.
Pd from B, *Darley cart.*, ii. 538–40; and *Mon. Ang.*, vi. 360, part only.

The date of the *conventio* is given as 'anno dominice incarnationis mclxxv mense Septembri x kalendarum eiusdem mensis apud Wig''. This curious form makes it uncertain whether the writer had in mind the kalends of Sept. or Oct.

14. Darley Abbey

23 Aug. or 22 Sept. 1175. *Notification in impersonal form, similar to, but not identical with no. 13. Mentions the advowson of the church of Crich, and notes that the settlement was made before papal judges-delegate, Roger bishop of Worcester and Robert prior of Kenilworth. (Witnesses omitted.)*

B = Bodl. Gough MS Derby 1 (Darley cart.) fo. 26. s.xiv.
Pd from B, *Darley cart.*, ii. 541.

> On the date see no. 13.

15. Daventry Priory

6 Oct. 1176 in St Augustine's church, Droitwich. *Notification as judge-delegate, with Adam abbot of Evesham, that Alan de Glen, clerk, has voluntarily renounced the rights which he had claimed in the church of Foxton against the prior and monks of St Augustine's, Daventry.*

B = BL MS Cotton Claudius D. xii (Daventry cart.) fo. 149^{r-v}. s.xiv ex.

Universis sancte matris ecclesie filiis Rogerus dei gratia Wigorn' ecclesie minister et Adam eadem gratia dictus abbas de Evesham salutem. Delegata nobis a domino Alexandro papa iii cause cognitione que vertebatur inter priorem et monachos sancti Augustini de Daventr' et Alanum de glen' clericum super ecclesia de Foxton', diem congruum partibus prefiximus. Prefatus vero Alanus, a nullo coactus set ut publice protestabatur spontaneus, omni iuri quod se in prescripta ecclesia habere dicebat inperpetuum renunciavit et eandem ecclesiam iuramento corporaliter prestito abiuravit, iuramento annectens se nunquam questionem prefatis monachis moturum super predicta [fo. 149^v] ecclesia, nec per se vel per alium eos super ipsa ecclesia quacunque occasione vexaturum. Facta est abiuratio ista in ecclesia beati Augustini de Wich' anno verbi incarnati millesimo c septuagesimo sexto, pridie nonas Octobris. Testibus Roberto tertio Heref' episcopo, Simone Wigorn' archidiacono, magistro Moise, magistro Hugone de Sutwelle, magistro Nicholao de Atingham et multis aliis.

> Comparison with no. 12 suggests the possibility that a litigant was being forced to abjure a benefice claimed by some sort of hereditary right. Pope Alexander III confirmed the church of Foxton, among others, to Daventry on 5 May 1160 x 1176 (*PUE*, i. 396 no. 126).

16. Daventry Priory

Early 1167. *Report to Pope Alexander III on the execution of a commission to hear a case between Walter, clerk, and the prior of Daventry about the church of West Haddon.*

APPENDIX I

B = BL MS Cotton Claudius D. xii (Daventry cart.) fo. 151ʳ (follows fo. 138ᵛ owing to misplacement of quires). s.xiv ex.

Summo pontifici episcopus Wig'.
Causa pater que vertebatur inter Walterum clericum et priorem de Daventre super ecclesia de Haddon nobis a sanctitate vestra delegata fuit, non absolute set conditione ut si pro veritate nobis constaret prefatum W. ad vestram audientiam appellasse ab examine domini Londonie super eadem ecclesia, partibus ante nos convocatis eandem causam cum omni studio decideremus remota appellatione, alioquin eidem Londoniensi episcopo ex parte vestra iniungeremus ut prescripte cause debitum finem cessante appellatione inponeret. Evocatis itaque partibus et facta nobis fide de appellatione prefati W. ab examine domini Londoniensis idem Walterus poscebat sibi restitui ecclesiam de Haddon' qua se iniuste spoliatum conquerebatur; prior vero eidem transactionis exceptionem opposuit quam in presentia domini Londoniensis, cui olim causa delegata fuit, in hunc modum factam fuisse dicebat: cavit prior fide super hoc interposita se predicto clerico statutis terminis .iii. marchas argenti daturum ut a lite recederet et super iamdicta ecclesia nec se nec ecclesiam suam ulterius inquietaret, quod ipse Walterus tractis (*sic*) iuravit euuangeliis cum ei satisfactum esset ad plenum de predicta summa, et sic est a lite recessus. Super hoc scripsit nobis dominus episcopus Londoniensis testimonium perhibens de transactione facta in modo predicto; et cum ei denuo cognitio cause a vobis commissa esset et testibus prioris adiudicata esset probatio, et quidam monachus post celebratam xiiii solidorum solutionem se xxvi solidos eidem exsolvisse tractis iurasset euuangeliis, ceteris testibus sese probationi offerentibus, Walterus abscessit. Walterus vero transactionem factam fuisse respondit et se ecclesiam abiurasse, non absolute set ea conditione, si prior scilicet ei satisfecisset statutis terminis de predicta summa; quod quia non fecit, ut asserebat, voluit habere regressum ad principalem causam, xii solidos tantum se inde suscepisse confidens, nec statuto termino, reliquum dicebat insolutum. Prior vero copiam producens testium se pactis stetisse et tres sibi in integrum marchas solvisse respondit. Inquisitus Walterus si testes cognovisset,

negavit se opinionem eorum cognoscere—cum obiecisset prior illos de eadem villa esse de qua et ipse, et eum tanto tempore inter eos fuisse conversatum quo posset ei satis de vita eorum liquere—et petiit sibi inducias dari ut de vita testium et opinione diligentius inquireret. Cum itaque super hoc haberemus consilium, Walterus dicens sibi satisfactum fuisse super mandato nostro prefatum priorem appellavit de inobedientia et contemptu domini pape quia non fuit prosecutus appellationem quam fecerat adversus eum coram domino Londoniensi et de violenta intrusione ecclesie quam sibi petebat restitui, diem prefigens appellationi *Quasi modo geniti*. Prior vero, quia cognitionem cause nobis commissa fuit cessante appellatione, instabat ut iuxta mandatum vestrum procederemus in causam, super quo consuluimus fratres nostros episcopos qui venerant apud Oxoneford' ad audiendum mandatum vestrum per magistrum Iohannem decanum Sarespesberie (*sic*), qui dicebant probationem prioris debere suscipi et eum a petitione sepedicti Walteri absolvi. Testibus itaque prioris diligenter examinatis, assidentibus viris religiosis abbate scilicet Persorensi, priore Coventrensi, priore Kinildewird', et aliis multis, suscepta est eorum probatio et prior a petitione Walteri absolutus est.

> The bishop's report to the pope is recited in a letter of the prior and archdeacon of Worcester to Hilary bishop of Chichester (d. 13 July 1169), presumably in connection with further developments in the case after Bishop Roger's departure from England. The letter states that Prior Ralph and Archdeacon Simon were present when the case was heard. The precise date of the meeting at Oxford is not recorded. It was probably held as soon as possible after the return of John of Oxford, dean of Salisbury, to England at about the end of Jan. 1167. Walter presumably set the term for his appeal for Quasimodo, the first Sunday after Easter, in the following year, that is 7 Apr. 1168.

17. Master David of London

? 1171. *Letter to Pope Alexander III on behalf of Mr David of London.*

B = Vatican, Bibl. Apost. MS vat. lat. 6024 fo. 153[v]. s.xii/xiii.
Pd Liverani, *Spicilegium Liberianum*, p. 757.

(R)everentissimo domino et patri suo .A. dei gratia[a] summo pontifici sanctitatis eius servus devotus Rogerus eadem gratia Wigorn' ecclesie minister licet indignus devotam cum debita subiectione salutem. Presumptionis argui non timemus cum id a serenitate vestra petere decrevimus quod hinc placere debeat ex honestate, hinc offensam non incurrat ex rei facilitate. Pro dilecto itaque et familiari nostro magistro David de Lund', viro siquidem litterato et honesto, qui ecclesie Romane semper devotus extitit et personam vestram digno extollens preconio acta vestra magnificavit, vestre discretionis pedes amplectimur ut iuste et nulli denegande petitiones[b] pro eo consequi mereantur[c] effectum. Venerabilis namque frater noster .G. Lund' episcopus, considerata mediocritate immo parvitate redditus sui et viri honestate et litteratura, ei decem libras argenti in archidiaconatu Middelsexie annuatim percipiendas assignavit, donec eidem in pari vel ampliori beneficio ecclesiastico provideret, quod et carta sua quam inspeximus confirmavit, et litteris a sigillo dependentibus ut memorato magistro David solveret prefatas .x. libras .R. archidiacono Middelsexie precepit, qui de mandato suo ei per biennium continuum et ultra[d] terminis statutis persolvit. Ortis autem quibusdam controversiis inter iamdictos episcopum et archidiaconum et magistrum David, episcopus et archidiaconus arbitrium commutaverunt, ut quod archidiaconus ante magistro David solvere consuevit, deinde episcopo persolveret. Archidiachono (sic) itaque a solutione magistro David cessante, quod episcopus prius magistro David in debitum constituit, ei ad novam gratiam revocavit. Quia vero huiusmodi solutio in dampnum et detrimentum magistri David poterit converti, a celsitudine vestra impetrare[e] desideramus, si quid humilitas nostra in tante maiestatis conspectu potest efficere, vel zelo saltim iustitie, sub urgentis districtione mandati sepedicto episcopo iniungatis ut magistro David, qui sepius cum multo studio coram maiestate vestra pro eo stetit ut averteret indignationem vestram ab eo, in primo beneficio ecclesiastico quod ei vacaverit .x. illas libras assignet, cum magister David iuxta intellectum et interpretationem cartarum suarum dudum sibi credidit provideri debuisse in aliquo beneficio certiore et utique in primo quod vacaverit, iuxta sepememorati episcopi promissum. Plurima quidem postea vacaverunt, in quorum nullo ei est provisum. Interim vero donec vacaverit beneficium in quo sufficienter .x. libre ei recompensentur, districte precipiatis predicto archidiacono ut illas de archiaconatu in quo ei constat fuisse assignatas absque vexationis molestia persolvat. In huius ergo interventus pro viro digno exhibiti exauditione experiatur nostre parvitatis devotio, pater reverende, consuete benignitatis affectum, et ne tanti viri labores alicuius tergiversatione deludantur, in severitate et districtione mandati precipiatis prenominato archidiacono ut .x. libras quas magistro David solvere consuevit occasione et appellatione cessante integre persolvat.

>   a *om.* dei gratia B.   b petitionis ut B.   c mereatur B.   d utra B.
>   e impetrasse B.

>   No. 17 occurs only in Master David's letter-collection, on which see Z. N. Brooke, 'The register of Master David'. The letter may be incomplete at the end; it may be copied from a draft. David was receiving his £10 yearly from the archdeaconry of Middlesex in 1187–8 (Brooke, pp. 238–9); it is not known whether the pope intervened on his behalf. Gilbert Foliot's original grant may have been a reward for David's services in 1169 (Brooke, p. 240); if so, no. 17, which refers to payment for two years and more, may belong to 1171. Brooke (p. 243) suggested 1173, and connected it with a letter of Gilbert Foliot to Bishop Roger, complaining of David and his desire for the 'chief dignity of our church' (*Letters of Foliot*, p. 313 no. 240). As Roger's letter to the pope does not mention this matter, Foliot's letter has not been considered as relevant to the dating of no. 17. David himself may have composed the letter.

18. Durham Cathedral Priory

12 Nov. 1174 at Warwick. *Notification as judge-delegate with John treasurer of Exeter, their fellow-judge Robert dean of York being absent, of the settlement of the case between the prior and monks of Durham and the monastery of St Albans about the church of Tynemouth.*

A = Durham, D. and C. Mun., 1.3.Pont. 9, lower half of chirograph. Endorsed: Scriptum iudicum de composicione inter nos et monachos sancti Albani (s.xii ex.) de ecclesiis de Bivelle et Edelingham (s.xiii); Prima 3e Pont. J (s.xv med. in rough box over erasure:— ... 4a prime); I (red ink, ?s.xv); Bywell' (s.xiv ex.). Endorsements facing in opposite direction: .iii. (s.xiii); 4a prime iij (s.xiv ex.); C I Bywell' (s.xiv ex.). Approx. 220 × 206 + 12 mm. Sealed *double queue* (seal tags folded lengthways), two seals remain, described in *Catalogue of the ecclesiastical seals in ... Durham, by William Greenwell*, ed. C. H. Hunter Blair, Soc. of Antiquaries of Newcastle upon Tyne (1917–19), p. 489

APPENDIX I

no. 3216 (Bishop Roger, and see p. 229 above), and p. 526 no. 3336 (John).

B = ibid. Cartuarium vetus fo. 118^{r-v}. s.xiii in.

C = ibid. Cartuarium II fo. 39^{r-v}. s.xv in.

D = BL MS Cotton Tiberius E. vi fo. 126^v. (St Albans cart.) s. xv in.

Pd from A., J. Raine, *Historiae Dunelmensis Scriptores Tres*, Surtees Soc. (1839) liv no. 38.

Pd here from A; cartularies not collated.

+ CYROGRAPHUM : (cut through)

Rogerus dei gratia Wigorn' episcopus et Iohannes exoniensis ecclesie thesaurarius universis sancte matris ecclesie filiis presentibus et futuris ad quos presens scripta pervenerit ? salutem. Ne semel sopita litigia denuo suscitentur et bonum pacis contentio recidiva perturbet ? in publicam volumus noticiam devenire quod controversia quam movebant prior et fratres Dunelmenses monasterio sancti Albani super ecclesia de Tynemuth' et pertinentiis eius . cuius nobis et venerabili fratri nostro . Roberto eboracensis ecclesie decano de mandato summi pontificis Alexandri tercii cognitio fuit et decisio delegata sub hac forma ut si tres interesse non possemus duo nostrum in eadem causa procederent . hoc tenore et ordine conquievit. Videlicet quod tam venerabilis pater noster Hugo dei gratia Dunelmensis episcopus quam supradictus prior et totus conventus eiusdem ecclesie liti prescripte et repeticioni ecclesie de Tynem' et ad eam pertinentium in perpetuum renuntiarunt . et ipsam ecclesiam cum universis pertinentiis suis monasterio sancti Albani scriptis suis autenticis confirmarunt . Abbas vero et fratres sancti Albani pro bono pacis et prenominata renuntiatione concesserunt ecclesie Dunelm' ecclesiam de Biwella salvo iure Salomonis presbiteri quoad vixerit . et ecclesiam de Eduluingeham salvo tenemento Ade de Dunbar et post eum Engelerii clerici iure perpetuo possidendas. Instrumenta autem quibus Dunelmensis ecclesia uti poterat adversus monasterium sancti Albani ad repetendam ecclesiam de Tynem' prior Dunelmensis in manus nostras resignavit . preter ea in quibus ecclesia de Tynem' cum aliis possessionibus Dunelmensi fuerat ecclesie confirmata . que quidem adversus transactionem istam nichil roboris aut virtutis habebunt . et monachi sancti Albani versa vice munimenta que super ecclesiis de Biwell' et de Eduluingeham habebant priori et fratribus Dunelmensibus reddiderunt . exceptis his quibus ecclesie ipse monasterio sancti Albani cum aliis sunt possessionibus confirmate . que utique quantum ad articulum illum viribus carebit . Episcopus sane Dunelmensis intuitu et consideratione pacis istius sepedicto abbati tam suo quam ecclesie sue nomine indulsit . ut ab ecclesiis ad ecclesiam de Tynem' pertinentibus liceat eidem abbati et fratribus fructus solito uberiores percipere et pensiones earum decedentibus personis presentibus supra quam prius solvere consueverant . ad quadraginta marcarum summam augere. Nos igitur prefato coniudice nostro absente sed absentiam suam ex causis necessariis et sufficientibus excusante transactionem istam ratam habentes auctoritate nobis et potestate concessa monasterium sancti Albani ab impeticione Dunelmensis ecclesie super iam dicta ecclesia et pertinentiis eius inperpetuum absolvimus . et prefatam transactionem cunctis temporibus decrevimus valituram. Actum Warewici . anno dominice incarnationis .m°.c°.lxxiiii. pridie idus Novembris.

> A papal letter (App. II, 18) instructs the judges to ensure that the monks of Durham act with the consent of the bishop, so that he may not reopen the case if the monks lose. The judges' notification shows that the order was obeyed. John treasurer of Exeter is the celebrated John of Salisbury, who was active in England at this time (cf. no. 8). On the Tynemouth case see *Durham episcopal charters, 1071–1152*, ed. H. S. Offler, Surtees Soc. 179 (1968) 41 and *passim*, also H. H. E. Craster, *A History of Northumberland*, viii (1907), 64, where related documents are printed from transcripts of the damaged St Albans cart., BL MS Cotton Tib. E. vi. See also p. 186 above. Pope Alexander confirmed the settlement in 1177 (*PUE* iii. 369 no. 239, and Craster, op. cit., p. 66, for St Albans; *PUE* ii. 346–7 no. 158 for Durham).
>
> Mr Alan Piper of Durham University kindly gave me information about the endorsements of nos. 18 and 19, and the appearance of these texts in Durham cartularies.

19. Durham Cathedral Priory

Late Nov. 1174 x late July 1176. *Letter to Hugh bishop of Durham from Roger bishop of Worcester and John treasurer of Exeter about the exchange of muniments proposed in no. 18.*

A = Durham, D. and C. Mun., 2.2.Spec.2. Endorsed: Littera securitatis .R. episcopi Wyg' de permutacione facienda inter nos et monachos sancti Albani (s.xiv); de ecclesiis de Bywell' et Edlyngham (s.xiv ex.). On left: .ij. (?s.xiv ex.); centre: B 1, erased, (s.xiv ex.); right: .2a .2e . specialium (s.xv med., in rough box), 4 ... (erased), B 1 Bywell' (s.xiv ex.). Approx. 137 x 85 + 10 mm. Sealed *double queue*, two seals remain (as no. 18 but tags are not folded).

B = Ibid., Cartuarium II fo. 39ʳ. s.xv in.
Pd here from A; cartulary not collated.

Venerabili domino et patri .H. dei gratia Dunelmensi episcopo . R' . eadem gratia Wig' ecclesie humilis minister . et .I. Exoniensis ecclesie thesaurarius . salutem et copiose dilectionis affectum. Fidei nostre providendum commisit vestra serenitas quid ad securitatem ecclesie vestre comodius esse censeamus ׃ cum dilecti fratres nostri abbas et monachi sancti Albani specialia rescripta non habeant super ecclesia de Biwelle et de Edeluingeham que se habere sperabant tempore inite transactionis apud Warewich' ׃ et ea ecclesie Dunelmensi resignanda pepigerunt. Nos autem perfectam huius rei perspectionem absque vestre discretionis consilio et presentia ׃ nullatenus fieri posse attendentes ׃ negotii huius deliberationem usque in presentiam vestram duximus differendam . ut communi habito consilio ׃ commoditati utriusque ecclesie spiritu consilii previo ׃ provideamus . Verum autentica rescripta Dunelmensis ecclesie ׃ Gervasio monacho et magistro Osberto qui vice abbatis et monachorum sancti Albani ad nos accesserant . et versa vice rescripta autentica monasterii sancti Albani Hylario monacho et magistro Roberto clerico vestro manibus nostris tradidimus . securius estimantes ut a nobis qui iudices eramus traderentur ׃ quam si nobis absentibus esset facta tradicio. Ego quoque Wig' ecclesie minister me fideiussorem constituo . quod abbas sancti Albani iuxta vestrum et nostrum consilium utriusque ecclesie securitati providebit . et nobis etiam absens assensum super hoc prebebit. Valete.

> No. 19 was probably written within about three months of no. 18. Representatives of St Albans had travelled home from Warwick, failed to find

suitable muniments to transfer to Durham, and reported to the judges, who then wrote to the bishop of Durham, received his reply, and now write again after further action. The latest possible date is fixed by John's election to Chartres on 22 July 1176; the news may have reached him in about a week. The problem of the muniments was solved by a subsidiary agreement; St Albans undertook to defend the right of Durham to the churches of Biwell and Edlingham against claims by a third party (Craster, op. cit., p. 64).

20. Evesham Abbey

6 Sept. 1176 x c. 1 Jan. 1179. *Notification that Richard, knight, of Aldrintona has renounced his claim to the advowson of the chapel of Westona in favour of Adam abbot of Evesham and his successors.*

B = BL MS Harley 3763 (Evesham register) fo. 86^v. s.xiii/xiv.

C = BL MS Cotton Vespasian B. xxiv (Evesham register) fo. 16^r. s.xii/xiii.

Universis sancte matris ecclesie filiis R. dei gratia Wig' episcopus salutem. Cum controversia verteretur inter dilectum fratrem nostrum Adam abbatem Evesh' et Ricardum militem de Aldrintona super iure advocationis capelle de Westona, idem Ricardus in presentia nostra constitutus in ecclesia de Fladebur' presente prefato abbate advocationem prescripte capelle et quicquid sibi iuris in ipsa capella competere videbatur anno dominice incarnationis m^o c^o septuagesimo vii^a viii id' Septembr' abiuravit et eam absque omni reclamatione liberam inperpetuum dimisit memorato abbati et successoribus suis ita quod de cetero nichil iuris sibi^b in predicte capelle representatione vendicabit, nec consilium vel auxilium^c alicui prestabit qui contra monasterium Evesh' et abbatem sepedicte capelle representationem sibi vendicaverit. Facta est autem hec abiuratio^d presentibus Roberto capellano de Lench, Rogero presbitero de Fladebur', Roberto de Uppeton' capellano episcopi, Galfrido de Warneston^e, Roberto monacho persona de Clive, magistro Rad' filio Pagani de Evesh', Adam clerico de Fladebur', Samsone clerico episcopi,^{f} magistro Hugone clerico de Evesh', Philippo senescallo abbatis Evesh'. Postmodum prescripta capella vacante Ricardum clericum filium Ricardi ad representationem prefati abbatis personam eiusdem capelle constituimus. Ne igitur^g quod sollempniter actum est quacunque facilitate in irritum devocatur nec^h

alicuius malignitate evacuetur, presentis scripti paginam sigilli nostri appositione roboravimus. Testibus Roberto capellano nostro, magistro Moys', Sams', Willelmo de Glouc',[j] magistro Silvestro, clericis nostris, Reg' presbitero de Aldrinton', Ricardo milite de Aldrinton', Bertramo de Aldrinton'. Ricardus quoque prescripte capelle persona hiis omnibus presentibus preter magistrum Silvestrum, iuramento interposito promisit quod pensionem[k] eiusdem capelle scilicet dimidiam marcam absque consensu nostro vel successorum nostrorum non augmentabit.

a vi° C. b sibi *interlined* C. c auxilium *interlined* C.
d conventio *expunged* C. e *om.* Galfrido de Warneston' C.
f *add* Galfrido de Warneston' C. g ergo *for* igitur C. h ne B; ut C.
j Gloec' C. k promissionem B; pensionem C.

The single notification of the two events suggests that the institution of the new parson followed soon after the settlement of the dispute. B gives the date of the settlement as 1176, C as 1177; there is nothing to show which is correct. Richard of *Aldrintona*, probably from Alderton, Glos., occurs in *PR 32 Henry II* (*1185–6*), p. 122. *Westona* may be Weston-on-Avon, of which the church was paying half a mark to Evesham in 1248 (*Chron. Evesham*, p. xxvii). The bishop's manor of Fladbury lies between the two places.

21. Evesham Abbey

Jan. 1167 x *c.*1 Jan. 1179. *Confirmation of an agreement between Evesham Abbey and Kenilworth Priory about the chapel of Wixford.*

B = BL MS Harley 3763 (Evesham register) fo. 85^r. s.xiii/xiv.

C = BL Cotton MS Vespasian B. xxiv (Evesham register) fo. 15^r. s.xii/xiii.

D = Bodl. MS Dugdale 12 p. 445, transcript of C, dated 1 May 1652.

Universis sancte matris ecclesie filiis Rog' dei gratia[a] Wigorn' episcopus salutem. Ad notitiam[b] presentium et posterorum referatur nos ad instantiam venerabilis fratris nostri Ade abbatis Evesh' et dilecti nostri Roberti prioris de Kenilwrdie[c] transactionem inter monasterium Evesh' et ecclesiam de Kenild' factam et cirographo annotatam pontificali auctoritate ad perpetuam utriusque pacem confirmasse, quam sub eadem literarum serie quam in cirographo super[d] transactione conscripto continetur, in hac pagina fecimus annotari. A. siquidem dei gratia abbas Evesh' totiusque eiusdem cenobii conventus immutabiliter concedunt ecclesie beate Marie de Kenillewrth' et canonicis ibidem deo servientibus viii sol' quos annis singulis de decimationibus ville de Withlakesford' percipiebant et quicquid beneficii parochialis in prefata capella habebant exceptis decimis territorii quod specialiter ad dominium eorum pertinet. Preterea prenominatus abbas et sui monasterii conventus promiserunt predicte ecclesie de Kenillewrth' quod operam dabunt ne homines de parva Saltford' dampnum eis faciant de prato quod predicti canonici habent in eadem parva Saltford', sicut in cirographo quod factum est inter abbatem Evesh' et ecclesiam de Kineld' continetur. Canonici vero de Kenild' propter hanc concessionem singulis annis prenominate abbatie de Evesham x sol' reddere tenentur, v sol' ad festum sancti Michaelis et v sol' ad annuntionem[e] sancte Marie et tribus diebus in septimana in sepedicta capella divina celebrari facient, videlicet die dominica et die mercurii et die veneris. Test' Simone archidiacono Wig', Petro de Witald', Willelmo de Ponte Audem'[f] Samsone clerico, magistro Silvestro.

a *om.* gratia C.   b *om.* notitiam B.   c Kenildewrdie C.
d *om.* super B.   e in annuntiatione C.   f Aldom' C.

On Wixford and its chapel of St Milburga see *VCH Warwicks.*, ii. 189. The earliest possible date of no. 21 is fixed by Simon's appointment as archdeacon.

22. Eynsham Abbey

23 Aug. 1164 x 24 Mar. 1178. *Confirmation of the church of Tetbury to the church of Eynsham, as it was given by Reginald of St Valéry. 'His testibus, Matheo archidiacono de Gloec', magistro Moyse, Ricardo Luvel, Gill' capellano, Samsone clerico, Roberto monacho, Roberto de Camped' et multis aliis.'*

B = Oxford, Christ Church Chapter Library MS 31 (Eynsham cart.) fo. 23[r-v]. s.xii/xiii.
Pd from B, *Cart. of the abbey of Eynsham*, ed. H. E. Salter, i (OHS 1907), 65 no. 49.

The final date is fixed by the death of Archdeacon Matthew in 1177/8. The charter of Reginald of St Valéry is ibid. i. 70 no. 60, 1154 x 1161.

23. Gloucester Abbey

23 Aug. 1164 x 9 Aug. 1179. *Confirmation to the abbot and convent of St Peter of Gloucester of the church of Hatherop, with the tithe of the village and the land of the priest, given by Ernulf of Hesdin; also of the pension of five marks from the church of St Mary in front of the abbey, with all the tithes both of the villeinage and the demesne of Maisemore, Barton, Barnwood and Upton, to be converted to their own uses; also of pensions of twenty shillings from the church of St John of Gloucester and of ten shillings from that of Matson, to be paid by the vicars of those churches. (Witnesses omitted.)*

B = PRO C.150/1 (*Gloucester cart.*) fo. 82^v. s.xiii/xiv.
Pd from B, *Gloucester cart.*, i. 327, no. 305.

24. Gloucester Abbey

c. 1174. *Letter to Pope Alexander III about the claim of Gilbert of Muntfichet to the patronage of the churches of Wyrardisbury and Langley Marish, which Gilbert is trying to obtain from the abbot and monks of Gloucester by a papal rescript. Transcripts of charters are enclosed. The churches were given to Gloucester long before Gilbert's father received the estates in which they lie. The bishop asks the pope to consider whether arrangements confirmed by episcopal and royal authority, especially grants to religious houses, should be overturned at the will of a layman at every change of lordship.*

B = PRO C.150/1 (*Gloucester cart.*) fo. 176^v. s.xiii/xiv.
Pd from B, *Gloucester cart.*, i. 174–5.

> Nicholas bishop of Llandaff (cons. 14 Mar. 1148) wrote to the pope at the same time, and observed that he was now in his twenty-sixth year as bishop, hence the suggested date of no. 24. The churches had been given to Gloucester before May 1118. For charters relating to them see *Gloucester cart.*, i. 349–53; ii. 164–75, and *Letters of Foliot*, pp. 416–17. Cf. *VCH Bucks.*, iii. 300, 325. On the general principle raised at the end of the letter, see p. 190 above.

25. Gloucester Abbey

23 Aug. 1164 x c.1 Jan. 1179. (*Lost charter*) *Notification of the admission of Osmund, clerk, to the church of Uley at the presentation*

APPENDIX I 259

of the abbot and convent of Gloucester. Osmund shall pay an annual pension of one mark to Stanley Priory.

> Mentioned in *Curia Regis Rolls*, x. 226; the abbot produced a charter of Bishop Roger as evidence in legal proceedings in Trinity Term 1222. Stanley Priory was a dependency of Gloucester.

26. Gloucester Abbey

? 1178. *Richard archdeacon of Wiltshire records a composition between himself and the monks of Gloucester, made in the presence of Roger bishop of Worcester, about tithes of the demesne of Robert of Ewias in Clevancy. 'His testibus. Symone archidiacono . Magistro Moyse . Magistro Silvestro . Magistro Iohanne de Paris . Willelmo cantore.'*

A = Hereford, D. and C. Archives no. 784. Endorsed: De decimis Roberti de Ewias de Cliva. contra Ric' archid' (s.xii ex.); non indiget registrari (s.xv). Approx. 204 × 125 + 15 mm. Sealed *double queue*; tag remains, seal lost.
Pd from A by D. Walker in *PR Soc.* new ser. 36 (1960), 261 no. 6; also by W. St Clair Baddeley in *Trans. of the Bristol and Glouc. Arch. Soc.* xxxvii (1914), 228 no. 13.

> Though not a charter of Bishop Roger (and therefore not printed here) no. 26 appears to be written in the same hand as no. 28A (cf. p. 231 above). Clevancy was in Salisbury diocese, which was never vacant while Roger was bishop of Worcester; he must have been acting as papal delegate, or perhaps as arbiter. A composition was made in 1178 between the abbeys of Lire and Gloucester about tithes of Ewias, and Jocelin bishop of Salisbury confirmed to Gloucester gifts of Harold and Robert of Ewias, mentioning tithes of *Cliva Vancy, c.*1180 × 1184 (*Bristol and Glouc. Arch. Soc.* record ser. xi (1976), 49 no. 143, 52–3 no. 159). No. 26 is therefore tentatively assigned to 1178, Roger's last year in England. See also *VCH Wilts.*, ix (1970), p. 62.

27. Harrold Priory

23 Aug. 1164 × *c.*1 Jan. 1179 (*Lost charter*) *Sentence as judge-delegate in favour of the nuns of Harrold against the canons of Lavendon in a case* super iure et proprietate *of the church of Cold Brayfield.*

Mentioned only, in inventory of Harrold muniments BL MS Lansdowne 391 fo.15ʳ no.50.i. s.xv. Cf. *Records of Harrold*

Priory, ed. G. H. Fowler, Publ. Beds. Hist. Record Soc. xvii (1935), p. 46.

> In the 1170s and 1180s Harrold Priory was engaged in complex litigation about its relations with the abbey of Arrouaise and its control of some English churches. Cf. App. II, 15 and literature there cited.

28. Hereford Cathedral

19 Mar. 1177 at Westminster. *Confirmation of the churches of Moreton Valence and Whaddon to the cathedral of Hereford, reserving the rights of the church of Worcester and the diocesan.*

A = Hereford, D. and C. Archives no. 2773. Endorsed: Littera episcopi Wygorn' confirmantis appropriationem dictarum ecclesiarum (s.xiv). Approx. 180 × 110 + 20 mm. Sealed *double queue*; tag remains, seal lost.

Pd from A, *Hereford Charters*, p. 30 (dated 1176).

Universis sancte matris ecclesie filiis . Rogerus dei gratia Wigorn' ecclesie minister salutem in domino perpetuam. Approbate consuetudinis est . et rationi consentaneum esse videtur ׃ ut beneficia que pia largitione fidelium . locis deo dicatis . benigne devotionis intuitu conferuntur ׃ pontificalis autoritatis munimine roborentur ׃ quatinus ut equm (*sic*) est continua letentur tranquillitate . et perpetua stabilitate firmentur. Eapropter provida ducti consideratione . ecclesias de Morton' et de Waddon . quas Rogerus parvus . ecclesie Herefordensi in prebendam cum omnibus pertinentiis et libertatibus suis liberali munificentia rationabiliter dedisse cognoscitur . quarum etiam donationem Hugo parvus memorati Rogeri heres et filius . postmodum in domini Ricardi Cantuariensis archiepiscopi . totius Anglie primatis et apostolice sedis legati . et Gileberti Lund' . et B. Exon' . episcoporum presentia et nostra ׃ se ratam et inconvulsam habere professus est ׃ a deo nobis collata auctoritate prescripte Herefordensi ecclesie in perpetuum possidendas confirmamus . confirmationem nostram tam presentis scripti serie . quam sigilli nostri impressione munientes . salvo nimirum iure Wigorn' ecclesie . et diocesiani canonica iustitia . et tam dignitate quam libertate eiusdem ecclesie in omnibus reservata . et canonica eiusdem diocesiani obedientia. Facta est autem hec confirmatio apud Westmonasterium . anno verbi incarnati . m⁰ . c⁰ . septuagesima sexto . .xiii. Kal' . Aprilis . Testibus . Roberto capellano . Magistro Moise . Sansone . Magistro Silv' . Willelmo filio Osmundi . Reginaldo capellano domini Roberti Foliot Heref' episcopi . Waltero Mapp . Magistro Eustachio . Waltero scriptore . Theobaldo clerico . Mauricio filio Roberti . Rogero de Berchel' socero[a] eius.

a secero A.

Charters preserved at Hereford and a papal commission (App. II, 90A) show that there had been a dispute about the two churches between Hugh Parvus and the bishop of Hereford, and that the archbishop as judge-delegate had given sentence for the bishop *tam de proprietate quam de possessione* (D. and C. Archives 2770, *Hereford Charters*, p. 27). King Henry confirmed the sentence, describing it as a *finis* made before the archbishop and recorded before himself (ibid., p. 31). See Hugh's charter of ratification, no. 28A below. On the attitudes and principles underlying this dispute see p. 147 above. Pope Alexander confirmed the sentence on 5 February 1178 (*PUE*, ii. 362; misdated in *Hereford Charters*, p. 28).

28A. Hereford Cathedral

*c.*19 Mar. 1177. *Hugh Parvus records that he has accepted the sentence of Archbishop Richard, adjudging the churches of Moreton Valence and Whaddon to the church of Hereford. In the presence of the archbishop and Bishops Gilbert of London, Bartholomew of Exeter, and Roger of Worcester, Hugh renounced the rights he had claimed, and ratified his father's gift of the churches to form a prebend of Hereford.* 'His testibus. Ricardo Cant' archiepiscopo. Gillberto episcopo Lund'. Bartholomeo episcopo Exon'. Rogero episcopo Wigorn'. Hereberto Cant' archidiacono. Walerano archidiacono Baioc'. Petro Blesensi. Magistro Moyse. Magistro Silvestro. Magistro Eustachio. Teobaldo. Reginaldo capellano episcopi Heref'. Waltero scriptore. Amico et Willelmo domini Cant' notariis. Mauricio de Berkaleia. Rogero de Berkaleia.

A = Hereford, D. and C. Archives no. 2771. Endorsed: Littera Hugonis filii Rogeri parvi confirmantis factum patris sui (s.xiv). Approx. 270 × 180 + 20 mm. Sealed *double queue*, tag remains, seal lost.

Pd from A, *Hereford Charters*, pp. 28–9 (dated 1175–6).

Though not an act of Bishop Roger, and therefore not printed here, this charter is written in the same hand as no. 26 and possibly no. 55, cf. p. 231 above. Eight of the witnesses are common to nos. 28 and 28A.

29. Lanthony Priory

23 Aug. 1164 x 27 Feb. 1167. *Confirmation of freedom from services and customs due to the bishop or his officials, for St Mary of Lanthony and its appurtenances, namely the church of St Owen, Gloucester, with its chapels and one of the schools of Gloucester. The chapels are the castle chapel and those of St Kinburga, Hempstead, Elmore and Quedgeley. Confirmation also of a weir in the Severn.*

B = PRO C/115/L1/6689/A4 (Lanthony cart.) fos. 204^v–205^r. s.xv med.

C = PRO C/115/K2/6683/A1 (Lanthony cart.) fo. 33^r, section 1 no. 103, marked *dupl'* in margin. s.xiv med.

D = ibid., fo. 33^v, no. 104 *bis*. The rubricator noted: Carta R. Wig. episcopi que supra numero ciii scripta est non habet hic locum nec currit in numero nec copia tenet locum.

E = ibid., fo. 33^{r-v}, no. 104, in inspeximus of Baldwin bishop of Worcester.

Rogerus dei gratia Wigorn' episcopus omnibus sancte matris ecclesie filiis tam presentibus quam futuris salutem. Quod a predecessoribus meis bone memorie Symone, Iohanne et Alvredo episcopis propensiori cura novimus constitutum, nos quoque precipimus illibatum conservari, quod videlicet libertatem ab omni servitio et consuetudine ad episcopum vel eius ministros pertinentibus concedimus ecclesie sancte Marie de Lanthonia et regularibus fratribus ibidem deo servientibus tam ei quam eius appendiciis scilicet ecclesie sancti Audoeni cum capellis et una scolarum Gloecestrie^a ad eam pertinentibus, capella videlicet intra castellum, capella sancte Kineburge, capella de Heccamsteda, capella de Elmoura, capella de Quedesleia de eodem feodo, quam videlicet libertatem bone memorie Symon episcopus prefate ecclesie de Lanthonia in eius dedicatione prius concesserat. Preterea sedem unius gorti [fo. 205ʳ] in Sabrina apud Sestaneslade liberam et quietam concedimus eidem ecclesie de Lanthon', quam quidem predictus Symon episcopus dedit in excambium unius modii vini a Theoldo predecessore suo et nostro ecclesie de Lanthon' collati, et eidem ecclesie concessit, Osmundo etiam camerario concedente similiter eidem ecclesie partem sedis eiusdem gorti suo feodo pertinentem. Has itaque libertates et in ecclesiis et in gorto concedimus et episcopali confirmamus auctoritate et scripti nostri munimine et sigilli nostri impressione corroboramus. Hiis testibus, Roberto episcopo Hereford',[b] magistro Baldewino Exoniensi, magistro Symone Luvel,[c] magistro Moyse, magistro Silvestro, Gilleberto capellano, Sampsone clerico, magistro Ricardo de Inglesham, Rogero capellano de sancto Audoeno, Rogero filio Fulconis.

a et una scolarum Glouc' *interlined* C.   b *om*. Roberto episcopo Hereford' C.
c *remaining names replaced by* et aliis C.

Simon Luvel, who became archdeacon of Worcester in 1167, has no title. If this indication can be trusted, the bishop of Hereford must be Robert of Melun (d. 27 February 1167). The school is not mentioned in the charters of Bishops Simon, John and Alfred. Apart from this variation, Roger's charter is an almost verbatim reproduction of Alfred's (cart. A 1, fo. 33ʳ no. 102). The chapels are all within a few miles of Gloucester.
In the present work, the spelling 'Lanthony' is used for Lanthony by Gloucester, and 'Llanthony' for the original Welsh part of this bipartite convent.

30. Lanthony Priory

23 Aug. 1164 x Dec. 1165. *Confirmation to the canons of Lanthony of the church of Haresfield, given by Henry of Hereford.*

B = PRO C/115/L1/6689/A4 (Lanthony cart. A 4) fo. 44ʳ (formerly fo. 30ʳ). s.xv med.

C = PRO C/115/K2/6683/A1 (Lanthony cart. A 1) fo. 61ʳ. s.xiv med.

D = ibid., fo. 45ʳ in inspeximus of the prior and convent of Worcester of 1278.

R. dei gratia Wigorn' ecclesie minister universis sancte matris ecclesie filiis salutem. Officii nostri nos hortatur auctoritas ut beneficia que in nostra diocesi fidelium devotio venerabilibus locis pietatis intuitu contulit ipsis confirmare et scripto communire curemus. Hinc est quod ecclesiam de Hersefeld'[a] confirmamus[b] canonicis de Lanthonia sicut eam habent ex dono nobilis viri Henrici de Hereford' et carta sua quam inspeximus testatur, et eam presentis scripti munimine duximus roborandam. Testibus Radulfo priore Wig', Gervasio, Iohanne, monachis,[c] magistro Moyse, Ricardo Luvel, Gisleberto capellano, Roberto monacho, Samsone.[d]

<blockquote>
a Haresfeld' D.   b confirmavimus CD.   c remaining names replaced by et aliis D.
d Sampsone CD.

No. 30 was probably issued before the death in 1165 of Henry of Hereford, who is not called 'bone memorie'. For Henry's grant see David Walker, 'Charters of the earldom of Hereford 1095–1201', Camden Miscellany XXII, Camden 4th ser. i (1964), p. 47 no. 78, there dated 1161. Henry's gift was confirmed by his sister Margaret de Bohun in 1171 (ibid., p. 54 no. 91). Pope Alexander confirmed the gift 'ex dono Rogeri Wygorn' episcopi' on 1 Mar. 1177 (PUE, i. 414 no. 142).
</blockquote>

31. Lanthony Priory

1177 × 14 Apr. 1178. *Notification with Bartholomew bishop of Exeter, as papal judges-delegate, that the case between the canons of Lanthony and Roger, priest, about the church of Painswick has been ended by a composition. Roger resigned the church to the judges, who transferred it to the canons. Walter of Mayenne and Countess Cecily his wife, on whose land the church is situated, conceded and confirmed it to the canons.*

B = PRO C/115/L1/6689/A4 (Lanthony cart.) fo. 49^v. s.xv med.

C = PRO C/115/K2/6683/A1 (Lanthony cart.) fo. 293^r. s.xiv med.

D = PRO C/115/K1/6679/A9 (Lanthony cart.) fo. 139^r. s.xiii med.

Pd from C, Morey, *Bartholomew of Exeter*, p. 140 no. 17.

<blockquote>
No. 31 must have preceded no. 32, in which Roger the priest is reinstated at the presentation of Lanthony. See also App. II, 72 and p. 144 above. The concession by Walter of Mayenne and Countess Cecily is addressed to Bishop Roger and Matthew archdeacon of Gloucester (d. 1177/8); it is printed by David Walker (see no. 30), p. 40 no. 66. A charter of the Countess is ibid., no. 65. The church had been granted to Lanthony by Hugh de Lacy, Cecily's grandfather. Cf. VCH Glos., ii. 88, and W. E. Wightman, The Lacy Family (Oxford 1966), p. 181.
</blockquote>

32. Lanthony Priory

14 Apr. 1178 at Worcester. *Notification of the admission of Roger, clerk, as perpetual vicar of St Mary's church, Painswick, notwithstanding that his father ministered there.*

B = PRO C/115/K2/6683/A1 (Lanthony cart.) fo. 294^r. s.xiv med.

C = ibid. fo. 293^v in inspeximus of Archbishop Edmund of Canterbury and other bishops.

D = PRO C/115/K1/6679/A9 (Lanthony cart.) fos. 140^v–141^r in inspeximus as C. s.xiii med.

Universis sancte matris ecclesie filiis Rogerus dei gratia Wygorn' ecclesie dictus[a] minister salutem. Ad omnium cognitionem referatur nos ad presentationem dilectorum nostrorum Rogeri prioris Lanthon' et eiusdem loci conventus, secundum quod inter ipsos et Galterum de Meduana et Ceciliam eius uxorem convenit super iure presentationis ecclesie beate Marie de Wyka, Rogerum clericum in perpetuum vicarium eiusdem ecclesie admisisse, ut ecclesiam ipsam cum omnibus pertinentiis suis iure perpetuo nomine canonicorum Lanthon' possideat, eis annuam pensionem unius marce solvendo, non obstante quod pater memorati clerici in prescripta ecclesia[b] nomine alterius ministravit, cum super hoc mandatum domini pape Alexandri iii suscepissemus ne illud prefato Rogero preiudicium aliquod generaret. Ut igitur quod a nobis auctoritate apostolica rationabili est consideratione statutum inviolabili firmitate[c] perseveret, concessionem nostram presentis scripti serie et sigilli nostri impressione duximus muniendam. Facta est autem carta presens Wygorn' anno verbi incarnati m^o c^o lxxviii xviii kal' Maii . Testibus Petro de Wytind,'[d] Gilberto et Roberto[e] capellanis nostris et aliis.

    a *om.* dictus D.   b *om.* in prescripta ecclesia B.   c *om.* firmitate D.
    d Wrthindon C; Wydindon' D.   e B *ends here.*

    The admission of Roger as vicar of Painswick followed the settlement announced in no. 31. A letter of the prior of Lanthony to Bishop Roger announces the 'concession' of the church to Roger, 'in our chapter, in the presence of the lord William, your archdeacon of Gloucester'. The letter, like the bishop's charter, is dated 14 Apr. The letter is more precise than the bishop's charter about the details of Roger's tenure of the church. He is to meet all obligations due to the bishop and his officials, and stock the church with books, vestments and other necessities; it shall be restored to the canons fully stocked, when he dies or takes the religious habit (follows B).

33. Lanthony Priory

23 Aug. 1164 x c.1 Dec. 1176. *Notification that Robert, son of Richard, and Hawise his wife, have ratified the gift of her father, Richard Foliot, of the church of Tytherington to the prior and canons of Lanthony.*

B = PRO C/115/L1/6689/A4 (Lanthony cart. A 4) fo. 56^r (formerly fo. 41^r). s.xv med.

C = PRO C/115/K2/6683/A1 (Lanthony cart. A 1) fo. 301^r. s.xiv med.

Universis sancte matris ecclesie fidelibus Rogerus Wigorn' ecclesie dei gratia dictus episcopus salutem. Constituti in presentia nostra Robertus filius Ricardi et uxor eius Hawisa heres et filia Ricardi Foliot plenum assensum prebuerunt concessioni et donationi quam memoratus Ricardus Foliot fecerat dilectis fratribus nostris priori et canonicis Lanthonie super ecclesia de Tidrintona et carta sua confirmaverat. Qua inspecta et in communi audientia ipsis presentibus perlecta prescriptam ecclesiam petierunt a nobis predictis canonicis in perpetuam elemosinam confirmari. Nos itaque petitioni eorum satisfacientes et sepedictorum canonicorum securitati providere curantes ecclesiam de Tidrintona ecclesie Lanthon' cum pertinentiis suis episcopali auctoritate confirmavimus. Testibus Galfrido decano Hereford', Gilleberto capellano, Symone canonico Heref', Sampsone clerico,[a] magistro Silvestro, magistro Eustachio Heref', Randulfo Gansel, Willemo filio Godefridi, Willelmo de Wigornia.

<small>a *remaining names replaced by* et aliis C.</small>

<small>No. 33 was presumably issued before Pope Alexander confirmed the gift 'ex dono Rogeri Wygorn' episcopi' on 1 Mar. 1177 (*PUE*, i. 414 no. 142). The cartularies preserve, in proximity to no. 33, charters of Richard Foliot, addressed to Bishop John, two of his widow, and that of Robert and Hawise.</small>

34. Lanthony Priory

16 Mar. 1178 at Henbury in Salt Marsh. *Notification of the admission of Gilbert Cumin to the church of Tytherington at the presentation of Roger, prior of Lanthony. Gilbert shall pay an annual pension of one bezant to the canons within the octave of Easter.*

APPENDIX I

B = PRO C/115/K2/6683/A1 (Lanthony cart.) fo. 301^r, sec. 17 no. 6. s.xiv med.

C = PRO C/115/L1/6689/A4 (Lanthony cart.) fo. 56^r s.xv med.

Universis sancte matris ecclesie filiis Rogerus dei gratia Wygorn' ecclesie minister salutem in domino perpetuam. [fo. 301^v] Ad omnium volumus notitiam referri nos ad presentationem dilecti nostri Rogeri prioris Lanthon' admisisse Gilebertum Cumyn in ecclesia de Tydrintona et eiusdem prioris petitione prescriptam ecclesiam cum omnibus pertinentiis suis eidem Gileberto concessisse in perpetuum tenendam de canonicis Lanthon' sub annua pensione unius bisantii infra octavas Pasche nomine iamdicte ecclesie eisdem canonicis solvendi. Quod quia firmum et inconcussum esse desideramus scripti huius seriem sigilli nostri munimine roboravimus. Facta est concessio prescripta anno verbi incarnati m° c° lxxvii apud Hamber' in Saltem' xvii Kaln' April'. Testibus Symone archidiacono Wygorn', Willelmo Scotro priore sancti Augustini, Gileberto capellano, Algaro canonico, Henrico de Almari et aliis.

> The admission took place at the bishop's manor of Henbury in Salt Marsh, near Bristol.

35. Lanthony Priory

Mid-Apr. 1176 x 24 Mar. 1177. (*Lost charter*) *Confirmation of grant by Osmund reeve of Gloucester to the canons of Lanthony of land next to the church of Holy Trinity and two stalls under the church of St Michael, Gloucester, for the maintenance of two canons, who shall be approved by his heirs.*

Mentioned only, PRO C/115/K1/6681/A2 (Lanthony cart.) sec. 20 nos. 268 and 269, fo. 82^r (formerly 48^r). s.xiv med.

> Recording his gifts, Osmund notes: Hec autem feci per consilium domini Rogeri Wigorn' episcopi in cuius carta confirmantur hec in testimonium perpetuum. Anno incarnationis domini m° c° lxxvi ... Testibus Rogero Wygorn' episcopo, Roberto capellano eius, magistro Sampsone, magistro Silvestro et aliis. The bishop was in London on 28 Mar.; this piece of Worcester business is not likely to have been transacted until mid-Apr. 1176 at earliest.

36. Launceston Priory

23 Aug. 1164 × 1 July 1175. *Notification that Reginald earl of Cornwall in the bishop's presence granted to St Stephen of Launceston the land of* Karneduna, *a member of the manor of Rillaton, and as much more land of the manor as will make up one hundred shillings worth of land.*

B = London, Lambeth Palace Library MS 719 (Launceston cart.) fo. 217ᵛ. s.xv med.

Rogerus dei gratia dictus episcopus Wigorn' omnibus fidelibus ad quos presens scriptura pervenerit salutem. Noverit universitas vestra Reginaldum comitem Cornub' nobis presentibus pro salute anime sue et patris sui regis H. et Matillis imperatricis et filii eius regis H. et eius liberorum et pro salute uxoris sue et liberorum suorum et omnium antecessorum et successorum suorum concessisse et in puram et perpetuam elemosinam dedisse deo et ecclesie sancti Stephani de Lansteuatona et canonicis ibidem deo servientibus terram de Karneduna que est membrum manerii de Rillectuna ita quidem ut de reliqua parte ipsius manerii de Rilletuna (*sic*) perficiatur eis tantum quod bone et plenarie habeant centum solidatas terre adeo libere et quiete perpetuo tenendas sicut ipse unquam melius et liberius eam tenuit. Hiis testibus, venerabili fratre nostro Bartholomeo Exon' episcopo, Nicholao filio comitis, Bernardo clerico etc.

> The grant may belong to May 1175, shortly before the earl's death on 1 July, when Bartholomew, Roger and the earl, Roger's uncle, were all in London (Eyton, *Itinerary*, p. 190). But this is not the only possible occasion. *Karneduna* is probably Carnadon in Linkinhorne parish; Carnedon Lyer in the same parish was worth only five shillings at the time of the Domesday survey, while Carnadon rendered £7 to the king.

37. Lewes Priory

10 Feb. 1175 at Newbury. *Notification as judge-delegate, with Robert archdeacon of Surrey, of the settlement of the dispute between the monks of Lewes and William son of Ralph about estates called* Heselcrofta *and* Tilleberia.

APPENDIX I

A = PRO E/40/15488 (formerly Ancient Deeds A 15488), lower half of chirograph. Endorsed: transactio inter Lew' et Will' fil' Rannulfi (s.xiii); de fundis tillberi et heselcroft (s.xiv in.); $\frac{\text{xxiiii}}{\text{o}}$ (press mark, s.xiv). Approx. 120 × 110 + 18 mm. Sealed *double queue*; seals lost, remains of three tags.

B = BL MS Cotton Vespasian F. xv (Lewes cart.) fo. 78^r. 1444. Summary and English translation from B, L. F. Salzman, *The chartulary of* . . . *Lewes*, Part 1, Sussex Record Soc. xxxviii (1933), 140–1.

CIROGRAPHUM (cut through)

Universis sancte matris ecclesie filiis Rogerus dei gratia Wigorn' episcopus . et Robertus Winton' archidiaconus ꝉ salutem. Causa que vertebatur inter monachos Lewenses et Willelmum filium Randulfi . super fundis qui dicuntur Heselcrofta et Tilleberia remota appellatione a domino papa Alexandro tercio nostre cognitioni commissa . amicabili compositione interveniente ⸱ hoc modo finem sortita est. Memoratus Willelmus filius Randulfi terram viginti librarum apud Willelmum abbatem Ram' vel apud Ricardum de Luci . vel apud aliquem legalem virum si neuter predictorum custodiam terre predicte suscipere voluerit . communi consensu nostro videlicet et monachorum et Willelmi filii Randulfi eligendum deponet nomine suo custodiendam. Monachi similiter Lewenses custodie ipsius qui terram viginti librarum de manu predicti Willelmi susceperit . prenominatas terras . scilicet Heselcroftam et Tilleberiam nomine suo et monasterii servandas committent . hec interposita conditione . quod quisquis custos omnium terrarum prescriptarum fuerit universum censum videlicet viginti libras de terra Willelmi et xliv.^{a} sol' de terris monachorum Heselcrofte et Tilleberi ꝉ integre persolvet prefatis monachis de Lewes . donec centum marcas argenti acceperint . quibus solutis . omnes terre prescripte Willelmo filio Randulfi vel si ipse decesserit eius heredi libere et quiete absque omni reclamatione ꝉ resignabuntur. De his autem centum marcis terra alia in usus Lewensis monasterii convertenda . cum testimonio et consilio virorum fidedignorum comparabitur pro animabus predecessorum Willelmi et pro ipso . fratribus deo in prescripto monasterio servientibus conferenda. Cautio vero a monachis prestabitur ei cui custodia sepedictarum terrarum committetur quod pecunia predicta non in alios usus quam in terram comparandam expendetur. Sciendum etiam quod quandocunque infra triennium a die compositionis numerandum predicte centum marce persolute fuerint tota terra prenominata Willelmo vel heredi eius ⁑ libera et quieta restituetur. Hec autem compositio prout superius distincta est ⁑ a monachis Lewensibus verbo veritatis . a Willelmo filio Randulfi fide interposita ⁑ roborata est . Facta vero anno m⁰ c⁰ septuagesimo quarto verbi incarnati apud Neuberiam in ecclesia beati Nicholai iiii^{to} idus Februarii. Testibus Simone archidiacono Wig' . magistro Henrico de Norant' . magistro Moise . magistro Hugone de Cardunvilla . magistro Willelmo de Chine^b . magistro Nicholao de Hettingeam . Eduardo priore de Radinges . Lamberto sacrista Waltero monacho . Hugone filio cancellarii monacho.

> a *the scribe appears to have written* xlv, *and subsequently inserted a stroke, converting the number to* xliv.
> b *Chive or Thine could be intended; there are no abbreviation marks.*

> The archdeacon of Winchester in 1175 was Ralph, but Robert of Inglesham was archdeacon of Surrey in the diocese of Winchester. Assuming that the document is genuine (and it seems unlikely that so curious a transaction would be invented later), it was probably drawn up by the clerks of the bishop of Worcester as senior judge; possibly they were uncertain of Robert's title. 'It was not until the second half of the twelfth century that territorial titles were used regularly by the archdeacons of the diocese of Winchester.' (*Fasti*, ii. 91). Lewes owned the church at Tilbury, Essex; the *Tilleberia* of this text may be the same place. *Heselcrofta*, perhaps in the same area, has not been identified.

38. Lire Abbey

? June 1171 x Sept. 1172. *Confirmation and protection of possessions of Lire Abbey in the diocese of Worcester, saving episcopal rights, naming the churches of Feckenham, Hanley Castle and Chedworth, also tithes of the demesne of Crowle, Bisley, Forthampton, Eldersfield, Hempstead and Arlington, also two hides in Duntisborne Abbots.*

B = Évreux, Arch. dép. de l'Eure, microfilm (Eure 1 M 2/R 1) of Lire cart. in private possession, MSS de Dom Le Noir vol. 23, p. 448 no. 89.

APPENDIX I 271

Mentioned in Sheen Abbey inventory, BL MS Cotton Otho B. xiv fo. 25^r: In primis confirmatio Rogeri episcopi Wigorn' super ecclesiis de Feckenham et aliis in episcopatu suo, facta abbati de Lyra.

Rogerus dei gratia Wigorn' episcopus omnibus sancte matris ecclesie filiis salutem. Sciant tam presentes quam futuri nos omnes possessiones ecclesie de Lira ubicumque fuerint in nostro episcopatu sub nostra protectione suscepisse et eidem ecclesie nos easdem confirmasse, has videlicet, ecclesiam de Fekeham cum appendiciis suis, ecclesiam de Hanleg' cum appendiciis suis, ecclesiam de Chedeworda cum appendiciis suis et decimam foreste de Malvernia et decimam totius dominii de Cohulla et decimam totius dominii de Bisseleg' et decimam totius dominii de Forthelmestona et decimam totius dominii de Elderesfeld' et decimam totius dominii de Hechamestod' et decimam totius dominii de Aluerintona et duas hidas apud Duntesburn'. Volumus itaque ut possessiones predictas ecclesia de Lira libere et quiete salvo iure episcopali teneat, episcopali auctoritate prohibentes ne quis ei super his aliquam iniuriam faciat. His testibus: Giliberto capellano nostro, Roberto monacho clerico nostro, Willelmo clerico de Trum, Gaufrido, Radulfo, Tostino, Roberto de Hereff', Alberico, Roberto de Almenasch', Ricardo, monachis de Lira.

No. 38 is witnessed by seven monks of Lire, and by William of Trun, who witnesses no. 7, which was probably issued in Normandy in 1171 or 1172. No. 38 probably belongs to approximately the same period.

39. Lire Abbey

23 Aug. 1164 x 9 Aug. 1179. *Permission to the monks of Lire to have the churches of Hanley Castle, Feckenham and Chedworth for their own uses, saving proper maintenance for the vicars.*

B = Évreux, Arch. dép. (as no. 38), p. 493 no. 102.

Rogerus dei gratia Wigorn' episcopus universis sancte matris ecclesie filiis salutem. Quia ad nostre amministrationis spectat officium locis religiosis pia dispensatione providere ut qui divino in eis mancipantur officio habundantius habeant unde pauperibus et necessitatis incommoda sustinentibus largius amministrent, iccirco omnium cognitionem tenere desideramus nos religionis et hospitalitatis intuitu ecclesiam de Hanleia, ecclesiam de Fecheham, ecclesiam de Chegcheworda cum universis decimationibus et ceteris obventionibus et omnibus ad eas de iure pertinentibus usibus monachorum Lirensium salva honesta sustentatione vicarii in ea ministraturi in perpetuum concessisse, et ne futuris temporibus in irritum debeat revocari hanc nostre concessionis largitionem episcopali auctoritate roborasse. Testibus.

Cf. no. 38 and p. 79 above.

40. Lire Abbey

23 Aug. 1164 x 9 Aug. 1179. *Confirmation to the monks of Lire of their churches in the diocese of Worcester, Hanley Castle, Feckenham and Chedworth, for receiving guests and increasing works of charity. The vicars shall have a third of all tithes and offerings.*

B = Évreux, Arch. dép. (as no. 38), p. 488 no. 90, in inspeximus by Bishop William of Worcester.

Universis sancte matris ecclesie filiis Rogerus dei gratia Wigorn' ecclesie dictus episcopus salutem quam in domino speramus. Ex suscepte sollicitudinis officio viris religiosis provida dispensatione providere teneamur ut tanto liberius contemplationi et orationi vacare debeant quanto in exterioribus victualium necessitatibus uberius habundant. Eapropter Lirensis monasterii mediocritate considerata cuius fundatio non in amplis terrarum possessionibus sed in ecclesiis potius et decimationibus consistere noscitur, monachis in eodem monasterio divino mancipatis obsequio ad hospitum susceptionem et ad diffusioris caritatis amplificationem ecclesias quas in nostro habere noscuntur presulatu, videlicet ecclesiam de Feecham, ecclesiam de Hanleia, ecclesiam de Cheddewrd' votive pietatis studio concedimus et eis pontificali auctoritate roboramus. Verum ut vicariis onus et curam regendarum animarum suscepturis honesta et sufficiens sustentatio de prescriptis ecclesiis ministretur, ipsis tertiam portionem omnium decimarum oblationum et omnium obventionum ad iamdictas ecclesias sive ad altare aut cimiterium spectantium assignamus. Ne ergo posteritas evacuet quod equitate previa statutum esse cognoscitur, illud presentis scripti serie et sigilli nostri impressione duximus muniendum.

Cf. nos. 38, 39 and p. 79 above.

41. Lire Abbey

c.May 1170 x Sept. 1172. *Notification as judge-delegate with Giles bishop of Évreux of the termination of the case between the abbots of Bec and Lire about the church of* Brue(r)land.

B = Évreux, Arch. dép. (as no. 38) p. 491 no. 96.

Notum sit tam presentibus[a] quam futuris quod ego Rogerus Wigorn' episcopus et Egidius Ebroicensis episcopus consilio et assensu dilecti fratris nostri Victoris abbatis sancti Georgii et Ivonis archidiaconi Rothomagensis qui nobiscum arbitri assidebant super questionem que vertebatur inter abbatem Beccensem et abbatem Lirensem de ecclesia de Brueland et omnibus pertinentiis eius, inspectis instrumentis et presumptionibus et testibus hinc inde diligenter examinatis et depositionibus eorum in scripto redactis, in presentia domini et patris nostri Rotrodi Rothomagensis archiepiscopi absolvimus abbatem Lirensem et monasterium eius a petitione abbatis Beccensis et monasterii sui, venientesque Beccum in presentia eiusdem abbatis Beccensis et quorundam monachorum, scilicet Eustachii prioris, Roberti de Aureis Vallibus cantoris, Isembardi sacriste, Ricardi camerarii, Hunfridi elemosinarii, Rogeri de Bardovilla, Henrici de Buketot, magistri Willelmi de Aspravilla, Hugonis de Sarniaco, qui de parte conventus late sententie assenserunt, eandem sententiam absolutionis iteravimus, prefatam ecclesiam de Bruerland cum omnibus decimis et pertinentiis suis, et nominatim decimis de feudo Gudonis, abbati Lire et monasterio Lirensi adiudicantes. Ne ergo super eadem re inposterum possit eis controversia moveri, prefatam sententiam presentis scripti attestatione et sigilli nostri munimine corroboravimus.

a *posteris* B.

Giles became bishop of Évreux early in 1170, and was absent from Normandy with Bishop Roger on a mission to the Curia from late Jan. 1171 to *c*.May. An annotator has written '1172' in the margin of the cartulary, and this could be correct. For the dating compare nos 7 and 38.

42. Lire Abbey

c.Aug. 1173 x 6 Oct. 1174. (? *Lost charter*) *Notification as judge-delegate with Robert elect of Hereford of the settlement of the dispute between the abbey of Lire and the church of Wimborne about tithes of the demesne of the earl of Leicester at Shapwick and Kingston Lacy. Wimborne abandoned its claim; Lire undertook to offer a candle worth 12 pence annually on the feast of St Cuthberga (31 Aug.).*

Mentioned only, Évreux, Arch. dép. de l'Eure, H 590 (Titres de Lyre), p. 325 no. xx, s.xviii; also in confirmation of the *transactio* by Pope Alexander III, JL 13987, Loewenfeld, *Epistolae Pontificum*, p. 203 no. 340; also in confirmation of Pope Lucius III, *PUF*, ii. 320–1 no. 221. Perhaps noted in BL MS Cotton Otho B. xiv (inventory of Sheen Abbey muniments) fo. 38ʳ: Antiqua scriptura iudicum delegatorum de causa mota inter abbatem de Lyra et canonicos de Wymburne super decimis de dominio comitis Leic' in Kingeston et in Sapewyke.

> None of these texts explicitly mentions a document in the name of the bishop of Worcester and the elect of Hereford. The document imperfectly summarized in *Titres de Lyre* is a letter of the dean of Hereford and the prior of Kenilworth, who were commissioned to hear the dispute, but apparently reported to the pope (probably Lucius) that the matter had been settled by Roger bishop of Worcester and Robert elect of Hereford. Further litigation was ended by definitive sentence, confirmed by Lucius III (*PUF*, ii. 348 no. 254). There can be no doubt that Roger and Robert were commissioned to hear the case, and presided over a settlement; only the form of the ensuing document is uncertain. The tithes were paid to Lire's cell at Wareham, which like Lire's other cells in England, passed to Sheen.

42A. Lire Abbey (Rejected)

Mon. Ang., vi. 1094 no. 13 is an incomplete text deriving from a transcript by André Duchesne, of a notification by 'R. bishop of Worcester' of a settlement between the abbeys of Lire and Saumur about the chapels of Little Lydney (St Briavel's) and Hewelsfield in the diocese of Hereford. The full text is in Bodl. MS Rawlinson B.329 (Hereford register) fo. 162ʳ. The bishop was A(lfred) of Worcester, acting as delegate of Pope Adrian IV.

Lire Abbey *see also* **Carisbrooke Priory, no. 9**

43. Luffield Priory

c. July 1167 x *c.*1 Jan. 1179. *Announcement of the settlement of the case between the prior of Thetford and the monks of Luffield about the church of Dodford. The case had been committed to the bishop of Worcester and Simon, abbot of St Albans.*

B = London, Westminster Abbey, Muniment Book 10 (Luffield cart.) fo. 23ᵛ. s.xv ex.

Pd *Luffield Priory Charters*, ed. G. R. Elvey, vol. i Northants Record Soc. xxii (1968), p. 39 no. 29, dated 1167–74.

Universis sancte matris ecclesie filiis R. dei gratia Wigornensis ecclesie minister salutem. Ad universorum referimus notitiam quod controversia que vertebatur inter priorem de Thefford' et monachos de Luffelde super ecclesia de Dodeford' et nobis et dilecto in Christo fratri Sim' abbati sancti Albani ab Alexandro papa tertio commissa fuerat communiter terminanda sub hoc fine quievit. Memoratus siquidem prior de Thefford' compatiens paupertati monachorum de Luffeld' iuri quod sibi vendicabat in ecclesia de Dodeford' penitus renuntiavit et eandem ecclesiam predictis monachis cessit. Hanc autem renuntiationem viva voce fecit Christianus prior de Thefford' in presentia nostra constitutus et postmodum eandem plenius protestatus est per litteras sui conventus quas nobis destinavit. Valete.

> Luffield's opponent was the Cluniac priory of St Mary of Thetford. The nature of Thetford's claim is not stated. These proceedings could possibly have taken place in the summer or autumn of 1167, between the election of Abbot Simon *c.*21 May and the departure of Bishop Roger from England at an unknown date in 1167, but on general grounds 1172 x 1178 is more probable. A dispute about Dodford church between Luffield Priory and A., clerk, was ended by a settlement made before other judges-delegate on 9 Apr. 1176. This dispute might have been related to, and followed upon, the proceedings before Bishop Roger, but this is not certain, since in the same period (*c.*1167 x 19 Feb. 1177) Prior William and the convent of Merton also renounced rights claimed in Dodford church (*Luffield charters*, pp. 38–9). The Luffield cartulary preserves a letter to Bishop Roger and Abbot Simon from the prior and convent of Thetford, appointing an agent to act for them in this case (*Luffield charters*, i. 38).

44. Maiden Bradley Hospital

1167 x *c.*1 Jan. 1179. *Confirmation of Kidderminster church to the leper women of Maiden Bradley, with permission to appropriate after the death of Robert the parson.*

APPENDIX I

A = original formerly in the College of Arms.

B = BL Add. MS 37503 (Maiden Bradley cart. fragment) fo. 30^v. s.xiv.

Pd from A, *ex autographo in officio armorum, Esc. 4 Ric. II n.*, *Mon. Ang.*, vii. 644, and by Sir Richard Colt Hoare, *A modern history of Wiltshire* (1822–37), i. 97, apparently from *Mon. Ang.*

Pd here from *Mon. Ang.* with select variants from B.

Universis Christi fidelibus ad quos presens scriptum pervenerit, Rogerus dei gratia Wygorn'[a] episcopus eternam in domino salutem.[b] Cum ad omnes sollicitudini nostre commissos ex suscepto officio bonum operari teneamur, specialius quodam modo ad eorum promotionem et provectionem[c] teneri nos credimus qui ex occulto dei iudicio continuis cruciatibus affliguntur et quos arctioris vite propositum et religio immaculata deo efficit acceptos et in facie omnium commendat[d] laudabiles. Attendentes itaque et diligenter perpendentes[e] honestam conversationem mulierum leprosarum de Bradeleia[f] et ministrorum suorum ibidem deo servientium et curam eorum gerentium[g] inspecta carta Manseri[h] Biset dapiferi H. regis Angl' qua idem Manserus Biset predictis mulieribus leprosis ecclesiam de Kedeminstre[j] tanquam advocatus concessit, et nobilis rex H. secundus eis carta sua confirmavit, eandem ecclesiam ad petitionem predicti Henrici regis et Manseri Biset eius dapiferi sepedictis mulieribus et earum ministris pietatis intuitu concedimus et presentis scripti patrocinio communimus et confirmamus, statuentes ut ipsam ecclesiam de Kedeminstre[k] cum omnibus pertinentiiis suis post decessum Roberti persone possidentis[l] in usus suos proprios sine aliqua contradictione salvis consuetudinibus episcopalibus convertant. Hiis testibus,[m] Simone archidiacono Wigorn', magistro Moyse, et Silvestro magistro de Leche (*sic*), Ricardo Lumple, Ernaldo decano de Sumerford, Radulfo filio Stephani, Bartholomeo Biset, Ricardo Talebot, Radulfo de sancto Germano et multis aliis.

a Wygorn' B, Wigorniensis *Mon.*   b eternam salutem in domino *Mon.*
c provexionem B.   d *add* acceptos *Mon.*   e attendentes B.
f Bradeleghe B.   g *om.* gerentium *Mon.*   h Manasseri *Mon.*   j Kyd' B.
k Kyderm' B.   l possident B.   m *all names replaced by* etc B.

Manaser's gift was contested by his heirs in 1265 and 1336 (*VCH Worcs.*, iii. 175, *VCH Wilts.*, iii. 295–302). The appropriation was finally effected in 1335 (*Liber Albus ... of Worcester*, calendar by J. M. Wilson, Worc. Hist. Soc. (1919) no. 1275).

45. Malmesbury Abbey

? c.Sept./Oct. 1178. *Confirmation of a pension of ten shillings from the church of Shipton, issued when Roger came with Bishop Bartholomew of Exeter to make peace between the abbot and brethren, by order of Pope Alexander.* 'Actum in capitulo de Malmesburia coram his testibus, Augustino Watreford' episcopo, Thoma abbate de Hyda etc.'

B = PRO E/164/24 (Malmesbury cart.) fo. 183^v–184^r. s.xiii ex.

Pd from B, *Reg. Malmesbury*, ii. 15 no. 153.

> Augustine, bishop of Waterford (elected 6 Oct. 1175) was with Bishop Roger c.24 Sept. 1178, cf. no. 2 above. No. 45 has therefore been assigned to approximately the same date. App. II, 14 is a commission to the bishops of Worcester and London (?*recte* Exeter) concerning the dispute between the abbot and monks. Shipton has not been identified.

46. Newnham Priory

20 or 25 Jan. 1177 at Windsor. *Notification as judge-delegate that the case between the canons of St Paul's, Bedford (later Newnham Priory) and the incumbent of the church of Holcot has been ended by an agreement made in the bishop's presence in the king's chapel at Windsor. The canons recognized the right of Gilbert Passelewe and his heirs to present parsons to the church, but retained an annual payment of five shillings from it. Nicholas the parson swore to make this payment, and his successors shall make a similar promise before institution. Gilbert Passelewe, for himself and his heirs, swore to observe the agreement. Adam abbot of Evesham, the second judge, was absent.*

'Teste Nicholao archidiacono de Hunt', Sym' archidiacono Wig', magistro Moise et aliis'.

B=BL MS Harley 3656 (Newnham cart.) fo. 56^v s.xv.

Pd from B, *Cart. of Newnham Priory*, ed. J. Godber, Publications of the Bedfordshire Hist. Rec. Soc. xliii (1963), p. 58 no. 94.

The date is not perfectly clear in B; it may be either viii or xiii Kal. Feb'. As the bishop was at Warwick on 17 Jan. it is perhaps more probable that he was at Windsor on 25 than on 20 Jan. The canons had evidently brought their complaint against Nicholas the parson, described obliquely as 'him who was said to occupy the church of Holcot'. A following document shows that he was a brother of Gilbert Passelewe, who does not appear to have been named in the papal commission. It is not clear whether the canons had intended to dispute the right to the advowson, or simply to force the parson to pay a pension.

47. Northampton, Priory of St Andrew

c.1166 x *c*.1. Jan. 1179. *Notification as judge-delegate that Hugh, clerk, has renounced his claim that he was violently despoiled of the chapel of Potton. The prior and convent of St Andrew, Northampton, have been absolved from his charge. Richard archdeacon of Ely, the second judge, was absent.*

B = BL MS Royal 11 B. ix (cart. of St Andrew's, Northampton) fos. 27^v–28^r. s.xiii ex.

Universis sancte matris ecclesie filiis Rogerus dei gratia Wig' episcopus salutem. Causa que vertebatur inter dilectos fratres nostros monachos sancti Andree de Norht' et Hugonem clericum super capella de Potton' qua se Hugo spoliatus esse absque ordine iudiciario asserebat, a domino Alexandro papa tertio nobis pariter et dilecto nostro R. Heliensi archidiacono fuerat delegata. In fine vero mandati apostolici erat annexum si uterque interesse non posset alter nichilominus in causa procederet. Coniudice itaque nostro urgentibus negotiis occupato, cum prenominatus Hugo se a priore sancti Andree violenter eiectum a prescripta capella proponeret [fo. 28^r] nos ab ipso modum illate violentie requisivimus. Ille autem super hoc habita deliberatione, in iure professus est se nullam violentiam a memorato priore sustinuisse, et incontinenti tam monasterio sancti Andree quam priori et monachis questionem violentie quam sibi super capella Pottone illatam proposuerat penitus remisit. Nos itaque ut qui plena potestate et iurisdictione, acceptis litteris college nostre quod cause illius cognitioni non posset adesse, fungebamur ab impetitione prescripte violentie prescripti loci monachos absolvimus.

This investigation took place in execution of a papal commission (App. II, 12) which required a particular course of action if Hugh had been despoiled. The commission was at least the fourth obtained by one or other party to this case.

The time required for the various stages of the dispute makes it unlikely that Bishop Roger's charter was issued before about 1166; more probably the whole affair took place in the 1170s, perhaps after the capture of the King of Scots in July 1174, since the papal commissions show that Hugh's opponent was a clerk of that king. See also p. 153 above.

Richard archdeacon of Ely is Richard FitzNeal, author of the *Dialogus de Scaccario*, royal justice, treasurer, and later bishop of London.

48. Nostell Priory

1167 x *c*.1 Jan. 1179. *Confirmation to Prior Asketil and the convent of Nostell of the church of Newbold Pacy, given by Aytropius de Hasteng, to hold* in usus proprios *with all appurtenances after the death of Henry, son of Peter of Northampton.*

B = BL MS Cotton Vespasian E. xix (Nostell cart.) fo. 112^v. s.xiii ex.

Rogerus dei gratia Wigorniensis episcopus universis sancte matris ecclesie filiis salutem. Noverit universitas vestra nos caritatis intuitu et causa hospitalitatis fovende concessisse et presenti scripto nostro confirmasse Asketillo priori et canonicis sancti Osuualdi regis et martiris de Nostl' in puram et liberam [fo. 113^r] et perpetuam elemosinam in usus proprios ecclesiam de Neubold quam habent ex dono Aytropii de Hasteng cum terris et decimis et omnibus pertinentiis suis cum vacaverit post decessum Henrici filii Petri de Norhamton', salvis in omnibus episcopalibus et sinodalibus. Eapropter volumus et precipimus quatinus predictam ecclesiam de Neubolt bene teneant et in pace et honorifice tanquam liberam elemosinam et nullus eis contra concessionem nostram et confirmationem super predictam ecclesiam iniuriam facere presumat vel contumeliam. Siquis vero contra hanc paginam nostram aliquid attemptare presumpserit indignationem dei omnipotentis se noverit incursurum. Hiis testibus etc.

Bishop Roger's charter must be later in date than the institution of Henry, son of Peter of Northampton, as parson of Newbold. This was effected by Prior Ralph and Archdeacon Simon of Worcester by authority of Bishop Roger, perhaps during his absence of 1167-72, certainly after Simon's appointment in 1167. Their charter recording the institution, at the presentation of the prior and convent of Nostell, is on fo.1 14^v. Charters of Aytropius Hasteng, father and son of the same name, are on fo. 114^r. The bishop's charter has a rubric: 'Carta Rogeri [Nor expunged] Wigorniensis episcopi', and a note:

'Ista carta scriba' in tercio fol' sequenti', i.e. fo. 114ᵛ, where a note shows that the writer intended the bishop's charter to follow that of the prior and archdeacon. Robert Hasteng, son of the second Aytropius, tried to reclaim the advowson by assize *de ultima presentatione* in 1221 (*Rolls of the justices in eyre for Gloucestershire* ..., Selden Soc. lix (1940), pp. 264–5). Perhaps the family had already shown a wish to reclaim the church, hence the unusual prohibition and threat against disturbance of the gift. The final threat uses the formula of papal confirmations.

49. Osney Abbey

? Sept. 1172 x *c.* Apr. 1175. *Notification as judge-delegate, with Hugh dean of St Paul's, London, that the dispute over the church of Shenstone, between the canons of Osney, claimants, Ralph of Tamworth archdeacon of Stafford, occupier, and William de Brai, patron, has been ended by agreement. Ralph shall hold the church from Osney, paying an anuual pension. After his death, William shall present a clerk to the abbot who shall pay to Osney 23 shillings annually. After the death of this clerk, William or his heirs shall present vicars to the abbot.* 'Huius rei testes sunt Thomas archidiaconus Wellensis, Iohannes Cumin, magister Moyses, magister Gilebertus, magister Helias, Rogerus, Iohannes, canonici de Kirkeham et plures alii clerici et laici.'

B = BL MS Cotton Vitellius E. xv (Osney cart.) fo. 36ᵛ. s.xiii in.
Pd from B, *Oseney cart.*, v. 71–2 no. 578D.

Thomas became archdeacon of Wells *c.*Michaelmas 1169 (J. Armitage Robinson, *Somerset Hist. Essays* (1921), p. 82), but Bishop Roger returned to England only *c.*Sept. 1172. The final date is suggested by the appearance of a papal commission of 31 July 1175 (*Oseney cart.*, v. 70 no. 578B), which probably followed this settlement. Ralph of Tamworth died, at latest, early in 1176. The cartulary is much damaged. The amount of the payment to be made by Ralph is illegible, as are some of the provisions about later vicars. Possibly they were to receive a fixed portion, whereas Ralph and his first successor were to receive all the revenues except for the fixed pension.

50. Osney Abbey

? July x Dec. 1176. *Notification with Gilbert bishop of London, as judges-delegate, of their definitive sentence in the case between Osney Abbey and St Frideswide's Priory about the church of St Mary Magdalen, Oxford. Pope Alexander's commission (App. II, 52) is* recited. *The bishop of London adjudged possession to Osney, following proof of violent dispossession. The hearing on the question of right was delayed, and later the canons of Osney brought a second commission (App. II, 4 of ?12 Apr. 1176), also recited, reproving the judges for delay. When the parties appeared before the bishop of London, the prior of St Frideswide's asserted that a letter of Robert, late bishop of Hereford, to Pope Eugenius, was forged. A sentence delivered by Eugenius* (Oseney cart., ii. 217–18, PUE, iii. 368) *is recited. When the parties met at Oxford, the judges rejected a demand from St Frideswide's for restoration of possession, because possession had been lost by judgement, and decided that the charge of forgery could not be admitted. Perpetual silence was imposed on St Frideswide's, which was condemned to pay four marks in respect of profits received during occupation of the church.* 'Sententie vero diffinitive tam de proprietate quam de possessione apud Oxenford' late affuerunt viri auctoriate graves, abbas videlicet Gloecestrie, abbas de Hegensh', magister Ricardus de Stortford', Ricardus de Salesberi, Radulfus de Alta Ripa, magister Silvester, magister Sanson et alii quamplures.'

A = Oxford, Christ Church, Osney Charter 625, lost.

B = BL MS Cotton Vitellius E. xv (Osney cart.), fos. 14^v–15^r, damaged. s.xiii in.

Pd from A and B, *Oseney cart.*, ii. 219–23; also, after the loss of A, *Letters of Foliot*, pp. 463–7.

> The pope confirmed the sentence on 4 Mar. 1177 (*Oseney cart.*, ii. 226 no. 785); the sentence cannot be much later than the end of Dec. 1176. The earliest date is suggested on the assumption that the date of the second commission (App. II, 4, *q.v.*) has been correctly copied in the cartulary. No. 50 may be the work of clerks of the bishop of London, the senior judge, hence the unusual insertion of the papal commissions, and the title *magister* given to Samson. The judges received written evidence from John bishop of Poitiers, and Laurence prior of Coventry, who had been present in the Curia when Pope Eugenius gave judgement. (*Oseney cart.*, ii. 216–17.) Other documents relating to the case are pd in *Oseney cart.*, ii. 224–6. See also App. II, 86A.

51. Osney Abbey

25 Mar. 1173 x Apr. 1174. *Notification and confirmation of the settlement made before Bartholomew bishop of Exeter, as judge-delegate, between the churches of Worcester and Osney about the church of Bibury. Osney shall possess the church, saving diocesan rights,*

paying to Worcester 60 shillings annually. The bishops of Worcester shall have the right to place one canon in the abbey, and the abbey shall pray for bishops of Worcester as for its founders and abbots. The bishop has sealed this document with the consent of his chapter. 'Hiis testibus, Radulpho priore Wigorn', Simone archidiacono Wigorn', Gileberto capellano, magistro Moyse, magistro Silvestro, Rand' Gansello, *clericis nostris,* Roberto et Rogero canonicis Oseneye, Bertremmo clerico de Verdun, Petro presbitero de Tilebrouke, Nicholao clerico de Ravesned'.

B = BL MS Cotton Vitellius E. xv (Osney cart.) fo. 18^v, damaged, in inspeximus of Bishop William of Worcester. s.xiii in.

C = Oxford, Christ Church, unnumbered (Osney cart.) fo. 171^r. s.xiii ex.

D = ibid. fo. 170^r in inspeximus as B.
Pd from D and B, *Oseney cart.,* v. 2–3 no. 512.

>No. 51 probably followed closely upon the settlement arranged by arbiters at Salisbury 'anno incarnationis domini mclxxiii', as announced by Bishop Bartholomew (*Oseney cart.,* v. 3–4 no. 512A, *Worc. cart.,* pp. 119–20 no. 226 with references to older editions and related documents). Bartholomew's charter is witnessed by John dean of Chichester, elected bishop of Chichester late in Apr. 1173. This should indicate that the settlement, and Bishop Roger's confirmation, belong to late Mar. or Apr.
>
>Bibury was a manor of the bishops of Worcester. Bishop John of Pagham granted the church and its chapels to Osney, without the consent of his chapter, that is, of the monks of Worcester; the validity of the grant could therefore be challenged. On the case see App. II, 36 and pp. 106, 183 above. Bishop Roger assigned the annual payment of 60 shillings to the monks of Worcester for food (no. 84 below).

52. Hamo Peche

Sept. 1164 x *c.*1 Jan. 1179. (*Lost charter*) *Notification as judge-delegate of the settlement of a case between Adam, clerk, and William de Careville about the church of Badmondisfield. William shall hold the church, paying forty shillings a year to Adam, and if Adam dies first, William shall possess the church. The composition was made in the presence and with the consent of Robert Burdel, patron of the advowson of half the church, and of William Giffard similarly, and in the presence of Hamo Peche, patron of the advowson of the other half.*

Mentioned only, in *Curia Regis Rolls* x (1221–2), pp. 242–3, in record of proceedings about the last presentation to the church of Wickhambrook, in Michaelmas Term 1221, in the course of which Hamo Peche produced Bishop Roger's charter. William of Careville was still alive, and was said to have been parson for forty years. If his tenure depended on the settlement reached before Bishop Roger, the settlement belongs to 1172 x 1178 rather than to the 1160s. Adam the clerk had died recently, and it was alleged that William had been his vicar. The record is obscure about the relationship of the two clerks to the patrons of the moieties of the church, but it would appear that William had been presented by Hamo Peche, and Adam by Robert Burdel and/or William Giffard, predecessors of Eularia Trussebut who in 1221 was claiming the presentation. Badmondisfield probably had a chapel attached to a manor in the parish of Wickhambrook; it seems to have been assumed by both parties in 1221 that a charter relating to the one was evidence of the status of the other.

53. Plympton Priory

27 June 1175 at Lambeth. *Notification with Richard archbishop of Canterbury, as judges-delegate, of their sentence in the case about patronage of the church of Sutton, between the canons of Plympton and Joel of Vautort, knight, on behalf of a nephew in his custody. Perpetual silence has been imposed upon Joel.*

B = Oxford, Bodl. MS James 23 p. 163, among extracts from lost Plympton cartulary. s.xvii in.

Universis sancte[a] matris ecclesie filiis ad quos presentes littere pervenerint Ricardus dei gratia Cantuariensis archiepiscopus totius Anglie primas et apostolice sedis legatus et Rogerus eadem gratia Wigorn' episcopus salutem in domino. Delegavit nobis dominus papa Alexander 3 causam que vertebatur inter canonicos de Plimton' et Iohelem militem de Valletorta super ecclesia de Sudtona, in qua ut idem miles domino pape suggesserat sibi et nepoti suo cuius erat tutor ius patronatus vendicabat, appellatione remota terminandam sub certa forma videlicet quod si nobis constaret per autenticas litteras bone memorie Willelmi quondam Exoniensis episcopi, quarum rescriptum prefati canonici domino pape ostenderant, prescriptam ecclesiam ipsis fuisse adiudicatam, predicto Ioheli et suis super eadem ecclesia perpetuum silentium appellatione postposita imponeremus. Die igitur et loco partibus constituto cum iamdictum Iohelem quarto edicto peremptorio citassemus ipse nec comparuit nec pro se responsalem destinavit. Unde absentiam ipsius ita solenniter citati pro contumacia reputantes et apostolicum mandatum secundum formam nobis prescriptam exequi cupientes, autenticas litteras prefati Willelmi episcopi Exoniensis nobis a canonicis oblatas diligenter inspeximus, super quarum veritate plena fide certificati tum ex nostra inspectione tum ex testimonio venerabilis fratris nostri B. Exoniensis episcopi, qui ut de veritate magis liqueret sigillum huius instrumenti aliis sigillis prenominati episcopi W. extantibus contulerat, tum ex sacramento Stephani canonici iurantis quod ex transcripto predictarum litterarum W. Exoniensis episcopi litteras commissorias a domino papa impetraverat secundum quarum formam nos in causa ista procedere oportebat, tum etiam ex sacramento ipsius et alterius canonici iurantium quod ipsi et totus conventus ecclesie Plimton' a maioribus eiusdem ecclesie acceperant instrumentum illud esse autenticum scriptum prefati episcopi, continentiam prescriptarum litterarum ratam haberi iudicavimus et memorato Ioeli et hiis qui nomine ipsius super hoc actionem contra predictos canonicos instituerunt[b] super eadem ecclesia autoritate domini pape et nostra perpetuum silentium imposuimus, prohibentes ne ipse Iohel vel per se vel per suos super eadem ecclesia ipsos molestare vexare vel inquietare presumat. Data est autem sententia ista apud Lamhed' anno dominice incarnationis mclxxv v kal. Iulii assidentibus nobis venerabili fratre nostro G. Lundon' episcopo, domino Roberto de Novoburgo, Yvone et Amico archidiaconis Rothomagensis ecclesie.

a The transcriber regularly writes *ae* according to classical usage.
b instituent B.

The judges' commission is App. II, 37. Joel's custody of his nephews is recorded on the Pipe Roll (*PR 18 Henry II (1171–2)*, p. 102). No. 53 may have been composed and written by clerks of the archbishop of Canterbury, as the senior judge.

54. St Albans Abbey

22 Nov. 1174 at London. *Notification with Bartholomew bishop of Exeter, as judges-delegate, of the settlement of the case between Simon, abbot, and the monks of St Albans, and A., clerk, about a third part*

of the church of Luton. A. had asserted that he had been wrongfully despoiled, but renounced his claims in return for an undertaking by the abbot and convent to pay him a hundred shillings a year for life.

B = BL MS Cotton Otho D. iii (Cart. of St Albans) fo. 115^v (damaged). s.xiv ex.

B.[a] dei gratia Exon' et R. eadem gratia Wygorn' dicti episcopi omnibus fidelibus ad quos presens scriptum pervenerit salutem. Noverit universitas vestra quod dominus papa delegavit nobis causam que vertebatur inter dilectos fratres nostros S. abbatem et monachos sancti Albani et A. clericum de Luytona super tercia [parte] ecclesie de Luitona et [? pertinentiis qui]bus idem A. se iniuste spoliatum conquerebatur cognoscendam et fine canonico terminandam. Partibus itaque in presentia nostra constitutis et allegationibus hinc inde auditis, tandem intervenientibus amicis sub hac transactionis forma lis tota sopita est. Predictus A. clericus liti et iuri quod dicebat se habere in prefata ecclesia et ablatorum repetitioni renuntiavit. Abbas vero et conventus sancti Albani sepedicto A. clerico quoad vixerit .c. solid' ... annuatim nomine transactionis solvent [per] manum cellerarii sui quisquis is fuerit, l. videlicet infra octabas Pasche[b] et alios l. ad festum sancti Michaelis, incipiens solvere ad proximum Pascha post factam transactionem. A. vero clericus se hoc fideliter et firmiter observaturum in presentia nostra fide corporaliter prestita obligavit, et abbas pro se pro conventu suo hoc idem in verbo veritatis repromisit. Quod ut ratum inconvulsumque perma[neat] nos qui iudices aderamus delegati auctoritate qua fungebamur approbavimus et attestationis nostre munimine fecimus roborari.[c] Facta est autem hec transactio anno domini m⁰ c⁰ lxxiiii in festo sancte Cecile (*sic*) apud Lund' [Testibus] magistro Iohanne de Sar', Nicholas priore [? de] Waringf', magistro Ambrosio, magistro ... redo de Hamelamest', magistro Nigello [fo. 115vb] de Redgrave,[d] Radulfo de Bertona, m' Lowys,[d] Alexandro de Luitona, Ricardo de Falda, Willelmo de Linleia.[d]

    a R. B.   b Pache B.   c roborarari B.   d *reading uncertain*.

    The history of Luton church in this period is told, from the point of view of the abbey, in *Gesta abbatum sancti Albani*, ed. H. T. Riley (RS 1867), i. 113–24; cf. L. F. Rushbrook Williams, 'William the Chamberlain and Luton church',

EHR xxviii (1913), 719-30. Adam the clerk, probably the A. of this transaction, held a portion of the church for some years, but was ejected when King Henry II took possession of it as part of the domain of his predecessors. Abbot Robert then granted Adam's portion to the king's servant Richard of Ilchester, as a bribe for his help in regaining the whole church for St Albans. This history explains the substantial payment to Adam, and the date of the proceedings; Richard presumably relinquished his portion on his consecration as bishop of Winchester on 6 Oct. 1174. This episode is not mentioned in the *Gesta*.

55. Abbey of Saint-Évroul

25 Mar. 1174 x 24 Mar. 1175. *Notification as judge-delegate of the settlement of the case between Walter, clerk, of Hazelton and the monks of Saint-Évroul about the church of Rowell.*

A = Alençon, Arch. dép. de l'Orne, H 925. Endorsed: R' Wirgornien' episcopi de Rauuella et de Halling'. Quedam conposio (*sic*). s.xii ex. Approx. 253 × 160 + 15 mm. Sealed *double queue*; tag and seal lost.

Pd M. M. Bigelow, *History of procedure in England, 1066–1204* (1880), p. 370. Summary in *Cal. Docs. France*, p. 226 no. 645.

.R. dei gratia Wig' episcopus universis sancte matris ecclesie filiis salutem. Omnium cognitioni notum esse volumus . quod controversia per Walterum clericum de Haseltona adversus monachos Sancti Ebrulfi mota super ecclesia de Rawella . et nobis a domino papa Alexandro delegata . quam idem Walterus insubiectione ecclesie sue de Hallinghis sibi petebat ׃ hunc finem coram nobis sortita est. Ecclesia de Rawella ecclesie de Hallinghis vigilia Pasche unam libram incensi persolvet inperpetuum . ita quod ecclesia de Hallinghis ab ecclesia de Rawella nichil amplius poterit exigere. Et monachi predicti Waltero clerico in recompensationem laboris et expense sex solidos de redditu suo de Rawella per manum procuratoris sui quamdiu Walterus vixerit duobus terminis in Pascha videlicet . et in festo Sancti Michaelis annuatim persolvent. Abbas autem et conventus Sancti Ebrulfi litteris suis nobis transmissis . se ratum habituros insinuaverunt . quicquid Ricardus monachus eorum in Anglia generalis procurator existens ׃ in presentia nostra iudicio vel compositione susciperet. Hanc conventionem se servaturos confirmaverunt hinc inde

APPENDIX I

Ricardus scilicet monachus in verbo veritatis . et Walterus clericus fide data in manu nostra. Facta est autem hec conventio anno ab incarnatione domini. M⁰ . C . lxxiiii. His testibus . Adam abbate Evesh' . Roberto priore de Kenillewrtha .[a] Sym' archidiacono Wig' . Magistro Moyse . Magistro Waltero . Magistro Silvestro . Gilleberto capellano . Samsone clerico.

a A employs the Anglo-Saxon crossed *d*.

The document, very much wider than it is deep, is written in a stiff, upright hand, almost a 'book' hand, on which see p. 230 above. The village and church of Rowell have disappeared, though Roel Gate and Roel farm survive near Hawling. Hazelton lies some four miles to the south. The case is mentioned by D. J. A. Matthew, *The Norman monasteries and their English possessions* (1962), p. 61. See also App. II, 45.

56. Abbey of Saint-Évroul

Mar. 1176 at London. *Confirmation to the abbot and brethren of Saint-Évroul of possessions in the diocese of Worcester in proprios usus, naming the church of Rowell, so long as the monks cause it to be properly served, and specified tithes, reserving episcopal rights.*

B = Alençon, Arch. dép. de l'Orne, H 925, original inspeximus of I. abbot of Lire, of 1236.
Mentioned in inventory of Sheen muniments, BL MS Cotton Otho B. xiv fo. 108r, under Ware.
Summary in *Cal. Docs. France*, p. 227 no. 650.

Universis sancte matris ecclesie filiis R. dei gratia Wygorniensis ecclesie vocatus episcopus salutem. Ad universorum notitiam volumus pervenire quod nos per assensum et consensum capituli Wygorniensis ecclesie concessimus et presenti scripto confirmavimus abbati et fratribus monasterii sancti Ebrulfi omnia bona ecclesiastica[a] subscripta que in episcopatu Wygorniensi ante tempora nostra possederunt in eorum proprios usus in perpetuum habenda et retinenda. Videlicet ecclesiam sancti Petri de Rowella cum suis pertinentiis ita tamen quod dicti abbas et fratres sancti Ebrulfi dictam ecclesiam ut decet honeste faciant deserviri.[b] Apud Quenton' duas partes omnium decimarum dominici eiusdem ville. Apud Weston' duas partes omnium decimarum dominicorum eiusdem ville. Apud Wibetote similiter. Apud Pebworthe duas partes decimarum dominici eiusdem ville et ad Merston' le Botiler similiter duas partes decimarum dominici. Apud Hostehulle duas partes decimarum dominici eiusdem ville et ad Haleford similiter duas partes decime dominici[c] et decimam molendini eiusdem ville. Apud inferiorem vero villam de Pilardinton' duas partes omnium decimarum dominici et francolanorum ipsius ville et similiter duas partes decimarum francolanorum ville superioris Pilardinton'. Ad ultimum autem concessimus et confirmavimus dictis abbati et fratribus decimas nutrimentorum suorum et omnium bonorum que habent in eadem villa in suis usibus retinendas et in perpetuum possidendas. Salva nobis et successoribus nostris dignitate nostra et ecclesie nostre Wygorniensis. Ne ergo rationabiliter concessa et confirmata oblivionis obscuritas posteris invideat aut inquieta contentiosorum malitia quacunque occasione perturbet, ea presentis scripti serie et sigilli nostri impressione duximus munienda. Facta est hec nostra concessio et confirmatio ad instantiam et petitionem nobilis viri Roberti comitis Leicestrie anno verbi incarnati m° c° lxxv Lond' tempore celebris congregationis archiepiscoporum, episcoporum, abbatum et priorum Angl' regum patris et filii et magnatorum regni Anglorum facte per vocationem Hugonis Petri Leonis sancti Angeli diaconi cardinalis apostolice sedis legati. Teste Roberto comite Leic', Roberto abbate Croilandie, Iohanne de Saresb' thesaurario Exon' ecclesie, Simone archidiacono Wygorniensi, Roberto capellano nostro et Roberto monacho, magistro Moyse et magistro Silvestro et aliis.

a ecclesiastica *added above the line* B.   b deservire B.
c dom. dec. *marked for transposition* B.

The council mentioned in the text was summoned for 14 Mar. 1176, but broke up on the first day; apparently no further sessions were held. Robert earl of Leicester, successor to the founders of Saint-Évroul, was involved in other business connected with the house at this time; cf. no. 58. For Rowell see no. 55.

57. Abbey of Saint-Évroul

6 Oct. 1174 x Nov. 1175. *Robert bishop of Hereford and Roger bishop of Worcester, as judges-delegate, order R. prior and the brethren*

of Bermondsey to persuade the earl of Leicester to satisfy the monastery of Saint-Évroul about the church of Widford. If he does not, they are summoned to appear on the second Monday after St Hilary at Cricklade.

A = Alençon, Arch. dép. de l'Orne, H 937. Endorsed: Rob' Hereford' et R. Vigornie episcoporum de quadam monitione (s.xiv). Approx. 150 × 50 mm. Tag for sealing *simple queue* torn away, seal(s) lost.

Summary in *Cal. Docs. France*, p. 226 no. 644.

Robertus Hereford' et Rog' Wigorn' dei gratia dicti episcopi . dilectis in domino fratribus . R' priori et fratribus de Beremundeshea salutem. Dilectioni vestre autoritate apostolica mandamus quatinus illustrem virum comitem Legecest' monasterio sancti Ebrulfi super ecclesia[a] de Wideford' satisfacere moneatis et modis omnibus inducere studeatis . et nisi eidem monasterio satisfecerit vobis prescripta auctoritate precipimus ut secundo die lune post festum sancti Hilarii sufficienter instructi presentiam vestram nobis aput Criccheladam exhibeatis procuratori illius monasterii[b] super iamdicta ecclesia secundum formam mandati apostolici quod vobis satis innotuit responsuri. Si autem evidenti causa prepediti die statuto ad nos accedere forte non poteritis sufficientem responsalem cum litteris patentibus et rati cautionem pretendentibus pro vobis dirigere curetis . hunc namque diem vobis peremptorium prefigimus . Valete.

a ecclesia *interlined*. A
b procuratori illius monasterii *added over erasure*. A

If the bishops are named in the correct order of precedence, no. 57 must be dated *c*.Oct. 1164 x *c*.Nov. 1166. But the order is reversed in a letter from the earl of Leicester: 'Carissimis amicis suis Wigorn' et Hereford' episcopis Robertus comes Legr' salutem. Sciatis quod tantum feci versus monachum de Wares quod quiete clamavit monachis de Bermundsey clamationem quam monachus de Wares habuit erga monachos de Bermundsey super ecclesiam de Wideford. Valete.' (BL MS Cotton Claudius A. viii fo. 121ᵛ). The letter is clearly related to the settlement made in Mar. 1176 (no. 58). It is probable that no. 57 was issued between Robert Foliot's consecration and *c*.Nov. 1175, which would give time for action before the peremptory day on 26 Jan. (1176). Possibly no. 57, which had already contained two mistakes, was superseded by a corrected version, hence its survival at Saint-Évroul. The prior of Bermondsey to whom no. 57 is addressed, was probably Roger II (1167–75); the elaborate R of the text may have been intended for *Ro. Cal. Docs. France* reads Robert, which cannot be correct. The monk of Ware, mentioned in the earl's letter, was the proctor of Saint-Évroul, perhaps the Richard of no. 55. Saint-Évroul had a small cell at Ware, four miles from Widford. On its claim to the church see D. J. A. Matthew, *The Norman monasteries and their English possessions* (1962), p. 33; the claim went back to the early years of the Norman occupation. The church had been granted to Bermondsey by the earls of Leicester, and twice taken away in exchange for Enderby; *Mon. Ang.*, v. 88 refers to a regrant in 21 Henry II (1175), which may be connected with this litigation.

58. Abbey of Saint-Évroul

28 Mar. 1176 or soon after, in London. *Notification as judge-delegate of the settlement of the dispute between the abbot and monks of Saint-Évroul and the monks of Bermondsey about the church of Widford. (Imcomplete).*

B = BL MS Cotton Claudius A. viii fos. 121^v–122^r, transcript of extracts from a lost cartulary of Bermondsey. s.xvii in.

Universis sancte[a] matris ecclesie filiis Rogerus dei gratia Wigornensis ecclesie vocatus episcopus salutem. Manifeste improbitatis est a transactionibus [fo. 122^r] quibus equitas patrocinatur recedere et per quietis inpatientiam contentiones sopitas in nova litigia suscitare. Unde omnium cognitioni volumus innotescere controversiam que vertebatur inter dilectos nostros abbatem et monachos sancti Ebrulfi et fratres de Bermundesey super ecclesia sancti Iohannis de Wideford absque spe litis restaurande fine pacifico conquievisse. Cum enim dominus Alexander papa tertius venerabili fratri nostro Roberto Herefordensi episcopo et nobis pariter causam que agebatur inter prefatos fratres super prescripta ecclesia cognoscendam et appellatione remota terminandam sub certa forma delegasset, illustris comes Legrecestrie Robertus, quem ex maxima parte causa contingebat, iamdictorum fratrum paci et tranquillitati studuit et ante litis ingressum omnem contentionis occasionem liberali munificentia precidit. In mandato namque domini pape continebatur insertum sibi ab abbate et fratribus sancti Ebrulfi fuisse suggestum quod cum fratres de Bermundesey et Robertus quondam comes Legrec', iunioris Roberti pater, duas villas adinvicem commutassent etc....

Facta est hec concessio anno verbi incarnati 1175 Londini tempore celebris congregationis archiepiscoporum, episcoporum abbatum et personarum[b] Anglie regum patris et filii et magnatum regni Anglorum facte per vocationem Hugonis Petri Leonis sancti Angeli diaconi cardinalis apostolice sedis legati. Testibus de concessione comitis Roberto abbate de Croyland, Simone archidiacono Wigorn', Roberto capellano nostro, magistro Moise, Ernaldo de Bosco, Willelmo de Chiray, Willelmo de Diva, Willelmo de Wibetot, Hugone de Campames.[c] Obligationi vero Roberti capellani comitis interfuerunt in ecclesia sancti Bartholomei Bartholomeus Exoniensis episcopus et Iohannes de Salesburia thesaurarius Exoniensis ecclesie et Simon archidiaconus Wigorn' et Robertus capellanus et Robertus monachus, magister Silvester, feria quinta post dominicam qua cantatur Letare Ierusalem [27 March]. Fecit comes concessionem suam super prescripta ecclesia in domo Roberti de Fuleham hospitis nostri. Robertus autem capellanus se obligavit sexta feria post dominicam predictam [28 March] in ecclesia sancti Bartholomei de Smethefelde in parte aquilonari.

a the transcriber sometimes uses *ae* for *e*.
b ? *recte* priorum *as in no. 56*.
c *reading uncertain, possibly* Canpaines.

The transcriber sometimes notes the folios of the cartulary from which he was copying; this text appeared between fos. 202 and 205. He omitted the whole core of the document, with the previous history of the church, and the details of the satisfaction given to Saint-Évroul.

On the complicated story of Widford church, see no. 57. No. 56 has an almost identical dating clause and some of the same witnesses. Professor C. N. L. Brooke kindly drew my attention to this transcript, on which his pupil Miss J. Foster was working. Cf. *Councils and Synods*, i *s.a.* 1176.

59. St Neots Priory

17 Jan. 1177 at Warwick. *Notification as judge-delegate of the settlement of the case between the monks of St Neots and Alan de Valeines, clerk, about the church of Heveningham.*

B = BL MS Cotton Faustina A. iv (cart. of St Neots) fo. 6^v. s.xiii med.

C = ibid. fo. 44^v.

Universis sancte matris ecclesie filiis R. dei gratia Wig' episcopus salutem. Ne lites semel sopite in rediviva[a] litigia suscitentur, scripture beneficio malingnantium improbitati[b] est obviandum.[c] Inde est quod omnium cognitioni duximus innotescendum quod cum dominus Alexander papa[d] III nobis et dilecto fratri nostro Ade abbati Evesham' causam que agebatur inter monachos de sancto Neoto et Alanum clericum de Valeines[e] super ecclesia de Heveningeham appellatione remota terminandam delegasset, memorato abbate coniudice nostro quod cause decisioni interesse non posset competenter excusato et litteris ratihabitionis ab ipso susceptis, lis habita inter prefatos monachos et Alanum clericum huiusmodi transactione interveniente coram nobis conquievit; videlicet quod iamdictus Alanus prescriptam ecclesiam de Heveningeham nomine monachorum de sancto Neoto quamdiu vixerit sub pensione viginti solidorum duobus terminis solvendorum, in Pasca[f] decem et[g] in festo sancti Michaelis decem, tenebit. Prior autem sancti Neoti et conventus prenominato A. iustum patrocinium tanquam clerico suo super prescripta ecclesia prestabunt. Hec transactio ex parte prioris et fratrum in verbo veritatis in nostra presentia est firmata, et ab Alano iuramento super sacrosanctum altare prestito roborata. Facta vero anno verbi incarnati m⁰ c⁰ septuagesimo sexto apud Warewich' in ecclesia beate Marie xvi kal' Februarii. Prescriptam itaque transactionem auctoritate qua fungimur salvo iure prelatorum quod habent confirmamus, nostra confirmatione dignitati diocesiani in nullo derogante. Testibus[h] Conano abbate Margan, Waltero abbate de Neth, Roberto priore de Kinildewrda, magistro Silvestro et Willelmo de Gloec' clericis nostris, magistro Nicholao et magistro Waltero, Hunfrido de Caune, Sim', clericis domini Norwic', Roberto capellano de Evertona et Waltero capellano de Wedon' et Willelmo Britone, Saverico de Valeinis, Absalon de Felesham, Alfredo presbitero de Rindham, Henrico Butenn,[j] Ricardo de Falesham, Henrico de Falesham, Ricardo filio Hugonis, Hugone de Suetling', Willelmo de Debeham.

<small>a iure divina B.   b malignantium inprobitati C.   c obviandu B.
d papa *erased* B.   e Valeins C.   f pascha C.   g *om.* et B.   h B *ends here*.
j *reading uncertain* C.</small>

Bishop Roger's charter was produced in proceedings about the last presentation to Heveningham in 1200 (*Curia Regis Rolls Richard I—2 John*, p. 137). It was then stated that Alan de Valeines had been parson for forty years and more, and had died twenty years previously, and that the church had been vacant ever since owing to litigation between William Pirho (and his father before him) and Robert FitzWalter (and his father Walter FitzRobert before him). St Neots claimed the church as the gift of Walter FitzRobert. Alan of Valeines must have become parson in about 1140. It is not clear what was the question at issue before Bishop Roger, but the later developments suggest that a dispute over patronage lay behind the litigation between St Neots and the clerk. Alan de Valeines could perhaps claim life tenure of the disputed church under the rule mentioned in *Glanvill*, iv. 10 (ed. Hall, p. 50).

60. Cathedral Church of Salisbury

16 Oct. 1173 at Bath. *Notification as judge-delegate, with Geoffrey dean of Hereford, of the settlement of a dispute between Jocelin bishop of Salisbury and William son of Alexander about land in Potterne and Bishop's Cannings.*

Ai = Salisbury, D. and C. Mun., Chapter Records, Press iv, C.3 Potterne 16, lower half of chirograph. Endorsed: Poterna et Kanniges. s.xiii in. Tanget episcopum. s.xiv. Scr'. s.xiv. Old pressmark, C.3 with 16 below. Approx. 180 × 124 + 12 mm. Sealed *double queue*; triple slit at left of bottom fold with tag and cloth bag, no remains of seal; single slit on right of fold, seal and tag lost.

Aii = ibid. Potterne 21, upper half of chirograph. Endorsed: Wortona et Poterna. s.xiii. Tanget episcopum. s.xiv. De Azo (*sic*), Scribitur. s.xv. Old pressmark, C.3 with 21 below. Size as Ai. Sealed *double queue*; triple slit at left of fold, with tag, seal lost. No trace of slit for second seal.

B = ibid. Diocesan Record Office, Liber Evidenciarum B fo. 42^r. s.xiv.

C = ibid., D and C. Mun., Liber Evidenciarum C p.132. s.xiii ex.

D = ibid., Liber Ruber fo. 38^v (copy of B). s.xiv.

E = ibid., Reg. Vetus (Reg. St Osmund) fo. 33^v. s.xiii in.

F = London, Inner Temple Library, Petyt MS 511.18 fo. 23^r. s.xiii ex.

Pd from E, *The Register of St Osmund*, ed. W. H. Rich Jones (RS 1883), i. 253 misdated.

Pd here from Ai and Aii; registers not collated. See plate I.

APPENDIX I

CIROGRAPHUM (cut through)

Rogerus dei gratia Wigorn' episcopus . et G. Hereford' ecclesie decanus omnibus sancte ecclesie filiis salutem. Ne iurgia que legitime terminata sunt denuo suscitentur in litem . vel posteris dubia relinquantur sollicita decrevit providentia modum decisionis scripto commendare . et posterorum memorie tradere. Sciant itaque tam posteri quam presentes ׃ quod causa que vertebatur inter .Ioc'. Sar' episcopum et Willelmum filium Alexandri super quibusdam terris quas tenuerat Alexander in socha Poterne et in Canniggis (sic) de dominico episcopi . nobis a summo pontifice delegata ׃ sub hoc tandem fine quievit. Prefatus[a] episcopus ut .W. a lite recederet ׃ dedit eidem .c. sol' et preterea medietatem terre Azonis fratris predicti .W. cum omnibus pertinentiis . consensu ipsius Azonis . exceptis managiis duobus . quorum unum ׃ scilicet capitale managium quod est in Wrtona Azo sibi retinuit . et W. habebit managium quod mater ipsius habet in Poterna . reddendo annuatim dimidiam libram piperis et dimidiam thuris pro omni servitio . nec ipse nec homines eius respondebunt ministris vel prepositis episcopi . uterque etiam tenebit in capite de episcopo ׃ quamdiu vixerit . terra predicta nullo modo ad heredes eorum transeunte ׃ post mortem eorum. Et quicunque supervixerit terram premortui habebit. Et post mortem utriusque ׃ tota terra cedet in dominicum episcopi ׃ et tam Azo quam .W. iuraverunt se firmiter observare predictam pactionem. Iuravit etiam .W. se non moturum litem alicui super querela quam intendebat adversus episcopum. Et Rogerus filius Everardi cognatus Azonis et W. eorundem petitione et assensu promisit ׃ quod si alterutrum á pacto resilire vellet ׃ cum eo staret qui pactum servare vellet. Predictorum etiam scilicet .W. et Azonis petitione promisit episcopus ׃ quod iudicio et districtione curie sue . cogeret illum stare pactioni ׃ qui ab eadem presumeret recedere. Recepit etiam dominus episcopus homagium sepedicti .W. de medietate terre quam Azo ei concessit . et utrique eorum cartam suam et capituli Sar' de confirmanda pactione inter eos facere promisit׃ Facta sunt hec anno ab incarnatione domini m.c.lxxiii. xvii kal' Novembris . apud Baton' ׃ Testibus . Willelmo abbate de Kainesham . Symone archidiacono Wigorn' . Gaufrido archidiacono Sar' . Baldewino de sancto Genesio . Magistro Radulfo . magistro Moyse . Gilberto capellano Sar' . Willelmo de Cicestria . Gilberto capellano Wigorn' episcopi . Sampsone clerico . Rogero[b] filio Everardi . Roberto[b] filio Turoldi . Radulfo[b] de Hedeleia . Ricardo[b] de Rughedirna . Rogero[b] filio Osmundi . Bernardo de Benacra . Waltero de Lideh'.

    a *The copy sent to the pope (no. 61) begins here.*
    b *initial only* Aii.

    This is the only case in which both halves survive of a chirograph issued by Bishop Roger. One part belonged from the first to the bishop of Salisbury; the other part presumably returned to the muniments when William and Azo were dead and the disputed land returned to the bishop. There is no obvious reason why the two parts were sealed differently. Both parts were written by one scribe, with minor variations in the elaboration of letters and the rendering of names. The settlement was reported to the pope for confirmation (no. 61). The charters promised to the brothers, confirming the settlement on behalf of the bishop and the chapter, are pd *Salisbury Charters*, pp. 37–8; the original of the bishop's charter is BL Add. ch. 37665.

61. Cathedral Church of Salisbury

c.16 Oct. 1173 *Roger bishop of Worcester and Geoffrey dean of Hereford send to Pope Alexander a copy of the settlement made before themselves as judges-delegate, between Jocelin bishop of Salisbury and William son of Alexander (no. 60). They ask the pope to confirm the settlement, so that it may have perpetual validity.*

B = Salisbury Dioc. Record Office, Liber evidentiarum B fo. 41^r. s.xiv.

C = ibid. D. and C. Mun., Liber evidentiarum C p. 130. s.xiii ex.

D = ibid. Liber ruber fo. 33^v, copy of B. s.xiv.

E = London, Inner Temple Library, Petyt MS 511.18 fo. 23^r. s.xiii ex.

Edited from B, C, D, *Salisbury Charters*, p. 37.

    No papal confirmation of the settlement survives. No. 61 is perhaps incomplete, or a draft. It consists of an introductory passage, followed by the effective part of no. 60, with the dating clause. C alone copies the terms in full and gives the name of the first witness. It seems unlikely that there was no respectful termination, but cf. no. 6. Confirmation was needed because a *transactio* made by a prelate concerning the possessions of his church did not bind his successors unless confirmed by a superior (X 1.36.8 = App. II, 93).

62. Cathedral Church of Salisbury

Sentence given 14 Nov. 1177 at Leigh near Worcester. *Notification as judge-delegate of sentence in the case about the church of Burbage, between Alan of Hurstbourne and Richard Barre archdeacon of Lisieux. Two commissions were received; the first obtained by Alan, the second by the archdeacon. After the* litis contestatio *the case was thoroughly examined. After nearly two years and many peremptory summonses, issued at longer intervals than the canons and the* leges *allow, a peremptory day was set, to which Alan neither came nor sent a representative. The case had been sufficiently disputed, the attestations published, and both parties had renounced the right to challenge the witnesses or their sayings. The bishop of Worcester therefore, with the advice of Robert bishop of Hereford, Peter bishop of St David's and other wise men, has by sentence absolved the church of Salisbury and the archdeacon, who is a canon of Salisbury, from Alan's claim, and imposed perpetual silence on Alan.* 'Testibus Roberto capellano nostro, Samsone, Roberto monacho, magistro Silvestro, clericis nostris, Rad' Foliot et Willelmo de Stoche et magistro Eustachio, clericis domini Hereford', magistro Erardo, magistro Ivone Cornub', magistro Rad' Lumbard', magistro Henrico de Rowelle, Ada filio prepositi de Wygorn'.

B = Salisbury Dioc. Record Office, Liber evidentiarum B fo. 41^r. s.xiv.

C = ibid. D. and C. Mun., Liber evidentiarum C, p. 130. s.xiii ex.

D = ibid. Liber Ruber fo. 33^v, copy of B. s. xiv.
Pd from B, *Charters of Salisbury*, p. 11 no. 48.

> The first commission, obtained by Alan, is lost. The second, obtained by Richard Barre, is perhaps App. II, 62, which gives more information about the conduct of the case. App. II, 69B is another commission obtained by Alan, complaining of an incorrect decision by Bishop Roger on a subsidiary question. Richard Barre became archdeacon of Ely in 1188 x 1190. At the date of these proceedings he was archdeacon of Lisieux. The Salisbury registers show the usual confusion between *Lexov'* and *Exon'*; the editor of *Salisbury Charters* mistakenly corrected them to *Eliensis*.

63. Shrewsbury Abbey

Sept. 1172 x Apr. 1173. *Notification of the conclusion of a case between Adam abbot of Shrewsbury and Robert son of Robert, about the burial of his men at Aston Eyre. Robert has renounced all right in the matter, and the bishop, having inspected a charter of Robert of Bethune bishop of Hereford, has confirmed burial rights to the mother church of Morville, whose priests shall decide which bodies shall be buried at the church and which at the chapel. 'Teste Radulfo priore Wig', Humbaldo priore de Wenel' et aliis.'*

B = Aberystwyth, Nat. Libr. of Wales MS 7851 (Shrewsbury cart.), pp. 303–5 no. 343. s.xiii ex.

Pd *Cartulary of Shrewsbury Abbey*, ed. Una Rees (Aberystwyth 1975), ii. 311 [p. 311 line 3, for *ecclesie* read *esse*; line 8 for *iuris iquid* read *iuri si quid*; line 15, delete *per*].

> Adam abbot of Shrewsbury was elected not before 1168, when Bishop Roger was abroad. Roger returned *c.*Sept. 1172; Adam was deposed at latest by July 1175. But the bishop was probably acting during the vacancy of the see of Hereford, before the election of Robert Foliot late in Apr. 1173. If the words 'auctoritate qua fungimur' are intended to imply a papal commission, the final date would be 8 July 1175, when Adam's successor was elected. Robert of Bethune's charter is pd op. cit., p. 302; it shows that the chapel was one of several consecrated *c.*1138 'pro imminenti bellorum tumultu . . . pro defensione pauperum'. On Morville see *VCH Shropshire*, ii. 29, and Brett, *English Church*, p. 131, where *Estona* is identified with Astley.

64. Southwark Priory

23 Aug. 1164 x 9 Aug. 1179. *Grant to the church of St Mary, Southwark, of land which Gerard the tanner holds in the soke of Worcester, paying eight pence annually at Mid-Lent.*

A = BL Harley charter 43. I. 35. Endorsed: Karta concessionis Rogeri Wigon' (*sic*) episcopi (s.xii ex). Approx. 196 × 82 + 23 mm. Sealed *double queue*; seal and tag lost, but see below.

Pd *Sir Christopher Hatton's Book of Seals*, ed. Lewis C. Loyd and Doris M. Stenton (Oxford 1950), pp. 84–5 no. 123, with particulars of the seal from the drawing in Sir Christopher's book, now Finch Hatton MS 170 fo. 30^v, deposited in Northants Record Office.

Noverit universitas fidelium quod ego Rog' gratia dei Wigorniensis episcopus concedo conventui ecclesie sancte Marie de Sutwerch' illam terram quam Gerardus tanarius tenet in soca

Wigorniensi reddendo inde singulis annis octodecim denarios finabiliter in media qudragesima (sic). quam soror eorum Cristina contulit secum in predictam ecclesiam . Teste magistro Barthol' Exoniensi episcopi et Galfr' Blundo bailivo suo eiusdem socche . magistro Petro Picot . magistro Petro de Mandavill' . Petro filio Ric' . Walt' filio Driu . Henr' de Tantona . Nichol' eius connato (sic).

> This odd, untidy and amateurish document carried a genuine seal and may record a genuine grant; it was not composed or written by any of Bishop Roger's, or Bartholomew's, clerks. See p. 230 above. The suggested site of the bishop of Worcester's soke in London is shown on the map in William Page, *London: its origins and early development* (London 1923), p. 133.

65. Order of the Knights Templar

23 Aug. 1164 x 9 Aug. 1179. (*Lost charter*) Confirmation to the Knights Templar of an annual payment of one mark from the church of Sherbourne.

> Mentioned only, in H. Cole, *Documents illustrative of English history in the thirteenth and fourteenth centuries* (1844), p. 229, from PRO E/142, 'Corrodia petita de domibus Templariorum'. After the dissolution of the Order, Henry vicar of Sherbourne, to prove his right to a payment, produced a charter of John bishop of Worcester recording that he had allowed the Templars to appropriate Sherbourne church 'qua Rogerus beate memorie predecessor noster episcopus unam marcam per cartam suam confirmavit'.

66. Tewkesbury Abbey

23 Aug. 1164 x 9 Aug. 1179. (*Lost charter*) Confirmation to the monks of Tewkesbury of the church of Atherstone on Stour.

> Mentioned only, in BL MS Cotton Cleopatra A. vii (Tewkesbury inventory) fo. 74^v. s.xiii med. *Mon. Ang.*, ii. 69 no. xxv. The charter of the lay donor, Roger de Rupa, is noted before Bishop Roger's confirmation. This information supplements *VCH Warwicks.*, v. 4.

67. Tewkesbury Abbey

Sept. 1172 x July 1176 at Bristol. (*Lost charter*) Evidence that Picard held churches in Cornwall of the monks of Tewkesbury, paying an annual pension of one aureus.

Mentioned only, in BL MS Cotton Cleopatra A. vii (Tewkesbury inventory) fo. 74ᵛ. s.xiii med. Pd *Mon. Ang.*, ii. 69 no. xxv. In the inventory the note of no. 67 is followed by a reference to a charter of Bartholomew of Exeter giving the same evidence. Bartholomew's charter survives (Morey, *Bartholomew*, p. 146, also in *Trans. of the Bristol and Glos. Arch. Soc.*, lv (1933), 260). It certifies that on the day when he and Roger dedicated the church of St Augustine's Abbey, Bristol, Picard clerk of William earl of Gloucester confessed to them that he held all the churches which he had of the earl's fee in Cornwall 'in the name of the monks of St James of Bristol', paying one *aureus* annually. St James was a cell of Tewkesbury. Bartholomew's charter was issued when he and Roger were together, since three of Roger's clerks and Simon archdeacon of Worcester are witnesses. John of Salisbury also witnesses, as treasurer of Exeter, before his election to Chartres in July 1176. Simon became archdeacon in 1167, but John was abroad from 1164 to Nov. 1170, while Bishop Roger was abroad from 1167 to ?Sept. 1172. All the evidence suggests that no. 67 and Bartholomew's charter were issued more or less at the same time, at Bristol. The dedication was commemorated between 28 Aug. and 8 Sept. (*Trans. of the Bristol and Glos. Arch. Soc.*, lxxv (1953), 36). If this was the dedication in question, it and the two charters must belong to Aug.–Sept. 1173, 1174 or 1175.

68. Tewkesbury Abbey

16 May 1177 at St Peter's church, Winchcombe. *Notification of a settlement between Tewkesbury Abbey and the church of Beckford about the chapel of Washbourne and specified tithes.*

B = BL MS Cotton Cleopatra A. vii (Tewkesbury inventory) fo. 83ʳ, long abstract. s.xiii med.
Pd *Mon. Ang.*, ii. 74–5 no. lxx.

Compositio facta inter ecclesiam de Theok' et de Bekkeford in presentia Rogeri Wigorn' episcopi anno gratie mclxxvii° xvii kal' Iunii in ecclesia sancti Petri apud Winchecumbam de capella de Wasseburna et decimis rusticorum de Dudicote que magister Silvester rector ecclesie de Bekeford [. . .]ᵃ et Reginaldo Bathon' episcopis.ᵇ Ecclesia de Bekeford remisit in perpetuum ecclesie de Theok'ᶜ omne ius quod vendicabat in capella de Wasseburna ita quod si aliquod instrumentum haberet super his que petebat in prescripta capellaᵈ nullas decetero vires haberet. Ecclesia vero Theok' remisit ecclesie de Bekeford decimas messium et nutrimentorum et omnium que per annum renoventur de xii virgatis terre in Dudicote cumᵉ istam excolunt qui sunt parochiani ecclesie de Bekeford. Preterea ecclesia de Theok' concessit ecclesie sancti Andree de Estona omnes decimas tam maiores quam minores cuiusdam virgate terre quam Willelmus francus tenuit de ecclesia de Theok' in eadem villa de Estona. Si autem forte processu temporis aliqua pars de xii predictarum virgatarum terre in dominicam versa fuerit, nichilominus inde decimas persolvent. De xxx vero acris terre quas tempore huius transactionis monachi Theok' in dominico excoluerunt in eadem villa de Dudicote non solvent ecclesie de Bekeford decimas, si autem villanis tradite fuerint decimas inde solvent sicut et de aliis ecclesie de Bekeford.

    a *In B the text is continuous, but makes nonsense. Possibly a line was omitted. A highly conjectural emendation would be*: et ecclesia de Bekeford petebat adversus ecclesiam de Theok' coram iudicibus delegatis Rogero Wigorn' *which might give two lines beginning with* et, *and makes sense of the next three words.*
    b *om.* Reginaldo Bathon' episcopis *Mon. Ang.*   c Bekeford B.
    d prescripto capitulo *Mon. Ang.*   e in B.

69. Warwick, Priory of the Holy Sepulchre

15 Nov. 1173 at Reading. *Notification as judge-delegate, with Adam abbot of Evesham, of the settlement of the case between the church of the Holy Sepulchre, Warwick, and William Cumin about the church of Snitterfield.*

B = Bodl. MS Dodsworth 65 fo. 34^{r-v}, *ex cartis penes Simonem Archer militem.* s.xvii med.

Universis sancte matris ecclesie filiis Rogerus dei gratia Wigorn' episcopus et Adam eiusdem gratia abbas Evesham salutem. Causam que^a vertebatur inter ecclesiam sancti Sepulchri de Warewic et Willelmum^b Cumin super ecclesiam de Snettenefeld' a domino Alexandro papa tertio nobis delegata transactione huiusmodi interveniente in nostra presentia sopita est. Videlicet quod Willelmus Cumin parsona ecclesie de [fo. 34^v] Snitenefeld' unam marcam argenti infra octabis sancti Michaelis de ecclesia predicta nomine ecclesie annuatim prestabit ecclesie sancti Sepulchri de Warwic. Vacante vero ecclesia prescripta presentatio parsonarum ad Walterum Cumin advocatum ecclesie sepedicte et eius heredes iure perpetuo pertinebit. Persona vero per Walterum memoratum vel eius heredes presentata unam marcam argenti prenominate ecclesie de Warwic' sicut Willelmus Cumin prestabit, et de illa prestatione iuramento interposito priori et canonicis sancti Sepulchri de Warwic' antequam instituatur parsona securitatem faciet. Hec autem transactio utrobique fide mediante roborata est. Quamvis etiam prior de Warwic' kartam iocunde memorie Simonis predecessoris nostri super confirmatione ecclesie de Snithenefeld' habeat, contra Willelmum Cumin vel eius successores nullam ei de ecclesia^c sepius dicta auctoritatem poterit prestare vel aliquid amplius quam unam marcam argenti in ipsa debeat optinere. Facta est autem transactio prescripta apud Rading anno dominice incarnationis M C lxxiii xvii kal' Decembris in ecclesia sancte Marie. Testibus Simone Wig' archidiacono, Willelmo de sancto Petro, Ricardo decano, Iordano de Wirec', Rad', Badduino, Rogero, Ailmero capellano, magistro Baldwino etc.

a quae B; *the transcriber writes ae dipthong throughout.*
B Willelmi B.   c ecclesiis B.

There is some doubt whether William Cumin the parson, or Walter Cumin the lay patron, was the second party. Directly or indirectly, the patronage of the church was in question, but the case may have been presented as a dispute about the parson's liabilities.

70. Warwick, collegiate church of St Mary

23 Aug. 1164 x 9 Aug. 1179. *Confirmation of arrangements made by Simon bishop of Worcester for the churches of St Mary and of All Saints, Warwick.*

B = PRO E 164/22 (Warwick cart.) fo. 23^v (formerly 22^v) no. 39. s.xv med. Abridged with reference to Bishop Simon's charter.

Rogerius dei gratia Wigorn' episcopus universis sancte matris ecclesie filiis in domino salutem. Quoniam ad nostre pondus sollicitudinis spectat quatinus ea que ad utilitatem et pacem ecclesiarum nostrarum statuta sunt nostre auctoritatis munimine inviolata permaneant, ideo nos vestigiis bone memorie Simonis episcopi predecessoris nostri inherentes, que ad utilitatem et pacem ecclesie sancte Marie de Warewic ab ipso sunt statuta et a Rogerio quondam comite Warewici concessa necnon a domino archiepiscopo Cantuar' roborata, sicut carte eorum testantur, nichilominus nostra episcopali auctoritate concedimus et in perpetuum confirmamus et sigilli nostri impressione communimus. Videlicet ut clerici ecclesie Omnium Sanctorum de Warewic propter importunitatem castelli in quo sita est, in predicta ecclesia sancte Marie que ad honorem ipsius virginis et omnium sanctorum consecrata est, cum ceteris clericis eiusdem ecclesie more canonicorum et concessa sibi libertate deo et sancte Marie inperpetuum famulentur, item ut et ipsi clerici habeant in eadem ecclesia sancte Marie capitulum et fraternam congregationem et decanum quem sibi fraterna [fo. 24ʳ] et canonica eliget deliberatio et easdem libertates et consuetudines quas Londoniensis gaudet habere[a] ecclesia, aut Lincolniensis vel Salesberiensis aut talis institutionis ecclesia, item ut nullus in eadem ecclesia potestatem aliquam vel alicuius prebende investituram sibi vendicare presumat nisi per licentiam decani vel alicuius ex sua parte, communicato prius fratrum consilio. Preterea ad tenacis[b] memorie firmitatem et nostre confirmationis recordationem dignum duximus in scripti nostri pagina possessiones vocabulis subnotare que adiacere ecclesie sancte genetricis et Omnium Sanctorum de Warr' dinoscuntur et sicut carta Simonis episcopi predecessoris nostri testatur. Hee sunt ecclesia sancti Nicholai, ecclesia sancti Laurentii cum x acris terre etc ut antea in carta confirmationis dicti Simonis que[c] sic incipit 'Simon dei gratia'. His testibus Haymone abbate Bordeslea, Rogero capellano domini regis et Safredo eius medico et magistro Rogero eius clerico,[d] et Gisleberto capellano nostro et Sansone clerico nostro.

> a *Bishop Simon's charter reads* libere (fo. 13ᵛ).   b *Simon*: tenacioris.
> c qui B.   d Rogero *follows* clerico B.

> Bishop Simon's charter, which Roger confirms and cites, is on fo. 13ʳ no. 13 (pd *Mon. Ang.*, viii. 1327 no. x); it is abridged in the cartulary with reference to Earl Roger's charter on fo. 12ᵛ no. 12 (pd ibid. no. ix). The archbishop's charter mentioned by Roger is ascribed in the cartulary to Thomas (pd A. Saltman, *Theobald, archbishop of Canterbury* (London 1956), p. 500. Roger's charter was confirmed by Baldwin as bishop of Worcester and as archbishop of Canterbury (fo. 24ʳ, 24ᵛ); these confirmations are abridged in the cartulary and do not offer additional texts of Roger's charter.

71. Cathedral Church of Wells

?Mar. 1176. *Record of Richard de Camville's grant of the church of Henstridge to the church of Wells as a prebend.*

B = Wells, D. and C. Mun. Liber albus (Reg. I) fo. 21ᵛ. s.xiii med.
C = ibid., Liber albus II (Reg. III) fo. 161ʳ. s.xvi in.
Summary in *HMC Wells*, i. 22 no. lix.

Universis Christi fidelibus ad quos presens scriptum pervenerit Rogerus dei gratia Wingor'ᵃ episcopus salutem. Quod scimus loquimur et quod vidimus testamur et quod in presentia nostra sollempniter actum est ut firmius roboretur inposterum testimonio veritatis prosequimur. Noverit itaque universitas vestra Ricardus de Camvill' in presentia venerabilis patris nostri Ricardi Cantuar' archiepiscopi et Gilberti Lond' et B. Exoniensis, Roberti Hereford', Iohannis Cicestr', Ricardi Cestren', Adam de sanctoᵇ Asaph' episcoporum et nostra donasse et concessisse quantum ad laicum et dominum fundi spectat ecclesie beati Andree Well' ecclesiam de Hengestr' inperpetuam prebendam, libere et quiete cum omni integritate sua et omnibus pertinentiis suis perpetuo possidendam, et in manu venerabilis fratrisᶜ nostri Reginaldi Bathonieᵈ episcopi quicquid iuris idem Ricardus vel aliquis antecessorum suorum cognoscebatur habuisse in prescripta ecclesia de Hengestr' sollempniter resignasse. Quod ne aliquo tempore possit inposterum malitiose interverti nostri id roborandum duximus auctoritate testimonii quod et scripti ac sigilli nostri indicio omnibus volumus patefieri.

    a Wygorn' C.   b sancta B, sancto C.   c patris B, fratris C.
    d Rainaldi Bathoniensis C.

    Richard de Camville's charter (Reg. I fo. 21ʳ, Reg. III fo. 159ᵛ) was witnessed by the archbishop and the six bishops named in Bishop Roger's charter. The archbishop and Hugh Pierleone also issued charters recording the grant, which was probably formally made and recorded at the time of the abortive council summoned for 14 Mar. 1176, when the bishops and the legate were together in London. No. 71 cannot be earlier than the consecration of Adam of St Asaph (12 Oct. 1175) or later than the legate's departure from England c.3 July 1176.

72. Cathedral Church of Wells

14 Mar. 1165 at Bath. *Notification of the settlement about lands of the church of Wells claimed by the nephews of Reginald the precentor.*

B = Wells, D. and C. Mun. Liber fuscus (Reg. IV) fo. 10ᵛ. s.xiv med.

C = ibid., Liber albus I (Reg. I) fo. 36ᵛ. s.xiii med.

D = ibid., Liber albus II (Reg. III) fo. 102ᵛ. s.xvi in.

E = ibid., Liber albus II (Reg. III) fo. 15ᵛ, copy of B. s.xvi in.
Summary in *HMC Wells*, i. 39.
Pd here from B with select variants from D.

Superne provisionis clementia controversia mota aliquando ecclesie Wellensi a nepotibus Reginaldi precentoris super quibusdam terris eiusdem ecclesie videlicet Wynesham, Wormestorr, Mudesleya cum una virgata de Bidesham ad eam pertinente et Merka et servitio Rainerii de Wandestr', hunc finem feliciter sortita est. Anno siquidem incarnationis dominice m c sexagesimo quarto, pridie idus Martii, dominica videlicet qua cantatur Letare Ierusalem, constituti Bathon' in presentia venerabilium Roberti Bathon' et Rogeri Wygorn' episcoporum, Paganus de Penebrigg' cum filio suo Henrico, Rogerus Witeing cum fratribus suis Willelmo scilicet et Roberto et Gilberto de Almari, Osbertus quoque de Bathon' sed et Radulfus Denebold' cum Roberto fratre suo, tacto sacrosancti ewangelii textu et sanctorum reliquiis, omnes quidem universo iuri quod se in prescriptis Wellensis ecclesie prediis habere pronuntiabant spontanea voluntate renuntiaverunt et illud absolute abiuraverunt. Pro ista vero renuntiatione Ricardus decanus et canonici iamdicte ecclesie fideiussoriam eis de sexaginta et decem marcis numerandis cautionem prestiterunt, ex quibus eodem die reddiderunt quindecim marcas et decem solidos. Prescripte igitur renuntiationi interfuerunt qui subscripti sunt: Ricardus tunc decanus Wellensis, Reginaldus precentor, Gaufridus succentor, Godefridus Wygorn'[a] et Thomas Bathon' archidiaconi, Aluredus de Chyv[b], Nicholaus de Wynesham, Baldwinus de sancto Genesio, Robertus filius Willelmi, Paris,[c] Odo, Samson clericus domini Wygorn', Ilbertus de Northon', Robertus de Aldomaro (*sic*), Iohannes de Ken, Willelmus Flamang', Iohannes filius Richildis, Iocelinus de Wynesham, Gaufridus franc', Alexander cocus, Symon filius Ricardi, Willelmus Godardus, Thomas homo cantoris, Gaufridus filius Roberti de Westbury, Ricardus de Glaston', Elias homo Thome archidiaconi et multi alii.

    a C ends here.   b Chiev D.   c *for* Willelmi, Paris *read* Baldwini, Henr' D.

B, D, and E note that no. 72 was in chirograph form. It carried the seals of the bishops of Bath and Worcester, the church of Wells, and the two knights, Paganus de Penebrigg' and Rogerus Witeing ('Historiola de primordiis episcopatus Somersetensis', ed. Joseph Hunter, in *Ecclesiastical Documents*, Camden Soc. (1840), p. 27.) The 'Historiola' describes the laymen named in the text as 'vi milites et duo iuvenes strenui et magnanimi militum fratres', and mentions that the precentor's nephews had sued the church 'in curiam laycam coram iudicibus contra canones'. The settlement was made in the chamber (*thalamus*) of Bishop Robert. Robert died on 31 Aug. 1166; Knowles, *Episcopal colleagues*, p. 31, suggests that he was incapacitated in his later years. Bishop Roger may have had the status of coadjutor, hence his appearance here in the chamber of the elderly bishop, and his involvement in a dispute over the archdeaconry of Bath (above, p. 32).

Wooton Wawen *see* Conches, nos. 11, 12

73. Cathedral Church of Worcester

23 Aug. 1164 x 9 Aug. 1179. *Grant of the church of Wolverley to the monks of Worcester* in usus monachorum, *saving episcopal rights and a sufficient portion for the vicar. Of the established pension of five marks, three are assigned to the chamberlain, two to the precentor. With the same reservations, the pension may be increased later.* (*Witnesses omitted.*)

B = Worcester, D. and C. Mun. Reg. I (A 4) fo. 6ʳ. s.xiii med.
Pd *Worc. cart.*, p. 23 no. 33, and Nash, *Worcester*, ii. 475.

> *Worc. cart.* gives the final date as 1174 (correctly May 1173) on the view that no. 73 precedes no. 74, which was issued before the election of Bishop Richard of Winchester. The sequence of events is not, however, beyond doubt, and a wider range of dates must be admitted.

74. Cathedral Church of Worcester

23 Aug. 1164 x 1 May 1173. *Notification as judge-delegate, with Richard archdeacon of Poitiers, of the settlement of the case between the monks of Worcester and Thomas, clerk, about tithes of the church of Wolverley. Thomas shall hold the church of the monks with all its land and tithes, except tithes of the monks' demesne, paying a pension of two marks a year, and a third mark as one third of the tithes which from of old belong to the chamberlain.* (*Witnesses omitted.*)

B = Worcester, D. and C. Mun. Reg. I (A 4) fo. 6ʳ. s.xiii med.
Pd from B, *Worc. cart.*, pp. 23–4 no. 34, and Nash, *Worcester*, ii. 475.

Worc. cart. dates no. 74 '1164–74'. Archdeacon Richard was elected bishop of Winchester on 1 May 1173, and would probably thereafter have styled himself 'elect of Winchester'. The case must therefore belong to 1164 x 1167 or to Sept. 1172 x May 1173. Cf. no. 73.

75. Cathedral Church of Worcester

23 Aug. 1164 x 9 Aug. 1179. *Notification of arrangements made about the church of St Helen and its chapels. Charters of Bishops Wulfstan and Simon are inspected and recited. Grants that the church may pass* in usus fratrum, *half the obventions being assigned to the monks' food and half to the sacristy, the bishop's rights and dues being reserved. The charter has been read before the brethren. (Witnesses omitted.)*

B = Worcester, D. and C. Mun. Reg. I (A 4) fo. 8ᵛ. s.xiii med.
Pd from B *Worc. cart.*, p. 34 no. 55.

> Wulfstan's and Simon's charters are pd. ibid., nos 52 and 54. In the cartulary Roger's charter is abbreviated with references to these earlier texts. Confirmations of Pope Lucius III relating to St Helen's are pd ibid., nos 59, 60 and *PUE*, ii nos. 230, 239.

76. Cathedral Church of Worcester

23 Aug. 1164 x 9 Aug. 1179. *Notification of the grant by Simon de Mans of the right of advowson of the chapels of Doddenham and Knightwick to the prior and convent of Worcester, who shall have that right without any claim by Simon or his heirs. Commends Simon's devotion and ratifies his grant.* 'Testibus Roberto de Bernaio et Gaufrido* de Corton' presbyteris, Roberto Blundo, Roberto de Porta, Daniele et pluribus aliis clericis et laicis.'

B = Worcester, D. and C. Mun. Reg. I (A 4) fo. 14ʳ⁻ᵛ. s.xiii med.
C = ibid., fo. 14ᵛ in inspeximus of Bishop Henry, which gives the names of the witnesses from *; B replaces these with *etc.*
Pd from B and C, *Worc. cart.*, pp. 56–7, nos 95, 96. Also pd from C by Nash, *Worcester*, ii. 68, and W. Thomas, *Worcester*, appendix p. 17 no. 29. Mentioned, *Reg. Prioratus*, p. 20*b*.

77. Cathedral Church of Worcester

9 Apr. 1175 at Worcester. *Inspeximus of charter of Hugh son of Osbert, by which Hugh confirmed his father's gift to the monks of Worcester of Boraston and the church of Dodderhill and a salt pit in*

Droitwich. Osbert son of Hugh, and Hugh de Saio his brother, have confirmed their consent to the gift.

A = Worcester, D. and C. Mun. B 306 (formerly 311). Endorsed: .iii. Carta Rogeri Wig' episcopi de Duderhull'. s.xiv. Approx. 205 × 125 + 30 mm. Sealed *double queue*; seal lost, fragment of tag remains.

B = ibid., Reg. I (A 4) fo. 22ᵛ. s.xiii med.
Pd from A in *Worc. cart.*, p. 90 no. 165, with facsimile.

Universis sancte matris ecclesie filiis . Rog' dei gratia Wigornensis episcopus . salutem in domino perpetuam. Que semel recte statuuntur ne temporum lapsu a memoria recedant . et posteris habeantur incognita ⁖ posteritati scripti serie est subveniendum. Universorum itaque teneat cognitio quod cartam Hugonis filii Osberti autentico sigillo roboratam sub hac forma inspeximus. Omnibus sancte ecclesie fidelibus . omnibusque suis successoribus . filiis . parentibus . et omnibus heredibus suis . Hugo filius Osberti ⁖ salutem. Sciatis me plenarie concessisse et perpetualiter proprio sigillo meo confirmasse priori et monachis Wyrecestrie elemosinam patris mei Osberti quam ipse dedit eis . scilicet Burestonam . et ecclesiam de Dudrenhulla cum omnibus que ad eam pertinent . insuper etiam dedi eis pro remedio anime mee . et patris mei Osberti . et matris mee Nest . et omnium parentum meorum unam salinam in Wich . de viginti solidis. Volo itaque ut eadem libertate perpetualiter teneant hanc donationem patris mei et meam qua prius eam tenuit pater meus et ego. Teste Ailrico archidiacono . Hugone archidiacono . Fritherico . Colebrando decano . Wilfwio presbitero supranominate ecclesie de Dudrenhulla . Thancredo capellano meo . Adam fratre meo . Thurstino avunculo meo . Ricardo de Escrop . Radulfo de Coleshulla . Ricardo filio Hyldewini . Aldwino de Bureford . Ernsi de Codderugia. Hanc cartam Osberti filii Hugonis inspectam et manibus propriis contrectatam in presentia nostra ratam habuit . et sub presentia subscriptorum testium patris sui concessioni assensum plenum prebuit. Quod quia presentibus et posteris certum esse volumus ⁖ presentis scripti seriem sigilli nostri testimonio roboravimus. Hec autem acta sunt anno incarnationis dominice .m.c.lxxv. v. idus Aprilis . in cripta

Wigornensis ecclesie ante altare sancti Petri. His testibus . Thoma suppriore . Gervasio camerario . Senato cantore . Alano . Iohanne de Beiberi . Waltero de Omnibus Sanctis . Magistro Moyse . Magistro Silvestro . Magistro Godefrido . Abel . Roberto de Cliftuna . Hugone de Saio . Roberto de Luci . Hugone Poer . Adam filio Edwini prepositi et multis aliis . prefato Hugone de Saio presente et cum fratre suo Osberto consensum suum fide in manu nostra interposita confirmante.

> Pope Lucius III, confirming the church of Dodderhill to the monks, noted that it had been restored to them by authority of Bishop Roger 'from him who had invaded it' (*Worc. cart.*, p. 36 no. 60). On the arrangements concerning this church see no. 78 and p. 93 above.

78. Cathedral Church of Worcester

9 Apr. 1175 at Worcester. *Notification that the monks of Worcester have granted to Osbert son of Hugh, and one heir only, the presentation to St Augustine's, Dodderhill. The parson shall be presented by Osbert to the prior, and by the prior to the bishop. The first parson shall pay half a mark yearly to the monks, and the second twenty shillings. After the death of Osbert and his next heir the church shall be converted* in usus monachorum *as perpetual alms, saving the possession of the parson already instituted. (Dating clause as no. 77, witnesses omitted.)*

B = Worcester, D. and C. Mun. Reg. I (A 4) fo. 23^r. s.xiii med.

Pd from B, *Worc. cart.*, p. 91 no. 167.

> Copies of no. 78 were given to Osbert and his brother Hugh, and later returned by them to the monks (*Worc. cart.*, pp. 93–4 no. 173). In 1178 Osbert presented a parson, in accordance with the terms of no. 78 (see no. 83). In 1221, following the death of that parson, Osbert's great-niece claimed the presentation, but the prior of Worcester defeated the claim, citing Bishop Roger's charter among others (*Worc. cart.*, p. 100 no. 189 with other references). On the earlier history of the church of Dodderhill see *VCH Worcs.*, iii. 67. See also no. 77.

79. Cathedral Church of Worcester

9 Apr. 1175 at Worcester. *Notification of the settlement of a dispute between the monks of Worcester and Osbert son of Hugh about the patronage* (super iure advocationis et patronatus) *of All Saints'*

church, Worcester. The patronage shall belong to Osbert and his heirs, with the condition that the parson shall be presented by them to the prior, and by the prior to the bishop, and shall pay half a mark yearly to the monks. (Dating clause as no. 77, with first witness only.)

B = Worcester, D. and C. Mun. Reg. I (A 4) fo. 24^r. s.xiii med.

C = ibid., Reg. Prioratus (A 2) p. 133b. s.xiv in.

D = ibid., Liber Pensionum (A 3) fo. 1. s.xv med.

Pd from B, *Worc. cart.*, p. 96 no. 178; from C, *Reg. Prioratus*, pp. 133b–4a. Summary from D, *Liber Pensionum*, no. 1.

> A charter of Osbert in similar terms, of the same date, refers to presentation to the bishop, not to the prior (*Worc. cart.*, p. 95 no. 177). Nos 80 and 81 show that the settlement recorded by no. 79 was part of a general settlement of disputes between the monks and Osbert. The church of All Saints had been confirmed to the prior and monks by Bishop Simon, with other possessions, on 26 Jan. 1149, and was also included in a privilege of Pope Alexander III (*Worc. cart.*, p. 42 no. 73, and p. 47 no. 77).

80. Cathedral Church of Worcester

? c. Apr. 1175. Notification of a settlement concerning the churches of All Saints and St Clement, Worcester. After a dispute in the bishop's presence between Osbert son of Hugh and Ralph prior of Worcester, the prior stated that St Clement's did not belong to All Saints. Osbert formally admitted that he claimed no rights over St Clement's. Hugh Poer lord of the estate (dominus fundi ecclesie sancti Clementis), *granted all his rights to the church of Worcester. Walter the dean, parson of All Saints, was present and made no protest. The bishop has therefore confirmed St Clement's to the church of Worcester, and freed it from subjection to All Saints, so that it shall be the monks' own demesne chapel. 'Hiis testibus, magistro Silvestro etc.'*

B = Worcester, D. and C. Mun. Reg. I (A 4) fo. 24^v. s.xiii med.
Pd from B, *Worc. cart.*, p. 98 no. 182.

> No. 80 appears to record part of the general settlement between the monks of Worcester and Osbert son of Hugh, finalized on 9 Apr. 1175 (nos. 77–9).

81. Cathedral Church of Worcester

? c.Apr. 1175. Notification that Hugh Poer and Richard of Grafton have conceded to the prior and convent of Worcester the advowson of

St Clement's church, Worcester, which they had claimed. The bishop makes their concession valid by episcopal authority, and confirms it.

B = Worcester, D. and C. Mun. Reg. I (A 4) fo. 24^v. s.xiii med.
Pd from B, *Worc. cart.*, p. 99 no. 184.

> No. 81 records part of the same settlement as no. 80, and the same considerations apply to the date. Only in this period were canonists formulating the rule that gifts of advowsons required episcopal consent. The rule appears in canon 9 of the Third Lateran Council (1179): 'Ecclesias et decimas de manu laicorum sine consensu episcoporum ... religiosos recipere prohibemus'. Cf. Landau, *Ius Patronatus, passim.*

82. Cathedral Church of Worcester

2 Aug. 1164 x 9 Aug. 1179. *Notification that Hugh Poer has granted to the monks of Worcester two shillings a year from his chapel at Whittington, to be paid by the parson. The bishop has confirmed the grant by episcopal authority, placing his seal on it so that it shall endure for ever. 'Hiis testibus, magistro Baldwino etc.'*

B = Worcester, D. and C. Mun. Reg. I (A 4) fo. 25^r. s.xiii med.
C = ibid. Reg. Prioratus (A 2) p. 92a. s.xiv in.
D = ibid. Liber Pensionum (A 3) fo. 1^v. s.xv med.
Pd from B, *Worc. cart.*, p. 100 no. 187; from C, *Reg. Prioratus*, p. 92a. Summary from D, *Liber Pensionum*, no. 3.

> Hugh Poer figures in the arrangements recorded in nos. 80 and 81, of ? Apr. 1175, but there is no certain indication that no. 82 is connected with them and of the same date.

83. Cathedral Church of Worcester

4 Nov. 1178 at Worcester. *Notification of the institution of Adam son of Edwin, the bishop's clerk, to the church of Dodderhill, saving the vicarage of Ernald the priest, who shall pay 13 pence yearly to Adam, and saving the monks' pension of half a mark yearly. Adam shall hold the church with all appurtenances, saving the composition between the monks of Worcester and the nuns of Westwood. 'Fuit hec institutio facta anno ab incarnatione domini mclxxviii pridie non' Novemb' apud Vigorn'. Hiis testibus, Gilleberto capellano etc.'*

B = Worcester, D. and C. Mun. Reg. I (A 4) fo. 23ʳ. s.xiii med.
Pd from B, *Worc. cart.*, p. 92 no. 169.

> The agreement with the nuns of Westwood, made in the bishop's presence on the same day as the institution, is recorded in a charter of the prior of Worcester, of which the original survives (*Worc. cart.*, p. 89 no. 164). This charter has a long list of witnesses, many of whom, like Gilbert the chaplain, probably also witnessed no. 83. The agreement and the institution were the final stages in the settlement between Worcester and Osbert son of Hugh about the church of Dodderhill, which Osbert had withdrawn from Worcester and given to Westwood some twenty years earlier (above, p. 95).

84. Cathedral Church of Worcester

? 25 Mar. 1173 x *c.*Apr. 1174. *Confirmation to the monks of the 60 shillings to be paid by the canons of Osney according to the composition made between Osney and Worcester about the church of Bibury. The payment is assigned to the monks' food.* 'His testibus, Symone archidiacono Wigorn', magistro Moyse, Gill' capellano, Rodberto monacho, magistro Silvestro, Aluredo, clericis episcopi, magistro Gaufrido de Fulri, Osberto de Henberi, Rodberto de Uppetona, magistro Godefrido.'

B = Worcester, D. and C. Mun. Reg. I (A 4) fo. 30ᵛ. s.xiii med.
C = ibid., Liber Pensionum (A 3) fo. xx. s.xv med.
Pd from B and C, *Worc. cart.*, p. 120 no. 227; summary from C, Liber Pensionum, no. 45.

> C preserves the full witness list printed above; B gives only the first name. For the composition about Bibury see no. 51. No. 84 probably followed soon after the composition, as a decision would have to be made about the use of the pension.

85. Cathedral Church of Worcester

1167 x *c.*1 Jan. 1179. *Notification that lawful men have recognized on oath in the bishop's presence that a hide of land called* Herdewicha *should belong to the demesne of the church of Hartlebury. Absalon who had held it, resigned it to the prior of Worcester; the prior granted it to Absalon to hold for his life only, for six pence yearly.* 'Testibus, Simone archidiacono Wigorn' etc.'

B = Worcester, D. and C. Mun. Reg. I (A 4) fo. 36^r. s.xiii med.

C = ibid. Liber albus (A 5) fo. 122^v. s.xiv–xv.

Pd from B, *Worc. cart.*, pp. 141–2, no. 268; from C, Nash, *Worcester*, i. 574.

> The earliest date is fixed by the appearance of Simon as archdeacon, the latest by the bishop's last departure from England. His exile of 1167–72 makes it probable that no. 85 belongs to the 1170s. Cf. *VCH Worcs.*, iii. 386.

APPENDIX II

CALENDAR OF LETTERS OF POPE ALEXANDER III TO BISHOP ROGER, AND EVIDENCE FOR LOST COMMISSIONS TO THE BISHOP AS JUDGE-DELEGATE

INTRODUCTION

1 The letters

This Appendix is designed to present a conspectus of Pope Alexander's correspondence with Bishop Roger, and at the same time to make it easier for readers to follow up the numerous references to decretals and other papal letters. A comprehensive work, *Regesta decretalium saeculi XII*, ed. S. Chodorow and C. Duggan, will be published in *Monumenta Iuris Canonici* (Biblioteca Apostolica Vaticana); it has not therefore been thought necessary to duplicate here the exhaustive study of the manuscript tradition of each decretal, or to discuss the details of every text. By the generous permission of Professor Stephan Kuttner, use has been made of the working papers and photographs of manuscripts of the late Professor Walther Holtzmann, who had already, before his death in 1963, listed every decretal and pseudo-decretal of this period, and had in nearly all cases identified the issuing pope, the addressees, the places, and the earliest and best surviving texts, and noted the occurrence of each letter in decretal collections up to 1234. Before I knew the extent and exact nature of his work in this field, I had worked over much of the material independently, and was glad to find only a few items to correct or add (I should have missed no. 38 but for his careful analysis of the burnt *Collectio Cottoniana*); in a few cases I have preferred a different identification of places or persons. It is hoped that the conclusions presented here in summary form will seldom differ seriously from those which will appear with full scholarly apparatus in the forthcoming *Regesta*, and its accompanying volume of hitherto unprinted texts.

In this Appendix reference is given to the number of each letter in the *Regesta Pontificum* (JL) for letters listed there, and to a printed text or texts where such exist. The printed texts are generally sufficient for the purpose of the present work, but they are seldom derived from the earliest manuscripts, and very often present an abbreviated, corrupt, or deliberately rewritten version.

This Appendix includes all papal letters that have come to my notice, from whatever source, which may concern Roger of Worcester. A warning must be given about items which have been excluded. The decretal collections, printed and unprinted, of *c.*1170–1234 contain alleged pronouncements of Pope Alexander III addressed to the bishop of Worcester, which do not appear here. Some of these are well-known letters which were certainly addressed to other prelates (above, p. 128). Some are fragments, often reworked, or summaries, of letters appearing here; some are not papal letters, but conciliar decrees, stray glosses and other material. A few of these items are noticed here for special reasons, but as this material will be dealt with comprehensively in the *Regesta Decretalium*, it seems unnecessary to add thirty or forty items to this list merely in order to dismiss them.

2 *The dating of the letters*

Decretals were simply papal letters, issued in the same form as others (solemn privileges had of course their own form), with an address, often to an office-holder (*episcopo Wigorn'*) rather than to an individual (*Rogero Wigorn' episcopo*), and at the end a dating clause. Before 11 February 1188 the dating clause of letters indicated only the place of issue, with the day and month expressed in Roman fashion, but not the year. Most letters in this Appendix are known only from decretal collections, and unfortunately for the historian the canonists soon learned to lighten their labours by abbreviating addresses and omitting dating clauses altogether. There are therefore many letters of Pope Alexander III of which it can only be said with certainty that they were issued during his pontificate (7 September 1159–30 August 1181), always assuming that they have not been confused with those of his predecessor Adrian or his successor Lucius III.

In dealing with letters of Alexander III to a bishop of Worcester, it is often possible to narrow the limits of date considerably. Bishop Alfred died on 31 July 1160, only nine days after Alexander was recognized by the kings of France and England; from that time there was no bishop, as opposed to a bishop-elect, till Roger was consecrated on 23 August 1164, and this event will hardly have been known at the Curia, then at Sens, till September. It is theoretically possible that a few papal letters were addressed to the bishop of Worcester before that date, but none has been identified, and it seems reasonable to give September 1164 as the earliest probable date, except in a few cases which present special problems. The latest possible date is a more complex matter. Some papal letters of unknown date may have been addressed to Bishop Baldwin during the period of about eleven months that elapsed between the time when his consecration (10 August 1180) was known at the Curia, and the pope's death. It is therefore necessary to give 30 August 1181 as the latest possible date for many letters, though the probability in any given case is in favour of the address to Roger rather than Baldwin. In the present state of knowledge, the decretal collections themselves give little help in this problem. Some are thought to have been compiled before the Lateran Council of March 1179, because they show no knowledge of its decrees; letters to a bishop of Worcester in such collections could not be addressed to Baldwin. But as the decrees at first circulated independently and must have been known to collectors in separate texts, I have been chary of using this evidence to assign letters to Roger rather than Baldwin.

As regards letters addressed to Roger, it is not known whether the Curia continued to address letters to him between January 1179 when he left England, and August when he died at Tours. Letters on which he is known to have taken action must have been issued at latest some three months before his departure, and the probabilities are in favour of an even earlier date. It is improbable that he received commissions to act as judge-delegate in England during his exile, between about the beginning of 1168 (when – at latest – his departure from England must have been known at the Curia) and the final settlement at Avranches in September 1172. But both these dates are approximate. We do not know exactly when the pope was informed of

Roger's exile, or to what extent normal traffic may have begun to flow between England and the Curia in the summer of 1172. It is impossible to express these considerations satisfactorily in summary form. Some undated letters have therefore been dated simply 1164 x 1179 (for example), and the reader must bear in mind the possible effect of the bishop's movements on the dating of papal letters.

Where a commission was addressed to more than one prelate, the order of precedence may give evidence of dating. For example, a commission of Pope Alexander to the bishops of Hereford and Worcester could have been issued between c.1 September 1164, when Roger's consecration should have been known at the Curia (at Sens), and late March 1167, when Robert of Melun's death was known there; or it could have been issued between late September 1180 and late August 1181. But a commission to the bishops of Worcester and Hereford will probably have been issued between November 1174, when the Curia knew of Robert Foliot's consecration, and September 1179, when it knew of Bishop Roger's death. The Curia observed the rules of precedence, and it is only rarely that a copyist must be suspected of altering the order of the names. Precedence has therefore been used regularly as a guide to dating.

It would be absurd to note every occasion on which use has been made of basic works of reference for dating purposes. It is assumed, unless there is a note to the contrary, that dates are as given in the new *Le Neve's Fasti*, as available, for prelates and dignitaries; where the new *Fasti* is not yet published, *The Handbook of British Chronology* is used for English bishops, as also for earls. *Heads of Religious Houses* is used for abbots, and priors of houses having no abbot.

In expressing dates, x is used to indicate a point in time between two limiting dates: e.g. the first letter in the calendar was issued between September 1164 and 1 January 1181. The hyphen indicates a continuous period: e.g. Roger was in exile 1167–1172.

3 The Calendar

Entries are arranged in order of incipits, and cross-referred where texts give variants. This order will be used in the *Regesta*

Decretalium, and it should be easy to refer from this calendar to the *Regesta* in due course. Decretal collections are listed on p. xv in summary style; a full list appears in Holtzmann's *Studies*. Some papal letters are included which concern Bishop Roger, though they were not addressed to him; these are normally distinguished by the letters A, B, etc. e.g. no. 3A. Some letters are more fully calendared than others, according to their interest for the present work; those who wish to study the history of law and procedure, and the use of particular *clausulae*, must of course refer to the best and earliest texts, as indicated in the *Regesta*.

Unprinted decretal collections are cited according to published analyses, or, where these are not available, according to the numbers assigned to the item in unpublished analyses made by Holtzmann and Dr Duggan, with folio references.

CALENDAR OF PAPAL LETTERS

1. Abbas sancti Edmundi. To the bishop of Worcester.

Sept. 1164 x *c*.1 Jan. 1181. Commission to hear the complaint of R., that the abbot of Bury, from whom he holds his patrimony, forced him to renounce his church by threat of expulsion from his possessions.

> JL 14131. Pd X 1.40.2 and ACL 22.7. Occurs in many decretal collections of English provenance or associations.
>
> The abbot of Bury is not styled *bone memorie*, so the commission was probably issued before Abbot Hugh's death on 14 or 15 Nov. 1180 was known at the Curia. His successor was elected in Feb. 1182.

2. Accedens ad presentiam. To (Roger) bishop of Worcester and one or two others.

? 1175 x Sept. 1179. Master Hugh complains that after he had been put in possession of the church of Whittlesea on the authority of a papal mandate, he and his witnesses were brought before the secular court and suffered serious losses. His opponent, O., has refused for a year to appear in the ecclesiastical court. Hugh shall be absolved from the claim of O. as regards possession. When O. has restored the losses, he may plead as to right. If he again takes Hugh before the secular court, the addressees shall impose perpetual silence on him.

JL——. Pd Wig. 7.72; occurs here only.

> No. 2 is a further development of nos. 27 and 68A. Wig. names only the bishop of Worcester as addressee, but the forms are plural throughout. No. 27 was addressed to the bishop and the prior of Kenilworth; the prior was perhaps the second addressee of no. 2 also. Odo, son of Odo de Chambai received the church of Whittlesea at the presentation of Abbot Solomon of Thorney (1176–95), perhaps after Bishop Roger's death. (Cambridge Univ. Libr. Add. MS 3020 fo. 423^r.)

3. Accepimus litteras venerabilis. To the bishop of Worcester.

Late 1174 x 30 Aug. 1181. Commission to hear the complaint of A., who has appealed from the synod of Archbishop Richard of Canterbury, fearing a sentence of divorce. Witnesses there said that he and his wife were related in the fourth and fifth degree of consanguinity, though none had spoken when the banns were published three times by the parish priest, as is customary, before the marriage *in facie ecclesie*. The couple shall be absolved from the charge, and silence imposed on the witnesses.

JL——. Pd Wig. 1. 48; occurs here only.

3A Accepimus querelam T. clerici. To the bishops of ?London and Exeter.

? Mar. 1174 x early 1177. Commission to hear the complaint of T., clerk, that G., priest, who has benefices worth at least forty marks, troubles him improperly about the church of Holy Cross of Bungay. If G. wishes to begin legal proceedings, the addressees shall hear the case.

JL——. Flor. c. 171 fo. 179vb, unprinted; occurs here only.

> No. 59 refers to an earlier letter to the bishops of Exeter and *Worcester* in terms which seem to fit no. 3A. See no. 24 and notes, also no. 88.

4. Accepta querela abbatis. To G(ilbert) bishop of London, and R(oger) bishop of Worcester.

? 12 Apr. 1176. Second commission to the addressees in the case between the abbot and canons of Osney and the prior and canons of St Frideswide about the church of St Mary Magdalen, Oxford. The addressees had already adjudged possession to

APPENDIX II 319

Osney; the prior then appealed. The judges are reproved for delay and ordered to proceed notwithstanding appeal or letters obtained by fraud; one may act alone. Clerks and laymen who attacked the canons (of Osney) shall be sent to the pope.

JL——. Pd *Letters of Foliot*, pp. 464–5, *Oseney cart.*, ii. 220–2, *PUE*, iii. 364 no. 234.

The commission is recited in the judges' sentence, App. I, 50. The incipit is conjectural, as proposed in *PUE*. See also nos. 52 and 86A. Nos. 4 and 52 have the same dating clause; one or other may have been miscopied, cf. *Letters of Foliot*, p. 463, n. 2. At least eighteen months, and more probably two years, must have elapsed between the issuing of the two commissions.

5. Ad audientiam nostram noveritis. To the bishops of Exeter and Worcester.

*c.*Nov. 1174 x 30 Aug. 1181. Commission to hear the case between Hugh, clerk, and N., chaplain of the king, about the chapel of *Suttona*. Earlier judges had adjudged possession to Hugh; N. then got a commission to Archbishop Richard, and regained possession. The addressees shall examine the two earlier commissions. Hugh shall have possession, appeal being forbidden, if the second commission did not mention the first sentence; if it revoked or cast doubt on the sentence, the addressees shall approve the archbishop's decision if just, or hear the whole case, appeal being forbidden, if the decision was clearly unjust. One judge may act.

JL——. Pd Wig. 7.70 (occurs here only) and Holtzmann and Kemp, p. 48 no. xix, with translation.

This commission must have been issued at least three or four months after Archbishop Richard's return to England in Aug. 1174. The one text reverses the precedence of the bishops, or possibly names one, or both, incorrectly.

6. Ad audientiam nostram pervenit. To (Bartholomew) bishop of Exeter and (Roger) bishop of Worcester.

27 July 1176. Commission to hear the case about the chapel of Leaveland, previously committed to the abbots of Faversham and Boxley, between the monks of Saint-Bertin and firstly Nathaniel, a knight, and secondly Richard, archbishop of Canterbury, who has appealed. If the knight admitted before the previous judges that he had no rights, silence shall be imposed on him, without right of appeal. The addressees shall then

hear the allegations of the monks and the archbishop. If Archbishop Theobald gave the chapel to the monks, and he and St Thomas the martyr confirmed the gift in writing, silence shall be imposed on Archbishop Richard. One judge may act.

> JL——. Pd *Les chartes de S. Bertin*, ed. D. Haigneré, i (1890), 125, no. 275. Cf. *Cal. Docs. France*, p. 486 no. 1339, and *Archaeologia Cantiana*, 4 (1861), 215.

> The date, given by Haigneré as *Anagnie, vi° Kalendas augusti*, could refer to 1174 or 1176; but Archbishop Richard was out of England till Aug. 1174, so that the later date is more probable. There is no trace of a sentence, but agreement was reached; the archbishop confirmed the chapel to the monks (Haigneré, i. 123 no. 269), who presented it to William Baiuin (ibid., i. 148 no. 336). William was perhaps a minor clerk of Archbishop Thomas (*MTB*, iii. 131).

7. Ad aures nostras pervenit. To the bishops of Exeter and Worcester.

Late 1174 x 30 Aug. 1181. Commission to hear the case between the parson of East Grinstead and the archbishop of Canterbury. The archbishop claimed that the parson had been instituted by officials of the bishop (of Chichester) before presentation to the bishop, and thus incurred the general sentence he had pronounced against those entering upon churches without the approval of the diocesan. If the bishop later approved of the parson's institution, he shall retain the church, appeal being forbidden; if not, the judges, or one of them, shall hear the case. If the parson was excommunicated after appeal, the sentence is invalid.

> JL——. Pd Wig. 4.50, inc. *Pervenit ad aures*. Also occurs in Chelt. 4.23 and Cott. 6.49, both of the 'Worcester' group, and 1 Alc. c.66, which alone gives the clause permitting one judge to act if the other cannot, 'adhibitis sibi viris honestis et discretis'.

> On the general sentence pronounced by Archbishop Richard see M. Cheney, 'Council of Westminster', p. 64.

8. Ad aures nostras perlatum. To Roger bishop of Worcester.

Sept. 1164 x *c.*Mar. 1179. Replies to legal problems posed by the bishop.

(a) *Ad aures . . . constringas*. A man has left his wife and lives with her relative. On being sued by his wife, he appealed to the

APPENDIX II 321

pope. If the two women are related in the first or second degree, the man must be compelled to leave both, appeal being forbidden, and may never marry; if in the third degree or beyond, he must return to his wife.

> JL 13163. Pd 1 Comp. 4.13.2. Occurs in many collections.

(b) *Illas vero terras ... conferri.* The bishop may grant newly-cleared woodland on rent-paying hereditary tenancies, to those who cleared them, or their relatives, unless the land can be conferred on others to greater advantage to his church.

> JL 14132. Pd X 3.13.7. Occurs in many collections.
>
> The letter occurs undivided in many early collections, among them Belv. 1.13, which gives the bishop's initial (pd *Gilberti epistolae*, ii. 102). All the datable decretals in this part of *Collectio Belverensis* were probably issued before 1175 (Duggan, *Collections*, p. 72); the same *terminus ante quem* may apply to this letter. It is cited by Simon of Bisignano in his *Summa*, thought to have been composed before the Lateran Council of March 1179.

9. Ad hec quia (or *cum*, or *quod*). To the bishops of Exeter and Worcester.

Sept. 1164 x 30 Aug. 1181. Instruction to summon witnesses, lay and clerical, because the clerks have no documents (*scripta autentica*), and to warn them to tell the truth without fear or favour.

> JL 13927. Pd ACL 8.19, 1 Comp.2.13.22. Occurs in a few other collections. No. 9 may be the concluding sentence of no. 42.

10. Ad tue discretionis. To Thomas archbishop of Canterbury.

22 Apr. 1167. Notification that the bishops of Winchester and Worcester have been ordered to hear the case between Hugh, earl of Norfolk, and the canons of Pentney. The bishops shall absolve the earl, but if he does not within forty days restore what was taken from the canons, they shall excommunicate him afresh.

> JL 11346. Pd *MTB*, 6.557. Cf. Foreville, *Église et royauté*, pp. 206–9; *Letters of Foliot*, pp. 210–14.

11. Archidiaconis de ecclesiastica. ? To the bishop of Worcester.

? 7 Sept. 1159 x 30 Aug. 1181. According to the law (*de ecclesiastica institutione*) archdeacons may not pronounce sentence (of excommunication) without consent of the bishop.

> JL 13166, in which this text is treated as the end of no. 18. Pd X 1.23.5, and ACL 36.4. Occurs in many collections.
>
> No. 11 appears in several early collections with address to the bishop of Worcester. It became attached to a genuine letter, no. 18, which has nothing to do with archdeacons. No surviving letter to the bishop of Worcester raises just this problem. The gloss notes that law and custom might be opposed on this point.

12. Audita querela dilecti (or *Aud. olim quer.*). To R(oger) bishop of Worcester and R(ichard) archdeacon of Ely.

1165 x Summer 1178. The bishop of London and the archdeacon of Ely had been commissioned to hear the complaint of Th. clerk of the king of Scots, that Hugh parson of Sandy troubled him unlawfully about the church of Potton, though he had sworn not to bring any case. Later, Hugh's messenger arrived, and asserted that Hugh was violently despoiled; he obtained a commission to the same archdeacon and the bishop of Worcester, to hear the case notwithstanding other letters or the instructions (*forma*) therein, and to revoke action taken after the messenger set out. The first judges now report that they had obeyed the instructions, and imposed silence on Hugh. Although Hugh's messenger (*Licet autem nuntius*) obtained a second commission, yet it was not intended to revoke what had been done by judges-delegate by papal authority, but only anything done by force, or improperly. The sentence shall stand if it was issued before the arrival of the second commission; if not, the addressees shall act according to the instructions of that commission, always provided that Hugh was violently despoiled and then swore his oath.

> JL 14143. Pd X 2.13.4 (with some confusion) and ACL 22.4. Occurs in very many collections, sometimes starting at *Licet autem nuntius*.
>
> The judges' initials are given in Chelt. 19.10. Reg. c.95-6 and 1 Berol. c.47 give Th. for the name of one party, where others give T., confirming an identification suggested by Professor G.W.S. Barrow, with Thomas de Paraviso, who witnesses a number of Earl David's charters in the honour of Huntingdon.

See also no. 84. Bishop Roger's sentence (App. I, 47) shows that Hugh's complaint of violent spoliation was made not against Thomas, but against the prior of St Andrew's, Northampton, who (at an uncertain date) granted the church of Potton with the chapel of the manor to Thomas for an annual pension of seven marks (BL MS Cotton Vespasian E. xvii (cart. of St Andrew's) fo. 276ᵛ). The dispute may have followed the grant of the earldom of Huntingdon to Simon of Senlis after the capture of the king of Scots in July 1174. Simon tried to oust clerks presented by the king (cf. JL 13764).

The lawyers were interested in the pope's ruling that Hugh's renunciation, though made on oath, was ineffective if made after he had been despoiled of the church.

13. Auditis olim a multis. To (Bartholomew) bishop of Exeter, (Roger) bishop of Worcester, and (Clarembald) abbot of Faversham.

25 May, 1174 or 1176. Confirms the deposition of Clarembald, formerly abbot-elect of St Augustine's, Canterbury, and orders the addressees to excommunicate him if he troubles the monastery.

JL 12706. Pd *Hist. Mon. S. Augustini*, p. 414, and Thorne, p. 1817, curtailed.

The commission to the judges is no. 33; their report to the pope is App. I, 8. No. 13 was dated at Anagni, where the pope was in residence on 25 May in 1173, 1174 and 1176. 1173 is probably too early, since the sentence was, it seems, announced in the summer of that year.

13A. Audivimus quod decimas. See *Sicut vobis iura* no. 85 below.

14. Causam que inter dilectum. To the bishops of London (or Exeter) and Worcester.

Summer 1174 x Oct. 1178. Commission to hear the case, previously committed to the bishop of Worcester, between R(obert) abbot of Malmesbury and some of his brethren. If Robert's election was properly conducted, it should be confirmed, although he is not very learned.

JL——. Pd Wig.2.34; occurs only here.

There may be an omission from the text (after *audiendam* p. 100, line 3), since a reason was normally given for the issue of a fresh commission naming an additional judge. Wig. gives address to the bishops of London and Worcester, but Giraldus mentions proceedings before Bartholomew of Exeter and Roger and a decision following the instructions of this commission (*Giraldi opera*, ii. 34). See also App. I, 45. If this was the commission on which Bartholomew and Roger acted, it must have been issued in time for action before *c*.1 Jan. 1179. Robert was blessed by the bishop of Llandaff, May x Oct. 1174.

15. Causam que inter dilectos. To the bishop of Norwich and the abbot of St Edmunds.

1165 x Sept. 1179. Commission to hear the case between the brethren of Arrouaise and R. priest, about the church of Harrold. The case had been committed to the abbot and the bishop of Worcester. Because the bishop was absent, the abbot consulted the pope, who had sent instructions (*certam formam*). The history of the case is recounted. R. the priest had sworn not to claim the church of Harrold if he was left in occupation of that of 'Bratfeld' (Cold Brayfield).

> JL——. Pd Claustr. c.197 (a bad text, inaccurately printed). Also in Wig.7.6 and Sang.2.1.8 (pp. 598–9) part only.

> This was at least the fourth, and it was not the last, commission in a complex dispute. Bishop Roger was named only in the first, on which he did not act because he was absent. He is not called *bone memorie*. He did however give sentence in favour of Harrold Priory concerning *proprietas* of the church of Cold Brayfield (App. I, 27), in a dispute with the canons of Lavendon; it is not clear where this sentence fits into the string of commissions concerning R. the priest. Harrold was a priory of Arrouaise, but was trying at this time to obtain independence, and to keep control of its subject churches (L. Milis, *L'ordre des chanoines réguliers d'Arrouaise*, i (1969), 598–9 and *passim*).

16. Causam que inter nobiles. To the bishop of ?Exeter, and the bishop of Worcester.

Sept. 1164 x 30 Aug. 1181. Instructions about a case between two noblemen concerning patronage of the church of *Waltona*. The pope would prefer the case to be heard by ecclesiastics, rather than by secular authorities. If either party fails to appear they shall be compelled by ecclesiastical censures. One judge may act.

> JL——. Cott.6.40 f.280, damaged, unprinted. Occurs only here.

> Only the *on*' of the first bishop's title remains. The letter is explicitly curtailed at one point; probably there are omissions of considerable passages which rehearsed the earlier stages of the case. The names of the parties appear to be Fr. de Thelpald (or Thelwald) and R. de Bic; neither reading is certain and neither has been identified.

17. Causam que inter Patricium. To (Richard) archbishop of Canterbury.

Late May 1174 x Sept. 1179. The case about the church of Buckworth between Patrick, clerk, and Nigel (*sic*), archdeacon of Huntingdon, and William of Hastings, had been committed to the bishop of Worcester and the abbot of St Albans. Patrick asserts that they have not acted 'and, which we cannot believe, have applied themselves less diligently to the case than is proper'. The archbishop is to admonish them to proceed, without respect of persons, and to hear the case if they do not act within forty days. William is dead, and Nigel is said to have been intruded into the church; the case is therefore to be heard according to the instructions (*formam*) for the dispute between Patrick and William.

JL——. Pd Wig. 7.81, also occurs in 1 Alc. c.70. For the last sentence, see no. 73 below.

The archdeacon was Nicholas, not Nigel, de Sigillo, a royal official, recorded as justice in 1173, 1174, and 1179, hence the order to proceed without respect of persons. In King Richard's time there were proceedings about Buckworth *de ultima presentatione* in the king's court, and a papal commission was met with a writ of prohibition (*Curia Regis Rolls* v. 173). William of Hastings was perhaps the king's dispenser, who disappears from the Pipe Rolls after 1168–9, but may have been alive later. The identification is the more probable, since on his death another royal official obtained the church.

18. Causam que vertitur. To R(oger) bishop of Worcester and ? the abbot of Evesham.

Jan. x Aug. 1174. ? Commission to hear the case between the brethren of Durham and the monks of St Albans about the church of Tynemouth. The monks of Durham must act with the authority and consent of their bishop, so that he may have no grounds for reopening the case later.

JL 13166, cf. no. 11 above. Pd ACL 36.3 which gives the bishop's initial; also X 2.1.9 without address, ascribed to Pope Celestine III. Occurs also in Wig. 2.11, and other collections.

The terse form of the letter suggests that it has been curtailed and reworked. It may be a supplement to an earlier commission, cf. p. 186 above. Only Wig. names both addressees; some collections name the bishop only, some the abbot only. But the final settlement (App. I, 18) was made before the bishop and John, treasurer of Exeter, their fellow delegate Robert dean of York being absent. Therefore either the collections err in naming the abbot, or there was a fresh commission.

The earliest possible date of this letter is determined by that of a letter to Bartholomew of Exeter and others, of 14 Mar. 1173; this was followed by a fresh appeal, with the feast of St Hilary, 13 Jan. 1174, as term. The final *transactio* is dated 14 Nov. 1174; the commission on which the judges acted can hardly have been issued later than the end of Aug.

18A. Ceterum de rigore. 1 Par. c.68. Part of no. 36 below.

18B. Ceterum quia clerici. ACL 15.4. See no. 72B below.

19. Conquerente nobis Milone. To the bishop of Worcester.

Sept. 1164 x Sept. 1178 (or Sept. 1180 x *c*.Apr. 1181). Commission to hear the complaint of Milo, clerk, that his institution to the church of St Mary of (Droit)wich is impeded by Roger, priest, son of Roger the previous parson. Milo says he was presented to the bishop by the lord of the estate, Richard Panceford (many spellings). If it is notorious that the father held the parsonage, his son must not be allowed to hold it, and must be removed if instituted. If Milo was presented by the lawful patron, he is to be instituted provided that he is suitable.

> JL 14138. Pd X 1.17.4 and ACL 19.1. Better texts in 1 Alc. c.60 and Sang. 4.8.1. Occurs also in other collections.

> No. 60 shows that the bishop investigated and reported. In view of the time required for the various stages, the bishop concerned is more likely to be Roger than Baldwin. In 1203, Reginald Pauncevaut made a final concord with the monks of Worcester by which he retained the advowson of the church of St Mary, Droitwich, but compensated them with a grant of land (*Worc. Cart.*, p. 97 no. 181). See p. 76 above.

20. Conquestionem abbatis et fratrum. To (Gilbert) bishop of London and (Roger) bishop of Worcester.

25 Feb. 1177. Commission to investigate the complaint of the abbot and monks of Malmesbury, that they are pursued by merchants who frequent the Curia, about debts contracted without proper authorization.

> JL 12787. Pd *Reg. Malmesbury*, 1.374.

21. Conquestionem Albini presbiteri. To the bishop of Worcester and the abbot of Ramsey.

Sept. 1164 x 1177 or Sept. 1180 x 30 Aug. 1181. Commission to hear the complaint of Albinus, priest, that W. Tosti (many spellings) has had his mother's corpse buried in another church, although she was his parishioner, and after appeal to the pope. W. also refuses to render to the church what she had bequeathed. He is said to have taken the cross, and withdrawn without permission. He shall be punished, and sent to the pope with a letter from the judges.

>JL——. Pd Sang. 6.1.19, p. 251. Occurs also in a few other collections.
>
>The abbot of Ramsey was probably William, elected abbot of Cluny in 1177, and the bishop probably Roger, but their successors cannot be absolutely ruled out.

22. Conquestus est nobis Herbertus. To (Bartholomew) bishop of Exeter and (Roger) bishop of Worcester.

5 July 1177. Herbert complains that his wife's uncle, Robert of *Manestun*' (many spellings) tries to disinherit her because she was born before the marriage of her mother. If her father later married her mother, the addressees shall declare her to be legitimate, appeal being forbidden, and shall forbid her uncle to trouble her husband or her heirs about her inheritance, using ecclesiastical censures if he disobeys.

>JL 14167. Pd X 4.17.1, without address, and ACL 33.3. Cf. JL 13929, no. 43B below. No. 22 is dated in 1 Par. c.156, Duac. c.37 (*Repert.*, p. 280) and elsewhere. Occurs in very many collections.
>
>The Lincoln MS of ACL alone gives the full name of the offending uncle. Robert of Manneston' occurs in *PR 21 Henry II* (*1174–5*), p. 22, under Suffolk, owing 26 shillings and eight pence for default, and in the next year (p. 68) paying his debt. This Robert probably took his name from Manston in Suffolk, and he may be the uncle of this case, since he had evidently been engaged in litigation in the king's court. See also pp. 138, 149 above.

23. Conquestus est nobis Rad'. To R(oger) bishop of Worcester and (Robert) prior of Kenilworth.

Mar. 1173 x Sept. 1179. Commission to hear the complaint of Ralph, clerk, that he was dispossessed of the church of St Hippolytus, Dinsley, by Richard de Lovetot, during the exile of the blessed Thomas the martyr. If Ralph was canonically instituted, and was despoiled without judgement, the church shall be restored to him with the revenues received, unless he voluntarily renounced it. The addressees shall not allow him to be disturbed illegally (*citra formam iuris*).

>JL 14049. Pd Brug.31.1; and 2 Comp.2.7.2 in abbreviated form with incorrect address and garbled names. 1 Alc. c.65 gives the bishop's initial and the last sentence, which is often omitted. Occurs also in a few other collections.

No. 23 must have been issued between the canonization of St Thomas and the death of Bishop Roger. Two dedications to St Hippolytus are recorded in England; one belonged to the church, now All Saints, of the village now called Ippolitts, formerly part of the manor of Dinsley (*VCH Herts*, iii. 10). For the Lovetot family and its relations with Dinsley, see *Early Yorkshire Charters*, iii. 4–6, where the death of a Richard de Lovetot is noted in 1171.

24. Conquestus est nobis magister. To (Bartholomew) bishop of Exeter and (Roger) bishop of Worcester.

Mar. 1174 x Feb. 1177. Commission to hear the complaint of Master T(homas), clerk of Earl Hugh of Norfolk, against Wi(mer), priest, about armed attack on T.'s house on the land of the church of Bungay. The addressees shall also investigate the allegation that Wi. was excommunicated by St Thomas, and improperly absolved by the late bishop of Norwich.

> JL——. Flor. c.169 fo. 179ᵛ, unprinted. Occurs only here.
>
> See nos. 3A, 59, 88. The sequence of events is not clear, but no. 24 was issued after the Curia had heard of the death of Bishop William of Norwich (16 Jan. 1174), and before news arrived of the death of Earl Hugh in the Holy Land, which was known in England by 1 Mar. 1177. But as nos. 59 and 88 seem to refer to later stages of the case, and do not mention the earl's death, no. 24 probably belongs to 1174 or 1175. The defendant was Wimer *capellanus*, a royal official who had been excommunicated by Archbishop Thomas (*MTB*, vii. 99). Wimer was sheriff or under-sheriff of Norfolk from 1170 to 1187.

25. Conquestus est nobis venerabilis. To the bishops of Exeter and Worcester.

Jan. 1177 x Sept. 1179. Commission to hear the complaint of Adam bishop of St Asaph that the bishop of St Davids dedicated the church of St Michael of Kerry (*Ken*), said to be in the diocese of St Asaph, after appeal to the pope. If the dedication was carried out after appeal, this is to be reported promptly, so that the contempt of the pope and the Roman church may be suitably punished.

> JL——. Pd Wig.4.44; occurs only here.
>
> Adam of St Asaph tried to dedicate the church of St Michael of Kerry, and to claim the surrounding area, during the vacancy of St Davids, 8 May–7 Nov. 1176, but was prevented (*Giraldi opera*, i. 32–40). The new bishop may have carried out the dedication himself, giving rise to this protest. Kerry remained in the diocese of St Davids, so that Adam's claim failed. But there is no evidence of action on this commission.

APPENDIX II

26. Constitutus in presentia ... G. To (Roger) bishop of Worcester and (Robert) prior of Kenilworth.

1172 x Sept. 1179. Commission to hear the complaint of G., clerk, that R., knight, despoiled him without judgement of the chapel of Stretton on Fosse. G. sued before the bishop, but could get no redress, because it was said that his father had ministered in the chapel. If G. was ejected by a layman, and if his father was not parson or perpetual vicar, the chapel shall be restored to him with the revenues received, appeal being forbidden. Other papal letters, if any, shall not prejudice truth and justice. One judge may act.

> JL 14145. Pd X 1.17.8, with address to the bishop only; also ACL 19.9, with plural forms and garbled version of 'Kenilworth'. 1 Alc. c. 61 preserves the address in original form. Occurs also in a few other collections.
>
> This case is the subject of no. 49A below, to Bishop Baldwin; it seems likely therefore that no. 26 belongs to Bishop Roger's later years. See also nos. 26A, 93A, and above, pp. 73–4. Variant spellings might suggest Stratton, Stretton, Street or even one of the many Stantons. But nos. 26, 26A, 49A and 93A agree in referring to a chapel. Stretton on Fosse, in Blockley deanery, still had a chapel in 1291 (*Tax. Pap. Nich.*, p. 219), and seems to be the most likely locality. No. 93A certainly, and no. 26A almost certainly, concern Stretton on Fosse.

26A. Constitutus in presentia ... G. To the abbot of Stratford and the prior of Ashby.

1173 x 30 Aug. 1181. Commission to hear the case between G. and Alan, clerks, about the chapel of *Strata* (many variants). G. asserts that A. refuses to keep the agreement by which a dispute had been ended. The addressees shall quash the agreement and bring the case to a lawful end.

> JL 14103. Pd X 1.36.4 and ACL 28.6. Occurs also in a few other collections.
>
> No. 26A probably relates to the same case as no. 26, and to a later date. It may be one of the forged commissions mentioned in no. 49A.

27. Constitutus in presentia ... Hugo. To (Roger) bishop of Worcester and (Robert) prior of Kenilworth.

? Sept. 1172 x *c*.Dec. 1177. Commission to hear the complaint of (Master) Hugh that, although he had canonically obtained the church of Whittlesea, O. *nepos* of Roger the last incumbent has been intruded into it, against the wish of the monks of

Thorney, to whom it is said to pertain. If this is so, silence shall be imposed on O., appeal being forbidden.

> JL——. Pd Wig. 7.80; occurs here only.

> Nos. 68A and 2 relate to later stages in this case. No. 68A shows that the addressees acted on no. 27, but that difficulty had arisen, or was expected, in executing the sentence. The defendant then took the case to the secular court, and more than a year elapsed before the issue of no. 2. Dates are suggested for no. 27 on the assumption that the archbishop addressed in no. 68A was Richard, and that no. 2 was addressed to the same bishop of Worcester as no. 27.
> The Thorney cartulary (Cambridge University Libr. Add. MS 3020 fo. 172^v) contains a report from William, formerly archdeacon of Ely, to T., archbishop of Canterbury, stating that Roger was never instituted to Whittlesea, and that the abbot and convent of Thorney had the patronage. William, archdeacon of Ely, was deposed $c.$1151; the date of his death is unknown. He was probably the author of the report. His successor (d. $c.$1158) was also named William. No. 27 may therefore arise from the reopening of an old quarrel, but did not necessarily follow an appeal from the archbishop's hearing.

28. Constitutus in presentia ... Ric'. To (Gilbert) bishop of London and (Robert) prior of Kenilworth.

1165 x Sept. 1179. Commission to hear the complaint of Richard, deacon, that O., priest, sues him before the bishop of Worcester and the abbot of Evesham about half the church of St Peter of Preston (? Preston Capes), although silence had been imposed on O. after proceedings before the archdeacon of Northampton.

> JL——. Pd Brug. 45.7; see also Wig. 7.67. 1 Alc. c. 72 is a good text, possibly from Bishop Roger's archives (above, pp. 203–6).

> The commission to the bishop and abbot is lost. The dates of the bishops, abbot and prior would make it almost certain that the bishop of Worcester in question is Roger, apart from the additional evidence of 1 Alc.

29. Consuluit nos tua. To the bishop of Winchester or Worcester.

Nov. 1159 x 30 Aug. 1181. Ruling on the case of William, the bishop's parishioner, who promised *in manu tua* to marry a certain woman, but later took to himself another. Penance shall be imposed for breach of faith, but William should not be separated from the second woman.

> JL 14136. Pd 1 Comp. 4.1.3.

The address to Worcester occurs in Flor. c.159, ACL 6.2, Bamb.50.2, and 1 Comp.; Winchester appears in Bridl. c.24, Dertus. c.7, 1 Cant. 31, Wig.1.9, 1 Paris c.53. Winchester seems marginally better attested. This part of Dertus. is thought to be earlier in date than the Third Lateran Council; if this is correct the letter must have been issued before March 1179.

30. Continebatur in litteris. To R(oger) bishop of Worcester.

13 May x 15 Oct. 1177. The bishop has reported that when Master Herbert and Master Nicholas pleaded before him, as judge-delegate, it appeared that tithes of W. had been given to Herbert by Emma, abbess of Winchester, with the convent's consent, and that Ralph, archdeacon of Winchester, invested him with book and bread (or key). But it was proved that the same abbess had earlier given the tithe to Nicholas, the convent not objecting, and the bishop had confirmed the grant. The first grant should stand, if the convent knew of it and did not protest.

> JL 14033. Pd X 3.10.2, with address to the bishop of Norwich; also ACL 47.5. Occurs in many collections.
>
> Three collections preserve the place-date, Venice, at the Rialto (*Cus.* c.5, *Duac.* c.36, *Francofort.* 53.2). In *Duac.* this letter is the second of a group of four, all issued from Venice; the first on 30 June, the third on 3 July. Possibly it was issued between these two dates. The evidence of the early collections is clearly in favour of the address to Worcester; 1 Paris. c.72 has *Idem eidem*, that is Alexander III to R. bishop of Worcester. Winchester and even Toledo appear among the variants. The place from which the tithes were paid certainly lay in Hampshire, and probably began with 'W'; Chelt.17.26 gives *Werth*, which suggests 'Wetham', where the abbey had land but not the church (*VCH Hants.*, ii. 126).

30A. Cum aliquam causam. 1 Dertus. c.8 = no. 63d.

30B. Cum aliquibus adiudicata. JL 14035, X 2.27.6, part of no. 39.

31. Cum causam que. To (Bartholomew) bishop of Exeter.

Jan. 1165 x Apr. 1167. Informs the bishop that the case between him and some clerks of the archdeaconry of Barnstaple has been committed to Hen(ry) bishop of Winchester, R(obert) bishop of Hereford and R(oger) bishop of Worcester. The bishop's *responsalis* (Peter) canon of Plympton has explained that the bishop proceeded against the clerks for incontinence, that they were contumacious, and later began proceedings against him before Archbishop Thomas. A vicar deposed while at the Curia must be restored. Orders the bishop to compel all clergy of his diocese to live chastely.

> JL——. Pd Morey, *Bartholomew*, p. 134, from 1 Alc. c.76.
>
> No. 31 must have been issued before the Curia knew of the death of Robert of Hereford (27 Feb. 1167), and after it knew of Bishop Roger's consecration. But the parties had been ordered to appear before the pope on the feast of St Lucy (13 Dec.), at which date Peter appeared and waited a long time. The commission to the three judges is lost.

32. Cum de tua. To (John) bishop-elect of Chichester.

28 Apr. 1174 x Aug. 1174. Informs the bishop-elect that the objections raised against his election have been considered. The pope has granted a dispensation in the matter of his birth; as regards his eye defect, the archbishop of Canterbury shall act on the advice of his suffragans, particularly the bishops of Exeter and Worcester.

> JL 12367. Pd X 1.20.2. Occurs in many collections.
>
> The archbishop is entitled legate of the apostolic see. The title was granted on 28 April 1174 (*PUE*, ii. 327–8 no. 135). John was consecrated, presumably after the arrival of this letter, and some consideration of it, on 6 Oct. 1174 (cf. pp. 214–5).

33. Cum ex suscepti. To B(artholomew) bishop of Exeter, R(oger) bishop of Worcester and (Clarembald) abbot of Faversham.

Oct. 1170 x 26 Jan. 1173. Commission to investigate the state of St Augustine's Abbey (Canterbury). The addressees, in whom the pope has great confidence, shall if possible go together to the monastery, and promptly correct what needs correction, without respect of persons, appeal being forbidden. If necessary, they shall remove the abbot-elect and certain monks, appeal being forbidden.

> JL 12179. Pd *Acta pontificum Romanorum inedita*, ed. J. von Pflugk-Harttung, iii (1886), 229; also with many faults Liverani, p. 546. Mentioned by Thorne (Twysden, *Hist. Ang. SS X*, col. 1817).
>
> The possible dates are those of the pope's residence at Tusculum, only the place-date being preserved. The political situation in these years makes it

unlikely that the commission was issued before *c*.April 1171, when Bishop Roger was himself at the Curia. A date after May or even Sept. 1172 is more probable. The abbot-elect was deposed in 1173; the judges' report is App. I, 8.

34. Cum homines de Hortona. To the bishops of Exeter and Worcester and another.

Sept. 1164 x 30 Aug. 1181. Commission to compel the men of Horton to pay tithes in the autumn to St Michael's church, without deduction of wages, according to English custom, and to make good past deductions.

> JL 13928. Pd X 3.30.7 (a poor text, with address to Exeter only), and ACL 4.4 (a poor text, abbreviated, with corrupt address). Occurs in other collections, of which Wig.4.4 and Bridl. c.16, fo. 84ra (= Claud. c.16) seem to be good texts, with a final sentence authorizing excommunication of offenders until payment is made in full.
>
> Many early collections give the address to the two bishops, and the plural forms show that this is correct. The form *discretioni vestre*, which appears in all texts, shows that there was also a third, non-episcopal, judge. Horton has not been identified; dedications to St Michael are found at Horton near Colnbrook, Bucks, and near Leek, Staffs. See pp. 138, 186 above.

35. Cum iampridem si(cut) bene. To (Bartholomew) bishop of Exeter and (Roger) bishop of Worcester.

Sept. 1164 x ? 1177. Commission to hear the complaint of the prior of Barnwell (or Kenilworth) that the case about tithes claimed by Walkelin, clerk, of Mord' (or Morton) had been committed to the abbot of Ramsey, who did not proceed because of the king's justices. After a year, the abbot summoned the canons, though the case was committed with a time limit of two months. They eventually 'refused' the judge, and appealed against him. If the other party refuses to appear, the canons shall be put in possession.

> JL——. Pd Sang.5.4.11 (p. 228), and Claustr. c.221. Occurs also in Wig.7.22 (a good text), and other collections.
>
> The abbot of Ramsey must be William, elected abbot of Cluny in 1177. Sang., being a French text, converts Ramsey into Reims. William's successor at Ramsey was elected at an uncertain date in 1180. It is difficult to be sure of the places concerned. Barnwell and Kenilworth were both houses of canons; the latter, however, possessed no church which corresponds to Mord' or Morton. Barnwell had long owned the church of Guilden Morden. There is much of technical interest in the account of the proceedings, which cannot be summarized satisfactorily.

36. Cum nos tibi. To R(oger) bishop of Worcester.

1165 x Jan. 1174. Reply to the bishop's communication. The bishop had obtained from the pope permission to revoke the gift of Bibury church to Osney Abbey, made by Bishop John of Worcester in spite of protests by his chapter. Later, forgetting that document, the pope at the request of the brethren of Osney issued a letter ordering the bishop to leave them in peaceful possession. The pope hopes that the bishop will give up the church, out of reverence for St Peter and himself, but the letter to the bishop remains effective, since the grant was invalid if made against the wish of the chapter.

> JL 13164. Pd X 3.10.3; also *Gilberti epistolae* ii. 103, from Belv.1.16. Occurs in many collections.

> The case came before Bartholomew of Exeter as judge-delegate and was settled by a composition made between 25 Mar. 1173 and 24 Mar. 1174. Bishop Roger's charter of confirmation is App. I, 51. The last sentence of this letter interested lawyers and ensured its preservation. The old law had severely restricted alienation of church property, but conflicting statements were preserved. Alexander's ruling was noted as a recent statement allowing alienation with the approval of the chapter.

37. Cum nuntius canonicorum. To R(ichard) archbishop of Canterbury and R(oger) bishop of Worcester.

7 Apr. 1174 x Feb. 1175. Commission to hear the case between Johel, knight, and the canons of Plympton about the patronage of the church of Sutton. The canons' messenger produced a charter of William, bishop of Exeter, recording his judgement for them in a dispute over the church with Reginald, Johel's grandfather. Johel's messenger said that he and his predecessors had held the patronage up to the present time, and that the charter had never been seen before. Neither party came fully prepared; the pope therefore commits the case to the addressees, in whose prudence and honesty he trusts. If they find that the church had been adjudged to Plympton, they shall impose silence on Johel and his party, and enforce the interdict laid by Bishop Bartholomew of Exeter on Johel's land because of injuries inflicted on the canons. If he does not repent, they shall excommunicate him, notwithstanding any letters obtained by suppression of the truth. The addressees will be aware that the canons should not be excluded from giving evidence, unless

there is some lawful impediment. If one judge cannot act, the other shall do so promptly, with the assistance of prudent men.

> JL 13249. Pd X 2.20.12 (one sentence only). Full text in Regalis c.86 fo. 113^v and Cus. c.39 fo. 76^r unprinted. The single sentence, allowing the canons to give evidence, occurs in many collections.
>
> Before the canons' messenger arrived at the Curia, Johel's messenger obtained a commission to the archbishop, no. 52A. No. 37 stresses that both messengers have now appeared, and quashes letters obtained surreptitiously. The judges gave sentence on 27 June 1175 (App. I, 53).

38. Cum nuntius Serlonis. To the bishop of Worcester and the abbot of Cirencester.

Sept. 1164 x 30 Aug. 1181. Commission to hear the case (unspecified) between Serlo, priest, and the prior of *Oteri*. Separate commissions had already been issued to the judges on behalf of each party, first to Serlo's messenger, then to the prior's, then again to Serlo's, because he had been robbed. The parties tell different stories, and the pope is confused and uncertain. The addressees shall inspect the letters of each party, and hear their statements, as is contained in the other letters, and give sentence, unless the parties make a composition. R. (? *recte* S.) shall be absolved from the sentence laid upon him after appeal.

> JL—. Cott. c.59 fo. 236ra unprinted.
>
> *Oteri* has not been identified; the name may be hopelessly garbled. Otterton, Devon, springs to mind; its cartulary provides no relevant information.

39. Cum olim inter. To the bishop of Worcester and (Adam) abbot of Evesham.

Oct. 1164 x 30 Aug. 1181. Commission to hear the case between the Knights Templar and the prior of Wenlock about tithes (unspecified). The case had been delegated to the bishop of Exeter, but the prior had again appealed. If possession had been adjudged to the Templars, they must be put in corporal possession, pledges not being sufficient. The question of right may then be heard. If the prior is contumaciously absent, the judges shall proceed none the less.

> JL 14035. Pd X 2.27.7 (small part only), in full Sang.6.1.14 (p. 247). Occurs in whole or part in other collections.
>
> The prior's appeal had had Michaelmas as its term, so no. 39 was probably issued after 29 Sept.

40. Cum omnes taillie. To (Richard) archbishop of Canterbury and the bishop of Worcester.

Apr. 1179 x 30 Aug. 1181. Commission to hear complaints about payments demanded by R(obert) archdeacon of Essex, contrary to the decree of the Lateran Council.

> JL——. Pd Wig.3.40. Occurs only here.
>
> It is barely possible that this commission, which mentions the Lateran Council of Mar. 1179, was intended for the archbishop and Bishop Roger; probably the second recipient was Bishop Baldwin, and the date of issue after Sept. 1180.

41. Cum sicut ex rescriptis. To (Gilbert) bishop of London and (Roger) bishop of Worcester.

11 Feb. 1177. Commission to inspect the privileges of the monastery of Malmesbury and the bishop of Salisbury, and if it is proved that the monastery pertains directly to the jurisdiction of St Peter and the pope, the bishop shall be forbidden to claim any rights over it. He shall dedicate it without demanding (profession of) obedience, otherwise the addressees shall do so, appeal being forbidden.

> JL 12780. Pd *Reg. Malmesbury*, i. 370.
>
> There seems to be no record of action by the addressees. Archbishop Richard, writing to the pope, suggested that Malmesbury's claim to exemption was based on forged privileges (PL 200.1456). See also no. 79.

42. Cum (iampridem) Simon clericus. To the bishops of Exeter and Worcester.

Sept. 1164 x 30 Aug. 1181. Commission to admonish the monks of Castleacre to give a benefice to Peter and his brother, as requested by the pope when Peter renounced the church of (Long) Sutton and the chapel of Lutton after proceedings at the Curia between himself and Simon, proctor of the monks. If the monks refuse, the addressees shall investigate the clerks' complaint of unlawful ejection from the church and chapel, notwithstanding the pope's confirmation of them to the monks. The clerks had given up their charters (*autentica instrumenta*) to the pope.

JL 13924. Pd X 1.35.4. Occurs in many collections, sometimes divided into two sections, as e.g. Wig. 4.25. No. 9 may be the final sentence of no. 42.

The identification of the church and chapel was suggested by W. Holtzmann in unpublished work. The church had been in dispute in the time of Bishop Robert of Lincoln (BL MS Harley 2110 (Castleacre cart.) fo. 116ʳ).

42A. Cum tibi aliquam. See no. 63c.

Friedberg, editing Cantab. c.45, produced an astonishing address to the bishop of Avignon. The MS has *Uvigornien'*.

43. Cum venerabili fratri. To R(oger) bishop of Worcester.

3 or 17 Apr. 1178. Order to bless the abbot-elect of St Augustine's, Canterbury, if the archbishop fails to do so within the prescribed time, notwithstanding appeal or letters to the contrary.

JL 13048. Pd *Hist. Sancti Augustini*, p. 423 dated iii° ii° Aprilis, and p. 428 dated xv kal. Madii. Also *Hoveden*, ii. 149 and PL 200.1229, no. 1413.

The date is uncertain. *Hist. Sancti Augustini*, pp. 423–4, amends iii° ii° Aprilis to xvii Aprilis, which cannot have been the form of the original; iii non. Aprilis would give 3 Apr., the date of the parallel letter to the archbishop. But the date of the copy on p. 428 agrees with Hoveden. Possibly two copies were issued on different days. The bishop of Worcester did not obey the order (above p. 223).

43A. Cum venerabilis frater. Claud. c.70 (= Bridl. c.88), a reworked extract from no. 45.

43B. De nata ante. Cantab. c.98, a reworked version of part of no. 22.

43C. De sacerdote vero. ACL 26.3 (JL 14146) a chapter on forgers of papal letters, with address to the bishops of Worcester and Norwich. See JL 12253, to Bishop William of Norwich.

44. Dilecti filii nostri abbas. To (Richard) archbishop of Canterbury and the bishop of Worcester.

c.1177 x 30 Aug. 1181. Commission to hear the case, previously committed to other judges, between the brethren of Newhouse and the nuns of Elstow about the church of East Halton.

JL 13825. Edited from all texts, with translation, Holtzmann and Kemp, pp. 12–17 no. 6. Also pd X 2.8.1, altered. Occurs in many collections.

Holtzmann and Kemp, by close study of the MSS, disentangled two commissions with the same incipit and much material in common. One, the second commission in this case, was addressed to the abbot of Rievaulx and the prior of Bridlington; the other is no. 44. The archbishop announced a composition between the parties in 1177 x 1182, perhaps after Roger's death or departure from England (F. M. Stenton, *Documents . . . of the Danelaw* (British Academy 1920), p. 216). No action by a bishop of Worcester is recorded; the sequence of events in this protracted dispute is still not perfectly clear.

44A. Dilecti filii nostri abbas. To the abbots of St Albans and St Mary of Leicester.

Sept. 1164 x 30 Aug. 1181. Commission to hear the complaint of the abbot and brethren of Saint-Évroul that A. (or W.), priest, obtained a commission to the bishop of Worcester to hear a case about their church of *Cerletune* (many variants), naming as defendant not the convent but their vicar. The bishop is said to have adjudged the church to A. in spite of protest and appeal, *quod vix credere possumus*. If this is true, the addressees shall restore the church to the monks, with revenues received from it. They shall then hear the question of right (*proprietas*) if the monks wish to plead.

JL 13729. Pd 2 Comp. 2.18.1, ACL 42.2. Occurs in many collections.

The place may be Carlton Curlieu or Charlton-on-Otmoor. The texts offer equal authority to *Cerletune* and variants, and to *Aleton* and variants. The priest's name is regularly A. at the beginning of the text, but sometimes W. later. The combination of Saint-Évroul, W. and *Aleton* suggests a connection between no. 45 and the case recorded in App. I, 53, but the two cases seem to be quite distinct.

45. Dilectorum filiorum nostrorum. To (Roger) bishop of Worcester and (Odo) abbot of Battle.

10 May 1178 or 1179. Commission to hear the complaints of the prior and convent of Christ Church, Canterbury, against Ivo of Charing, knight, who illegally detains their manor of Westwell, Ralph of Allington, knight, and W. his brother, who detain their manor of Bredhurst and the same W. who detains their manor of Stisted. Any person who resists the judges shall be excommunicated, without right of appeal. One judge may act, with the assistance of prudent men.

JL——. Pd *PUE*, ii. 367 no. 176, from Canterbury, D. and C. Mun. Reg. D fo. 300ᵛ.

No. 45 was issued from the Lateran, therefore a date in 1166 or 1167 would be possible, but the monks are not likely to have started proceedings in those years. In May 1178 and/or Feb.–May 1179 the convent impetrated a dozen letters, in two of which Abbot Odo, formerly prior of Christ Church, was named as judge-delegate. No. 45 must belong to the same period. Reg. D contains no trace of action on this commission, but shows that the convent established its right to Westwell only in 1241, in the king's court.

45A. Diocesis donationem. Regalis c.43 (fo. 111ʳ); a clumsy reworking of no. 91d.

45B. Discretioni vestre. Claud. c.91 (= Bridl. c.104); an extract from no. 12.

46. Etsi a sacris. To Roger, bishop of Worcester.

16 Mar. 1167. Authority to establish, for the salvation of his relatives and especially of Robert his nephew, a house of canons regular in the diocese of Bath, which is now vacant, in the church of Keynsham. The church is in the bishop's patrimony, and he has long held it in his own hands.

JL——. Pd *PUE*, ii. 313–14 no. 123, from Bodl. MS Tanner 3 fo. 1 (Dialogues of Pope Gregory, s.xi). Also pd in H. M. Bannister, 'Bishop Roger of Worcester and the church of Keynsham', EHR xxxii (1917), 387–93.

47. Ex conquestione prioris. To the bishops of Exeter and Worcester.

Sept. 1164 x 30 Aug. 1181. Commission to hear the complaint of the prior and brethren of Huntingdon (*Hitunde*) that R. Piel granted them the patronage of the church of Isham (*Hisam*) and then presented a clerk himself. The addressees shall remove the clerk, appeal being forbidden, and shall allow no one to be instituted except at the presentation of the prior and brethren. If any person resists the execution of the commission he shall be subject to ecclesiastical censures, on papal authority, appeal being forbidden. One judge may act, with the advice of learned men.

JL——. 1 Alc. c.56 fo. 17ᵛ.

No. 47 was probably copied from the bishop's archives, along with other material in this part of Alcobacensis I (cf. p. 206). These proceedings may have led to division of the patronage. In the early thirteenth century Huntingdon presented to half the church of Isham, while half remained in lay hands.

47A. Ex constanti relatione. To (Roger) archbishop of York and (Hugh) bishop of Durham.

*c.*Apr. 1177. Mandate to punish Master Hugh of Southwell for forgery of papal letters, by deprivation of benefices and seclusion in a monastery.

> JL——. Pd G. Scammell, *Hugh du Puiset* (Cambridge 1956), p. 251, from Bridl. c.152 fo. 123^v.

> The mandate is recited in a report from the recipients to Bishop Roger, whose connection with the business is obscure. Hugh witnessed a charter of the bishop of 6 Oct. 1176 (App. I, 15). The mandate was issued after, and probably soon after, the return to the Curia of the legate Hugh Pierleoni, cardinal deacon of St Angelo, who left England early in July 1176, but seems to have rejoined the pope only in Apr. 1177 at Venice. Hugh of Southwell occasionally witnesses charters of Archbishop Richard; none appears to be later than the end of May 1177.

48 Ex litteris fraternitatis. To (Richard) archbishop of Canterbury.

Sept. 1179 x 30 Aug. 1181. Commission to hear the case between H. and A., clerks, about the church of *Lega*. A., a clerk of Richard de Lucy, had been instituted upon a false report of H.'s death. The case had been committed to the late bishop of Worcester and the abbot of St Albans, who had put A. in possession *causa rei servande*. The archbishop had asked for instructions on the procedure to be followed *in possessorio ipsius H.*; he is reminded of the parallel with the case of a woman who remarries, thinking her first husband is dead.

> JL——. Pd Sang. 6.1.15, p. 248. Occurs in a few other collections.

49. Ex litteris quas. To the bishops of Worcester and ?Coventry.

1165 x 30 Aug. 1181. The addressees had received a commission to hear the case between Master Alan of Idsall and R(alph) de Alta Ripa about the chapel of *Cambritona*, appeal being forbidden, but Ralph claimed that the commission was not issued by the papal chancery, because there was an erasure in the statement of the facts. The judges appointed a day for him to swear that he was not making this claim merely to cause delay, and when he failed to appear, adjudged possession to Alan, *causa rei servande*. Ralph then got a fresh commission to the bishops of London and Norwich, concealing the truth. Alan appealed again, claiming that those judges were hostile, since Ralph was the bishop of London's nephew, and ate daily at his table. The pope declares the first commission genuine, returning it closed under seal to the addressees, who shall revoke anything done to Alan's disadvantage on the authority of the second commission, and condemn Ralph to pay Alan's costs in sending again to the pope. They shall then hear the case.

> JL 14142. Pd X 2.22.3, omitting the last third of the commission. ACL 49.3 omits only a few words. Roff. c.75 (fo. 146ʳ) gives the full text. X has altered the wording as well as abbreviating (cf. S. Kuttner in *Traditio* xxii (1960), 481).

> Claud. c.207 gives address to the archbishop of Canterbury and bishop of Worcester. 'Worcester and Coventry' cannot be correct, as the order of seniority is wrong. If the archbishop was one addressee, this would put the commission, with its reference to action before a bishop of Norwich, after *c*.March 1176. Master Alan of 'Ideshale' occurs *c*.1177 x 1182 (*Magnum Reg. Album of Lichfield*, p. 80 no. 174); he is probably the Alan of Hidesh', Hillesdale, Bilsdale and many variants, of this text. Master Ralph de Alta Ripa was a canon of St Paul's, London, and later Master of the Schools.

49A. Ex litteris tue fraternitatis. Pope Lucius III to B(aldwin) bishop of Worcester.

1182 x 1183 (Velletri). Commends the bishop's refusal to enforce a sentence of judges-delegate in the case between G. and A. about the chapel of Stretton on Fosse, because the commission, on which they had acted, could not be produced. A. had been presented to Bishop Roger, but G., son of the last minister, contested his institution, and obtained a commission to the abbot of Missenden, the prior of Canon's Ashby and Master Ambrose, who gave sentence in his favour. G. is said also to have obtained another false commission. If convicted of forgery he shall be imprisoned in a monastery.

> JL 15204 (part only). Pd in full Sang. 7.11, p. 268. Occurs in whole or part in many collections.

> On the case see above, p. 73, and no. 26. Cf nos. 26A, 55A, 93A. No. 77 concerns a similar but probably distinct case.

49B Ex litteris venerabilis. To Gilbert bishop of London and S(imon) abbot of St Albans.

1174 x July 1176. From the bishop of Worcester's letter the pope has learned that the case between the monks of Alcester and Henry, son of Adam the priest, about the chapel of Yardley, had been committed to the abbot of Leicester and the former abbot of Lilleshall. The bishop of Worcester forbade them to act, because Henry was the son of the priest who had been parson of the mother church, and because the chapel was in Worcester diocese, but was claimed as subject to a church in the diocese of Coventry. The monks of Alcester refused the judges. If sentence was given after appeal, it shall be revoked, and the case heard by the addressees, or one of them, appeal being forbidden.

>JL——. Pd Brug. 46.4, with corrections in Wig. 7.64. Occurs also in other collections.
>
>There was a change of abbots at Lilleshall in the course of the case. Abbot William died after 1173, and his successor was in office at latest by June 1176 (cf. no. 58B). The sequence of events is not perfectly clear, but 49B must precede 58B, which confirms the sentence of the first judges. See also p. 75 above.

49C. Ex litteris venerabilis. To B(artholomew) bishop of Exeter.

Sept. 1164 x Sept. 1179. From the letter of R(oger) bishop of Worcester the pope learns that Ralph, priest, was presented to the perpetual vicarage of Salford Priors by Henry sacristan of Kenilworth. The bishop admitted him, reserving the amount of the vicarage for discussion with the prior. But when Ralph stated his claim, the prior asserted that he was only an annual vicar, and tried to assign to him a portion on which he could not live decently, and prepared to eject him. Ralph appealed, setting as term the feast of St Faith (6 Oct.) but the other party did not appear. The addressee shall hear the case and decide the amount of the vicarage. The pope wishes for the appointment of perpetual, not annual, vicars.

>JL——. Pd Wig. 4.42; occurs only here.
>
>On this case see p. 80.

APPENDIX II

50. Ex litteris vestre fraternitatis. To R(oger) archbishop of York and R(oger) bishop of Worcester.

1165 x Sept. 1179. From the addressees' letter the pope has learned that a settlement had been made before the bishop as judge-delegate in the case between R. and A., clerks, about the church of Rempstone and the chapel of Costock. Later, G., who had been A.'s advocate, got a commission about the same church and chapel to the bishop of Durham and the dean of York, concealing the fact that he was not a tonsured clerk, and had been present at the settlement. The parties appeared before the pope, who imposes perpetual silence on G.

> JL 13159 Pd X 1.36.6. Occurs in other collections. 1 Alc. c.53 fo. 17^r gives the full address, with the prelates' initials.

> The places, both in the diocese of York, were identified by W. Holtzmann in unpublished work.

51. Ex multiplici conquestione. To (Roger) bishop of Worcester and (Robert) bishop of Hereford.

Nov. 1174 x Sept. 1179, probably 1177. Commission to hear the complaint of William, priest of Treton, that the monks of Bruern, having obtained a privilege and a royal charter, turned out all the peasants of the village, and have for four years refused to pay certain tithes, contrary to a composition made twenty years ago by Abbot William, with the consent of the convent. Unless the privilege mentioned the composition, the composition must be observed, appeal being forbidden, and arrears must be paid, or a new agreement must be made.

> JL 14144. Pd X 3.30.3, with incorrect ascription to Pope Adrian; also ACL 13.11. Occurs in many collections. 1 Alc. c.71 is a good text, from which the numbers given above (four years, twenty years) are taken.

> Two indications place no. 51 in the 1170s. In 1174–9 the bishop of Worcester was senior to the bishop of Hereford, and c.1173 Nicholas Basset gave to the Cistercian abbey of Bruern his manors of Treton and Nethercote, with the church of Treton (*VCH Oxford*, ii. 79–81). It must have been after this that the monks turned out the peasants and ceased to pay tithes. The appeal to the pope, after four years' non-payment, must have been in about 1177. William priest of Treton witnessed a grant to Bruern before May 1175 (Madox, *Formulare Anglicanum* (1702), p. 252 no. 426). The papal privilege is lost. For the royal charter see *Cartae antiquae rolls 11–20*, ed. J. Conway Davies, PR Soc., new ser. (1960) p. 185 no. 601. The village of Treton has disappeared.

52. Ex parte abbatis. To G(ilbert) bishop of London and R(oger) bishop of Worcester.

? 12 Apr. 1174. Commission to hear the complaint of the abbot and brethren of Osney, that they were violently ejected from the church of St Mary Magdalen, Oxford, by the canons of St Frideswide's, in spite of a sentence of Pope Eugenius and a decision of Bartholomew, bishop of Exeter and John dean, now elect, of Chichester, that Osney had perfect proof both of possession and right. Possession shall be restored to Osney, and if Eugenius made no reservation on the matter of right, perpetual silence shall be enjoined on St Frideswide's.

> JL——. Pd *Oseney Cart.*, ii. 219, *PUE*, iii. 346 no. 213, and *Letters of Foliot*, p. 463. See no. 4 for discussion of the date, which must be before the end of Nov. 1174, and after June 1173, and cf. App. I, 50.

52A. Ex parte nobilis. To (Richard) archbishop of Canterbury.

1174 x Mar. 1175. Commission to investigate the complaint of J. de Valle Dei (*recte* Valle Torta) that the bishop of Exeter laid an interdict on the churches of his estates after his appeal to the pope in the proceedings between himself and the prior of Plympton about the patronage of the church of Sutton.

> JL——. Pd Sang. 6.8.12 p. 270. Occurs also in 1 Abr. 6.8.12, Tan. 5.7.10, Cott. 3.40 ascribed to Lucius III.
>
> Cf. no. 37, which was probably issued soon after no. 52A.

53. Ex parte prioris. To the bishop of Worcester.

Sept. 1164 x Sept. 1179. Commission to hear the complaint of the prior and brethren of Wallingford that their vicar of Aston Rowant keeps a concubine and visits taverns.

> JL 14135. Pd 1 Comp. 3.2.11, and ACL 18.15. Occurs also in 1 Alc. c.54, and other collections.
>
> There are many variants of the name of the priory, including forms resembling Welbeck. But 1 Alc. has *barrengeforde*, and Wallingford was a priory, Welbeck an abbey. For Wallingford's connection with Aston, see *VCH Oxford*, viii. 35.

54. Ex parte tua. To R(oger) bishop of Worcester.

Sept. 1170 x Sept. 1171. Replies to questions put by the bishop:
i. Monks may accuse their abbot, and may receive payment from the convent for necessary expenses.

APPENDIX II 345

ii. Judgement may not be given against the terms of papal confirmations, unless a fresh mandate has been obtained, or the confirmations were certainly obtained by fraud.

> JL 11872. Pd ACL 50.16, marked in *12 libro Registr'*. Also X 5.1.11 = i, and 2.30.2 = ii. Occurs in many collections.

> On the references to the papal registers in ACL, pars 50, see W. Holtzmann in *QFIAB* xxx (1940), 13–87. See also p. 80 above.

55. Ex relatione dilecti. To (Roger) bishop of Worcester and (Godfrey) abbot of Eynsham.

Jan. 1165 x ?Dec. 1175. From William Giffard, and from letters from the addressees, the pope learns that acting on a papal mandate they adjudged half the church of *Kemest'* to William, and condemned R., clerk, to make a payment for costs and for revenues received. The pope enjoins perpetual silence on R., and orders the judges to enforce payment, notwithstanding any papal letter obtained by the other party.

> JL——. Pd Wig. 4.49. Occurs here only.

> A William Giffard, apparently a canon of Salisbury, had been dead at least two years in Nov. 1177 (*Salisbury Charters*, p. 40 no. 48). The bishop of Worcester received some ten commissions to act with the abbot of Evesham, and this one only with the abbot of Eynsham. Possibly the copyist wrote *Einesham* for *Euesham*.

55A. Ex relatione R. Lucius III to the abbot of Missenden, the archdeacon of Winchester and the prior of St Frideswide's.

Sept. 1181 x 25 Nov. 1185. Commission to hear the case between R. and W. about the church of *Fernham*. Quashes an agreement made before the abbot of Missenden, the prior of Ashby and Master Ambrose, by which R. renounced the church in return for payment, and *dispensative* allows R. to hold the church, although his father held it immediately before him.

> JL——. Pd Sang. 6.1.21 p. 253; occurs here only.

> The abbot of Missenden, the prior of Ashby and Master Ambrose are mentioned as judges in no. 49A. Possibly no. 55A concerns the same case; if so, all the names are corrupt. Forged letters are mentioned in no. 49A. Possibly this was one of them; the dispensation is unlikely to be genuine.

56. Ex transmissa conquestione. To the bishop of Worcester and another (or others).

Sept. 1164 x 30 Aug. 1181. Order to protect R., who was granted the church of ?*De* by the monks of ?*Dene* when William, clerk, was said to have contracted leprosy. Witnesses named by R. shall be admonished to give evidence for the love of justice.

> JL 14134. Pd 2 Comp. 3.7.1; also ACL 37.1, and Claustr. c.342, poor texts. Occurs in many collections.
>
> The names are so garbled as to offer little basis for identification. There were certainly two or three addressees, of whom one or two were not bishops. The Lincoln text (Lincoln Cathedral MS 121 fo. 43^v) of ACL gives *Dene* in full; Chelt. 13.12 gives *Will'm* for the leper. Flaxley Abbey (Glos., O. Cist.) was also called Dene.

57. Ex transmissa nobis. To R(ichard) archbishop of Canterbury and R(oger) bishop of Worcester.

Apr. 1174 x Apr. 1178. Commission to hear the complaint of Walter, clerk, that the bishop refused to admit him to a benefice in the church of Wootton (Wawen) at the presentation of the abbot of Conches, because Walter's father had ministered in the church. If another person held the benefice after the father's death, Walter shall be admitted, since this would not infringe the apostolic decree against hereditary succession. One judge may act.

> JL 13248. Pd, with many variants, X 1.17.7, and ACL 19.8. Occurs in many collections. 1 Alc. c.52 has the full address.
>
> No. 57 probably preceded by some months Walter's formal renunciation of his claim, recorded by Bishop Roger on 25 June 1178 (App. I, 12; see also p. 74). The 'apostolic decree' may be JL 13802, X 1.17.11; this allowed a son to hold his father's benefice if a third person had held it in the interval. If so, that undated decree must have been issued at latest before about Feb. 1178.

58. Fraternitatis tue litteras. To Roger bishop of Worcester.

1165 x Sept. 1179. The pope has granted the bishop's petitions, as he will learn from B. his messenger and from letters. Urges him to continue to be diligent in hearing lawsuits of the poor and others, committed to him by the apostolic see; he could do nothing more pleasing to God.

JL 13161. Pd *MTB*, vi. 81, no. 256; also *Epistolae S. Thomae*, ed. J. A. Giles, ii. 108. See also pp. 124–5 above.

58A. Fraternitatis tue per. Bridl. c.25; part of no. 60 (sections b, c, d).

58B Iampridem si(cut) bene. To Abbot R(obert) and the convent of Marmoutier and Henry their clerk.

12 Aug., 1174 x 1176. Confirms the sentence of the abbots of Leicester and Lilleshall in the case between Marmoutier and the monks of Alcester about the chapel of Yardley, which is dependent on their church of Aston. One abbot of Lilleshall died and was replaced by another after the parties were cited; the substitution of the successor as judge-delegate is approved. The bishop of Worcester was present when sentence was given; his officials inducted the monks and Henry, their proctor, into corporal possession.

> JL 14145; also 14009, a short form beginning *Quoniam abbas*. Pd X 1.29.14 (much abbreviated and reworked) and ACL 46.4 (full text, corrupt at the beginning). Cf. Wig. 7.57. Occurs in many collections. Claud. c.97 and Reg. c.136 preserve the date, *xi idus Augusti*, at Anagni.
>
> No. 49B shows that Henry the monks' proctor was probably identical with Henry, son of Adam the priest and former parson of Aston. There was litigation in the king's court about the advowson in 1220 (*Curia Regis Rolls*, ix, p. 148). Canonists were interested in the ruling on the substitution of the successor for the defunct abbot. See p. 128 above.

58C. Illas vero terras. See no. 8b.

59. Insinuavit nobis per T. To (Bartholomew) bishop of Exeter and (Roger) bishop of Worcester.

*c.*July 1174 x Feb. 1177. Commission to hear the complaint of Hu(gh) earl of Norfolk, brought by T(homas) his clerk, against Wimer, priest. A papal letter had been obtained to the effect that if Wimer had revenues of forty marks, or had several churches, the addressees should compel him to abandon his claim to the church of Bungay. Wimer later obtained from the pope another letter about the church, not mentioning the former letter. If this is proved, the bishop of London shall be instructed not to act on the second letter, and the terms of the first shall be enforced, appeal being forbidden. One judge may act.

> JL——. Flor. c.1.72 fo. 179ᵛ, unprinted; occurs here only.
>
> The first letter may be no. 3A; cf. nos. 24 and 88. The letter to the bishop of London is not preserved.

60. Intelleximus ex litteris. To the bishop of Worcester.

*c.*Mar. 1165 x 30 Aug. 1181. Acknowledges the bishop's report of action on no. 19. R(oger), clerk, was not conceived when his father was a priest, nor did the father hold the church of St Mary (Droit)wich, as vicar or parson. Silence shall be enjoined on his opponent, Milo.

> JL——. Pd Wig. 4.39; occurs here only.

61. Inter cetera sollicitudinis. To R(oger) bishop of Worcester.

26 Nov. 1164 (Sens). Rulings on clerical marriage and chastity.
a. Marriage is valid if contracted in minor orders (below the sub-diaconate). Clerks so married shall not leave their wives, or obtain benefices. (1 Comp. 3.3.4)
b. Marriage is invalid if contracted by subdeacons or clerks in higher orders. (1 Comp. 3.3.4)
c. The addressee shall not allow priests' sons to minister in their fathers' churches, but shall remove them, appeal being forbidden. (X 1.17.3)
d. The addressee shall admonish clergy keeping concubines; if they refuse to give them up, he shall despoil them of office and benefice, appeal being forbidden. (1 Comp. 3.2.6)

> JL 12254. Pd *Gilberti epistolae*, ii, 97, no. 368, whence PL 200.930 no. 1050. Occurs in various forms in many collections. Wig. alt. c.3 preserves the date. Translated and discussed above, pp. 69–70.

61A. Licet nuntius Hugonis. See no. 12.

61B. Mandamus fraternitati vestre. See no. 67.

62. Meminimus iampridem Alanum. To (Roger) bishop of Worcester.

1165 x 1175, probably 1175. Order to end without delay the case between Alan, clerk, of Hurstbourne and Richard (Barre), archdeacon of Lisieux, about the church of Burbage, already committed to the addressee. Recounts earlier proceedings, as reported by him and other great men. Alan is said to have got a commission to other judges in which the earlier commission was not mentioned; if so, he shall pay Richard's expenses in sending again to the pope.

JL——. Pd Wig. 7.73; also occurs without address in Chelt. 4.18 fo. 25v.

The dispute was protracted. There had been a settlement before Pope Adrian between Alan and William Giffard, then a commission to the bishop of Worcester got by Alan, then a commission to other judges, perhaps no. 69A also got by Alan, in which the first was not mentioned, and finally no. 62, got by Richard Barre. There was then an interval of some two years before the sentence. Because the first commission is lost, there is no indication of the nature of Alan's original claim. The bishop's sentence, dated 14 Nov. 1177 is App. I, 62.

63. Meminimus nos ex. To R(oger) bishop of Worcester.

4 Sept. 1167 x 1169. Replies to questions on law and procedure.

a. Those who promise before a bishop to enter a monastery, and then marry, should not be forced to enter it, so long as they had not received the habit or made profession. (X 4.6.3)

b. i. The addressee shall receive no vicar at the presentation of monks, unless enough of the benefice is assigned to him, in the bishop's presence, to provide suitable maintenance and pay episcopal dues.

ii. Vicars already instituted may be removed if this condition has not been met. (X. 3.5.12)

c. Those who receive annual pensions from churches have no legal claim, unless the pension was authorized by the bishop or by his officials (*ministeriales*) who have authority to institute parsons. (X 3.39.8)

d. When appeal is forbidden in a commission, the bishop may proceed even though the defendant appeals or sets out for the Curia after citation. (X 2.28.9)

e. If a case is committed with a time limit, the limit cannot be extended without the consent of the parties. (1 Comp. 1.21.12)

JL 13162. Occurs in very many collections, of which several preserve the bishop's initial (e.g. Belv. 1.10), and three the date; of these the best seems to be Paris. BN MS lat. 15001 fo. 122 (*Repert.*, p. 286), which gives *Benev' ii non. Sept.* Cf. Font. 1.4, *Ben. v. R non Sept'.*, and Biberach an der Riss, Spitalarchiv B 3515 fo. 77vb, *Bn' so (? secundo) non' Sept'*.

Pd *Gilberti epistolae*, ii. 99 no. 369 with no. 91 below, as one letter. For the view that nos. 63 and 91 may have been originally two distinct letters, see *BMCL* iv (1974), 66–70. See also pp. 172–9 above.

64. Nosti sicut vir. To (Roger) bishop of Worcester.

June 1173 x Aug. 1175. Mandate to prevent Geoffrey, called elect of Lincoln, from disposing of the archdeaconry of Northampton and the prebend held by William, because his election is not yet confirmed. Any grant made shall be revoked, and the addressee shall press the dean and chapter to carry out the pope's wishes.

> JL 12753. Edited from all texts, and translated, Holtzmann and Kemp, pp. 18–19 no. vii. Pd X 1.6.9. Occurs in many collections.
>
> The mandate must have been issued between Geoffrey's election in Apr. (known at the Curia *c*.June), and his confirmation on 1 July 1175, known *c*.mid-Aug. On the new importance attached to episcopal confirmation in this period, see Robert L. Benson, *The bishop-elect* (Princeton 1968), *passim*.

65. Omnino nobis placeret. To R(oger) bishop of Worcester.

? Late May 1168. Permits the bishop to return to his diocese if if he can act freely there, but if he fears that he will have to observe 'those evil customs' he should on no account put his foot in the trap or himself into prison. If the king will not listen to the pope's envoys, the pope will no longer restrain the archbishop.

> JL 11406. Pd *MTB*, vi. 390, and PL 200.488 no. 489.
>
> The words of no. 65 resemble JL 11404, *MTB*, vi. 437, of 22 May 1168. It certainly falls between late 1167 and 1170.

65A. Pervenit ad aures. See *Ad aures nostras*, no. 7.

66. Pervenit ad audientiam (or *ad aures*). To the bishops of Worcester and Norwich.

Feb. 1176 x Sept. 1179. Commission to investigate the alleged division of the church of Caddington, belonging to St Paul's, London, and the claims of Hen' and Robert Pullus, nephew of R., the late chancellor of the Roman church. Robert is said to have no other benefice. If Hen' has other benefices and secular revenues, the addressees shall assign his portion to R. and induct him into corporal possession of the whole church, as O. his predecessor held it, appeal being forbidden.

> JL——. Pd Sang. 4.5.1, p. 190; also in Abr. 4.4.1, and Wig. 4.43.
>
> Sang. names only the bishop of Worcester, but the closely related Abr. names the two bishops, confirming the reading of Wig. The bishops must be Roger and John (consecrated 14 Dec. 1175). Parisius, nephew of Robert Pullus, held the prebend of Caddington Minor until 1190 after Odo. Hen' does not occur in this prebend in the lists (*Fasti, St Paul's*, p. 34), nor does Robert.

67. Pervenit ad nos. To G(ilbert) bishop of London and R(oger) bishop of Worcester.

Sept. 1164 x Sept. 1179. Commission to hear the complaint of R., an old priest, who had brought to the addressees an earlier commission ordering them to restore to him the church of *Giddingia*, which he had possessed for forty years, but renounced because of pressure (*per vim*) from T., clerk, and fear of the king. T. then obtained a commission to other judges. The addressees shall hear the case according to the first commission, unless the second stated explicitly that the case was withdrawn from their hearing.

> JL 13160. Pd 1 Comp. 1.21.13 and ACL 7.15. Occurs in many collections. The last part of the commission sometimes occurs separately (beginning *Mandamus fraternitati vestre*).
>
> Several collections preserve the bishops' initials. Pet. 2.26.2 gives *Te* for the name of the defendant. The church seems likely to be Steeple, Great, or Little Gidding. The patronage of Little Gidding was in dispute in the time of Hugh de Welles, bishop of Lincoln, which may indicate a conflict reaching back into the twelfth century (*Rotuli Hugonis de Welles*, iii. 49, Lincoln Record Soc., ix, 1914).

68. Pervenit ad nos. To (Roger) bishop of Worcester and (Robert) bishop of Hereford.

1175 x Sept. 1179. Commission to enforce the sentence already issued by the addressees in the dispute between Herbert, knight, and And', parson of *Hacfor'* (or *Acforde*) about the chapel of *Caldenvalle*. The lord of Hacfor' is trying to sue Herbert about patronage in the lay court. The addressees shall forbid the lord or his heirs to take Herbert before a layman; he may pursue his claim before them or before the diocesan.

JL——. Pd Wig. 4.48. Occurs here only.

The places involved may possibly be Hackford, Norfolk, and the chapel of Bawdeswell. The wording of the last sentence suggests that the chapel was not in the diocese of either of the judges.

68A. Pervenit ad nos. To the archbishop of Canterbury.

Apr. 1174 x Sept. 1179. Order to enforce the sentence of Roger bishop of Worcester and the prior of Kenilworth, who have absolved the monks of Thorney and Hugh, clerk, from the claim of O., clerk, to the church of Whittlesea and imposed silence on O.

JL——. Pd Wig. 7.75; occurs only here.

The commission to the bishop and prior is no. 27; see also no. 2.

69. Precipimus ut No. To the archbishop of Canterbury and the bishop of Worcester.

Sept. 1164 x 30 Aug. 1181. Commission to restore the church (unnamed) to No., even if it was objected after his eviction that he was the son of the previous parson, and to remove anyone placed in it within a year of the appeal or within seven months after No. set out (for the Curia).

JL 13825. Pd ACL 22.8, with addition in Sang. 6.1.9 p. 246. Occurs in a few other collections, of which Wig. 4.57 reads No. where the rest read N.

No. 69 is clearly part, possibly reworked, of a commission which has not been identified. The *No.* of Wig. suggests that the claimant's name was Nicholas. No. 5, which mentions a commission to the archbishop alone, and no. 81 to the bishops of Exeter and Worcester, deal with similar cases; either or both may be connected with no. 69.

69A. Querelam Ade clerici. To the bishop of Chichester and the abbot of Ford.

*c.*1176. Commission to hear the complaint of Adam (*recte* Alan) that the bishop of Worcester, to whom was committed the case between him and the bishop of Salisbury about the church of Burbage, had condemned him to pay expenses incurred by R(ichard) archdeacon of Lisieux in attending a hearing to which Adam did not come, being sick. Adam says that he sent a priest and a deacon to the meeting to give proof of his sickness. If it is proved that the bishop gave costs against Adam solely because, being sick, he did not appear on the appointed day, he shall be absolved from the sentence, appeal being forbidden.

> JL 14196. Pd X 1.38.2 without address. Occurs also in other collections.

> No. 62 mentions a commission obtained by Alan's son and presented to other judges, not mentioning the earlier letter(s). No. 69A does mention the earlier letter to Bishop Roger, so the number and sequence of the papal letters is not certain. Roger's sentence on the main issue (App. I, 62) does not mention this point, on which, if the facts were as stated, he had made a mistake. The pope's ruling interested lawyers because it dealt with the problem of the litigant's duty to appoint a proctor.

70. Querelam monachorum de Acra. To R(oger) bishop of Worcester and the prior of Pentney.

1172 x Sept. 1179. Commission to hear the case between the monks of (Castle)Acre and St Stephen of Caen about the lease of the manor of Wells and the church of Gayton. The prior of Castle Acre had resigned the manor, church and relevant charter in return for payment, without the consent of the chapter. The case may be settled by agreement or judgement, provided always that just as the church could not be bought, so it could not be redeemed. One judge may act.

> JL 13165. Pd X 5.3.15 and ACL 2.12. Occurs in many collections. The bishop's initial is given in Roff. c.140, Bamb. 1.6, Tan. 2.6.

> The cartulary of Castle Acre (BL MS Harley 2110 fo. 37^{r-v}) shows that an agreement was made between the two monasteries by which Jordan prior of Castle Acre renounced the case about the manor of Wells and the church of Gayton. Jordan's predecessor was in office in 1170, and possibly as late as 1174, so that the commission was probably issued after bishop Roger's return to England *c*.1172.

71. Querelam R. canonici. To (Gilbert) bishop of London and the bishop of Worcester.

Sept. 1164 x 30 Aug. 1181. Commission to hear the complaint of R. canon of Lincoln, that William Selvagius no longer pays the two bezants promised on oath in the name of the church of *Stantuna*. If William broke his promise, voluntarily and not of necessity, the addressees shall remove him and put R. in possession.

JL 14001. Edited from all texts, with translation, Holtzmann and Kemp, p. 26 no. 11. Pd X 2.24.10.

The place is perhaps Stainton by Langworth, where Simon Selvagius occurs as a landowner in 1203 x 1219 (*Reg. Antiq. Lincoln*, v.74, no. 1568). Holtzmann and Kemp assume that Bishop Roger was the second judge.

72. Querimoniam prioris et fratrum. To (Roger) bishop of Worcester.

? *c.* 1176. The prior and brethren of Lanthony have complained about loss of rights in the church of Painswick. The grant by H(ugh) de Lacy, their founder, was recognized by R(oger) formerly earl of Hereford, his son-in-law, and J(ohn) bishop of Worcester invested the brethren with the church. But the earl was divorced from C(ecilia) his wife, in whose land the church lay, and her second husband, W(illiam) the Poitevin, gave the revenues of the church to R(oger) the priest, without episcopal authority, and after his death, her third husband, W(alter) of Mayenne, continued to support the priest against the prior, saying that what was done by Bishop J(ohn) before the divorce should be invalid, because his wife's full inheritance had not passed to him, if he could not do as he wished with the church. It is absurd that changes should be made in arrangements about churches at every change of patron. The bishop shall restore the church to the brethren, and prevent such changes in future in his diocese, by means of excommunication, appeal being forbidden.

JL 14141. Pd X 3.38.9, and ACL 15.7. Occurs in other collections.

The dispute was ended by a settlement, made before Bartholomew of Exeter and Bishop Roger as judges-delegate, before 14 Apr. 1178, possibly in Mar. 1177 (App. I, 31). But the decretal collections agree in addressing no. 72 to Roger alone, with the exception of Cott. 6.51, and even Cott. has singular forms throughout. Cott. gives address to the bishops of Exeter and Worcester. Presumably there was a second papal letter; possibly the compiler of Cott. knew the later history of the case. See also above, p. 144.

72A. Qui ecclesiam non suo nomine. To the bishop of Worcester.

Font. 2.54 (Holtzmann's numeration) = 28 (Duggan's numeration) gives this fragment, which appears to be a garbled extract from no. 45 above.

APPENDIX II

73. Quia Willelmus qui. To the bishop of Worcester and the abbot of St Albans.

1172 x 1178. Because W(illiam of Hastings), who was said to have obtained the church of Buckworth by violence, is dead and Nigel (*recte* Nicholas) has been intruded into it, the addressees shall hear the case between Patrick and Nigel according to the instructions (*forma*) of the letter about the case between Patrick and W(illiam).

> JL 14140. Pd X 2.1.11 (a poor text), and ACL 22.9. Occurs also in 1 Cant. c.56 f.56ra (unprinted) and other collections.
>
> This mandate, or fragment of a mandate, closely resembles the end of no. 17.

73A. Quoniam abbas. JL 14009. Part of no. 58B above.

74. Recepta conquestione A. mulieris. To Roger bishop of Worcester and Adam abbot of Evesham.

? July 1175 x Sept. 1179. The pope had committed to the addressees the complaint of A., that she had been forced as a child to marry H. son of W. son of R., that she had renounced this upon reaching the age of discretion and married B., and that after proceedings before the archbishop of Canterbury the case had been taken to the pope on appeal. Later, the other party asserted that A. was fourteen when married, had lived with H. for over a year, and been carried off by B., who appealed when he saw that the judgement of the archbishop's court would go against him, setting 2 July last as term. The pope does not know who to believe. If A. was fourteen, or even twelve, when she married H., and lived with him voluntarily, then B. must give her up.

> JL——. Pd 1 Par. c.176 (a poor text). Also in Aureaevall. c.40 (p. 88). Fragments occur in other collections, with incipit 'Si (puella) nondum xii annorum'.
>
> Consideration of the various stages of the case makes it probable that the archbishop mentioned was Richard, and that this commission belongs to the later 1170s.

75. Recepta olim querimonia. To R(oger) bishop of Worcester and another or others.

Nov. 1174 x Sept. 1179 or, less probably, Sept. 1164 x Apr. 1167. The bishop of Hereford and the abbot of Evesham had been commissioned to hear the complaint of the dean of Lincoln, that he had been despoiled of a prebend in Hereford cathedral. Later, Master Geoffrey of Winchester asserted that the chapter had granted the prebend to him at the request of King Henry. With the consent of G. and of R. representing the dean, the case is now committed to the addressees, in whose experience the pope has confidence. The addressees shall take into account the dean's large revenues.

> JL——. Edited from all texts, with translation, Holtzmann and Kemp, pp. 28–9 no. xii. Pd Sang. 6.1.16 p. 249.

> The commission refers to a vacancy, probably recent, at Hereford, and therefore is most likely to have followed the long vacancy of Feb. 1167–Oct. 1174. At least one judge was not a bishop. Master Geoffrey does not appear as a canon or witness in *Hereford Charters*.

76. Referente magistro Henrico. To the bishops of London and Worcester.

Sept. 1164 x 30 Aug. 1181. Master Henry complains that the Hospitallers of Hardwick refuse to pay tithes of the increase of animals and from some lands pertaining to his church. The Hospitallers must restore unpaid tithes and pay in future, or appear before the judges, appeal being forbidden. No document shall prejudice Henry's rights.

> JL 14000. Pd 1 Comp. 3.26.22. Occurs in other collections.

> Hardwick is not mentioned in King John's charter confirming grants to the Hospitallers (*Rot. Chart.*, I.i.15b), but before 1279 they had a small house at Hardwick (*VCH Beds.*, iii. 302). The form of the commission, resembling the English writs *Praecipe*, is unusual though not unique.

77. Referente nobis dilecto. To the bishop of Worcester and the abbot of Evesham.

c. Jan. 1175 x 30 Aug. 1181. Commission to hear the complaint of D. (or M.) that G., clerk, has long troubled him with claims to the church of *Fossoria*, though he swore to renounce it, and is believed to be the son of the priest who was formerly parson. G. got papal letters to the bishop of Bath, the abbot of Stanley and the prior of Monkton Farleigh, stating that he was absolved from his oath, and later to the same effect to the bishop of Worcester, the abbot of Stanley and the prior of Bradenstoke. These letters and dispensations are not likely to be genuine. The

APPENDIX II

addressees shall order the judges to whom these letters came, to reveal the truth without fear or favour of any man, whether G. appears or not.

> JL——. Pd Brug. 37.1, p. 157. Also in Cott. 5.66, fo. 27ra, which alone preserves the last sentence.

> Bishop Robert of Bath is thought to have been incapacitated for some time before his death in Sept. 1166; this and the protracted nature of the case suggest that no. 77 was issued during the pontificate of Bishop Reginald, not before about the end of 1174. A date in 1164 or 1165 is just possible.

78. Referente nobis I. To the bishop of Worcester and the prior of Kenilworth.

? 1172 x ? Sept. 1179. Commission to investigate the complaint of R., priest, of Yelvertoft, that he was violently ejected from his church by R. clerk of *Botendun* on the authority of Master G. de *Ailestun* then vice-archdeacon, after appeal. R.'s messenger to the pope was delayed, and he was forced by unjust excommunication to promise to do as R. and G. wished, if they would provide for him. The judges appointed by the pope refused to act because of his promise. Now his opponent withholds some of the promised provision, so that he has nothing to keep him in his old age. The addressees shall restore him to his church; any papal letter not mentioning this one shall be of no effect. One judge may act.

> JL——. Pd Wig. 7.79. Occurs also in Chelt. 4.42 fo. 27ra, and Rome, Vatican MS Pal. lat. 652 fo. 60 (information from papers of W. Holtzmann).

> Of the twelve letters at the end of Wig. (7. 70–81), eight are almost certainly of the 1170s. This letter, which has no internal evidence of dating, has therefore been assigned to the same period. The vice-archdeacon seems to be unknown.

79. Relatum est nobis. To (Gilbert) bishop of London and (Roger) bishop of Worcester.

22 Dec. 1174. Commission to investigate the alleged exemption of Malmesbury Abbey. If the facts are as reported, the addressees shall not allow Abbot Robert or the bishop who blessed him to be troubled by the bishop of Salisbury. They shall send copies of Malmesbury's privileges to the pope under seal, and assign the tribute due to St Peter to the abbot of St Germain of Paris. One judge may act alone if one cannot or will not act.

APPENDIX II

JL 12401. Pd *Reg. Malmesbur.* i.371.

> Copies of Malmesbury's privileges were in the pope's hands by 11 Feb. 1177 at latest. There is no certain indication of action on this commission. The abbot and the bishop who blessed him were suspended by the archbishop, and the bishop made an abject apology for his action (*Salisbury Charters*, p. 41). See nos. 14 and 41, also David Knowles, 'The growth of monastic exemption', *Downside Review* l (1932), 225–31.

80. (Re)Scripsimus vobis ad suggestionem. To R(oger) bishop of Worcester and (Adam) abbot of Evesham.

Sept. 1164 x Sept. 1179. At the suggestion of Hugh, clerk, the pope wrote to the addressees with precise instructions (*sub certa forma*) committing to them the case between Hugh and Robert, clerk, of Mansfield about the chapel of Woodhouse, forgetting that it was already committed to the dean of York and the abbot of Rievaulx, who have pronounced sentence. If this is so, the sentence shall stand, and silence shall be imposed on Hugh.

> JL 14035; by a curious error, the editors included under this number the decretal fragment *Cum aliquibus*, no. 30B, and all their references refer to that fragment, and not to no. 80. Pd ACL 36.1 (abbreviated, with address to Norwich and Evesham), Brug. 44.5 (without address and with some corruption of names), Claustr. c.265 (also poor text). Reg. c.71 fo. 113vb is a good text with recognizable names, and address as above. Occurs also in Cant. 3.7 and other collections. 1 Rot. 26.12 has address to William, bishop of Norwich. The readings of Reg., supported by Cant., are to be preferred.

> King William II gave to Lincoln Cathedral Mansfield with its four chapels, of which Woodhouse, now Mansfield Woodhouse, was one. The litigation left no trace in surviving Lincoln records.

80A. Si diversa pars. *Repert.*, p. 288 notes this item with inscription *Alex. iii episcopo Vigoriensi*, in Troyes, Bibl. municipale, MS 103, fos. 265^v–266. It appears to be a reworking of no. 91a below.

81. Si qui testium. To B(artholomew) bishop of Exeter and R(oger) bishop of Worcester.

Sept. 1164 x Sept. 1179. Instruction to send suitable persons to take evidence from witnesses, if any are old or ill, or if Nicholas, being poor, cannot convey them to the judges' presence.

> JL 13926. Pd X 2.20.8, reworked so as to refer to poverty of the witnesses, not of the plaintiff. Bridl. c.92 fo. 106^v has the rubric 'Pro Nicholao clerico de

Mendlesham pro ecclesia eiusdem loci contra W. de Luci'. Occurs without the rubric in other collections.

Bridl. supplies the bishops' initials, the instructive rubric and the mention of Nicholas in the text. This evidence suggests that no. 81 was part of a commission dealing with the church of Mendlesham, one of the 'dower' churches of Battle Abbey. Nicholas, son of the previous rector, figures in the account of Abbot Walter de Lucy's efforts to regain control of the church (*Chron. de Bello*, pp. 122–7). Perhaps the abbot presented a relative to the church (cf. the W. de Lucy of no. 89). The chronicle breaks off in 1176; there is no trace of this stage of the dispute.

81A. Si quis tonsoratus. To the archbishop of York and the bishop of Worcester.

Claud. c.116, fo. 206va, has this brief statement that if a tonsured man, who pretends to be a clerk, obtains a church, he may not keep it, even if he becomes a clerk later. Cf. no. 50, though the problem does not seem to be identical.

81B. Si (vero) quisquam. Reg. c.122 with address to the bishop of Worcester. Pd ACL 5.5, with address to the bishop of Exeter, elsewhere to Lisieux; cf. JL 13899. States the same rule as no. 63a.

82. Si vobis constiterit. To B(artholomew) bishop of Exeter and R(oger) bishop of Worcester.

Sept. 1164 x Sept. 1179. If the addressees find that the clerk claims the church on the authority of a simple gift by a knight, they shall impose silence on him. If he claims the patronage, they shall hear the case.

JL 13923. Pd ACL 47.9. The bishops' initials are given in 1 Alc. c.84. Occurs in other collections.

No. 82 is part of a lost commission.

83. Si vobis constiterit. To the bishop (or archdeacon) of Worcester and the archdeacon of Exeter (or Oxford).

? Sept. 1159 x 30 Aug. 1181. If G., clerk, is the son of the previous parson of *Cubton*', and N., a canon, was lawfully instituted, the addressees shall remove G. from the church.

JL——. Bridl. c.22, Claud. c.22 p. 191r.

No. 83 is part of a lost commission.

84. Sicut ex litteris tuis, frater episcope. To (Roger) bishop of Worcester (? and Richard archdeacon of Ely).

1165 x 1178.

a. Commends the bishop for referring to the pope, because the cord of the papal *bulla* was broken, and therefore the advocate of Th(omas), clerk, would not answer H(ugh), clerk. The letter in question (no. 12) was in fact composed in the chancery.

b. The addressees shall enquire whether H(ugh) was despoiled when he renounced the church.

> JL 14139. Pd 1 Comp. 2.15.3 = a, 2.9.1 = b, also X 2.13.2 = b. The two parts appear separately in very many collections, and as a single letter in a few, e.g. Reg. c.95–6, Cantab. c.44. The latter adds a final phrase on the oaths to be taken by witnesses.

> The address is uniformly given to the bishop alone. But his announcement of the end of the case (App. I, 47) refers to the archdeacon as his fellow-judge, and the words *frater episcope* indicate that the pope was addressing one of two or more addressees of a letter. Plural forms occur at two points in b, in Reg. which often provides good texts. These indications suggest that no. 84, like two earlier letters in the case, was addressed to Archdeacon Richard and another.

85. Sicut vobis iura. To the monks of St Mary and St Lawrence.

Sept. 1164 x Mar. 1179. The pope has heard that the monks do not pay tithes to the church of *Collingham* as fully as was done before they obtained the estate. They must pay in full, under threat of papal displeasure if further complaint is received. If they claim any legal right, they shall appear before the bishop of Worcester and the dean of Chichester, appeal being forbidden.

> JL 13978. Pd ACL 13.13, 1 Comp. 3.26.19 without address and reading *Cistrensis* for *Cicestrensis*. Occurs in many collections. A shorter form, beginning *Audivimus quod decimas* occurs in a few collections, e.g. Belv. 4.6, pd *Gilberti epistolae*, ii. 108 no. 376.

> The monks of Revesby were regularly described as 'of St Lawrence' in the twelfth century, and the complaint about unpaid tithes fits a Cistercian house. Revesby Abbey had land in Coringham, where the church was attached to a prebend in Lincoln Cathedral. The abbey does not seem to have had land in any other place recognizable as *Collingham*. There is no trace of this litigation in the Lincoln archives, or in the sparse remaining records of Revesby. The letter occurs in 2 Paris. 56.5; this collection is thought to have been produced before the Lateran Council of Mar. 1179.

APPENDIX II 361

86. Significatum est nobis. To the bishops of London and Worcester.

Sept. 1164 x 30 Aug. 1181. G., clerk, is suspected of the murder of William Sarracenus. If he cannot be convicted and yet is publicly defamed, he shall undergo canonical purgation. If he fails in purgation, or is judicially convicted, he shall be despoiled of his benefice and suspended from the service of the altar.

> JL——. Pd Brug. 42.5 with address to the archbishop of Toledo. Occurs also in other collections, mainly those of English origin or connections. The earlier collections agree in giving the address as above; some introduce the common confusion between Worcester and Norwich.
>
> On this letter see above, pp. 183–4.

86A. Significaverunt nobis dilecti. To (Richard) archbishop of Canterbury.

? late 1174 x early 1175. Commission to investigate the complaint of the canons of St Frideswide's that a commission (no. 52) was obtained by fraud, and that the bishop of London put the canons of Osney in possession of the disputed church after appeal.

> JL 13799. Pd ACL 10.32, 1 Comp. 2.20.35, Claustr. c. 290, and *Oseney Cart.*, ii. 223 from ACL. Occurs in many collections.
>
> No. 86A mentions no. 52, of ? 12 Apr. 1174 and action taken upon it. No. 4, of ? 12 Apr. 1176, mentions letters obtained by fraud, presumably no. 86A, and an appeal by St Frideswide's, which set 1 Nov., ? 1175, as term. On the case see no. 4.

87. Significavit nobis B. presbiter. To the bishops of Exeter and Worcester (or Winchester).

Sept. 1164 x 30 Aug. 1181. Commission on behalf of B. (variously A., O., or D.), priest, who says that he has held the church of Meppershall for thirty years, but now the monks of Lenton trouble him with a commission to the bishop of Hereford and Master Vacarius, asserting that he is the son of the former minister, although his father was not a priest, and the pope's decree was promulgated only against priests' sons. New constitutions affect future cases; therefore if the priest held the church long before the Council of Tours, the addressees shall absolve him from the monks' claim.

JL 14224. Pd ACL 41.2, Claustr. c.138. Occurs in other collections; good texts appear to be Claud. c.90, Bridl. c.102, Roff. c.31.

Lenton Priory owned the church of Meppershall. The decretal collections often reduce the name to *Map*' or similar forms; ACL has *Waplam*. Roff. and collections of the *Wigorniensis* group name the bishop of Winchester as the second judge; if this was correct the commission was issued after Nov. 1174. The rule about the effect of new law is from the Codex of Justinian, 1.14.7.

88. Significavit nobis dilectus. To (Bartholomew) bishop of Exeter, (Roger) bishop of Worcester, and (Hugh) abbot of Bury St Edmunds.

July 1174 x Apr. 1177. Commission to investigate the complaint of T(homas), clerk of Hugh earl of Norfolk, that a commission was issued to the addressees about the church of Bungay, with the consent of T.'s messenger and of the messenger of Wimer the chaplain and the monks of Thetford. After the departure of T.'s messenger, the chaplain got a commission to other judges. If this is true, G. (*recte* W.) must pay T.'s expenses in coming again to the pope, and any sentence arising from the second commission must be revoked.

JL——. Flor. c.170, fo. 179^v, unprinted. Occurs here only.

The previous commission may be no. 24, though that was addressed to the two bishops, while no. 88 adds the abbot. Some four months, at least, must have elapsed between the issue of nos. 24 and 88. See also no. 3A.

89. Significavit nobis dilectus. To the bishop of Worcester and (Adam) abbot of Evesham.

? Sept. 1164 x ? 30 Aug. 1181. Commission to investigate the complaint of W. de Luci, dean of N., that possessions of his deanery have been taken from it without the consent of his chapter. The addressees shall order W., clerk, to return the vill of *Ludlega* and the land of W. de Fonte, with fruits received, and Hel., clerk, to return other possessions. If they do not, they must appear before the judges. If either party appeals, the addressees shall receive the allegations and attestations of witnesses, and appoint a day for the parties to appear before the pope with copies.

JL——. Pd Löwenfeld, *Epistolae Pontificum*, pp. 207–8 no. 348.

Löwenfeld dated no. 89 '1178–81', because most of the papal letters in this part of the MS belong to those years. On the MS (Cambridge, Trinity College,

R. 9.17 fo. 108ʳ–129ᵛ) see Holtzmann, 'Die Register', pp. 69–80. The origin of this collection of papal letters is still obscure, and as it certainly includes one letter of Adrian IV and one of Lucius III, a wider range of dates has here been assigned to no. 89. The complaint seems likely to refer to possessions of the deanery of a cathedral or collegiate church. A W. de Luci was involved in the dispute over the church of Mendlesham (no. 81), which was the head of a rural deanery; *Ludlega* has not been identified in that area.

90. Significavit nobis Hen' Bram. To the bishop of Worcester.

Sept. 1164 x 30 Aug. 1181. Commission to investigate the complaint of Hen' Bram, knight, that the chapel of that vill is so far from the mother church that parishioners sometimes die without the last rites and children without baptism. If this is true, the bishop shall allow the inhabitants to have a chaplain to celebrate and baptize, appeal being forbidden, provided that the mother church suffers no loss.

> JL——. Pd Wig. 4.45. Occurs here only.
>
> The commission does not make it clear whether the village of *Bram* lay in the diocese of Worcester or elsewhere. Perhaps one of the Bramptons in Herefordshire was intended.

90A. Significavit nobis Hugo. To (Richard) archbishop of Canterbury and (Bartholomew) bishop of Exeter.

Sept. 1174 x Jan. 1177. Hugh of Moreton says that he was impleaded by the bishop of Hereford before the archbishop about the patronage of the churches of Moreton and Whaddon and that he appealed to the pope. As appeal was forbidden in the commission, the archbishop did not defer to it, but excommunicated Hugh and laid an interdict on the churches. The addressees shall relax the sentence when Hugh has given sufficient pledges that he will appear before them, and shall hear the case, appeal being forbidden, notwithstanding any letters obtained to the prejudice of truth and justice. One judge may act.

> JL 13812. Pd Lips. 52.11 in Friedberg, *Quinque Comp.* p. 203 (a poor text) with address to the archbishop only, and Claustr. c.195. Occurs also in other collections. 1 Alc. c.112 is a good text, preserving the final phrase.
>
> There is much confusion in the collections as to the address; Bridl. c.78 fo. 103ᵛ appears to be correct in giving, after a run of letters to Canterbury, *eidem et B. Exon'*. The archbishop alone pronounced sentence. Bishop Roger's confirmation as diocesan is App. I, 28.

90B. Sollicite cures. JL 14139. See no. 84.

90C. Suggestum est nobis. ? To the bishops of Salisbury and Exeter.

? Sept. 1160 x 30 Aug. 1181. Order to remove I., a priest's son, from his father's church.

> JL 14097, addressed to the bishops of Salisbury and Exeter; cf. JL 13815 to the archbishop of Canterbury and his suffragans, pd X 1.17.10. Wig. 3.23 gives address to Salisbury and Worcester, probably in error.

90D. Super causa cuiusdam. (Claud. c.74, Bridl. c.91.) See no. 37.

91. Super eo quod. To R(oger) bishop of Worcester.

1 Sept., 1167 or 1168 or 1169. Replies to questions on law and procedure.
a. Even in cases committed without right of appeal, an appeal on a related question (*ex incidenti questione*) is permitted, so long as it is not based on fraud. (X 2.28.10)
b. Appeals on even the smallest questions are lawful. (X 2.28.11)
c. If a man has intercourse with his wife's mother, sister or daughter, and the offence is notorious, the man and wife must be separated. If the offence is secret or the relationship less close, divorce is not required. (1 Comp. 4.20.6)
d. If part of a convent protests about a grant made by an abbot alone or with the consent of part of the convent, local custom and the size of the grant must be considered in determining its validity. (X 3.24.3)
e. A donor may not revoke a conditional gift to a church, unless it was explicitly stated that revocation would follow if the condition was not fulfilled. (X 4.5.4)
f. Documents have no validity if the named witnesses are dead, unless they are drawn up *per manum publicam* or have an authentic seal. (X 2.22.2)

> JL 13162, as part of no. 63. Occurs as a whole or in sections in very many collections.
>
> See no. 63 for the date and the question whether no. 91 was a separate letter. See also pp. 172–9 above.

APPENDIX II

91A. Sustinere nolumus. To the bishop of Worcester. Font. 2.16 has this item, which appears to be a reworking of part of no. 35.

92. Testes quos Radulfus. To the bishops of Exeter and Worcester.

Sept. 1164 x 30 Aug. 1181. Witnesses, lay or clerical, named by Ralph, shall, if necessary, be compelled to give evidence.

> JL 13925. Pd 1 Comp. 2.14.6, ACL 8.16. Occurs in very many collections.
>
> No. 92 is part of a lost commission. No. 56 differs at the vital point, since it does not order compulsion of witnesses. See P. Herde, 'Der Zeugenzwang in den päpstlichen Delegationsreskripten des Mittelalters', *Traditio* xviii (1962), 255–88.

93. Veniens ad apostolice. To (Roger) bishop of Worcester. ? 1173.

Commission to hear the case between Mr William of Flammeville and the monks of Marmoutier, who withhold tithes in the parish of St Mary of Marton, on the authority of an old agreement.

> JL 14137. Pd ACL 48.1. (JL 14102, pd X 1.36.8, is the same commission with incorrect address, and text altered to supply plural forms). Occurs in many collections.
>
> In 1173 an agreement was made between Mr William of Flammeville and William son of Walo about tithes and the rights of the chapel of Welham, 'about which they should have appeared before the Lord Bishop of Worcester on a writ of the Lord Pope' (*Early Yorkshire Charters*, iii. 495 no. 1888). Possibly Mr William obtained both commissions to Bishop Roger at the same time, for use against different opponents. Marmoutier had received land near Marton-cum-Grafton for its priory of Holy Trinity, York, early in the twelfth century. It is not known whether the monks, like William son of Walo, came to terms with Mr William.
>
> The long commission cannot be satisfactorily summarized. Its interest for lawyers appears from the rubric in ACL (*ed. princ.*): an agreement made with a predecessor does not bind a successor, unless confirmed by the pope, and tithes should be paid to the church from which sacraments are received.

93A. Veniens ad nos G. To R(ichard) archbishop of Canterbury.

May 1174 x 30 Aug. 1181. Commission to hear the complaint of G., a poor clerk, that he is being disturbed and threatened by R. Brito, who has bought the patronage of the chapel of

Stretton on Fosse (*Stratona*). The addressee shall compel R. to make good damage and loss suffered, or to stand trial before him, appeal being forbidden. As regards the right of patronage, which R. Brito is said to have bought, it is improper that patronage should be sold. The addressee shall declare the contract invalid, appeal being forbidden.

> JL 13798, pd X 3.38.16 and ACL 47.1, is the second part of this commission. The first part is printed 1 Abr. Appendices c.8 (p. 393). The two appear as one letter in 1 Alc. c.51, which preserves the archbishop's initial, and the surname of R. Brito in the first part.
>
> No. 93A concerns the chapel of Stretton on Fosse in the diocese of Worcester, for which see nos. 26, 26A, 49A, and p. 73 above. It probably belongs to an early stage in the case, before the death of Bishop Roger; this would be compatible with the fact that there are no items in this part of 1 Alc. which are certainly later than 1179. The identification of *Stratona* as Stretton on Fosse, and of this case with that described in no. 26A, is made certain by the record of proceedings in 1233, when Alan Brito claimed that Ralph Brito his uncle had presented Alan his brother to the chapel, and that a certain William had opposed him. According to the jurors, Alan agreed to pay 2s. yearly to William, and on Alan's death William occupied the chapel and held it for the rest of his life without ever being presented to, or admitted by, the bishop (*Curia Regis Rolls* xv, 1233–1237 (HMSO 1972), no. 756).

94. Veniens ad presentiam. To the bishop of Worcester. Oct. 1164 x 30 Aug. 1181. Order to allow G., priest, to minister in the diocese of Worcester, provided that he is personally suitable. G., who came from that diocese, had been ordained by the bishop of Moray, without licence of the bishop of Worcester, who has properly forbidden him to minister.

> JL——. Pd Wig. 3.38. Occurs only here.

95. To Hilary bishop of Chichester and Roger bishop of Worcester.

Oct. 1164 x late 1167. Commission with instructions (*certa forma*) concerning the case between Richard, Adam and Walter about the church of Harlington.

> Mentioned only, in JL 11306, pd *MTB*, v. 294 and *Letters of Foliot*, p. 196 no. 150.

96. To Roger bishop of Worcester.

Oct. 1164 x Oct. 1178. Commission to hear the case between Adam, clerk, and William of Careville about the church of Badmondisfield.

APPENDIX II 367

Mentioned only, *Curia Regis Rolls* x (1221), pp. 242–3. Bishop Roger's charter announcing a composition was produced in court in 1221; see App. I, 52. The commission must have been despatched in time for him to act before leaving England *c*.1 Jan. 1179.

97. To Roger bishop of Worcester and Robert archdeacon of Winchester.

1172 x 1174. Commission to hear the case between the monks of Lewes and William son of Ralph about land at *Haselcroft* and *Tilleberia*.

> Mentioned only, in the judges' notice of a composition, dated 10 Feb. 1175, App. I, 37.

98. To Richard archbishop of Canterbury, Gilbert bishop of London, Bartholomew bishop of Exeter, and Roger bishop of Worcester.

Before, and probably not long before, 15 Sept. 1176. Commission to visit Amesbury Abbey, and to advise and induce the nuns to accept the Order of Fontevrault. Any two of the addressees may act.

> Mentioned only, in JL 12623 to the abbess of Fontevrault (*PUF*, v. 251 no. 160), and *Gesta Henrici*, i. 135, 165.

99. To Roger bishop of Worcester.

c.1172 x 1173. Commission to hear the case between Master William of Flammeville and William, son of Walo, about tithes due to the church of Norton and the rights of the chapel of Welham.

> Mentioned only, in record of a settlement made *anno incarnationis* ... *1173*. See no. 93.

100. To Robert bishop of Hereford and Roger bishop of Worcester.

Sept. 1164 x late 1166. Commission to hear the dispute between A. and R., monks of Norwich, and William, bishop of Norwich.

> Mentioned only, in letter of Lawrence, abbot of Westminster (d. Apr. 1173) to Pope Alexander III (Liverani, p. 745, from MS Vat. lat. 6024 fo. 150). The two bishops arranged a settlement, so the commission must have been issued in time for action before Robert's death on 27 Feb. 1167.

101. To Robert elect of Hereford and Roger elect of Worcester.

Mar. 1163 x Feb. 1164. Commission to hear the case between Robert and Henry about the church of Whitbourne.

> Mentioned only, *Letters of Foliot*, p. 190 no. 145.

102. To Roger bishop of Worcester and Robert prior of Kenilworth.

*c.*1167 x *c.*May 1179. Commission to hear the case between the abbot and canons of Darley and William earl Ferrars, about the church of Uttoxeter.

> Mentioned only, in the undated announcement of a settlement made before Prior Robert, and Simon archdeacon of Worcester and Master Moses, the two latter acting as subdelegates of the bishop (*Darley cart.*, ii. 574–5). The case may have been heard during Bishop Roger's absence in 1167–72, or January–mid-August 1179.

103. To Roger bishop of Worcester and Simon abbot of St Albans.

? 1172 x 1176. Commission to investigate the complaint of the abbot and monks of St Edmund that pensions are being withheld, which are due from two churches in Colchester, Holy Trinity and Berechurch, and to remove the occupant if he will not obey, appeal being forbidden. One judge may act.

> Mentioned only, in an undated report from the bishop to the pope, pd *PUE*, 3. 372–4 no. 243 (App. I, 6).

104. To Roger bishop of Worcester and Robert prior of Kenilworth.

Sept. 1164 x *c.*Oct. 1178. Commission to hear the case between the monks of Lire (at Carisbrooke) and Jocelin de Insula, clerk, about the church of Newchurch, Isle of Wight.

> Mentioned only, in record of an amicable composition confirmed by the judges (App. I, 9).

105. To Roger bishop of Worcester and Robert prior of Kenilworth.

? 1174 or 1175. Commission to hear the case between Albinus, abbot of Darley, and Hubert son of Ralph about the manor of Crich.

> Mentioned only, in Bishop Roger's announcement, dated 22 Sept. 1175, of the ensuing settlement, App. I, 14.

106. To Roger bishop of Worcester and Adam abbot of Evesham.

? c. Jan. 1174 x July 1176. Commission to hear the case between the prior and monks of St Augustine of Daventry and Alan of Glen', clerk, about the church of Foxton.

> Mentioned only, in the judges' announcement, dated 6 Oct. 1176, of Alan's renunciation of his claim, App. I, 15.

107. To Roger bishop of Worcester and Adam abbot of Evesham.

? c. Jan. 1174 x July 1176. Commission to hear the case between the prior and convent of Daventry and Hugh le Poer about the church of Thrupp.

> Mentioned only, *Curia Regis Rolls* v p. 43, in record of a case in 1207. Possibly nos. 106 and 107 were obtained at the same time, hence the suggested date of no. 107. Hugh's charter, produced in 1207, states that his father's gift of the church had been renewed and recorded before the two prelates, and that it was confirmed with their seals. See also BL MS Cotton Claudius D. xii fo. 110.

108. To Roger bishop of Worcester.

? 1166. Commission to hear the case between Walter, clerk, and the prior of Daventry about the church of West Haddon.

> Mentioned only, in the bishop's report to the pope, which shows that judgement was given early in 1167, App. I, 16.

109. To Roger bishop of Worcester and Giles bishop of Évreux.

Spring 1170 x summer 1172. Commission to hear the case between the abbots of Le Bec and Lire about the church of *Brueland* (or *Bruerland*).

> Mentioned only, in the announcement issued by the bishops as arbiters, App. I, 41.

110. To Roger bishop of Worcester and Robert elect of Hereford.

? June 1173 x Nov. 1174. Commission to hear the case between the abbey of Lire and the church of Wimborne, about tithes of the demesne of the earl of Leicester at Shapwick and Kingston Lacy.

> Mentioned only, in later references to a settlement, App. I, 42.

111. To Roger bishop of Worcester and Simon abbot of St Albans.

1172 x *c*.Oct. 1178. Commission to hear the case between the prior of Thetford and the monks of Luffield about the church of Dodford.

> Mentioned only, in the bishop's notice of a settlement, App. I, 43.

112. To Roger bishop of Worcester and Adam abbot of Evesham.

? 1176. Commission to hear the case between the canons of St Paul's, Bedford, and the occupier of the church of Holcot.

> Mentioned only, in the bishop's notice of a settlement made late in Jan. 1177, App. I, 46.

113. To Roger bishop of Worcester and Hugh dean of St Paul's, London.

Sept. 1164 x autumn 1175. Commission to hear the case between the canons of Osney, and Ralph of Tamworth, archdeacon of Stafford with William de Brai, *advocatus*, about the church of Shenstone.

> Mentioned only, in the judges' announcement of a settlement. See App. I, 49, where the date is discussed.

114. To Bartholomew bishop of Exeter and Roger bishop of Worcester.

? 1173 x Sept. 1174. Commission to hear the case between the abbot and monks of St Albans and A., clerk, about a third of the church of Luton.

> Mentioned only, in the judges' announcement of a settlement, dated 22 November 1174, App. I, 54.

115. To Roger bishop of Worcester.

1172 x 1174. Commission to hear the case between Walter, clerk, and the monks of Saint-Évroul about the church of Rowell.

> Mentioned only, in the bishop's announcement of a settlement, dated '1174', App. I, 55.

116. To Roger bishop of Worcester and Robert bishop of Hereford.

c.Nov. 1174 x *c*.Dec. 1175. Commission with instructions (*certa forma*) to hear the case between the monks of Saint-Évroul and the brethren of Bermondsey about the church of Widford.

> Mentioned only, in a citation and in Bishop Roger's announcement of a settlement, late in Mar. 1176, App. I, 57, 58.

117. To Roger bishop of Worcester and Adam abbot of Evesham.

c.Jan. 1175 x *c*.Oct. 1176. Commission to hear the case between the monks of St Neots and Alan of Valeines, clerk, about the church of Heveningham.

> Mentioned only, in the bishop's announcement of a settlement, dated 17 Jan. 1177, App. I, 59.

118. To Roger bishop of Worcester and Geoffrey dean of Hereford.

c.1172 x *c*.Aug. 1173. Commission to hear the case between Jocelin bishop of Salisbury, and William son of Alexander, about land held of the bishop in Potterne and Bishop's Cannings.

> Mentioned only, in the judges' announcement of a settlement, dated 16 Oct. 1173, App. I, 60.

119. To Roger bishop of Worcester.

? *c*.1172 x *c*.May 1175. ? Commission to hear the case between Adam abbot of Shrewsbury, and Robert son of Robert, about burials of the men of Aston Eyre.

> Mentioned only, in the bishop's undated announcement of Robert's submission, App. I, 63. The announcement does not refer to a papal commission; the bishop may have been acting during the vacancy of the see of Hereford, 1167–74.

120. To Roger bishop of Worcester and Adam abbot of Evesham.

*c.*1172 x *c.*Aug. 1173. Commission to hear the case between the canons of Holy Sepulchre, Warwick, and William Cumin, about the church of Snitterfield.

> Mentioned only, in the judges' announcement of a settlement, dated 15 Nov. 1173, App. I, 69.

121. To Roger bishop of Worcester and Richard archdeacon of Poitiers.

Sept. 1164 x *c.*Feb. 1173. Commission to hear the case between the monks of Worcester and Thomas, clerk, about tithes of Wolverley.

> Mentioned only, in the judges' announcement of a settlement, undated but probably before 1 May 1173, App. I, 74.

122. To Bartholomew bishop of Exeter and Roger bishop of Worcester.

Sept. 1164 x *c.*Oct. 1178. Commission to hear the case about the church of Winterbourne Bassett.

> Inferred from letter of Jocelin bishop of Salisbury informing Bishops Bartholomew and Roger that Richard of Dunstanvill was never instituted parson or vicar in the church of Winterbourne by himself or by any of his officials with his consent. *Scripta autentica* about presentations and advowsons of churches in his diocese show that the advowson of Winterbourne belongs to the monks of Lewes. *Lewes Cartulary, Wilts., Devon etc. portions*, ed. L. F. Salzman and W. Budgen, Sussex Rec. Soc. (1943), no. 48.

123. To Roger bishop of Worcester and Baldwin abbot of Ford.

? 1172 x *c.*Oct. 1178. Commission to hear the case about the church of Marston.

> Inferred from letter of Simon abbot of St Albans, sending to Bishop Roger and Abbot Baldwin information obtained from a monk of Hertford about events 'almost forty years ago', before King Stephen besieged the empress in Oxford. The original letter is endorsed *Testimonium S. abbatis de ecclesia de merston' transmissum iudicibus* (Muniments of St George's chapel, Windsor, XV 7.2, cf. *HMC Reports, Var. coll.* vii. 34, and *Reg. Antiquiss.* ix. 256 n. 6), also J. M. A. Delaville Le Roulx, *Cartulaire... des Hospitaliers* (1894–1906), iv. 265 and note.

124. To Robert bishop of Hereford and Roger bishop of Worcester.

Sept. 1164 x Jan. 1167. Commission to hear the case about the church of Gamlingay, perhaps between St Botolph's Priory, Colchester, and Robert son of Warin, chaplain.

> Inferred from letter of Nigel bishop of Ely (d. 30 May 1169) informing the two bishops that when a claim was made before him against the church of Colchester about the church of Gamlingay, venerable persons in the general synod stated that St Botolph's had possessed the church for forty-five years and more (Oxford, Merton College muniments, no. 5525 face, copy headed *Littera testimonialis*). Merton mun. no. 5521, also copied on 5525, is an announcement by other judges-delegate (Feb. 1176 x Apr. 1180), which suggests that patronage was the underlying issue. Perhaps no. 124 was ineffective owing to Robert's death and Roger's departure from England.

125. To Roger bishop of Worcester.

Sept. 1164 x c.Oct. 1178. ? Commission to hear the case between Richard archdeacon of Wiltshire, and the monks of Gloucester, about tithes of the demesne of Robert of Ewyas in *Cliva*.

> See App. I, 26, where the case is discussed.

126. To (Roger) bishop of Worcester and R(obert) bishop of Hereford.

Dec. 1174 x Sept. 1179. Commission to hear the case between Stoneleigh Abbey and Kenilworth Priory about tithes of Stoneleigh.

> J(ohn) prior of Trentham (?1155 x ?1181) informs the bishops about a composition over tithes, confirmed by the late Bishop Walter (of Coventry, d. 1159) (BL MS Add. 47677 (Kenilworth cart.) fo. 128ʳ). Though the bishop of Worcester's initial appears to be written as 'A', this is impossible, since Bishop Alfred was not contemporary with any Bishop 'R' of Hereford. If the order of precedence is correct, the date of the commission must be as above.

APPENDIX III

THE PRIORS OF GREAT MALVERN, 1177–1191

Differing accounts have been given of the clash between Bishop Roger and the abbot of Westminster over the institution of the prior of Great Malvern. The crux of the matter is: did Roger institute a prior? Master Silvester, Roger's clerk, who claimed to have been present, stated that he did, and it will be as well to have his words before us:

Universis sancte matris ecclesie filiis, magister Silvester B. dei gratia Cant' archiepiscopi clericus salutem in domino. Noverit universitas vestra quod cum tempore bone memorie Rogeri quondam Wigorn' episcopi domini mei W. abbas Westm' W. priorem Malvern' auctoritate propria absque consensu episcopi clanculo instituisset, idem episcopus prefatum priorem suspendit, eumque suspensum tenuit donec idem abbas et prior ei de excessu suo satisfecerunt, ita quod omnibus que circa institutionem prioris facta fuerunt in irritum redactis, iussu prenominati episcopi per officiales suos institutus est. Cum itaque propter iter peregrinationis susceptum ad testandam veritatem cui interfui presentialiter interesse non possim, ad veritatis testimonium presentes litteras sub sigilli mei testimonio relinquo.[1]

Silvester's statement is supported by a letter of Gilbert Foliot who asks Bishop Roger to show favour to W. 'who, as I hear, you have already admitted and made prior on the election of the brethren of Malvern'. Foliot refers to the new prior's learning and virtue, and specifically to his humility, which would be appropriate after, but surely not before, his submission to the bishop of Worcester.[2] It should be noticed that both Silvester and Foliot refer to the prior as W.; the editors of Foliot's letters supply W(alter).

On the basis of Silvester's evidence and Foliot's letter, it would be reasonable to assume that Bishop Roger instituted a prior of Great Malvern at some time between July 1177, when the previous prior (another Roger) was elected abbot of Burton, and the bishop's death in August 1179. A prior William occurs

---

[1] *Worc. cart.*, p. 158 no. 301.
[2] *Letters of Foliot*, p. 311 no. 239 and notes.

in the Westminster records in 1184 x 1186, as noted by the editors of Foliot's letter, which agrees with the W. of our two texts. Why then did the editors of Foliot's letter call him Walter, and why did the compilers of *Heads of Religious Houses* list Walter (p. 90) as prior from *c*.1177 to *c*.1216, saying that he presumably succeeded Roger, but was not formally instituted until 1191?

A prior Walter was indeed instituted in the summer of 1191. Some years later, perhaps in 1194, he made and recorded a formal admission (*in iure confessi sumus*) that he had received the cure of souls and the administration of spiritualities in the church of Malvern from Robert, bishop of Worcester, in the presence of the lord William, bishop of Ely and papal legate.[3] It seems at first surprising that the institution of the prior of a cell in the west country took place in the presence of William Longchamp, the greatest man in England in both Church and State. Longchamp at that time was justiciar as well as legate; King Richard was in the Holy Land, and there was no archbishop of Canterbury. The obvious explanation is that once again there had been dispute over the status of Malvern Priory, with Abbot Walter of Westminster renewing his attempt to establish the exemption of the cell from the jurisdiction of the bishop of Worcester, and the bishop fighting to maintain his rights. The dispute could have come before the legate either by direct appeal, or by delegation from the pope, or the legate may have mediated between the parties.

Master Silvester's statement about the episode in Bishop Roger's time was made in writing because he could not give evidence in person on account of the pilgrimage which he had undertaken. Silvester was then in the service of Archbishop Baldwin, who left for the Holy Land in March 1190; perhaps Silvester went with him, and this was the *iter peregrinationis* which prevented him from testifying in person. All the pieces of evidence fall into place if it can be accepted that Bishop Roger instituted a prior, probably named William, in 1177 x 1179, and that this prior died, fell ill, or resigned early in 1190.

---

[3] *Worc. cart.*, p. 160 no. 303. Bishop Robert was consecrated by William Longchamp on 5 May 1191. Longchamp should have ceased to call himself legate when the news reached England of the death of Pope Clement III late in Mar., but at some uncertain date his commission was renewed by Pope Celestine III.

The bishop of Worcester at that time was William of Northolt, who had been archdeacon of Gloucester in Bishop Roger's last years. He must have asked for Silvester's evidence as ammunition for Worcester in the next round of litigation with the abbot Westminster. There is nothing here that requires us to suppose that a Prior Walter was elected to Great Malvern $c.1177$ and remained without formal institution till 1191.

The source of the trouble seems to be a transcript of Master Silvester's statement in the register of Bishop Godfrey Giffard.[4] Giffard, like so many bishops of Worcester, was involved in litigation over Great Malvern; his clerks collected evidence to support his case, and copied various items into his register among documents of the year 1283. The first item is Silvester's statement, the second the record of Prior Walter's admission in 1191. The copyist assumed that the W. of the first text was the Walter of the second, and extended the name accordingly; he also made confusion worse confounded by adding to Silvester's statement the words 'anno domini m. c. sexagesimo quinto'—an impossible date, since at that time the abbot of Westminster was L(aurence), not W(alter), and there was not, so far as is known, a vacancy at Malvern. The Worcester antiquary William Thomas reproduced Silvester's statement in his work on Great Malvern.[5] His text is taken from Giffard's register; he too gives the date 1165 and extends the prior's name to Walter.

Taken as a whole, the evidence makes it all but certain that no reliance can be placed upon the name and the date added to the copy of Silvester's statement in Giffard's register. If this interpretation is correct, there were two priors of Great Malvern: W., probably William, elected $c.1177$ and instituted by order of Bishop Roger before—at latest—9 August 1179, and Walter, elected $c.1190$ and instituted by Bishop Robert in the summer of 1191.[6]

---

[4] *Register of Bishop Godfrey Giffard*, calendared by J. W. Willis Bund (Worcs. Hist. Soc., 1902), ii. 198 (from fo. 179^r).
[5] William Thomas, *Antiquitates Prioratus Majoris Malvernie* (1725), appendix, Chart. orig., pp. 96–7.
[6] *VCH Worcs.*, ii. 138 states briefly that there were two priors, both named Walter.

APPENDIX IV

ITINERARY OF BISHOP ROGER

In expressing dates a hyphen indicates duration of time, while × indicates a point in time between two limiting dates.

1163
May 19–21	Tours	above, p. 15

1164
Jan. 14–19	Clarendon	above, p. 22
Aug. 23	Canterbury	ibid.
Oct. 6–20	Northampton	above, pp. 22–5
Nov. 2	Portsmouth	*MTB*, iii. 70
c. Nov. 5	St Omer	*MTB*, iii. 331
c. Nov. 12–16	Compiègne	ibid. p. 332
c. Nov. 25–7	Sens	ibid. p. 335–8 and above, p. 27
Dec. 24	Marlborough	*MTB*, iii. 75

1165
Feb. 2	Worcester	*Ann. Mon.*, i. 49, iv. 381
Mar. 14	Bath	App. I, 72
? Aug.	Oswestry	above, p. 28
? Dec.	Oxford	App. I, 16

1166
? Jan.	Oxford	App. I, 16

1167
c. Nov. 27–9	Argentan	above, p. 35
Dec.	? Tours	above, p. 38

1168
	? Tours	ibid.

1169
Jan.–Aug.	? Tours	ibid.
Sept. 1	Bures (near Bayeux)	*MTB*, vii. 72, 80
Sept. 8	Caen	*MTB*, vii. 75
c. Sept. 10	Rouen	*MTB*, vii. 80
Oct.–Dec.	? Tours	above, p. 38

1170
Jan.–May	? Tours	ibid.
c. June 7	Dieppe	*MTB*, iii. 103
c. June 21	Falaise	ibid.
July 21–2	Fréteval (near Vendôme)	*MTB*, iii. 107–8

APPENDIX IV

Aug.–Dec.	? Tours	above, p. 38
1171		
Jan. 25	Sens	above, p. 51
Early Mar.	Siena	*MTB*, vii. 471
After Mar. 28	Tusculum	ibid. p. 477
? July	Ste-Barbe-en-Auge	App. I, 7
Aug. 6	Winchester	above, p. 53
Aug.–Dec.	? Tours	above, p. 10
1172		
Jan.–Apr.	? Tours	above, p. 10
May 21	? Avranches	above, p. 54
Aug. 24	Southampton	ibid.
Aug. 27	Winchester	ibid.
Sept. 8	(to Normandy)	ibid.
Sept. 27	? Avranches	ibid.
Oct.	? (to England)	ibid.
1173		
Feb.	? London	*Gervas. Cant.*, i. 241 and above, p. 214–5
? Mar. 25 × Dec. 31	Salisbury	App. I, 51n
Late Apr.	? London	*Gervas. Cant.*, i. 243
June 3	? Westminster	ibid. i. 243
June 9–10	Canterbury	ibid. i. 244–5
Mid Aug. × mid Sept.	Bristol	App. I, 67n
Oct. 16	Bath	App. I, 60
Nov. 15	Reading	App. I, 69
1174		
? Jan. 1 × Mar. 24	Salisbury	App. I, 51n
July 14 × 19	Westminster	above, p. 217–8
Oct. 5–6	? Canterbury	*Gervas. Cant.*, i. 251
Nov. 12	Warwick	App. I, 37
Nov. 22	London	App. I, 54
1175		
Feb. 10	Newbury	App. I, 37
Apr. 9	Worcester	App. I, 77–9
May 11–18	Westminster	above, p. 218
June 25	Lambeth	App. I, 53
July *c.* 1–9	Woodstock	above, p. 215
Aug. 10	? York	*Hoveden*, i. 79
Aug. 23 or Sept. 22	Worcester	App. I, 13
? Oct.	Worcester	*Worc. cart.*, p. 133, no. 149
1176		
March 13–18	Westminster/Fulham	App. I, 56, 58
? Sept. 6	Fladbury	App. I, 20
Oct. 6	Droitwich	App. I, 15
Oct. 17	? Circencester	above, p. 61n
Nov. 7	Canterbury	*Gervas. Cant.*, i. 260

APPENDIX IV

1177
Jan. 17	Warwick	App. I, 59
Jan. 20 or 25	Windsor	App. I, 46
Mar. 14–19	Westminster	App. I, 28
? Sept. 6	Fladbury	App. I, 20
Nov. 14	Leigh, near Worcester	App. I, 62

1178
Mar. 16	Henbury in Salt Marsh	App. I, 34
Apr. 14	Worcester	App. I, 32
June 25	Alvechurch	App. I, 11
Sept. 24	Alvechurch	App. I, 2
Nov. 3–4	Worcester	App. I, 12, 83
Dec. 25	Winchester	above, p. 223

1179
c. Jan. 1	(to France)	above, p. 223–4
Early Jan.	Paris	ibid.
Aug. 9	Marmoutier (death)	ibid.

GENERAL INDEX

Numbers in this index refer to pages. Persons, and places if identified, appear in their modern English forms. Patronymics appear under the name of the son. Ecclesiastical office-holders are indexed under their personal names, or the place-names by which they were known: thus John of Salisbury, treasurer of Exeter and bishop of Chartres, appears under Salisbury. For place-names, the pre-1974 county is noted first, followed by the post-1974 county if different.

The following abbreviations are used: ab. = abbot, abbess; bp = bishop; ch. = church; dn = deacon; pr. = prior; HW = Hereford and Worcester (county of).

Abel 308
Abelard, Peter 60
Abingdon (Berks./Oxon.), Ben. abbey 119, 234
Absalon 97, 311
absolution, effect of 58–64
Adam ab. of Evesham 67–8, 84, 90–1, 255–7; as judge-delegate 126, 130–1, 146, 247, 277, 291, 300, 325, 330, 335, 345, 355–6, 358, 362, 369–72; as witness 287
—— Philip, his seneschal 255
— ab. of Shrewsbury 296, 371
— bp of St Asaph 308, 328
— clerk, of Badmondisfield 143, 282, 366
—— of Luton 285
—— of bp of Worcester 104, 296, 308, 310
— *recte* Alan 352
Adrian IV, pope 119–20, 168, 274, 349
advowson *see* patronage
Ailmer, chaplain 301
Ailred ab. of Rievaulx 67
Ailric archdn of Worcester 307
Alan 308
— ab. of Tewkesbury 23, 26
— clerk, of Glen 247
— Mr, of Idsall 340–1

and see Hurstbourne, Stretton on Fosse
Alanus Anglicus, canonist 61
Albert, papal subdn and *nuntius* 221
Albinus, ab. of Darley 246
— priest 326
Alcester (Warws.), Ben. abbey 342, 347
Aldomaro, Robert de 304
Aldrintona (? Alderton, Glos.)
— Bertram of 256
— Reginald, priest of 256
— Richard of, and Richard his son 255–6
Alexander *cocus* 304
Alexander III, pope 2, 4, 25–7, 29, 32–3, 41–2, 51–4, 57, 70–1, 73, 81, 117, 120, 133, 148, 151, 166–70, 205, Chapter 5 and Appendix II *passim*
Alexander of Luton 285
Alfred bp of Worcester 19, 45, 129, 262, 274
— chaplain 245
— clerk of bp of Worcester 311
and see Alured
Algar, canon (? of Bristol) 267
— steward of bp of Worcester 107
alienation of church property 111, 182

INDEX 381

Allington (Kent), Ralph of 338
Almari, Henry of 267
— Gilbert and Robert of 304
Almondesbury (Glos./Avon), ch. of 237
Alta Ripa *see* Hauterive
Alured ab. of Saint-Pierre-sur-Dives 241
and see Alfred
Alvechurch (Worcs./HW) 107, 236
Ambrose, Mr 285, 341, 345
Amesbury (Wilts.), Ben. abbey 216–7, 367
Amfrid of Bereford 244
Amicus archdn of Rouen 284
Andrew ab. of Cirencester 243
Anstey, Richard of 120
appeals to pope (judicial), Chapters 4, 5, passim
— in first instance 159–60
— motives for 155–8
— on small matters 175–6, 364
— royal licence for 118–20, 159
— *super incidenti questione* 177–8, 364
appropriation 78–9
arbiters 92, 162, 273, 281
archpriest 59, 66
Argentan (Orne) 35
Arlington (Glos.) 270–1
Arnulf bp of Lisieux 14, 47, 51, 54, 123, 208
Arrouaise (Nord) abbey and head of Order 260, 324
Ashby *see* Canons Ashby
Asketil pr of Nostell 279
Ashleworth (Glos.), ch. of 237
Aspravilla (Épreville), Mr William of 273
assarts 111, 182, 321
Aston (Warws./W. Midlands), ch. of 76, 347
— (Worcs./HW), chapel of 105
— (? Aston on Carrant, Glos.) ch. of 299–300
— Eyre (or Astley, Salop) 296–7
— Rowant (Oxon.) 344
Atherstone on Stour (Warws.) 298
Attingham, Mr Nicholas of 247, 270

audientia, audience, court of 91
Augustine, bp of Waterford 277, 236
— — his clerks, Osbert and John 277
— chaplain 237
aureus, pension of 298
Avranches (Manche) settlement at (1172) 54, 131, 150
Azo 294–5

B., messenger of bp of Worcester 124
Badduinus 301
Badmondisfield (Suff.), ch. of 282, 366
Baldwin, J.M.W. 62n, 65
Baldwin de Sancto Genesio 104, 294, 304
— Mr 104, 301, 310
— — archd. of Exeter 36, 41, 104; ab. of Ford 126, 131, 205, 244, 352, 572; bp of Worcester 74, 129, 197–9, 262, 336, 341, 364; archbp of Canterbury 116, 197–9, 374–5
— — of Dredona 104, 235
— — *Exoniensis* 104, 263
— — claimant of archdnry of Wells 32, 104
Baiuin, William 320
Barnstaple (Devon), clergy of archdnry of 72, 132, 139, 331
Barnwell (Cambs.), Aug. priory 333
Barnwood (Glos.) 258
Barre, Richard, archdn of Lisieux 296, 348, 352
Bartholomew archbp of Tours 54, 224
— bp of Exeter 25, 30, 34, 36, 46, 53, 72–3, 95, 101, 192, 201, 213, 217, 221, 260–1, 291, 299, 303, 334; as judge-delegate 2, 116, 130–9, 142, 149, 156, 160, 186, 242, 264, 277, 281–2, 284–5, 318–20, 323–5, 327–8, 331–3, 335–6, 339, 342, 347, 351, 354, 358–9, 361–5, 367, 370, 372; as witness 268, 298

Barton (Glos.), tithes of 258
Basset, Nicholas 343
Bath (Som./Avon) 294, 303
— archdnry of 32, 104
— archdn of *see* Cumin, John
— bp of *see* Reginald, Robert
— see of *see* Wells
— Osbert of 304
— Walter of 235
Bawdeswell (Norf.), chapel of 352
Bec, le (Eure), Ben. abbey 273
— obedientiaries and monks named 273
Beckford (Worcs./HW), ch. of 92, 105, 299–300
— cell of Ste-Barbe-en-Auge at 53
Bedford (Beds.), St Pauls ch. at 154, 277
Bellême, Robert of 6
Benacra, Bernard of 295
benefices, divided 284–5, 330, 366, 339
— hereditary succession to 69–78, 81, 153, 174, 219
— institution to 81–2, 320, 347
— pluralism of 105, 318, 347, 350, 356
and see patronage, vicarage
Benevento, Peter of 194
Berkeley (Glos.), Roger and Maurice of 261–2
— Hernesse, churches of 237
Bermondsey (London), Clun. priory 129, 288–91
Berechurch *see* Colchester
Bernay, Robert of 306
Bernard, clerk 268
Bertram clerk of Verdun 282
Bethune, William of, bp of Hereford 119, 281, 297
Beverstone (Glos.), ch. of 237
bezant, pension of 266
Bibury (Glos.) ch. of 106, 179, 181, 183, 281–2, 311, 334
— John of 308
Biddisham (Som.) 304
Billy (Calvados) 241
Bishops Cannings (Wilts.) 293–5

Bishop's Cleeve (Glos.), ch. of 106, 110
— Henry of 236
Bisley (Glos.) 270–1
Bisset, Bartholomew and Manaser 276
Blois, Peter of 261
Blund, Geoffrey 106, 298; Robert 306
Bologna, university of 167, 169, 194, 208
Boraston (Salop) 306–7
Bordesley (Worcs./HW), Cist. abbey 235–6; abbot of, Hamo 302; monks of, named 244
Bosham, Herbert of 1–2, 11, 20–1, 24–5, 28, 37–8, 56
Boxley (Kent), Cist. abbey, abbot of 319
Bradenstoke (Wilts.), Aug. priory, prior of 356
Brai, William of 280
Bram, village of 97, 363
Bredhurst (Kent) 338
Bretteville l'Orgueilleuse (Calvados) ch. of 240–1
Bridlington (Yorks., E. Riding/Humberside) Aug. priory, prior of 338
Bristol (Glos./Avon) 225
— Aug. abbey 237, 298–9; prior *see* William
— castle 7, 225
— Ben. priory of St James 8, 299
Brito, Alan and Alan, his uncle 366
— Ralph, knight 329, 365–6
— William 292
Bromfield (Salop), Ben. priory 75
Brooke, Z.N. 211
Brueland, Bruerland (? in Normandy), ch. of 273
Bruern (Oxon.) Cist. abbey 343
Buckworth (Hunts./Cambs.), ch. of 140, 143, 324–5, 355
Bungay (Suff.), ch. of 136, 140, 202, 318, 328, 347, 362
Burbage (Wilts.), ch. of 116, 153, 296, 348–9, 352

Burdel, Robert 282–3
burial rights 297, 326
Bury St Edmunds (Suff.) Ben. abbey 114–15, 161, 187–9, 238–40, 368; abbot of 137, 317, 324 *and see* Samson
Butenn, Henry 292
Bywell St Peter (Northumb.), ch. of 252–5
— Salomon, priest of 252

Caddington (Beds.), ch. of 350–1
— Minor, Odo prebendary of 351
Caen (Calvados), Ben. abbey of Holy Trinity 100
— Ben. abbey of St Stephen 240–1, 353
— Henry of 236
Caenegem, R.C. van 62n, 96, 148n, 159n
Caesarius of Heisterbach 175n
Calne, Mr Philip of 40
Cambrai (Nord) Odo bp of 200–1
Cambritona, chapel of 340
Campaines, Hugh of 291
Camped', Robert of 257
Camville, Richard of 302–3
candle, as payment 274
Canons Ashby (Northants.), Aug. priory 329, 341, 345
Canterbury (Kent)
— cathedral ch. and Ben priory
— — archbps of *see* Baldwin, Richard, Thomas, Stephen
— — archdns of *see* Ridel, Geoffrey; Herbert
— — prior and convent of 149, 218, 338–9
— — monks of, chroniclers, Gervase 7–8, William 20
— Ben. abbey of St Augustine 88–9, 119, 242, 332
— — abbots elect of *see* Clarembald, Roger
Cardunvilla, Mr Hugh of 270
Careville, William of 143, 282, 366
Carisbrooke (Isle of Wight), Ben. priory 242–3

Carlton Curlieu (Leics.) 338
Carnadon (Cornwall) 268
Castle Acre (Norf.), Clun. priory 336, 353; Jordan pr of 353; Simon, proctor of 336
Cecilia, countess *see* Hereford
celibacy *see* clergy
Chamberlains of bp of Worcester, Matthew, Roger, Osmund, Stephen 107; Gervase 308
chaplains, of king, N. 140 *and see* Wimer
— of bp of Worcester 103–6 *and see* Gilbert, Robert, Robert Monk
Charing (Kent), Ivo of 338
Charlton-on-Otmoor (Oxon.) 338
Chedworth (Glos.), ch. of 79, 270–3
Chester, bpric *see* Coventry
Chichester (Sussex), bp of *see* Hilary, John 'of Greenford'
— dean of *see* John 'of Greenford'
— Willaim of 294–5
Chiev, Chine, Chyv, Mr William of 270
— Alfred of 304
Chinchebouuilla, Richard of 240–1
chirograph 231, 305
Chiray (? Chimay) William of 291
Cirencester (Glos.), Aug. abbey 61n, 80–1, 243
— ab. of 131, 335, Andrew 243
— canons named 243
citations (*edicta*) 160–61
Clarembald ab. of Faversham 135, 242, 319, 323, 332
— ab. elect of St Augustine's, Canterbury 134–5, 180, 242, 323, 332
Clarendon (Wilts.), Council of (1164) 20, 142
— Constitutions of 22, 49, 118, 126, 139–40, 150, 159, 350
Claverdon (Warws.), ch. of 105
Cleeve *see* Bishops Cleeve
Clement pr. of Lanthony 237
clergy, celibacy and marriage of 68–77, 139, 219, 348
— accused of crime 141, 183–4

Clermont (? C. Ferrand, Puy-de-Dôme) 208
Clevancy, Clive Wancy (Wilts.) 249
Clifton, Robert of 308
Cliva *see* Bishops Cleeve
Colchester (Essex), dean of *see* Thomas
— churches of Holy Trinity and Berechurch 238–40, 368
— Ben. priory of St Botolph 373
Cold Brayfield (Bucks.), ch. of 146, 259, 324
Collectio Alcobacensis I 142, 203–7
— *Appendix Concilii Lateranensis* 196
— *Belverensis* 197, 202
— *Florianensis* 202
— *Parisiensis I* 205
— *Regalis* 197
— *Wigorniensis* 102, 142, 184, 198–200
— *Wigorniensis altera* 200–1
Collingham 360
composition, *compositio, conventio, pactio, transactio* 241, 243, 246, 248, 269, 277, 280, 285, 291, 294, 300, 325, 329, 338, 343
Conan ab. of Margam 291
Conches (Eure), Ben. abbey 74–5, 78–9, 244–6, 346; Thomas, monk of 244
confirmation, papal:
— of election 350
— of possessions 119, 155, 180–1, 183, 345
— of sentence 158
— of *transactio* 295
Cormeilles (Eure) Ben. abbey, ab. of 106
Cornwall, Reginald earl of 8, 268; Nicholas his son 268
Corringham (Lincs.) 360
Costock (Notts), chapel of 343
Coston', Geoffrey of 306
Coughton (Warws.), ch. of 204
Coventry (Warws./W. Midlands)
— archdn of *see* Ralph of Tamworth
— bp of 145, 246, 340 *and see* Peche, Richard

— pr. of 249 *and see* Walter, Laurence
Crich (Derbys.), manor of 146, 246; ch. of 246
Cricklade (Wilts.) 129, 289
— Robert of, pr. of St Frideswides 9, 21
— Waleran, Galerandus, of 243
criminous clerks *see* clergy
Cristina, sister, of Southwark 298
Cromhall (Glos./Avon), ch. of 237
cross, crusader's, 326
Crowland (Lincs.), Ben. abbey, Robert ab. of 288
Crowle (Worcs./ HW) 270–1
Cubton', ch. of 359
Cumin, Cumyn, Gilbert 266–7
— John 32, 280
— Walter 244, 300
— William 300
custom, validity of 178, 322, 364

Daniel 306
— chaplain 237
— pr. of Ste-Barbe-en-Auge 53, 240–2
Darley (Derbys.) Aug. abbey 145–6, 246–7, 368–9 *and see* Albinus, ab. of
Daventry (Northants.), Clun. priory 132, 146, 247–9, 369
David bp of St Davids 30
David, Mr, of London 10, 106, 115, 177, 201, 207–8, 249–51
Dean Colebrand 307
— Ernald of Sumerford 276
— Henry of Leckhampton 265
— Nicholas (? of Berkeley) 237
— Richard (? of Warwick) 301
— Thomas of Colchester 238
— Walter (? of Worcester) 309 *and see under bprics*
Debenham (Suff.), William of 292
debt, to Roman merchants 326
decretals, Chapter 5 *passim and see: Collection*
Dene (Flaxley, Glos.), Cist. abbey 346

INDEX

Denebold, Ralph and Robert 304
Derby, earls of *see* Ferrars
Diceto, Ralph of, archdn of Middlesex, 3, 14, 250-1
Dinsley *see* St Ippollitts
dispensation 332, 345
Dives (Calvados), William of 291
Dodderhill (in Droitwich, Worcs./HW)
— St Augustine's ch. 78, 93, 95, 247, 307-8
— — Adam, parson, and Ernulf, vicar of 310
— — Wilfwy, priest of 307
Doddenham (Worcs./HW) 306
Dodford (Northants.), ch. of 146, 275
dominus fundi 148, 303
Doulting (Som.) 364
Drichestuna *see* Atherstone
Droitwich (Worcs./HW)
— ch. of St Mary 76, 98, 143, 326, 348
— saltpit in 93, 307
Dudicote near Beckford (Glos.) 299-300
duel, judicial 61-5
Duggan, Charles 203, 209, 212
Dumbleton (Glos.), ch. of 234
— Geoffrey of 235
Dunbar, Adam of 252
Dunstable (Beds.), Aug. priory, Thomas, pr. of 177
Dunstanvill, Richard of 372
Duntisborne Abbotts (Glos.) 270-1
Durham, Cathedral and Ben. priory 137, 186, 251-5, 325 *and see* Hugh du Puiset, bp of

East Grinstead (Sussex), ch. of 320
East Halton (Lincs./Humberside), ch. of 337
Edlingham (Northumb.), ch. of 252-5
Edward 'the Confessor', king of England 208
— pr. of Reading 270
Eldersfield (Worcs./HW) 270-1

Eleanor queen of England 47
Elias, Mr 280
Elmore (Glos.), chapel of 262
Elstow (Beds.), Ben. nunnery 337
Ely (Cambs.), cathedral ch. of,
— archdn *see* William
— bps *see* Nigel; Longchamp, William; Ridel, Geoffrey
Emma, ab. of St Mary's, Winchester 183, 331
Enderby (Wood Enderby, Lincs.) 290
Engelerius, clerk 252
Erardus, Mr 296
Ernald de bosco 291
Erwarton (Suff.), Robert, chaplain of 291
Escrop, Richard of 307
Essex, Robert archdn of 336
— Mr Raymond vice-archdn of 239
Estona *see* Aston
Eugenius III, pope 100, 119, 138, 171n, 183, 281, 344
Eustace, Mr, of Hereford 261, 266, 296
Evertona *see* Erwarton
Evesham (Worcs./HW), Ben. abbey 80, 84, 255-7 *and see* Adam, ab. of
Ewias, Harold and Robert of 259
exceptio 123, 162, 176, 248
exemption, monastic 84-8, 138-9, 223
Exeter (Devon) cathedral ch. of
— archdn of 131 *and see* Baldwin
— bps of *see* Bartholomew, William
— canon of *see* Peter
— treasurer of *see* Salisbury, John of

Falda, Richard of 285
Feckenham (Worcs./HW), ch. of 79, 270-3
Felsham (Suff.), Absalon, Henry and Richard of 291
Feria prati 241
Fernham, ch. of 345
Ferrars, William of, earl of Derby 145, 368

FitzStephen, William 7, 13, 18, 23–6, 37, 47–8
Fladbury (Worcs./HW) 107; ch. of 255; Roger priest and Adam clerk of 255
Flamang, William 304
Flammeville, Mr William of 304, 365, 367
Flaxley *see* Dene
Foliot, Gilbert bp of London 4, 11–12, 18–35 *passim*, 42, 50, 61, 68–9, 82–3, 100–1, 155, 197, 205, 207, 213–4, 217, 220, 238, 250–1, 260–1, 284, 303, 341, 374–5; as judge-delegate 115, 119, 130–1, 134, 137, 140–1, 248, 277, 280–1, 318, 322–3, 326, 330, 336, 342, 344, 347–8, 353, 356–7, 361, 367
— Ralph 296
— Richard 266
— Robert bp of Hereford 73, 95, 129, 131–2, 142, 205, 222, 247, 274, 288–91, 296, 303, 343, 351, 355, 361, 363, 367, 370–1, 373
— — Roger and Reginald his chaplains 261
— — his clerks named 292
Fontevrault (Maine-et-Loire), abbey of 95, 217, 367
forgery of papal letters 185, 281, 340–1, 345, 356
Foreville, Raymonde 15, 17, 211
Forthampton (Glos.) 270–1
forma, certa forma, in papal letters 122–4, 322, 324–5, 358, 366, 371
Fowlmere (Cambs.), ch. of 177
Foxton (Leics.), ch. of 247
franklins 288
Frêteval (Loir-et-Cher) 49
Fritheric 307
Fruschelu, John 91, 234
Fulc', Mr 235
Fulham, Robert of 291

G., clerk 359 *and see* Stretton on Fosse
G., Mr, of Aileston, vice-archdn 357

Gamlingay (Cambs.), ch. of 132, 373
Gayton (Norf.) 353
gemipunctus in papal letters 128
Geoffrey, archdn of Lincoln 201, bp elect 215, 350
— archdn of Salisbury 294
— dean of Hereford 266, 293–5, 371
— franc 304
— Mr, of Fulri 311
— son of Robert 304
— of Warnestan (-ston) 236, 255 *and see* Ridel
Gerald of Wales 2, 4, 11, 38, 116–17, 124, 126, 131, 133, 323
Gerard the tanner 297–8
Gervase *see* Canterbury
Gidding (Hunts./Cambs.) 351
Giffard, Godfrey bp of Worcester 108, 376
— William 282, 345, 349
Gilbert, chaplain of Salisbury 294
— chaplain of bp of Worcester 103, 106; as witness 236, 245, 257, 263–7, 241, 244–5, 271, 282, 287, 295, 302, 310–11
— Mr 280
Giles bp of Evreux 51, 54, 224, 273, 369
Girold 111
Glanvill, Rannulf 65n, 145–6
Glastonbury, Richard of 304
Gloucester (Glos.)
— archdns of *see* Matthew, Northolt
— Aug. priory of St Oswald 37, 85–7
— Ben. abbey, 58, 75, 78–82, 87, 190, 237, 258–9, 373; ab. of 281
— castle chapel 262
— churches in, Holy Trinity 267; St John's 258; St Mary's 78, 258; St Michael's 267; St Owen's 262
— reeve of 267
— school in 262
— Robert earl of 1, 6–8, 46–7; Mabilia his wife 7
— William earl of 8, 13, 22, 225; Robert his son 8, 13, 339

— William of, clerk of bp of Worcester 104, 235, 256, 291
Godardus, William 304
Godfrey, Mr 93, 308, 311
Godfrey archdn of Worcester 100, 103, 304
Goldcliff (Monmouth/Gwent), Ben. priory 8
Grafton, Richard of 94, 309
Gratian, papal legate 44
Great Malvern (Worcs./HW), Ben. priory 85, 374–5
Great Leighs (Essex), ch. of 340
Great Washbourne (Glos.), chapel of 299
Gregory I, pope 125
Gregory IX, pope 169
Grim, Mr Edward 20
Guernes of Pont-Sainte-Maxence 20, 38–9
Guibert ab. of Gembloux 225
Guilden Morden (Cambs.) 333

Habendona, William of 236
Hackford (Norf.), ch. of 351–2
Halford (Warws.) 288
Hamo ab. of Bordesley 302
Hampton Lucy (Warws.), manor of 109
Hanley Castle (Worcs./HW), ch. of 79, 270–3
Harbledown (Kent), hospital of 218
Hardwick (Beds.) 356
Hardwick (Worcs./HW) 311
Haresfield (Glos.), ch. of 263–4
Hariulf ab. of Oudenburg 133
Harlington (Middlesex/London), ch. of 132, 366
Harrold (Beds.), Aug. priory 146, 259–60
— ch. of 324
Hartlebury (Worcs./HW), ch. of 97, 311–12
— manor of 107
Hasteng, Aytropius 279–80, Robert 280
Hastings, William of 325, 355

Hatherop (Glos.), ch. of 258
Hauterive, Mr Ralph of 134, 155, 281, 340–1
Hedeleia, Ralph of 295
Hel., clerk 362
Hempstead (Glos.), chapel of 262
— demesne of Lire in 270–1
Henbury in Salt Marsh (Glos./Avon) 267
— Osbert of 311
Henry I, king of England 6, 117–18, 268
Henry II, king of England 2, 7–8, 14, Chapter 2 passim, 86–8, 118, 120, 126, 139, 149–51, 207, 217, 224, 261, 276, 286, 350, 355–6
Henry the Young King 45, 54, 150, 213–14
— archbp of Reims 123, 127, 201, 210n
— archdn of Huntingdon 119
— bp of Bayeux 28
— of Blois bp of Winchester 11, 20–1, 23, 35, 45, 50, 53, 116, 119, 139, 171n, 321, 331
— bp of Worcester 306
— Mr 256
— of Hereford 263–4
— son of Adam 75–6, 342, 347
— son of Peter of Northampton 279
Henstridge (Som.), ch. of 302–3
Herbert 327
— doorkeeper of bp of Worcester 107
— archdn of Canterbury 261
— knight 351
— Mr 183, 331
and see Bosham
hereditary succession see benefices
Hereford (Hercfs./HW)
— bps of see Robert (of Bethune); Robert (of Melun); Foliot, Robert
— cathedral ch. of 147, 260–2, 256
— — canon of 266
— — dean of 131, 274 and see Geoffrey
— — prebend of 260–1, 355–6
— earl of, Hugh de Lacy 264, 354

—— Roger, William of Poitou, Walter of Mayenne, husbands of the countess Cecilia 144, 147, 264–5, 354
heretics 68–9
Herlo constable of the bp of Worcester 107
Hertford (Herts.), Ben. priory 372
Heselcrofta 268–70
Heveningham (Suff.), ch. of 291
Hewelsfield (Glos.), chapel of 274
Hilary bp of Chichester 25, 29, 35, 99, 132, 249, 366
Holcot (Beds.), ch. of 148, 154, 277–8
— Nicholas parson of 277
Horton, tithes of 186, 333
Hospitallers, Order of Knights 356
Hostehulle see Oxhill
Hoveden, Howden, Roger of 3
Hubert son of Ralph 246
Hugh ab. of Bury 362
— archdn of Worcester 307
— du Puiset, bp of Durham 30, 222, 253–5, 340, 343
— (St) bp of Lincoln 56, 116, 124, 137
— clerk 358
—— of Evesham 255
—— claimant of Sutton 319
— dean of St Pauls, London 280, 370
— Mr, claimant of Whittlesea 135, 163, 317, 329, 352
— parson of Sandy 153, 278, 322, 360
— (Parvus) of Moreton 95, 147–8, 260–1, 363
—— Roger his father 260
— son of Ralph 246
— son of the chancellor 270
— son of Osbert and his family 306–7
Humbald pr. of Wenlock 297
Hunfridus of Caune 292
Hundred, decision of 110
Huntingdon (Hunts./Cambs)
— archdn see Henry, Nicholas

— Aug. priory 142, 339
— Simon of Senlis earl of 323
— honour of 322
Hurstbourne, Husseburna, Alan of 161, 296, 348–9, 352–3

Ickleton (Cambs.), Ben. priory 177
Ilbert of Northon' 304
incense, payment in 286
Ilchester, Richard of 286, archdn of Poitiers 43, 65, 305–6, 371, bp of Winchester 72, 87, 177, 204
indulgences 59–64
Inglesham, Mr Richard of 263
— Robert of archdn of Surrey 268–9
Ingulph ab. of Abingdon 119
Innocent II, pope 133, 168, 171n
Innocent III, pope 66, 72, 137, 175n, 178–9
Inspeximus 112, 231
Ippollitts see St Ippollitts
Isham (Hunts./Cambs), ch. of 142, 339
Ivo, Yvo, archdn of Rouen 284
— Mr, of Cornwall 296
Iz' see Les Ifs

Jocelin bp of Salisbury 19, 30, 33, 35, 50, 149, 171n, 259, 293–5, 336, 352, 357, 364
— de Insula 242–3
Joel of Vautort 95, 143–4, 160, 283–4, 334–5, 344; Reginald his grandfather 334
John of Canterbury, treasurer of York 9, bp of Poitiers 28, 44, 281
— of Coutances, bp of Worcester 298
— of Pagham, bp of Worcester 144, 179, 262, 266, 282, 334, 354
— 'of Greenford', dean of Chichester 282, 360; bp of Chichester 214–15, 303, 320, 332, 344, 352
— pr. of Trentham 373
— son of Richildis 304
and see Oxford, Salisbury
Jordan pr. of Castle Acre 353
— of Worcester 301

INDEX

Karneduna *see* Carnadon
Kemest' (? Kempstone, Norf.), 345
Kempsey (Worcs./HW) 107, 110
Ken, John of 304
Kenilworth (Warws.), Aug. priory 80, 242, 256–7, 333, 373; prior 274 *and see* Robert; sacristan, Henry 342
Kerry, Ken (Montgomerys./Powys), ch. of 328
Keynsham (Som./Avon)
— Aug. abbey 13, 339; William ab. of 294
— ch. of 13
Kidderminster (Worcs./HW), ch. of 275–6
— Robert parson of 275–6
Kingston Lacy (Dorset) 274
Kirkham (Yorks. N. Riding/N. Yorks) Aug. priory, canons named 280
knights' fees, of Bpric of Worcester 108–9
— of earls of Gloucester 48
Knightwick (Worcs./HW), chapel of 306

Lacy *see* Hereford, earl of
Lambeth (Surrey/London) 284
Langley Marish (Bucks.), ch. of 258
Lanthony (Glos.), Aug. priory 80, 90, 119, 144, 147, 191, 262–7, 354; pr. Clement 237, Roger 266
Lateran councils, II, 71; III, 7n, 148, 221–2; IV, 66, 112
Launceston (Cornwall), Aug. priory 268
Laurence ab. of Westminster 367
Laurence pr. of Coventry 281
Lavendon (Bucks.), Prem. abbey 259
Leaveland (Kent), chapel of 319
Leckhampton (Glos.), Henry dean of 263
Lega *see* Great Leighs
legitimacy, litigation over 138, 149, 327

Leicester, Aug. abbey, ab. of 338, 342, 347
— Robert (d. 1168) earl of 28
— Robert (d. 1190) earl of 129, 138, 146, 274, 288–91
— — Robert his chaplain 291
— William of, *scriptor* 245
Lenton (Notts.), Clun. priory 361
Lepers 275, 346
Les Ifs, Iz' (Calvados) 241
Lewes (Sussex), Clun. priory 268–70, 367
Lideham, Walter of 295
Lilleshall (Salop), Aug. abbey, ab. of 342, 347
Lincoln, cathedral ch. of
— bps of *see* Geoffrey, Robert, Hugh
— canons of: R. 353, William 350
— dean of 355
— prebend in 207
Linleia, William of 285
Lire (Eure) Ben. abbey 78–9, 225, 242–3, 259, 270–4
— ab. of 287, Osbert 106
— monks of, named 271
and see Carisbrooke
Lisieux (Calvados), bp *see* Arnulf; archdn *see* Barre, Richard
litis contestatio 161
Littleton, Lutletona (? Glos.), chapel of 234
Lombard, Mr Ralph 296
— Peter 9
Londinton, Hugh of 244
London, bp of, dean of province 29 *and see* Foliot, Gilbert
— dean of St Pauls, Hugh 280
— ch. of St Bartholomew, Smithfield 291
— soke of bp of Worcester in 106, 297–8
Longchamp, William, bp of Ely 375–6
Long Sutton (Lincs.) 336
Louis VII, king of France 9, 26, 39, 54
Lovel *see* Luvel

390 INDEX

Lovetot, Richard of 141, 327–8
Lowys, Mr 285
Lucius III, pope 74, 274, 306, 308, 341, 345, 364
Lucy, Luci, Richard de 28, 43, 155, 269, 340
— Robert de 308
— W. de, dean 362
— Walter de, ab. of Battle 359
Ludlega 362
Luffield (Bucks.), Ben. priory 114, 275
Lumple, Richard 276
Luton (Beds.), ch. of 138, 284–5
— Alexander of 285
Luvel, Richard 257, 264
— Simon 46, archdn of Worcester 46, 99–101, 105, 171n, 199, 249; as witness 247, 257, 259, 263, 267, 270, 276–7, 279, 282, 287–8, 291, 294, 299, 301, 311, 368

Maiden Bradley (Wilts.) hospital of 78–9, 275–6
Maisemore (Glos.) 421
Malmesbury (Wilts.), Ben. abbey 80, 88, 96, 138, 154, 277, 326, 336, 357
— abbot *see* Robert
— William, monk of 125
Malton (Yorks. N. Riding/N. Yorks.), Gilb. priory 129
Mandaville, Mr Peter of 298
Mans, Simon of 306
Mansfield Woodhouse (Notts.), chapel of 358
Manston (Suff.), Robert of 327
Malvern, tithe of forest 271
Map, Walter 261
Margam (Glamorgan), Cist. abbey 8
— Conan ab. of 291
Mark, Merka (Som.) 304
Marmoutier (Indre-et-Loire), Ben. abbey 40, 76, 224–5, 347, 365; Robert ab. of 347
Marny, Robert 237

marriage, problems and litigation 151, 159, 178, 181, 318, 320–1, 330, 349, 355; bans of 318; of clergy *see* clergy; *and see* legitimacy
Marston (Bucks.), ch. of 372
Marston Butlers (Warws.) 288
Marton (Marton-cum-Grafton, Yorks. N. Riding/N. Yorks.) ch. of 365
Matilda the Empress 7, 268, 372
matricula 82–4
Matson (Glos.), ch. of 258
Matthew archdn of Gloucester 100, 257, 264
— de camera, chamberlain 106, 235–6
— Mr 7–8
Mayenne, Walter of *see* Hereford, earl of
Melun, Robert of, bp of Hereford 9–12, 14, 18, 21, 25, 28–31, 33–5, 75, 131–2, 139, 263, 331, 368, 373
Mendlesham (Suff.), ch. of 359
Meppershall (Beds.), ch. of 361
Merka *see* Mark
Merton (Surrey/London), Aug. priory 207n, 275
Milo, clerk 326, 348
Missenden (Bucks.), Aug. abbey, ab. of 341, 345
Monk, Robert, chaplain of bp of Worcester 103, 106; parson of Bps Cleeve 255; as witness 236, 243, 245, 257, 264, 271, 288, 291, 296, 311
Monkton Farleigh (Wilts.) Clun. priory, pr. of 356
Moray, bp of 366
Moreton Valence (Glos.), ch. of 97, 260–1, 363
Morville (Salop), ch. of 297
Moses, Mr 102, 368; as witness 245, 247, 256–7, 259–61, 263–4, 270, 276–7, 280, 282, 287–8, 291, 294, 308, 311
Mowbray, Roger de 137
Mudgley, Mudesleya (Som.) 304
Muntfichet, Gilbert of 146, 258

INDEX 391

Nathaniel, knight 319
necessitas 242, 353
Neufbourg, Novus burgus, Robert of 284
Neville, Alan de 28
Newbold Pacy (Warws.), ch. of 99, 279
Newburgh, William of 3, 68
Newbury (Berks.), ch. of 270
Newchurch (Isle of Wight), vicarage of 242–3
Newent (Glos.), Ben. priory 106
Newhouse, Newsham (Lincs./Humberside), Prem. abbey 337
Newnham (Beds.), Aug. priory 277
Nicholas archdn of Huntingdon 140, 277, 324–5, 355
— bp of Llandaff 139, 258
— clerk 185, 358
— clerk of Ravesned' 282
— dean 237
— Mr 183, 292, 331
Nigel bp of Ely 50, 132, 373
— Wireker 215–6
Norfolk, Hugh earl of 139, 321
— sheriff of, *see* Wimer
Northampton, archdn of 159, 330
— archdnry of 350
— Clun. priory of St Andrew 153, 278
— Council of (1164) 22–5
— Mr Henry of 270
Northolt, William of, archdn of Gloucester 101, 265; bp of Worcester 376
Norton (Yorks. N. Riding/N. Yorks) 367
Norwich (Norf.), bp of 324, 341 *and see* William; Oxford, John of
Nostell (Yorks. W. Riding/ W. Yorks.), Aug. priory 78–9, 279
— Asketil, prior of 279
notary-public 179

obedience *see* profession
Odo, ab. of Battle 338
— bp of Cambrai 200
— son of Odo de Chambai 318

Official, officials, of bp of Worcester 105
Osbert ab. of Lire 106
— son of Hugh 93–6, 307–10
Osmerley (Worcs.) 235–6
Osmund the chamberlain 263
— reeve of Gloucester 267
Osney (Oxon.), Aug. abbey 163, 183, 225, 280–2, 311, 318–9, 334, 361
— canons named 282
Otteri, pr. of 335
Oxford (Oxon.) 281
— council at 34, 101, 249
— ch. of St Mary Magdalen 138, 240–1
— St Frideswide's, Aug. priory 138, 163, 280–1, 318–9, 344–5, 361; Robert pr. of 9, 21
— John of, dean of Salisbury 34–5, 249; bp of Norwich 134, 216, 222, 341, 350; his clerks Simon and Hunfrid 292
Oxhill, Hostehulle (Warws.) 288

Painswick, Wyka (Glos.), ch. of 76, 97, 144–5, 148, 264–5
— Roger priest of 145, 264, 354
Pancevot, Pauncevaut, Richard and Reginald 326
Paris, schools of 9–10
— Mr John of 259
— Parisius (personal name) 304, 351
Parvus *see* Hugh
Paschal II, pope 117
Passelewe, Gilbert and Nicholas 277
Patrick, clerk 324–5, 355
patronage of churches 142–8, 165
Paucapalea 200
Pavia, Bernard of 194
Pebworth (Worcs./HW) 288
Peche, Hamo 282–3
— Richard, bp of Coventry 30, 53, 214, 303
Penebrigg (? Panborough, Som.), Paganus of, and Henry his son 304
penitentiary 66
pensions from churches 80–1, 174–5

Pentney (Norf.), Aug. priory 132, 321
— pr. of 129, 139, 353
Pershore (Worcs./HW), Ben. abbey 224
— ab. of 249
Peter bp of St Davids 216, 296, 328
— bp of Winchester 72
— Mr 243
— priest of Tillebroucke 282
— son of Richard 298
Picard, clerk 298
Picot, Mr Peter 298
Piel, R. 339
Pierleoni, Hugh cardinal-deacon of St Angelo 86, 141, 184, 221, 288–91, 303, 340
Pillerton Hersey and P. Priors, Pilardinton (Warws.) 288
Plympton (Devon), Aug. priory 95, 143–4, 186, 283–4, 334, 344; Peter, canon of 331
Poher, Le Poer, Hugh 94, 146, 308–10, 369
Poitou, William of see Hereford, earl of
Pontigny (Yonne), Cist. abbey 27, 31
— Roger of 19
Pont-Audemer, William of 257
possession, judicial treatment of 135, 158, 162–4
— of advowson 145
— *causa rei servandae* 161, 238, 340–1
Potterne (Wilts.) 293–5
Potton (Beds.), ch. of 153, 278, 322–3
Preston (Glos.), Jordan, vicar of 343
Preston Capes (Northants.), ch. of 160, 330
profession of obedience
— of ab. of Malmesbury 336
— of ab. of St Augustine's, Canterbury 223
— of Roger bp of Worcester 22, 228
Pullus, Robert 155, 350–1
purgation 361

Quedgeley (Glos.), chapel of 262
Quinton (Warws.) 287

R. de Bic' 324
R., knight see Brito
Ralph archdn of Winchester 331, 345
— Gansel 104, 237, 266, 282
— Mr 294
— Mr, son of Paganus of Evesham 255
— pr. of Worcester 93–4, 99–100, 249, 264, 279, 282, 297, 309, 368
— son of Stephen 276
Ramsey (Hunts./Cambs.), Ben. abbey
— ab. of 142, 326–7; William 269, 333
Raymond, Mr, vice-archdn of Essex 239
Reading (Berks.), Ben. abbey 237
— Edward, pr. and Lambert, sacrist of 270
— St Mary's ch. at 300
Red Book of Worcester 107–10
Redgrave, Mr Nigel of 285
Reginald archdn of Salisbury 53–4, bp of Bath 214, 222, 299, 303, 357, 364
— precentor of Wells 303–5
Rempstone (Notts.), ch. of 343
Rendham (Suff.), Alfred priest of 292
Revesby (Lincs.), Cist. abbey 360
Richard ab. of St Victor 29, 64
— archbp of Canterbury 74, 85–7, 101, 213–23, 303, 318–19, 332, 336–7, 355; as judge-delegate 131, 185–6, 260–1, 283–4, 319, 324–5, 334–8, 340, 342, 344, 346, 352, 361, 363, 365, 367
— — his clerks, Amicus and William 261
— archdn of Ely 278, 322, 360
— archdn of Wiltshire 259, 373
— bp of Bayeux 6
— bp of Coventry see Peche
— bp of Winchester see Ilchester

INDEX 393

— deacon 330
— dean 301
— dean of Wells 304
— son of Hugh 292
Ridel, Geoffrey archdn of Canterbury 43, bp of Ely 216
Rievaulx (Yorks. N. Riding/ N. Yorks.), Cist. abbey
— ab. of 338, 358, Ailred 67
Rillaton (Cornwall) 268
Robert ab. of Crowland 288, 291
— ab. of Malmesbury 180, 277, 323, 357
— ab. of Mont-Saint-Michel 6, 224
— ab. of St Albans 286
— archdn of Essex 336
— bp of Bath 27, 30, 32, 304, 357
— bp of Hereford *see* Bethune, Melun, Foliot
— bp of Lincoln 337
— bp of Worcester 235, 376
— chaplain of Lench 235
— chaplain of bp of Worcester 103, 106; as witness 236, 245, 256, 261, 265, 267, 288, 291, 296; called Robert of Upton 255, 311
— clerk 358
— de parco 236
— de porta 306
— dean of York 138, 243, 252, 358
— marshal 236
— pr. of Kenilworth 90, 246, 249, 256, 287, 291; as judge-delegate 73, 126, 131, 135, 140, 242–3, 274, 318, 327, 329, 330, 352, 357, 368–9
— son of Richard 91, 96, 266
— son of Robert 296
— son of Turold 295
— son of Warin 373
— son of William 304
— son of William son of Henry 236
Roger ab.-elect of St Augustine's, Canterbury 233, 337
— archbp of York 2, 8, 17, 25, 35, 37, 45–7, 50, 73, 85, 340, 343, 359
— bachelere 246

Roger bp of Worcester, contemporary accounts of 1–4, 56, 215
— — education 8–13; possible influence of Abelard 60, Richard of St Victor 64, Robert of Melun 10
— election 1, 13–14
— — death 223–4, obit celebrated 225
— — household as bp 99–105
— — seal 229–30
— — attitude to clerical celibacy 69–78; lay patronage of churches 147, 190–1; indulgences and theology of absolution 58–64; monastic exemption 84–9, 223
— — relations with Adam ab. of Evesham 67, 130; Pope Alexander III 2, 14, 124–6, 190; John of Salisbury 26, 101; King Henry II 2, 13, Chapter 2 *passim*, 48–9, 216–7; Archbp Richard 192–3; Senatus of Worcester 58–66
— — innovations made by 111–12
— chaplain of St Owen 263
— clerk 325, 348
— cook 107
— Mr, king's clerk 302
— priest, son of Roger 326
— pr. of Bermondsey 288–9
— pr. of Lanthony 266
— son of Everard 295
— son of Fulk 263
— son of Osmund 295
Rolandus 167n, 200 *and see*Alexander III
Rouen (Seine-Maritime) 44
— archbp Rotrou 45, 51, 54, 87
— archdns Ivo, Amicus 284
Rowell (Glos.), ch. of 79, 98
— Mr Henry of 296
Rughedirna, Richard of 295
Rupa, Roger de 298

Safred, the king's doctor 302
St Albans (Herts.), Ben. abbey 137, 186, 251–5, 325, 370
— abbots *see* Robert, Simon
— cellarer 285

St Asaph, bp *see* Adam
St Bertin (Pas-de-Calais), Ben. abbey 114, 319
St Briavels (Glos.), chapel of 274
St Cher, Hugh of 65
St Edmunds *see* Bury
St Evroul (Orne), Ben. abbey 79, 114, 129, 161, 286–91, 338; Richard, proctor of 286–9
St Genix (Savoie) 104
St Gennys (Cornwall) 104
St Germain of Paris, ab. of 357
St Germans (de sancto Germano) Ralph of 276
St Ippollitts (Herts.), ch. of 141–2, 327
St Mary and St Laurence, monks of 360
St Neots (Hunts./Cambs.) 291
St Peter, William of 301
St Valéry, Reginald of 257
St Victor of Paris, Aug. abbey 29
— Hugh of 200
Sainte-Barbe-en-Auge (Calvados), Aug. priory 9, 53, 225; canons named 241; pr. *see* Daniel
Salford Abbots (Warws.) 256–7
— Priors (Warws.), ch. of 80, 97, 152, 342; Ralph, vicar of 80, 342
Salisbury (Wilts.)
— cathedral ch. of 293–6
— — archdns *see* Geoffrey, Reginald
— — bp *see* Jocelin
— — chapter of 296
— — dean of *see* Oxford, John of
— John of 9, 26, 29, 31, 33–4, 36, 40–1, 46; treasurer of Exeter 138, 288, 291, 251–5, 325, bp of Chartres 61
— Richard of 281
Salvagius *see* Selvagius
Samson ab. of Bury 11–12, 111, 240
Samson clerk of bp of Worcester 102, 199; as witness 235, 253–7, 261, 263–4, 266–7, 287, 295–6, 302, 304; called Mr 281
Sandy (Beds.) *see* Hugh parson of
Sarracenus, William 141, 361

Saumur (Maine-et-Loire), Ben. abbey 274
Say, Sai, Hugh de 307–8
Scots, king of 246 *and see* Thomas, clerk of
seal, authenticity checked 284
— validates charter 179, 364
— of bp Roger of Worcester 229–30
Sées (Orne), John archdn of 241–2
Selvagius, William and Simon 353–4
Senatus pr. of Worcester 58–66, 308
Sens (Yonne) 14, 25–6, 51
— archbp of *see* William
Serlo, priest 335
Sestaneslade (on r. Severn) 263
settlement, judicial *see* composition
Shapwick (Dorset) 274
Sheen (Surrey/London), Carth. priory 271, 274, 287
Shenstone (Staffs.), ch. of 280
Sherbourne (Warws.), ch. of 298
Shifnal, formerly Idsall (Salop) 340
Shipton, ch. of 96, 277
Shrewsbury (Salop) 28
— Ben. abbey 296, abbot *see* Adam
Silvester, Mr, clerk of bp of Worcester 84, 92, 100, 102, 105, 199, 299, 374–6; as witness 244–5, 256–7, 259, 261, 263, 266–7, 276, 281–2, 287–8, 291, 296, 308–9, 311; called 'de Leche' 276
Simon ab. of St Albans 145–6, 186, 284–5; as judge-delegate 126, 131, 137, 188, 238–40, 275, 325, 338, 340, 342, 355, 368, 370
— archdn of Worcester *see* Luvel
— bp of Worcester 84, 110, 262–3, 301–2, 306, 309
— clerk of bp of Norwich 292
— son of Richard 304
Sinningfield (Berks.), ch. of 106
Snitterfield (Warws.), ch. of 98, 300–1
Southwark (Surrey/London), Aug. priory 297–8
Southwell, Mr Hugh of 247, 340
Stafford, archdn of *see* Tamworth, Ralph of

INDEX 395

— Robert of 244-5
Stainton-by-Langworth (Lincs.) 354
Stanley (Leonard S., Glos.), Ben. priory 81, 259
Stanley (Wilts.), Cist. abbey, ab. of 356
Stantuna *see* Stainton
Stanway (Glos.), flying crucifix at 102
Stephen bp of Tournai 194
— king of England 118, 152, 372
Stisted (Kent) 338
Stoke, William of 296
Stoneleigh (Warws.), Cist. abbey 373
Stortford, Mr Richard of 281
Stratford (S. Langthorne, Essex/London), ab. of 329
Stretton on Fosse, Strata, Stratona (Glos./Warws.), Alan and G. (William), claimants to chapel of 73-4, 329, 341, 365-6
Studley, Peter of 244
Sumerford (? Gt Summerford, Wilts.), Ernald dean of 276
Surrey, archdn of, Robert of Inglesham 268-9
Sutton (Devon), ch. of St Andrew 136, 283-4, 334, 344
Sutton (not identified), chapel of 319
Swallowfield (Berks.), ch. of 106
Swefling (Suff.), Hugh of 292
synod, diocesan 90, 151-2, 318, 373

Tamworth, Ralph of, archdn of Stafford 280
Talbot, Richard 276
Templars, Order of Knights 335
Teodelinus, clerk 236
Tetbury (Glos.), ch. of 257
Tewkesbury (Glos.), Ben. abbey 77, 92, 100, 205, 298-300; ab. of *see* Alan
Theobald archbp of Canterbury 60, 119, 302, 320, 330
— clerk 261
Thelwald (not identified) 324

Thetford (Norf.), Clun. priory 275, 362
— Christian pr. of 275
Theulf, Theoldus, bp of Worcester 109, 263
Thomas ab. of Hyde 277
— Becket, royal chancellor 8, archbp of Canterbury 15-16, Chapter 2 *passim*, 75, 85, 96, 100, 116, 120, 140, 184, 242, 320, 321, 328, 332, 350
— clerk of the king of Scots 153, 322, 360
— dean of Colchester 161, 188, 238-40
— Mr, clerk of the earl of Norfolk 318, 328, 347, 362
— pr. of Dunstable 177
— William 108, 376
Thorney (Cambs.), Ben. abbey 135, 160, 318, 329-30, 352; Solomon ab. of 318
Thrupp (Northants.), ch. of 369
Tilleberia (? Tilbury, Essex) 268
time-limit in judicial commissions 157, 178, 325, 349
tithes, method of calculating 222, 333
— payment by Cistercians 138, 343; by Hospitallers 138, 356
— conflict of jurisdiction over 141-2
— disputes over 151, 299, 305, 331, 333, 335, 343, 356, 360, 365, 373
Tours (Indre-et-Loire) 38, 40, 50, 244
— Council at (1163) 14-16, 98n, 361
— archbp *see* Bartholomew
Tosti, W. 326
Trian, Robert 236
Treton (Oxon.), William priest of 343
Trun (Orne), William of 104, 241-2, 271
Tunbridge, Mr William of 67
Tynemouth (Northumb.), Ben. priory 137, 158, 186, 251-5, 323
Tytherington (Glos./Avon), ch. of 266-7

396 INDEX

Uley (Glos.), ch. of 258–9
— Osmund clerk of 258–9
Upton-on-Severn (Worcs./HW), ch. of 106
— (U. St Leonards, Glos.) 258
— Walter of 236
Uttoxeter (Staffs.), ch. of 145, 363

Vacarius, Mr 361
Valeinis, Alan and Savery of 292
Veryan (Cornwall), ch. of 101
vicar, vicar's portion, vicarage 77–82, 152, 172–4
vice-archdn 239, 357
visitation, episcopal 88–9
Vivian archdn of Orvieto 44

W. de Fonte 362
Waleran archdn of Bayeux 261
Walkelin clerk of Mord' 333
Wallingford (Berks./Oxon), Ben. priory 344
— Nicholas pr. of 285
Walter ab. of Neath 291
— ab. of Westminster 85, 374–6
— bp of Rochester 21, 25
— clerk 74–5, 244–6, 346
— clerk of Hazelton 286
— Mr 287, 292
— pr. of Coventry 373
— pr. of Great Malvern 374–6
— *scriptor* 261
— son of Driu 298
— son of William of Stanes 235–6
Warwick (Warws.) 253–4
— Aug. priory of Holy Sepulchre 300–1, 372
— collegiate ch. of St Mary 291, combined with All Saints 301–2; Roger sacristan of 245
— earl of: Roger 301–2, William 105
— Godwin of 244
— Jordan clerk of 244
Walton (not identified) 146, 324
Wanstrow (Somerset), Rainer of 304
Ware (Herts.) 287, 289–90
Wareham (Dorset) 274

Washbourne (Glos.) 299
Wedon *see* Whitton
weir (in r. Severn) 262
Welham (Yorks. E. Riding/N. Yorks.) chapel of 365, 367
Welbeck (Notts.), Prem. abbey 344
Wells (Norfolk) 353
Wells (Som.), cathedral ch. of 280, 304
— archdn: Thomas 280, 304 *and see* Cumin, John
— bps *see* Bath
— chapter 302–5, dean Richard 304, precentor Reginald 303–5, succentor Geoffrey 304
Wenlock (Much W., Salop), Clun. priory, pr. of 335, Humbald 297
West Haddon (Northants.), ch. of 247–9
Westminster (London), Councils at, (1163) 20; (1175) 73, 86, 101, 218–22; (1176) 221, 288, 291–2
Weston (? Weston-on-Avon, Warws.), ch. of 91, 255–6
Weston Subedge (Glos.) 287
Westwell (Kent) 338
Westwood (Worcs./HW), priory of Fontevrault 95, 310
Wetham (not identified, ? Hants.) 331
Whaddon (Glos.), ch. of 97, 260–1, 363
Whitbourne (Herfs./HW), ch. of 368
Whittlesea (Cambs.), ch. of 216, 257, 263, 317–8, 329, 352
Whittington (Worcs./HW), chapel of 310
Whitton (Suff.), Walter chaplain of 292
Wibetot, William of 291
Wibtoft (Warws.) 288
Wick Episcopi (Worcs./HW) 107
Wickambrook (Suff.), ch. of 282
Widford (Herts.), ch. of 129, 289–91
William I, king of England 117
William II, king of England 61, 358
— ab. of Bruern 343
— ab. of Keynsham 294

INDEX

— ab. of Ramsey 269, 333
— ab. of St Etienne of Caen 241
— archbp of Sens 42, 51, 201
— bp of Exeter 144, 283–4, 233
— bp of Norwich 20–1
— 'bishop' of Caen 236
— cantor (? of Gloucester) 259
— Mr 101
— pr. of Great Malvern 374–6
— pr. of St Augustine's, Bristol 267
— son of Alexander 293–5
— son of Godfrey 266
— son of Osmund 261
— son of Ralph 268–70, 367
— son of Walo 365, 367
Wilton, Ralph of 236
Wimborne (Dorset), ch. of 138, 274, 370
Winchcombe (Glos.), ch. of 299
Winchester (Hants.) 54, 222; archdn Ralph 331, 345; bp of 365 *and see* Henry; Ilchester, Richard of; Peter
— Mr Godfrey of 355–6
Windsor (Berks.) 148, 277
Winsham (Som.), Nicholas and Jocelin of 304
Winterbourne Bassett (Wilts.), ch. of 372
Witald', Peter of 257
Witeing, Roger 304
Withington (Glos.), ch. of 106
— Peter of 104, 106, 199, 265
witnesses in ecclesiastical courts 185, 249, 318, 321, 346
— sued in secular court 317
Wixford, Withlakesford (Warws.) 256–7
Wolverley (Worcs./HW), ch. of 305, tithes of 97, 305
— Thomas clerk of 305
Wootton Wawen (Warws.), ch. of 74–5, 98, 244–5, 601
Worcester (Worcs./HW)
— archdns of 100–1 *and see* Ailric,
Godfrey, Hugh, Mr Simon Luvel
— bps of 330 *and see* Alfred; Baldwin; Giffard; Henry; Coutances, John of; Pagham, John of; Robert; Roger; Simon; Theulf; Northolt, William of; Wulfstan
— bpric, estates of
— — manors 89; Alvechurch 107; Bibury 106; Bps Cleeve 106, 110; Fladbury 265; Henbury 267; Upton 106; Withington 106
— — knights' fees 108–9
— — soke in London 297–8
— — survey of 107–10
— bpric, records of 56–7, 205–6; *matricula* 82; *Red Book* 107–110
— cathedral and Ben. priory 78–80, 114, 281–2, 305–12
— — chamberlain and precentor of 305
— — prior of *see* Ralph, Senatus
— — sacristy of 306
— — subprior 308
— churches in, All Saints' and Walter, parson of 93–4, 308–9
— — St Clement's 94, 309–10
— — St Helen's 306
— William of 266
Worminster, Wormestor (Som.) 304
Worton (Wilts.) 294
Wotton-under-Edge (Glos.), ch. of 237
Wulfstan bp of Worcester 66, 306
Wyrardisbury, Wraysbury (Bucks.), ch. of 258

Yardley (Warws./W. Midlands), chapel of 76, 97, 136, 342, 347
Yelvertoft (Northants.), R. priest of 357
York, archbp of *see* Roger
— dean of *see* Robert
— treasurer of 9
— Ben. priory of Holy Trinity 365